AF873913

CONGRESS

The Chester County Line

CONGRESS
The Chester County Line

by
Wayne C. Woodward

Chester County Historical Society • West Chester • Pennsylvania
1992

Library of Congress Cataloging-in-Publication Data
Woodward, Wayne C., 1930–
Congress—the Chester County line / by Wayne C. Woodward; foreword by Richard T. Schulze.
p. cm.
ISBN 0-929706-07-2 (hard cover : alk. paper)
1. Chester County (Pa.)—Politics and government. 2. United States. Congress. House—History. I. Chester County Historical Society (West Chester, Pa.) II. Title
F157.C4W66 1992
974.8'13- -dc20 92-32489
CIP

Cover illustration:

Desk and chair designed by Thomas U. Walter (ca. 1851) for the chamber of U.S. House of Representatives. This desk and chair were used from ca. 1857 until 1873. As a result of the 1870 census and reapportionment the number of Representatives was increased and the existing desks and chairs had to be removed. Most were sold or were taken home by the Representatives who used them. This desk and chair were used by Chester County's Washington Townsend (1813-1894) who served in Congress from 1869 to 1877. The desk and chair are in the collection of the Chester County Historical Society. *Photo by George J. Fistrovich*

Copyright © 1992 by Chester County Historical Society

All rights reserved. No part of this publication may be reproduced, stored in a retrieval system, or transmitted, in any form or by any means, electronic, mechanical, photocopying, recording or otherwise, without the prior written permission of Chester County Historical Society.

The paper used in this publication meets the minimum requirements of American National Standard for Information Sciences—Permanence of Paper for Printed Library Materials, ANSI Z39.48-1984 ♾

Printed by KNA Press Inc., Kennett Square, Pennsylvania

ACKNOWLEDGEMENTS

I am much obliged to the Chester County Historical Society for making possible the publication of *Congress—The Chester County Line*. For the advice and aid in the preparation of my manuscript I am indebted to Roland H. Woodward, the Society's director, and Douglas R. Harper, who edited the text. Special thanks also go to Teena Pescatore, who assisted in placing the manuscript on computer disks, and to members of the Society's library staff for their assistance during my research. I am also grateful to the Society's photo-archivist Pamela C. Powell for her help in providing photographs, and to Jan Friis, a staff member in the office of Congressman Schulze, for his assistance.

West Chester, June 1992 W. C. W.

CONTENTS

FOREWORD

From the very beginning of our great nation and the first American Congress, Chester Countians have served their southeast Pennsylvania constituents in the United States House of Representatives.

Not all have been nationally known leaders or internationally renowned legislators, but by and large, congressmen from Chester County have played a major role in American history. From the First Congress in New York and George Washington's inauguration in 1789, through the abolishment of slavery and the Civil War, through World War II to the present, Chester Countians have served with honor and distinction.

Author Wayne Woodward has painted a glowing and detailed history of our nation and region through a painstakingly researched book, *Congress—The Chester County Line*. Through the electoral process, Woodward has developed a concise political history of Chester County and the congressmen who have served the area.

This book will be vital to historians, essential to politicians who desire a historical perspective, and just plain enjoyable to those who live, work in and admire this area and its heritage. I am proud to have served in the United States House of Representatives and believe those who read *Congress—The Chester County Line* will better appreciate Chester County's role in our American history.

Richard T. Schulze, Member
United States House of Representatives
1975-1993

TO THE READER

Congress—The Chester County Line is an informal political history dealing with the selection of the men who have represented our county in the Congress of the United States from the days of George Washington to the days of George Bush. While it would be nice to be able to boast at the outset that there were a number of outstanding statesmen in this line whose contributions were of immense significance in our nation's history, such an assertion would be untrue. As a whole their legislative record was rather barren and in its long history the county has not produced a congressional giant of the stature of a Daniel Webster or a Henry Clay, nor has it had representatives of the caliber of a Nicholas Longworth, a Sam Rayburn, or a "Tip" O'Neill who made it to the top of the House leadership hierarchy. Still, even though not of the first order, most were high caliber men who did a creditable job of representing the people of Chester County in the national legislature, and it is the modest intent of this book to relate a little about their political careers.

Who were these legislators? Sandwiched between our first congressman, one Richard Thomas, a Friend by birthright who fought with the Continental Army, and today's Congressman Richard Schulze were three Darlingtons—William, Isaac and Smedley; two Hiesters—John and his son Daniel; two Everharts—William and his son James; attorneys Joseph Hemphill, Francis James, John Hickman, and Thomas S. Butler; and two physicians—Roger Davis and John A. Morrison. The legislative continuum also included Isaac Wayne, son of the Revolutionary War hero; Isaac Anderson, a youthful soldier in the Revolution and great-grandfather of a Pennsylvania governor; Joshua Evans, proprietor of the once famous Paoli Inn; David Potts, an ironmaster at the historic Warwick Furnace; Charles Miner, an influential newspaper editor and early anti-slavery crusader; Abraham McIlvaine, a well-to-do farmer from Springton Manor; Jesse Dickey, an educator and politician from the once thriving southern Chester County village of Hopewell; Washington Townsend, a West Chester banker; John H. Ware III, a wealthy utility executive and newspaper publisher from Oxford; and Paul B. Dague, a congenial politician from Downingtown.

Today even for the most serious and dedicated challenger it has become a near-impossible dream to defeat an incumbent congressman. This was not the case in the county during the nineteenth century. Competition for a seat in the national legislature was very keen. Defeated candidates sometimes returned to the ring and tasted victory. Also, the electorate (or party chieftains) deemed it advisable to limit tenure of a congressman. By contrast, in this century only four Chester Countians—Butler, Dague, Ware and

Schulze—have served in the Congress. Dague was serving as the county's sheriff when elected in 1946 to the first of ten terms in the House and Schulze, a onetime register of wills and state representative, was elected to a ninth term in 1990. For years of continuous service, though, top honors go to Thomas Stalker Butler, the "Fighting Quaker" from West Chester who served as a member of the House from March 4, 1897, until his death on May 26, 1928. An early advocate of military and naval preparedness, he was the Navy's greatest champion within the Congress and in his day a heavyweight among Washington's lawmakers.

Was Butler the most influential of Chester County's congressmen? Perhaps. But our vote goes to John Hickman, the West Chester lawyer whose voice was heard nationwide as the country divided over slavery. Elected first as a Democrat, Hickman broke with his party's leaders on the slavery issue. Not one to compromise, he angered politicians on both sides of the fence, yet managed to get re-elected without party endorsement from either the Democrats or Republicans in 1858. Two years later his popularity among Republicans was such that some felt he should be Abraham Lincoln's vice presidential running mate. A man of slight physique, he infuriated the South with his scathing taunts and sarcasm. After John Brown's raid at Harper's Ferry, for example, he upset his colleagues from the South by making light of the episode, saying "the whole state of Virginia was frightened by seventeen men and a cow."

Today the House of Representatives has 435 members from fifty states. In the beginning—in April of 1789 when the House met for the first time in New York—it was a small body of some sixty-five members from a dozen states. Eight of these members in the First Congress were Pennsylvanians whom Chester Countians helped to elect. Thus, we can truthfully boast that no county in the nation has been participating in the congressional election process longer than ours. In addition to relating a little about the lives and politics of our legislators, a main objective of *Congress—The Chester County Line* was to provide an insight into the county's congressional election battles and to touch upon some of the campaign issues. It was not intended to be a thorough history, however, and it ignores many important subjects. Unlike the situation today, there was a time when the competition for the Chester County seat in the Congress was very keen and a would-be lawmaker did not need a barrel of money to be able to toss his hat in the ring. Over the years a rich array of characters has marched across the county political stage with aspirations of going to Washington. These "also rans" were not forgotten in our history.

Another of the book's focal points is Chester County's congressional marriages (always very political and sometimes very unusual) with Lancaster,

Berks, Delaware and Montgomery counties. As a consequence of these "marriages" Chester County has had a say in the selection of some thirty House members from these neighboring counties in addition to her own twenty-five. Of these, the most famous is James Buchanan, our representative in the 1820s who later became the fifteenth president of the United States.

Lastly, it might be said that *Congress—The Chester County Line* is an attempt to present an American history synopsis with a Chester County perspective—a perspective gained from looking at Washington and the national political scene from a distance of some one hundred miles through the writings of editors and reporters of numerous county newspapers.

Wayne C. Woodward
June 13, 1992

CHAPTER 1

INDEPENDENCE

"Tell them they will live to see the hour when they will acknowledge it to have been the most glorious service that I rendered my country."

In April of 1777, less than a year after he signed the Declaration of Independence, John Morton sent from his deathbed the above message to friends in Chester County who had censured him for joining with the revolutionists and casting the deciding vote that put Pennsylvania on the side of independence. He was the first signer of the Declaration of Independence to die.

Morton's vote was a courageous one. Both he and his Chester County colleague, Charles Humphreys, agonized over Richard Henry Lee's independence resolution during the long month of June 1776 as the momentous proposition was debated both publicly and privately in Philadelphia. Then, when the crucial vote was taken on July 2, they rendered different decisions. Humphreys, a Quaker and a pacifist, voted against breaking ties with Great Britain.

Neither resided within the boundaries of Chester County as we know it today, yet John Morton and Charles Humphreys deserve more than casual mention in any account dealing with important personages on the county's political stage during the early phases of the American Revolution. In a chronicle dealing with county leaders who served in the United States Congress their names merit special recognition, for they were (if not our first congressmen) the forerunners to the parade of twenty-five Chester Countians who have served in the United States House of Representatives since its inception in early 1789.

Others occupied center stage in Philadelphia, the largest city in British colonial America, when our nation was born, but the supporting roles played by John Morton and Charles Humphreys in the historic and exciting independence drama should not be minimized or overlooked. They were among the eight Pennsylvanians who joined forty-seven delegates from eleven other colonies at Carpenter's Hall in September 1774, to form the First Continental Congress. Only Georgia was not represented at this assembly of some of colonial America's most prominent political figures. Morton and Humphreys were among those who favored conciliation, rather than resistance, at this initial gathering.

The two Chester Countians were also among the delegates who gathered in Philadelphia on May 10, 1775, for the opening session of the Second Continental Congress. By then militiamen from Massachusetts had confronted British redcoats at Lexington and Concord and the struggle for independence was underway. In fact, on the very day the delegates began their deliberations a Vermont revolutionist named Ethan Allen and his Green Mountain Boys demanded a British garrison at Fort Ticonderoga surrender "in the name of the Great Jehovah and the Continental Congress." Morton and Humphreys were unaware of this, of course, and did not realize then that the course they were pursuing would lead to a separation from Great Britain. During this difficult period both men continued to represent Pennsylvania in the Continental Congress until the early summer of 1776 when they were called upon to cast votes on eighteenth century America's most far-reaching and controversial issue—the question of independence.

Today when the Declaration of Independence is mentioned the names of Thomas Jefferson, John Adams, John Hancock, Benjamin Franklin, Richard Henry Lee and other luminaries of the American Revolution immediately come to mind. Less likely to be recalled, and frequently overlooked in accounts of the Second Continental Congress deliberations, is the name of the Chester Countian who made it possible for John Hancock to announce that the colonies "unanimously" declared their independence. There was anything but unanimity among the delegates when Lee proposed "these united colonies are, and of right ought to be, free and independent states."

Grandson of a Swedish adventurer who had settled along the Delaware some thirty years prior to the arrival of William Penn and the Quakers, John Morton was born and reared in what was then the Ridley Township section of Chester (now Delaware) County. It is unfortunate that historians usually overlook him in accounts of the struggle for independence since he probably worked longer and harder for the rights of colonists than many of the American Revolution's better- known patriots. Along with John Dickinson and George Bryan from Pennsylvania, Morton was a member of the famous "Stamp Act" Congress that met in New York in 1765 to protest parliamentary taxation. He shared in the writing of resolutions denouncing the Stamp Act and expressing other grievances, the most noteworthy of which were the colonial objection to taxation without representation and the use of admiralty courts to circumvent the right of trial by jury.

A onetime sheriff of Chester County and an assemblyman since 1756, Morton continued to serve in the Provincial Assembly after his Stamp Act Congress experience. He remained loyal to England as relations between the colonies and mother country deteriorated, and was not numbered among the radicals on the eve of the Revolution. His loyalty, though, did not prevent him from joining his fellow assemblymen in resolving that a congress of deputies from the several colonies should be held to adopt a plan for redressing American grievances, ascertaining American rights, and establishing union and harmony between Great Britain and the colonies.

The delegates to the First Continental Congress who gathered in Philadelphia, colonial America's leading commercial and cultural center, shared common complaints against the crown but brought with them a variety of political opinions. Coming from Chester County, where nonresisting Quakerism prevailed, Morton and Humphreys shared views much closer to those of Joseph Galloway, speaker of the Pennsylvania Assembly and a determined reconciliationist, than those expressed by the radical Samuel Adams of Massachusetts and Virginia's Lee. Public opinion, traditions, and customs in the different colonies made it difficult for the delegates to agree on a united plan of action, but the seven-week session in the late summer of 1774 provided an opportunity for the colonial leaders to get to know one another. Also, two significant measures were adopted by the First Continental Congress. The delegates declared American colonists were entitled to the same rights as Englishmen everywhere, and secondly they proposed an association of the colonies to boycott English trade until Parliament ended the infringement and violations of these rights. Both Humphreys and Morton signed all the resolutions and acts of the First Continental Congress.

The October election that followed this historic meeting in Philadelphia produced no surprises in Chester County, a politically conservative region of villages and farmlands that stretched to the Delaware River and included modern Delaware County. Although its citizens of Scotch-Irish background could usually be found in the forefront of the independence movement, the Quakers retained control of the county government. Morton and Humphreys were both returned to the General Assembly. So were Joseph Pennock, James Gibbons, John Jacobs, and Isaac Pearson, all of whom were members of the Society of Friends, and Benjamin Bartholomew, a Baptist from East Whiteland Township. The one new member elected was Anthony Wayne, a young and outspoken leader from Easttown Township. He sided with the "Whigs" or "Patriots" who would ultimately take up arms to win independence.

Elsewhere, though, the 1774 election weakened the hand of Speaker Galloway, Pennsylvania's ultra- conservative who had frustrated radicals from the other colonies during the First Continental Congress debates. The new assembly, controlled by moderates, appointed several new delegates to the Second Continental Congress, but retained both Morton and Humphreys. With fighting already underway in New England, the two Chester Countians found themselves swimming against the tide when they rejoined delegates from the other colonies in Philadelphia. Radical members were exerting the leadership. The new Congress took steps to equip an army, named George Washington as its commander-in-chief, devised a system of currency, and began seeking foreign alliances for aid in the struggle with Great Britain—actions opposed by a large segment of the constituency represented by Morton and Humphreys. Those who preferred the British connection and opposed resistance to the mother country became the "Tories" or "Loyalists" of the American Revolution.

John Penn, the colonial governor, and his Tory supporters exerted considerable influence in the Pennsylvania General Assembly. Dominated by moderates and conservatives, the Assembly ignored pleas from the patriots or radicals in other colonies and expressly prohibited Pennsylvania's delegation in the Second Continental Congress from doing anything that would change the colony's governmental structure or lead to a separation from England. The October election in 1775 did little to advance the cause of Pennsylvania's Whigs or bring about a change in the colony's political power structure. In Chester County, where Quaker influence and pacifist sentiment remained strong, seven of the eight assemblymen were re-elected; the only new member chosen being Joseph Pyle, a Quaker from East Marlborough Township who replaced the patriot Anthony Wayne.

This new Assembly, the last to be elected during the Penn proprietary reign, picked Morton as its speaker and reaffirmed the colony's opposition to a separation from Great Britain. Although responsible for appointing delegates to the Continental Congress, the General Assembly's power and influence steadily declined. The colony had moved to a war footing and for all practical purposes government in Pennsylvania, third largest of the colonies, was in the hands of the committees of safety that had been established in the various counties. It was through these committees, comprised mainly of radicals favoring independence, that the will of the Continental Congress was being carried out insofar as providing for the defense of the province and furnishing the Continental Army with men and supplies. In Chester County leadership in the Committee of Safety was provided by such men as Anthony Wayne, James Moore, Francis Johnston, Dr. Samuel Kennedy, Persifor Frazier, Richard Thomas, Caleb Davis and William Montgomery.

The General Assembly made a final effort to preserve its authority in 1776 when it removed the prohibition that prevented its members in Congress from voting on independence, but this change in thought or policy came too late. The radical leaders heading the various committees of safety were already at work preparing to organize a new government in Pennsylvania that would extend democracy to all its free male citizens. Under the old system the three original counties—Philadelphia, Bucks and Chester—elected twenty-four members to the Assembly while the other eight counties, with two-thirds of the colony's population, elected only fourteen. This injustice suffered by the western counties had long been a thorn in the side of the Scotch-Irish and other radicals who were meeting in Philadelphia at the same time the Second Continental Congress was debating independence. At their extra-legal constitutional convention, which lasted from June to September, these political revolutionists from throughout Pennsylvania drafted a new frame of government for the state and usurped the power of the elected Assembly.

At the time of Richard Henry Lee's call for independence (June 7, 1776) only seven colonies favored his proposal. Six were opposed or undecided. Pennsylvania was not among the seven favoring a break with the mother country. The war had intensified since the colonies had petitioned King George III to cease hostilities, but the ties to Great Britain were such that Pennsylvania's delegates had for months been under specific instructions not to assent to any proposition that might lead to a separation. The Society of Friends, which was very influential in Philadelphia, Bucks, and Chester counties, advocated peace and put pressure on its members to avoid any participation in revolutionary activity.

Only five of Pennsylvania's seven-member delegation occupied their seats in the Congress when the final historic vote on independence was taken. Morton provided Pennsylvania's tie-breaking vote. He joined Benjamin Franklin and James Wilson to put Pennsylvania on the side of the revolutionists. Ironically, two Pennsylvanians whose names are far more familiar than Morton's in American history—Robert Morris, the financier of the Revolution, and John Dickinson, the moderate Whig leader—absented themselves from the proceedings when Morton rendered his "most glorious service." Morton's decisive vote cost him friends in Chester County where there was a deep split between patriots and loyalists.

Up until the vote on independence Humphreys had taken an energetic part in the Continental Congress proceedings, siding usually with Dickinson and the other conservative or moderate Pennsylvania delegates. He was sixty-four and a respected political leader, but the patriots drafting the new state constitution wanted no parts of those who had not voted for independence. They quickly replaced him with one of their own. Picked by these revolutionists to serve with Franklin, Wilson and Morton in Pennsylvania's congressional delegation were Benjamin Rush, a thirty-year-old Philadelphian who would soon be recognized as the foremost physician in the United States, George Clymer, George Ross, George Taylor, and Col. James Smith. All affixed their signatures to the Declaration of Independence, as did Robert Morris, even though he had absented himself when the crucial vote was taken.

For the Quaker Humphreys, an assemblyman since 1763, the Declaration of Independence marked the end of his public service days. Neither his integrity nor his motives were questioned when he was removed (without an election) from the political stage. Since he had long championed the rights of colonists, some believe his vote against independence was due to conscientious scruples growing out of his affirmation of allegiance to the crown taken when he became a member of the Colonial Assembly. Humphreys, whose home was in Haverford Township in what was then part of Chester County, died in 1786 at age seventy-three.

For Morton, who was twelve years younger than Humphreys, the months following his vote for independence were extremely difficult ones. His health was poor and many of his friends and neighbors censured him for taking the stand that he did. His work in Congress kept him busy, though, as he and his colleagues attempted to equip the makeshift American army and at the same time look after their own survival, fleeing from Philadelphia to Baltimore towards the end of the year. One of Morton's assignments was helping to draft the Articles of Confederation, which were not adopted until seven months after his death in 1777.

DECLARATION SIGNERS

Pennsylvania had more signers (nine) of the Declaration than any other colony. Most historians maintain this was due to geography and historical circumstance rather than revolutionary ardor. Be that as it may, several of the signers had Chester County connections and a few words about these founding fathers are perhaps in order.

First, there was Thomas McKean, a native son of Chester County who later became a three-term governor of Pennsylvania. Born in 1734 in what is now Londonderry Township, McKean represented Delaware in the Continental Congress. Son of a ner-do-well tavern keeper, McKean received his early education at Dr. Francis Alison's school in New London before leaving the county at age sixteen to study law in nearby New Castle, a thriving transportation center on the Delaware as well as a court town and center of political activity. Here he prospered and made a name for himself as a lawyer. As was the case with Morton, his involvement in the colonial struggle with Great Britain dated back to the Stamp Act Congress days when he was a delegate from Delaware. Even after he took up lodgings in Philadelphia in 1774 and became embroiled in Pennsylvania politics, McKean continued to represent the neighboring colony and remained one of her most influential leaders. A dominant political figure in colonial America for fifty years, McKean never enjoyed great popularity among the conservative voters of his native Chester County.

Two other signers of the Declaration of Independence—James Smith of Pennsylvania and George Reade of Delaware—came under the tutorage of Dr. Alison at his New London Academy. So did Charles Thomson, the zealous radical who served as secretary of the Continental Congress. It is doubtful if any other teacher had as much influence over so many future leaders of the American Revolution as did Dr. Alison, and one would be remiss to exclude him from any account dealing with Chester County and the Declaration of Independence. Born in County Donegal, Ireland, and educated at the University of Glasgow in Scotland, Alison was thirty when he arrived in America in 1735 and found employment in Maryland as a tutor for the family of Samuel Dickinson, father of John Dickinson. Shortly thereafter he became pastor of the New London Presbyterian congregation and opened his remarkable academy, precursor of the University of Delaware at Newark. Not only did he train a number of future political leaders, but a goodly number of future ministers came under his influence at New London and later played important roles in the rebellion. These preachers, most of whom had no qualms about combining politics with religion, exerted much influence over their congregations, as is witnessed by the role of the Scotch-Irish Presbyterians in leading the reluctant Pennsylvania colony into the Revolution.

CONFEDERATION CONGRESSMEN

The Articles of Confederation provided a weak but very necessary framework of national government for the thirteen rebelling states during the war with Great Britain and immediately thereafter. Representing Chester County in the Confederation Congress during this period (1776 to 1789) were two ardent patriots—William Clingan and Joseph Gardner. Unfortunately, as with so many of their contemporaries, they are forgotten men of the American Revolution. Clingan, a resident of West Caln Township, was elected to the Congress in 1777 and served until 1779. He was one of Pennsylvania's five signers of the "Articles of Confederation and Perpetual Union" at Independence Hall on July 9, 1778. Gardner, also from the western end of the county, was a member of Congress after the war during the 1784 and 1785 sessions.

Pennsylvania's delegates to the Congress were chosen annually by the state legislature, not directly by the voters. Very little authority was conferred on the national government by the Articles and consequently political power rested with the individual state governments. Congress was more of an advisory assembly to the states than a governing body, and initially the main concern of its members was that of coordinating the armed resistance of the thirteen rebellious states. Under the Articles the states retained equality in Congress, each with one vote regardless of the size of its delegation.

Not a great deal has been written concerning the two Chesco congressmen who served during this critical period of the new nation's history. From historical footnotes and what little has been recorded about Clingan, however, one quickly gathers he must have been in the forefront of the independence movement. Although not a member of the General Assembly or the convention which drafted the state's first constitution in 1776, Clingan's appointment to the Congress indicates he was a man respected and esteemed by Pennsylvania's revolutionary leaders. A justice of the peace from 1757 to 1786, and president of the county courts during his last six years as a magistrate, he resided west of the village of Wagontown in a section of the county where the revolutionary cause had strong support. In their *History of Chester County*, J. Smith Futhey and Gilbert Cope state that Clingan "was one of the sufferers of the ravages of the enemy" and that he was appointed in 1779 "to receive subscriptions and transmit same to the loan officer, agreeably to the resolve of Congress on June 29th for the borrowing twenty million of dollars." After the war Clingan was one of the early advocates of moving the county seat from Chester, in what was then the extreme corner of Chester County, to a more central location. He died at an advanced age on May 9, 1790, four years after the county government was relocated to West Chester.

Concerning Dr. Joseph Gardner, who was much younger than Clingan, more has been written in the historical records of this era. Born in 1752, the son of Francis Gardner, an emigrant from Coleraine, Ireland, who settled in Nantmeal Township, Dr. Gardner was an early graduate of the University of Pennsylvania and one of the better-educated men of his day. Upon completing his study of medicine, he began his practice in the western section of the county and married Isabella Cochran, whose father and family were ardent patriots. Within a short time young Dr. Gardner not only gained respect as a physician but was recognized as a leader in the revolutionary cause.

He was elected to the General Assembly in Pennsylvania's first election after independence. In his mid-twenties, he was the youngest member of Chester County's six-man delegation. Like Clingan, he was representative of the new breed of politician who took over the governmental process in the county and state after the signing of the Declaration of Independence. Gone were the Gibbonses, Pennocks, Pyles and other prominent Quakers who had ruled for a century. In their place one found Scotch-Irish Presbyterian names such as Cunningham, Fulton, Mackey and Cochran.

Re-elected to the Assembly in 1777, Dr. Gardner was later made a member of the Supreme Executive Council, the executive branch of state government under the state's new constitution. He raised two companies of troops during the war and was one of the unsung heroes in the independence cause. His appointment to the Confederation Congress apparently brought him little satisfaction and after two terms Dr. Gardner gave up politics to concentrate on his medical practice. He moved to Elkton, Maryland, in 1792 to take over a retiring friend's medical practice and shortly thereafter died at age forty-two.

Fifty men represented Pennsylvania in the Continental and/or Confederation Congress between 1774 and 1789. In addition to Morton, Humphreys, Clingan, and Gardner, several had Chester County connections. One of these was David Jackson, who as a boy emigrated with his family from Ireland and settled in the southern section of the county. Jackson, who attended Nottingham Academy before going to Philadelphia to study to become an apothecary physician, was one of the long-suffering soldiers of the Continental Army. He lost an arm at the Battle of Trenton, but after recovering from this injury he rejoined the army and was present at Yorktown when Lord Cornwallis surrendered. He subsequently served as a Philadelphia delegate to the Congress in 1785 and 1786 before returning to Chester County and making his home in Oxford.

James McClene and William Henry, native sons of Chester County, also served in the Confederation Congress representing other sections of the state. Born in New London in 1730, McClene moved to Cumberland (now Franklin) County when he was in his twenties and took an active role in the frontier politics of western Pennsylvania. Henry, who was born near Downingtown, moved to Lancaster County where he also became politically active during the Revolution.

CHAPTER 2

THE EARLY YEARS

For the political leaders attempting to establish a national government from the thirteen sovereign states that comprised the United States of America, the late 1780s were a difficult and trying period. The Articles of Confederation, hastily written during the tumult of war, failed to meet the country's urgent needs. The union of the states under the Articles was a tenuous one and some leaders questioned just how long their new nation could survive. The national government had no viable executive authority and encountered all sorts of problems in attempting to pay off its war debts, finance its operations, and negotiate treaties with foreign powers. Power was lodged in thirteen virtually unrestrained state governments, held together under the loose coordination of the Confederation Congress. To address these perplexing and seemingly unsurmountable problems, leaders from twelve of the states gathered in Philadelphia during the hot summer of 1787 to strengthen the Articles. In what some historians have described as the most important event in our nation's history, they ended up writing the United States Constitution, a masterpiece that has endured two centuries.

The challenge facing the delegates sent to the convention in Philadelphia was one of no mean proportion. But when they completed their work a plan had been devised whereby central authority had been strengthened with national powers being carefully enumerated and other powers reserved to the individual states and the people. The story of the compromises that went into the writing of the Constitution is a familiar one as are the names of some of the men who helped draft this cherished document. George Washington presided over the convention that included such distinguished delegates as Benjamin Franklin, James Madison, James Wilson, Alexander Hamilton, George Mason, Gouverneur Morris and John Dickinson. Concerning these delegates, Alvin M. Josephy Jr., author of *On The Hill—A History of the American Congress*, said "they constituted one of the best-grounded and most astute group of political scientists the world has ever seen, with a maturity acquired not alone from what they had read, but from the long, tumultuous years in which necessity had made them experiment with self-government."

One of these political scientists was Dr. Hugh Williamson, a native Chester Countian who had come under the tutorage of the previously mentioned Dr. Francis Alison at Alison's remarkable Presbyterian academy at New London Crossroads. Born of Scotch-Irish immigrants who settled in West

Nottingham Township, Williamson represented North Carolina at the convention. A distinguished patriot and a zealous advocate of the proposed constitution, Dr. Williamson would later serve in the United States Congress during President Washington's first term.

The compromises that led to the Constitution and plan for governmental reorganization as envisioned in the document framed at Philadelphia were the source of much controversy. Sixteen of the fifty-five delegates would not subscribe to it, and there was no assurance the brilliantly devised plan of government would be accepted by the people back home in the states. While it was generally agreed the existing Articles were ineffectual, the widespread distrust of centralized power was just as prevalent in 1787 as it had been when the Articles were written a decade earlier.

RATIFICATION

Pennsylvania was the second state to ratify the Constitution, but this approval did not come about without a struggle. The revolutionists of the 1770s were now divided into two political camps. In the one were the more conservative republicans, the propertied men who realized the Articles could not guarantee a strong republic. They wanted checks and balances in their government. They were concerned with security, with order, and with good government. They reasoned that the power of the masses should be restrained, and some argued that the owning of property should be a qualification for voting and holding office. They called themselves Federalists during the prolonged ratification debate in which they supported the proposed Constitution.

In the second camp were the republicans of this revolutionary generation who feared a central authority whether it be king, president or governor. They were referred to as Anti-Federalists and they sought to bring government as closely as possible under the direct control of the people. They argued that the individual states were being asked to surrender too much of their sovereign power to the federal government. This opposition to the proposed Constitution was not peculiar to Pennsylvania. Some of the leading patriots in the colonial rebellion such as Sam Adams of Massachusetts and Patrick Henry of Virginia opposed ratification.

Anthony Wayne and a goodly number of Chester County's military heroes could be found in the conservative camp in favor of ratification. On Sept. 27, 1787, when the Pennsylvania General Assembly voted 43 to 17 to call a ratifying convention all six of the county's legislators—Richard Thomas, Robert Ralston, James Moore, Townsend Whelen, Samuel Evans and Richard Willing—cast "aye" votes. All six were re-elected a few weeks later after they campaigned on a "Friends to the Federal Constitution" ticket.

Chester County sent six delegates—Anthony Wayne, Thomas Cheyney, Thomas Bull, William Gibbons, John Hannum and Richard Downing Jr.—to the convention that had been called to decide the ratification question.

Unfortunately, there were no newspapers in the county at this time, and not much is known as to how these men came to be chosen. Were they elected by wide or narrow margins? Did the Anti-Federalists run men against them? In the years ahead Chester County would become known as a Federalist stronghold and the home of political conservatives, but the history buff can only look back and conjecture on the strength of ratification support in 1787. The common denominator then in the selection of persons for public office and conventions such as this one was participation in the Revolutionary War, but conspicuously absent from the county contingent sent to Philadelphia were the Scotch-Irish Presbyterians who had sacrificed so much and fought so bravely during the rebellion.

General Wayne, the hero of Stony Point and one of the young nation's top military leaders, was of course the best known of the county's delegates. After he led the attack that brought about the fall of the British stronghold on the Hudson, Dr. Rush had written to him: "Our streets for many days rang with nothing but the name of General Wayne. You are remembered constantly next to our good and great Washington."

Although not nearly as famous as the delegate from Easttown Township, four of the other county delegates had been deeply committed to the independence cause. 'Squire Cheyney, who at fifty-six was the oldest member of the county delegation, is remembered for his ride to warn Washington of advancing British troops during the Battle of the Brandywine. Frequently in great jeopardy as he worked as a spy for the colonial army, 'Squire Cheyney was sometimes unable to return to his Thornbury Township home for weeks at a time as the British employed various stratagems to capture him. Colonel Bull had assisted in organizing the county battalion of the "Flying Camp" (the term used for reserve units activated on an emergency basis) and later was captured and held prisoner on Long Island for a number of months. Hannum and Gibbons were also staunch patriots; only Downing among the six had followed the dictates of the Society of Friends and not involved himself in the struggle. However, his brother-in-law Richard Thomas had been an active Whig and was at this time one of the county's most influential politicos, which may account for Downing's being chosen as a delegate.

Regardless of how or why they were chosen to represent the county at the ratification convention, the familial and political backgrounds of the delegates are worthy of note in that they offer a clue as to how the county's conservative power structure was being established. General Wayne and Colonel Bull were Episcopalians; the other four had Quaker upbringings. Gibbons was disowned by the Society of Friends for the active part he took in the Revolution and Cheyney's antipathy to the Friends was such that he caused a burial place to be set aside on his farm lest his ashes might commingle with theirs. Although those who had remained loyal to King George or maintained a neutral position during the war were generally not considered worthy of holding public office, the makeup of the county delegation seems to indicate that political leadership in the county was reverting from the Scotch-Irish back to the well-fixed and well-established families.

The Quaker grandfathers of Cheyney, Gibbons and Hannum had emigrated from England about the time William Penn founded his colony. Their grandsons were fairly well-to-do farmers. Hannum owned a large farm on the Brandywine and Valley creeks in East Bradford; Cheyney's farm was in Thornbury; and Gibbons inherited a large property in West Nantmeal. The forebears of the other three delegates arrived a few years later in the early part of the eighteenth century. Wayne's grandfather, the first Anthony Wayne in America, purchased 386 acres in Easttown in 1724—two years after migrating with his family to this country from the county of Wicklow, Ireland. Like his grandson, he was a military man, having fought on the side of England's King William at the Battle of the Boyne. Here, not far from Paoli, his son Isaac built a magnificent stone mansion called Waynesborough, now a county showplace.

The Downing and Bull families were also well-established in Chester County before the Revolution. The Downing family, for whom the Borough of Downingtown was later named, operated mills along the Brandywine. Richard Downing Jr., who at age thirty-seven was the youngest of the county's six delegates to the ratification convention, was one of the most influential men in Milltown, as the small village in East Caln Township was called before it became Downingtown. Bull, a stone mason by trade, managed the Warwick Furnace prior to the war and at this particular time owned a large tract in what was then East Nantmeal on the headwaters of French Creek where he operated a saw-mill and grist-mill. Like the others, Bull was a man of means. The Bull name remains familiar today because of St. Mary's Episcopal Church in Warwick, founded in 1806 by his son Levi, and the historic Bull Tavern west of Phoenixville.

At the State House in Philadelphia the six Chester Countians joined sixty-three other delegates on November 21 and for the next three weeks listened as arguments for and against the new constitution were presented. Among their associates were such prominent Pennsylvanians as Thomas McKean, James Wilson and Dr. Benjamin Rush, all signers of the Declaration of Independence, and Frederick Augustus Muhlenberg, Joseph Hiester, Jonathan Roberts and Robert Coleman. Little has been recorded of the roles played by Wayne, Cheyney, Hannum, Gibbons, Downing and Bull during the ratification deliberations at Philadelphia, but when the vote was finally taken on December 12 all six cast affirmative votes. Strong opposition was voiced by delegates from the hinterlands beyond the Susquehanna and as a consequence the vote in favor of ratification was 46 to 23.

THE FIRST CONGRESS

For the Chester County history buff the first election of members to the

United States House of Representatives holds no special attraction since the county was without an entry on either of the tickets presented to the Pennsylvania electorate by the rival conservative and radical politicians. Nor did this first congressional election generate any great interest among the voters of Chester County. Less than twelve hundred of them went to the polls in 1788 on the last Wednesday in November to register their choices for congressmen. This poor voter turnout, however, was not peculiar to Chester County; the election was a failure everywhere.

Pennsylvania was allotted eight seats in the first House of Representatives. Some historians say there was not sufficient time after the federal Constitution was ratified to permit the state legislators to apportion the Commonwealth into eight congressional districts, and for this reason it was necessary to have an at-large election. Another explanation is that the conservatives or Federalists realized they could only be sure of success if the election was held on a statewide basis. Regardless, those Chester Countians who participated gave their overwhelming support to the Federalist ticket and provided Frederick A. Muhlenberg, George Clymer, Thomas Scott, Thomas Fitzsimmons, Thomas Hartley, Henry Wynkoop, Stephen Chambers, and John Allison with pluralities of roughly 700 votes. In passing it might be noted that Scott, a political leader in Westmoreland County, had been born in Chester County in 1739.

These Federalist winners in the county had been nominated in early November at a convention held in Lancaster. The radicals or Anti-Federalists convened in Harrisburg a short time later and came up with another list of nominees. Their list included the names of Gen. Peter Muhlenberg and Gen. Daniel Hiester, both of whom supported the recently adopted federal Constitution and held political views very similar to the nominees on the other ticket. In picking the two generals, both of German ancestry, the radicals hoped to attract the state's sizeable German vote. It was not the first time, nor would it be the last time, Pennsylvania politicians would sacrifice principles for votes. But this ploy on the part of the radical ticket-makers did not greatly help their cause. Instead it called attention to the lack of recognition given the Germans, who comprised one-third of the state's population. As a protest the German voters decided to support a hybrid ticket that included the two generals and all of the Federalist nominees but Chambers and Allison. Their strategy worked. Chambers and Allison lost out statewide by about 400 votes to Muhlenberg and Hiester; the other six Federalist nominees were successful.

The two Muhlenbergs—sons of the Reverend Henry Melchoir Muhlenberg, one of the most eminent Lutheran clergymen that Germany sent to America—led their respective tickets in the vote-getting. Frederick received 8,707 votes and Peter had 7,417. In all likelihood it was the two Muhlenbergs, both of whom had been educated for the ministry, who looked after the interests of Chester County in the First Congress. Both resided at Trappe,

Montgomery County. While serving as a preacher in the Shenandoah Valley of Virginia, Peter became deeply involved in the independence cause and finally discarded his ministerial robes for a military uniform. A friend of such political firebrands as Patrick Henry, he is reported to have told his congregation in a stirring farewell sermon "there is a time to pray and a time to fight." His younger brother Frederick was also active in the struggle for independence, but not as a military man.

Government of the thirteen states under the Articles of Confederation ended on March 3, 1789. The Confederation Congress intended that the new government would be organized immediately when the First Congress convened the following day at Federal Hall in New York City, but inclement weather and poor travel conditions delayed some legislators and it was not until April that the House and Senate finally had quorums and were able to get down to the business of organizing a new federal government. Frederick Muhlenberg was elected Speaker of the House. George Washington, the unanimous choice of the presidential electors, did not leave his Mount Vernon home in Virginia to assume his new duties until April 16 and was not inaugurated until April 30.

SENATOR MACLAY

Chester County did not have its own representative in the House until the midway point of President Washington's second term, but it did have a very vocal native son in the United States Senate when the First Congress met. William Maclay, a son of Charles and Eleanor Query Maclay, was born in the southern part of Chester County in 1737, three years after his parents emigrated from County Antrim, Ireland. In 1740, when he was only three, Maclay's family moved westward across the Susquehanna to Cumberland County. As was the case with so many of the Scotch-Irish patriots of this era, Maclay received his early education at one of Chester County's highly regarded Presbyterian schools. He studied under the Reverend John Blair at the Faggs Manor Classical School before taking up the study of law. His schooling completed, Maclay was admitted to the bar of York County in 1760, but the law did not appeal to him and he found employment as a deputy surveyor instead. During the French and Indian War he served as a frontier soldier. Afterwards he began devoting more and more time to politics, serving first as prothonotary and clerk of courts in Northumberland County. He later became a member of the Pennsylvania Supreme Executive Council and a power in Dauphin County politics.

Maclay's long and varied political career both before and after the Revolution well qualified him for a seat in the United States Senate. The selection of senators at this time rested with the General Assembly, and among the Pennsylvania assemblymen of 1788 Maclay could count many friends. After much backroom politicking his name and the names of Robert Morris, the financial genius of the American Revolution, and William Irvine, a moderate supported by the Anti-Federalists, were presented to the General Assembly for a vote. Maclay, with 66 votes, and Morris, with 37 votes, came out on top in the balloting and thus became Pennsylvania's first United States senators.

A strongly built man who stood over six feet tall, Maclay was also a strongly opinionated man. During his short but stormy two year stint in the Congress he was recognized as a leader in what was soon to become known as the Democratic-Republican Party. His views clashed with the Federalist majority in the Senate. Like Thomas Jefferson and James Madison, who are credited with founding the Democratic Party, he vigorously advocated agrarian interests and ridiculed those like Vice President John Adams who seemed to be expressing a preference for a kingly rather than a republican style of government. He made it very clear that he for one was opposed to calling Washington "His Highness the President of the United States and Protector of the Rights of the Same," as some people proposed to do. Although Maclay himself has been ignored in most history books, his diaries were the source of much first-hand information used later by historians in describing how the new federal government developed.

Futhey and Cope's *History* states Maclay "did much to develop those ideas which led to the formation of the Democratic party, and in this he, in fact, preceded Jefferson, although historians give the credit to the latter." The founding fathers had not envisioned a two-party system, but when the First Congress adjourned on March 3, 1791, the ideas and positions taken by such men as Senator Maclay were already beginning to crystallize in the form of political parties.

ELECTION OF 1790

Congressmen are normally elected in even-number years, but this was not the case in 1790. Probably due to bickering over apportionment or districting, the selection of Pennsylvania's representatives in the Second Congress was postponed until 1791. Nevertheless, the election that did occur in 1790 is noteworthy. It was Pennsylvania's first election following the adoption of a new state constitution, and in addition to choosing their first governor the Commonwealth's voters elected members to a bicameral state legislature for the first time.

Party lines were not clearly drawn and there were no real issues in this first gubernatorial election, which was won by Thomas Mifflin. Nor did the change in government structure result in any significant change in the makeup of Chester County's legislative delegation to the state capital in Philadelphia. Col. Richard Thomas, Richard Downing, Caleb James and John McDowell comprised the county's legislative foursome during the waning days of government under the state's first constitution. All four were returned to the General Assembly in 1790, Thomas as senator and the others as representatives. The only newcomer in the delegation was James Boyd, a

Revolutionary War veteran from Faggs Manor.

Governor Mifflin began his three-year term as the state's first elected chief executive on Dec. 21, 1790. Two weeks earlier the General Assembly had launched a lengthy 128-day session during which time the lawmakers tackled the problem of congressional districting. Under a plan finally approved on March 16, 1791, the state was divided into eight districts, one of which was comprised of Chester and Montgomery counties. The two counties had much in common, but their inhabitants differed on political matters. Chester County was a Federalist enclave; Montgomery County's voters had a preference for Anti-Federalist candidates. It should be emphasized, however, there was some strong Federalist sentiment in Montgomery County just as there was a resolute Anti-Federalist opposition in Chester County, largely concentrated in the northern and western townships.

Chester County had no newspapers in 1791 and the researcher today is hard pressed to find details pertaining to the election of Israel Jacobs to the Second Congress from this Chesmont district. The *Biographical Directory of the American Congress* states he was born in 1726 in Providence Township, Montgomery County, and was "one of the first to advocate the union of the colonies." Prior to the Revolution he served as an assemblyman from 1770 to 1774. The historian Edward W. Hocker writes in his *Montgomery County History* that Frederick Muhlenberg had changed his residence to Philadelphia, but that his brother Peter was active in Montgomery County politics and wanted to be returned to Congress. Although he does not paint a clear picture as to why Muhlenberg was cast aside and how Jacobs won the election, Hocker wrote:

> "Members of the Second Congress were not chosen until three years after the election of the First Congress. On October 4, 1791, a meeting of Democratic Republican citizens of Montgomery and Chester Counties was held at Warren Tavern, on Lancaster road, to select a congressional candidate, these two counties then constituting a district. A committee was delegated to choose the candidate. The committee reported in the evening that its vote was as follows: General Muhlenberg, 9; Thomas Ross, a Norristown lawyer, 8; William Moore Smith, 4; Israel Jacobs, 3; John Hannum, 3. However, at the election Israel Jacobs, a Federalist nominee, was elected. He was a member of the Society of Friends and lived at what is now Mont Clare, five miles south of Muhlenberg's home at Trappe."

Jacobs was elected to only one term in Congress, after which he resumed his agricultural pursuits on his Montgomery County farm. He died in 1796.

GEN. WAYNE'S ELECTION

Although the keepers of history neglected to save records pertaining to the congressional election in Chester County in 1791, they did a very good job in preserving materials relating to a controversial election in Georgia that year involving Chester County's illustrious military hero—General Anthony Wayne. But Wayne's election to the Second Congress was not one of his crowning achievements. Quite the contrary; it removed some of the luster from the hero image and presented the Second Congress with unpleasant problems it would have gladly done without.

The years following the war were difficult ones for Wayne; his marriage had soured, he was heavily in debt, and Waynesborough—his Chester County plantation—offered too tame a life for the restless soldier who a few years earlier had won gold medals and the praise of the Continental Congress for his daring capture of Stony Point. At times Wayne lived in Pennsylvania and at other times he resided in Georgia where the state legislature, in appreciation for his military service, had presented him with a large plantation twelve miles northwest of Savannah. He was active politically in both states. As already noted, Chester County voters elected him to the state assembly in 1784, restoring him to the political office he had held before the Revolution, and they later made him a delegate to the state convention that ratified the United States Constitution. During this same period Wayne claimed to be a Georgia resident and when the new federal government was established he was disappointed when the Georgia legislature passed over him and picked another man to represent the state in the United States Senate. He subsequently ran for congressman in a Georgia district and defeated the incumbent, James Jackson, in January 1791.

The voting irregularities in this election were so flagrant they are almost unbelievable. Using his authority as judge, one of Wayne's campaign managers ordered a polling place reopened after it had been closed for several hours in order to permit eight men to cast sixty-four votes for the general. In Savannah the mayor threw out the regularly chosen election board and installed men of his own choosing to count the ballots. These and other illegal means employed to obtain the desired result were initially overlooked when Wayne presented his credentials as the duly elected representative from the Georgia district to the Second Congress. Shortly after the session began, however, a petition from ex-Congressman Jackson was read in the House of Representatives complaining of the "undue election and return of Anthony Wayne." Congress had never dealt with a problem such as this, so the matter was referred to the Committee of Elections with instructions to bring in a bill for establishing a uniform mode of proceeding in case of contested elections.

Congress appears to have been in no hurry to act on the complaint. Initially, Wayne endeavored to persuade his colleagues to dismiss the petition on grounds that Jackson had waited too long (eleven months) to make his complaint. Other delays occurred as evidence pertaining to the case was gathered in Georgia. It was not until March of 1792 that the election case was heard and a decision rendered against Chester County's hero. On March 21, 1792, by a unanimous vote, the House declared he had not been duly elected to its membership and declared the Georgia seat vacant. Jackson, however, did not get his seat back. A resolution to make the former congressman a member of the Second Congress failed to pass when the Speaker of the House broke a 29-to-29 vote with his deciding nay vote.

THE THIRD CONGRESS

As a result of the 1790 census the size of the House of Representatives was increased to 106 members and the size of the Pennsylvania delegation was expanded to thirteen. However, this information was not available to the state's lawmakers before they adjourned in the spring of 1792. Not knowing how many men Pennsylvania would send to the next Congress the state legislators decreed (not unanimously) that all of the representatives sent to the Third Congress should be picked in an at-large election rather than by districts. Neither the Federalist nor Anti-Federalist kingpins saw fit to place a man from Chester County on their tickets even though it was the fifth largest of the Commonwealth's twenty-one counties with a population of 27,937.

Although Chester County was not represented in the national legislature, two of her native sons served in the Third Congress. Thomas Scott, of Westmoreland County, was again among the thirteen Keystone winners as was William Montgomery, a colonel in the Chester County militia during the Revolution. Born in Londonderry Township in 1736, Montgomery moved to Northumberland County after the war and became a leading political figure there. His previous legislative experience included memberships in the Confederation Congress and the Pennsylvania Senate.

CHAPTER 3

FEDERALISTS PICK THOMAS

From a distance of two hundred years it is difficult, if not altogether impossible, to single out Chester County's leading politician of the Revolutionary War era. Among her native sons the two most famous were Anthony Wayne, one of General Washington's most capable military leaders, and Thomas McKean, a signer of the Declaration of Independence. Both had the honor of having Pennsylvania counties named after them. Neither, however, is remembered as a Chester County politician.

During the turbulent years before the colonies declared their independence Wayne was one of the most politically active young men in the county, but his political career was a brief one, overshadowed by his achievements as a military man. His political ventures after the war, particularly those in Georgia, were frequently motivated by selfish personal goals, tarnishing his long career of public service. As a politician McKean had few peers in Pennsylvania in the late eighteenth and early nineteenth centuries. He was the first chief justice of the Pennsylvania Supreme Court under the Constitution of 1776 and three times was elected governor, but his home base was never Chester County. In fact, his popularity at the polling places in his native county left much to be desired.

A more likely candidate for Chester County's "leading politician" honors during our nation's formative years was another outstanding patriot who was elected in 1794 to serve in the United States House of Representatives. His name was Richard Thomas. A Friend by birthright, he was one of the earliest, most active, and most reliable of the Quaker Whigs of the American Revolution. His political and military activities met with the disapproval of the Uwchlan Meeting of the Society of Friends, to which he belonged, but his dedication in the colonial struggle for independence earned him widespread respect and recognition throughout the county.

Born in Whiteland Township in October 1744 (just a few weeks before his friend and comrade Anthony Wayne was born in nearby Easttown Township), Thomas was among the first in Chester County to take up arms against Great Britain. In September 1775, three months after the battle of Bunker Hill, he was appointed lieutenant colonel of the first military force raised in Chester County, a regiment of reserves headed by Wayne. Shortly thereafter when Wayne accepted a commission in the regular Continental Army the command of the county's "flying camp" devolved on Colonel

Thomas. He was in charge of the unit during the campaign across New Jersey that culminated in a costly defeat for the American forces at Long Island. His men later fought at Princeton and saw much action in 1777 when Chester County was a main theater in the war.

As was the case with many of the patriot leaders, Thomas' involvement in the "glorious cause" carried with it great personal risk. He came from a family of considerable means as did his wife Thomazine, daughter of the prosperous East Caln mill owner Richard Downing. There were still Indians living in the vicinity when his grandfather, an emigrant from Whitford Garden in North Wales, obtained lands in Whiteland Township and built a house along Valley Creek. Over the years his grandfather and his father increased the family's land holdings and built several mills. As a Whig leader he risked losing his home and property if the British were successful in quelling the rebellion. But even though his political beliefs were considered radical by his Quaker neighbors, and even though his rashness in taking up arms against the crown met with their disapproval, when it came to business Thomas was still a shrewd Quaker. As a precaution, he made a conveyance of his lands, approximately 500 acres, to his pacifist younger brother George so as to protect his property from confiscation in the event the "glorious cause" developed into a miserable fiasco.

It is quite possible that Thomas was in Philadelphia when the vote on independence was taken. An early supporter of the Continental Congress, he served on the Committee of Safety in Chester County from the time of its inception and was one of the thirteen revolutionaries representing the county when the Provincial Conference assembled at Carpenters' Hall in Philadelphia in June of 1776 and usurped power from the duly elected General Assembly. He and the others in the Conference arranged for the constitutional convention to change the form of government in Pennsylvania and took it upon themselves to concur in the vote of the Second Continental Congress declaring the colonies free and independent states.

Details of his Revolutionary War activities are somewhat sketchy, but those who have researched the matter conclude that Thomas was associated with the Continental Army in one capacity or another for about six years, serving until the British army under Lord Cornwallis surrendered at Yorktown, Va. His political career was resumed shortly thereafter with his election to the Pennsylvania Assembly in 1786. Just as the outbreak of war with Great Britain brought into existence a new revolutionary central government, it also brought about new and revolutionary governments within the individual colonies. And just as the Articles of Confederation were proving to be an unsatisfactory vehicle for governing the new nation in the 1780s, Pennsylvania's hastily drawn Constitution of 1776 also had many shortcomings that were causing problems and dissension when Thomas became an assemblyman.

Most historians agree that the patriots who had hurriedly convened a state constitutional convention in the summer of 1776 had not done an exceptional job in preparing a new framework of state government. Thomas himself had not been a delegate, but it is very likely he had helped pick Chester County's seven delegates. The seven—Benjamin Bartholomew, Samuel Cunningham, John Jacobs, John Mackey, Robert Smith, Thomas Strawbridge and John Flemming—were his friends. In writing their constitution the 1776 radicals had ended the oligarchic rule Chester County had shared with neighboring Philadelphia and Bucks counties by providing for equal representation in the General Assembly. No one could fault them for this. But among the constitution's many unusual features was the typical colonial aversion to a strong executive. Rather than having a governor, they had placed executive authority in the hands of a Supreme Executive Council. The legislative branch continued to be a unicameral assembly.

One of the earliest and most vociferous critics of the state constitution was Philadelphia's ardent patriot, Dr. Benjamin Rush. He criticized the single-house legislature concept and objected to the use of an executive council. Other important figures in the revolutionary movement such as Anthony Wayne later agreed with him that the power of the masses should be restrained through checks and balances. Thomas shared this viewpoint. Agitation for a new constitution mounted and during his four years as an assemblyman Thomas watched the political pendulum swing from the radical to the conservative side. Finally, in March of 1789, at just about the same time the new federal government was being launched in New York, the Pennsylvania Assembly, by a 41 to 17 vote, decreed that the state's governmental framework should be re-examined by a constitutional convention. Thomas and the county's other lawmakers—James Moore, Mark Wilcox, John McDowell, Caleb James, and Richard Downing Jr.—favored having the convention. The following year a new state constitution was adopted that did away with the unicameral legislature and provided for a General Assembly consisting of a House of Representatives and Senate. Eighteen members were elected to this first Senate and Thomas was one of them.

Political power rested with those serving in the General Assembly then, not Congress. The new federal government was regarded by many as an experiment; state government was real. As a state senator Thomas was an influential figure. During his tenure as senator he was appointed brigadier general in the Pennsylvania Militia and placed in command of the Chester County contingent. One can only speculate as to why he decided to remove himself from the state political stage to serve in the national legislature. Little has been preserved regarding his election as congressman from Pennsylvania's new Third District in 1794, least of all his reasons for running. Under the congressional apportionment approved by the Assembly in April of that year the counties of Chester and Delaware were united in one district, but since the county was still without a newspaper not even the name of his opponent—if he had one—has been saved in the historical archives. Since he was running in a Federalist enclave, though, it is presumed that Thomas—a popular personage as well as a durable and seasoned politician—was elected with little difficulty. With only seven voting districts in the county—Chatham, Paoli, Gum Tree, Lower Oxford, Manor, Red Lion and West Chester—it might also be safe to conjecture that participation on the part of the voters was limited.

The Fourth Congress did not begin its first session until Dec. 7, 1795—a year after Thomas was elected. For most congressmen the 177-day session meant a long absence from home, but this was not the case with Thomas. With the national capital located in Philadelphia, it was fairly easy for him to slip home to see his family. Thomazine no doubt appreciated this; shortly after her husband was elected to Congress she gave birth to a boy, and when he left home to attend his first session in the House he left her with eight children (ranging in age from eight months to ten years) to look after as well as a sizeable plantation to manage.

The conflict between the ideas and economic interests personified by Treasury Secretary Alexander Hamilton and Secretary of State Thomas Jefferson were well understood when Thomas presented his credentials at the opening of the Fourth Congress. The people of the young nation had drifted into one or the other of the two political divisions. Hamilton's Federalists, with whom Thomas associated, were regarded as the party of conservatism, devoted primarily to the interests of capitalists and the mercantile class. Jefferson represented the agrarian element and those who feared a strong central government.

A number of serious problems confronted Thomas and his colleagues in the Fourth Congress, but most of the questions of procedure and organization had been worked out by their predecessors and the new government's machinery of administration was smoothly operating by 1795. The departments of Treasury, State and War had been organized; a judiciary system established; a Bill of Rights enacted; the Bank of the United States chartered and the United States Mint established; a census had been taken; and President Washington had firmly asserted his authority in foreign affairs. Fiscal policies had been argued and formulated to resolve the controversial problems of funding the national debt (over $50 million) and assumption of state debts. Thomas' predecessors had also settled the all-important question of their own remuneration by voting themselves a salary of six dollars per day while in session and had resolved the matter of a permanent location for the national government.

One of the most controversial issues debated in the House of Representatives during Thomas' early days as a congressman was a proposed treaty with Great Britain. In the early 1790s the British had six thousand troops stationed in North America, and in the eyes of many United States citizens it was the British who were responsible for the trouble being experienced on the frontier with the Indians. British ships of war were also interfering with American shipping and American sailors were being impressed. To avert another war, President Washington sent John Jay to England to negotiate with the British. In Congress the Anti-Federalists, or Democratic-Republicans as they were sometimes called, condemned the treaty Jay came back with as a sacrifice of American rights and honor. The ensuing debate over the treaty did nothing to assuage the political acrimony building up throughout the country. Strong opposition developed in the House to appropriating the necessary funds (about $90,000) to implement the treaty after it was ratified in secret session by the Senate. Thomas voted "yea" in the close (51-48) House vote for carrying the Jay Treaty into effect.

Representative Thomas was twice re-elected and served his last two terms in the House during the presidency of John Adams. He had the distinction, but not pleasure, of being the first Chester Countian sent to Washington as a congressman. In early 1800 the nation's capital was removed from Philadelphia (a pretty and cosmopolitan city with good hotels, restaurants, theaters, museums, bookshops and libraries) to a small and undeveloped settlement of muddy roads and crowded boardinghouses along the Potomac. Following the fall elections the Sixth Congress began its second session at the new capital on Nov. 17, 1800. One can only speculate as to whether the relocation of the seat of government had any bearing on Thomas' decision not to seek a fourth term.

During the Adams presidency Congressman Thomas was called upon to stand up and be counted on a number of controversial subjects that divided the young nation and did much to embitter party spirit throughout the country. Perhaps the most bitterly debated of all these measures were the Alien and Sedition Acts—regarded by many historians as the most intolerant laws ever passed by Congress. As a Federalist and a staunch supporter of President Adams, Thomas voted for these laws, which among other things increased the length of residence required for citizenship to fourteen years, authorized the deportation of aliens considered dangerous to public safety, and allowed for imprisonment of those who wrote or spoke out against the government in a scandalous or malicious manner. From all accounts the laws were very unpopular and contributed greatly to the success of the Democratic-Republican Party in the election of 1800.

There is nothing in the records to suggest that Thomas made any waves during his three terms as a congressman or that he was ever involved in any kingmaking role, but it should be noted he served in the national legislature during a period of much political skulduggery when congressmen had considerable say regarding the selection of the president. National conventions were still several decades away and the lawmakers took it upon themselves to nominate the men they wanted elevated to the nation's highest office. In all likelihood Thomas was among the group of Federalist lawmakers who met in congressional caucus in 1796 and pledged their support to John Adams for president and Thomas Pinckney of South Carolina for vice president.

The Federalists were successful in electing Adams, but the vice presidency went to his opponent, Thomas Jefferson, leader of the Democratic-Republicans, when a situation developed that had not been anticipated by the framers of the Constitution. No distinction was made between the votes cast for president and those for vice president, and when the electoral vote was counted Adams was elected president with 71 votes and Jefferson, the runner-up with 68, was elected vice president. The Twelfth Amendment, ratified in 1804, rectified this flaw by providing for separate balloting for the nation's two top offices.

During the closing days of his congressional career Thomas was most likely involved in the controversy and intrigue surrounding the presidential election of 1800. Virginia's Jefferson and New York's Aaron Burr, both leaders in the Democratic-Republican Party, received the same number of electoral votes and the question as to who should be president and who should be vice president was referred to the House of Representatives for an answer. The legislators did not vote individually on the two candidates, but in state groups, with each state entitled to one vote. Nine votes were needed to win. Thomas was no admirer of Jefferson as is evidenced in a letter he sent from Washington to a Federalist friend in Chester County three days before the House began its deliberations as to whether Jefferson or Burr should occupy the White House. In this letter to Jesse Jones, dated Feb. 8, 1801, Thomas wrote:

> "Thy Picture of the Democratic Arrogance exactly coincides with the same sort here. . . . They can't deny that we have a choice—'but you shall take Jefferson, the people meant him'—or 'you shall gratify the People'—is the Eternal Clamor with them. . . . Virginia is very arrogant & her members bitterly chagrin'd that we dare to slight her Darling. . . . The First Vote will not decide the Choice, and tis probable 8 States will be Jeffersonian—they will then be stubborn . . . and claim preponderance to justify a single member of Maryland to turn the scale."

His prediction proved accurate; Jefferson received eight votes on the first ballot. It was not until the thirty-sixth ballot was taken on February 17 that Jefferson finally was elected. As much as he disliked Jefferson and the "arrogance" of his followers, Thomas indicated he was inclined to abide by the desires of the people. He realized, of course, his vote was meaningless since Pennsylvania's congressional delegation was comprised mainly of Jefferson's followers.

In early March of 1801 Jefferson became president, the Sixth Congress adjourned, and Congressman Thomas returned to Chester County. He was fifty-six and in good health, but apparently had no desire to continue holding public office. He remained loyal to the dying Federalist Party and as late as 1812 served on the Chester County Federal Republican Committee. He died on Jan. 18, 1832, in his eighty-eighth year.

CHAPTER 4

THE JEFFERSONIAN ERA

In 1800—the year of the Democratic-Republican triumph that led to Thomas Jefferson being chosen as president of the United States—the voters of Chester and Delaware counties picked thirty-year-old Joseph Hemphill, an ardent Federalist, and the youngest congressman ever elected from Chester County, as their congressman. In the long history of the Democratic Party in Chester County no family has provided more leadership or been more involved in party affairs than the Hemphills. It is therefore rather surprising to find the youthful Hemphill on the side of the Federalists and not with Jefferson, the founder of the Democratic Party.

Grandson of the Irish immigrant Alexander Hemphill, Joseph was an up-and-coming attorney at the turn of the century. His abilities were readily recognized and appreciated by the county's older politicians. A graduate of the University of Pennsylvania, class of 1791, Hemphill was admitted to the bar in 1793 and elected to the General Assembly four years later on a Federalist ticket headed by Col. Thomas Bull. As a state legislator Hemphill was instrumental in obtaining passage of a law giving Chester County a poorhouse, the first of its kind authorized by the state.

Very little has been recorded concerning Hemphill's service in the Seventh Congress. His most noteworthy effort had to do with a speech delivered during House debate over repeal of a judiciary law passed during the administration of President Adams. It was the only debate he participated in and afterwards he was sometimes referred to as "Single-Speech Hemphill." As far as Chester County was concerned he was a single term congressman. Redistricting cut short Hemphill's political career in his native Chester County after three brief terms in the Pennsylvania House and one in Congress, but these legislative experiences were just the beginning of a long career of public service. Following adjournment of the Seventh Congress he moved to Philadelphia where he became immersed in politics and soon was recognized as one of the city's leading public figures. He was elected as a state legislator in 1805 and later had the honor of being appointed the first president judge of the district court of Philadelphia.

Hemphill also quickly advanced to the top of Philadelphia's social ladder. With his marriage to the beautiful and wealthy Margaret Coleman of Lancaster County, he moved in the best circles and came into ownership of Somerton, one of Philadelphia's residential showplaces. In her book *Strawberry*

Mansion, Sarah Dickinson Lowrie writes:

> "He had a certain dash and manner which made it perfectly evident that he had traveled in Europe, was a friend of other well-known French notables, besides the Marquis de Lafayette, and in fact, had gone very far afield from his parents' farm in Chester County. There seemed nothing of the plain Quaker left in him. Scarcely any of the mere Philadelphia World Quaker either. As Robert Coleman's son-in-law, he had grown too to have very much the air of a sportsman, and by now was obviously quite the man about town, with a regency cut to his clothes, and the regency wave to his hair."

Always active in civic and political affairs, Hemphill returned to Congress during President Monroe's administration and gradually parted company with the Federalists to become a booster of Gen. Andrew Jackson. Concerning Hemphill's emergence as a "states right" man and a Jackson enthusiast, Lowrie wrote:

> "Hemphill having long felt the wind of change on his cheek, permitted himself to change too. To be sure he had run for Congress as a Federalist, and he had before that succeeded as a Federalist on the Bench. But even the walls of Somerton had had to meet the new times with new faces, so why not Somerton's master? Alexander Hamilton's portrait was replaced in the small parlor by one of Thomas Jefferson. The mezzotint of Washington was placed in the dark shadow of the great front door, that door ever to swing open to a new visitor in the hospitable house. But both of the leaders were dead and gone; the new States Rights leaders that Congress was trying out, Clay, Calhoun, Randolph of Roanoke, and Carroll, were all of them Southerners. States Rights men. They found the newly elected Pennsylvania Congressman Hemphill sympathetic to their new party drive. . . . The military hero, Jackson was their favorite; the Adams adherents were on the wane. In fact with Hemphill to organize Pennsylvania, and Webster to sweep Yankeeland with his eloquence, if he could be annexed, their presidential candidate, Andrew Jackson, might not only be nominated, but elected."

Undoubtedly, Joseph Hemphill played a key role in Philadelphia and Pennsylvania politics during the 1820s and Jackson's presidency. On four occasions the voters of Philadelphia elected him to the federal House of Representatives. But from a Chester county perspective he was no longer a major political figure. On the county political stage, however, his younger brother William was very active. It was this younger Hemphill who was responsible for beginning the family's political dynasty in Chester County. William's son and grandson, both named Joseph and both attorneys, became leaders of the local Democratic Party.

ISAAC ANDERSON

Isaac Anderson, a veteran of the Revolutionary War and a supporter of President Jefferson, succeeded Hemphill in the Chester County congressional cavalcade. First of the county's Democratic-Republicans to serve in the Congress, Anderson was in his early forties when he arrived on the Washington scene. Known for his great physical strength (he stood over six foot four), Anderson was credited with having three terms of service in the Continental Army before his eighteenth birthday.

Born on Nov. 23, 1760, not far from Valley Forge in what was then Charlestown Township (now Schuylkill), Anderson grew up in a frontier environment. His grandfather James Anderson, who emigrated from the Isle of Skye, Scotland, was the first settler along the Pickering Creek in Charlestown, and his father Patrick Anderson was the first white child born in the township. Patrick was one of the local leaders in the revolt against Great Britain, serving on the first Chester County Committee of Safety and later as a major in Anthony Wayne's regiment of Chester County minutemen. He fought in the battles of Long Island, the Brandywine and Germantown.

Futhey and Cope's *History of Chester County* has this to say concerning Isaac's boyhood:

> "He was a great favorite with the Indians, who still frequented the valley of the Pickering, and often accompanied them on their fishing and hunting excursions. Though a mere boy when the Revolutionary war commenced, he was not of the temper to rest in quiet amid the exciting scenes occurring around him. . . . In the fall of 1777, during the British invasion, he led a company of militia to the assistance of Washington, and while the army lay at Valley Forge he carried dispatches to and from the Congress at York."

At an early age Isaac married Mary Lane, a daughter of Edward Lane, who had been a member of General Braddock's expedition against Fort Dusquesne during the French and Indian War. In 1780, shortly after their marriage, Isaac and Mary were converted to Methodism. In his later years Isaac frequently preached for the sect. The Andersons had eleven children, but their marriage was not always a happy one. It survived, but at one point Mary left her husband and went to live with one of her sons. In his *Notes of Family History*, Isaac Sutton wrote concerning the estrangement:

> "It is said the basis of the dispute was the fact that his wife refused to wear any but plain clothes after she became a Methodist and especially because she would not dress up when they went to Washington to attend the sessions of Congress."

Exactly when Anderson became actively involved in county politics is not recorded. His father served in the Pennsylvania Assembly after the war and was a member of the commission responsible for providing navigation on the Schuylkill River. It is very likely Isaac shared his father's interest in government and took an active part in township and county political affairs from an early age. In 1799 he was appointed justice of the peace for his township, a post he held when he became a candidate for Congress in 1802 after the establishment of the Chester-Lancaster-Berks congressional district.

NEW DISTRICT CREATED

Before touching upon Anderson's election a few words are perhaps in order relative to the general political situation in the county and state at the start of the nineteenth century. The Federalists had the upper hand in Chester County in 1800, but elsewhere in the state the party's power had slipped. Thomas McKean's election as governor in 1799 was more than just a personal victory; it was a revolt against the old and established Federalist ruling class and a victory for the small farmer, the frontiersman, the city working man, and the newly arrived immigrant. McKean, a shrewd politician, was the recognized leader of Pennsylvania's Democratic-Republican Party and the most powerful and influential man in the state political arena. The Federalists had no one of his stature to lead them, and with the transfer of the national capital to Washington in 1800, coupled with Jefferson's election as president, their party was further weakened in the Keystone State. McKean and his followers—they called themselves Republicans, but were frequently referred to as Democrats or Democratic-Republicans—had everything going for them in the state, including the power to establish new congressional districts.

Following the census of 1800 the United States House of Representatives was increased to 141 members. At the time of the nation's first head count in 1790 the population of the original thirteen states was recorded at less than four million. During the ten-year interval three new states—Vermont, Kentucky and Tennessee—were added and the population of the young nation climbed beyond five million. The decision to expand the House membership meant that Pennsylvania (with a population of slightly over 434,000) would be entitled to elect eighteen congressmen rather than thirteen.

A simple solution for accompiishing congressional redistricting in Pennsylvania would have been to divide the state into eighteen districts, each with a population of roughly 24,000 persons. Chester County, fifth largest of the counties with a population of over 32,000, would have been entitled to its own congressman if this had happened, and it is quite likely Joseph Hemphill would have been returned to Washington City for a second term. The Federalists were strong in the county and generally managed to carry the day by several hundred votes in their battles with McKean's Democratic-Republicans. But the political cartographers drew the district lines another way, and they made Federalist Hemphill's re-election impossible.

Chester County was combined with Lancaster and Berks, the state's third and fourth most populous counties, in a three-county district. Because of the political makeup in these neighboring counties a Federalist aspirant from Chester County had no chance of winning in this new Third District. The vast majority of Berks County's farmers, mechanics and merchants shared President Jefferson's agrarian outlook; they believed in the doctrine of popular rule and favored restricting federal powers to the bare essentials. In Lancaster County the strength of the Federalist Party had diminished. As with Chester County, it had been in the Adams column when the votes were counted in 1800, but the next year five of its six seats in the state legislature were taken from the Federalists by Jeffersonian Democrats.

The strategy behind the congressional redistricting in Pennsylvania was to emasculate Federalist representation in Congress. It worked perfectly. The Federalists were unable to elect a single congressman in 1802. Hemphill and Lancaster County's Thomas Boude, a wealthy lumber dealer who played a prominent role in building the Federalist Party in his Pennsylvania Dutch bailiwick, were both defeated. Berks County provided the Democratic-Republican ticket in the Third District with an unsurmountable 3,400 vote majority, paving the way to victory for Chester County's Anderson; Lancaster County's John Whitehill; and Joseph Hiester, Berks County's incumbent congressman. The Democratic- Republicans not only made a clean sweep in the congressional elections, but they also gave Governor McKean a landslide second term victory in 1802. McKean won the rematch against Federalist James Ross, whom he had defeated by only 5,400 votes in 1799, by an overwhelming 30,800 votes.

The election story in 1804 was very much the same. The Federalists were disorganized both nationally and in Pennsylvania, allowing the Democratic-Republicans to re-elect President Jefferson by an overwhelming 162 to 14 electoral college vote. A letter addressed to the citizens of Chester County that appeared in *The Aurora*, a Philadelphia newspaper, shortly before the election reviewed the changes that had occurred since Jefferson took office:

> "Unnecessary taxes have been abolished—useless officers have been taken from an idle subsistence at the expense of the people, and sent to add their stock of labor to that of their industrious fellow citizens—unnecessary armies and camps have been abolished—the faith pledged by the old congress to the virtuous unfortunate of other countries has been restored, by the abolition of wicked restraining laws, and a more liberal naturalization law has been established—the public expenditure has been reduced one half, at the same time that the public debt is reducing more rapidly than before—these are but a few of the blessings which have proceeded from the due exertions of the people in removing faithless public servants and chusing better men."

This same letter warned the county's voters "to be cautious of the arts of designing men" when they went to the polls.

"Examine your tickets, for they who support their cause by deceit in words will cheat if they are not watched; recollect in 1801 a sheriff was imposed upon you by means of counterfeit tickets; be careful therefore that you are not again so cheated."

If there was chicanery, the Democrats were not hurt by it in 1804. It was a disastrous year almost everywhere for the Federalists. They lost the presidency again and nationwide were able to take only twenty-five congressional seats. In Pennsylvania the Democrats took all but one of eighteen congressional seats. The Third District was among those in the Democratic-Republican column. At a party caucus in Chester County it was decided Congressman Anderson should be supported for another term. A similar decision in favor of Congressman Whitehill was made by Lancaster County's party leaders. And in Berks County the name of Christian Lower was brought forth when Hiester said he would not seek a fifth term. Conferees from the three counties then met at Morgantown, a convenient spot near the intersection of all three counties, and gave their blessing to an Anderson-Whitehill-Lower ticket.

From the outset the Federalists realized victory was not within their grasp. They could not persuade anyone in Berks County to be a candidate for congressman. Chester County's Federalists proposed Isaac Wayne, son of the Revolutionary War hero, and ex-congressman Thomas Boude was drafted by Lancaster County's Federalists. Both were subsequently clobbered at the polls in Berks County. Wayne received only 79 votes and Boude was given 74. Their opponents polled over 2,600. For the second time the heavy Democratic-Republican vote there was the deciding factor in the Third District, insuring an Anderson-Whitehill-Lower triumph.

A NEW ALLIANCE

The gubernatorial election of 1805 brought to a climax the quarrels and struggle for power within Pennsylvania's Democratic-Republican ranks. Since the quarrel impacted upon future Third Congressional District elections, a brief digression is perhaps in order. Beleaguered with problems during his second term, McKean was assailed for nepotism and his stand in defense of the state constitution as the election season dawned. The more radical Democrats opposing him felt there was a need for judicial reform (in their opinion judges and lawyers had too much power) and argued that the four-year term of state senators was too long and contrary to the best interests of the people. On top of this, from their perspective, McKean's wealth and aristocratic bearing was more benefitting to a Federalist than to a Democrat. As their candidate for the governorship these radicals chose Speaker of the House Simon Snyder at a legislative caucus, but the aging McKean (he was seventy-one) decided to fight back and run for a third term. Snyder's German background was regarded as a big asset and was one of the reasons he was nominated; but Scotch-Irish McKean had Peter Muhlenberg and Joseph Hiester, the state's two most influential German politicians, in his corner.

Running on a "Constitutional Republican" ticket, and supported by Federalists and a large segment of the German citizenry, McKean was elected to a third term.

Although it proved to be an on-again, off-again arrangement, the alliance of the Federalists with the more conservative Democrats made for an entirely new ball game in the Third District. The Federalists, after two disastrous outings, came back strong in 1806, marching under the new Constitutional Republican banner, and the Chester-Lancaster-Berks congressional district became a real battleground. Congressman Anderson retired after four years of service in the House and was not directly involved in these bitter struggles. His reasons for not seeking a third term in 1806 are not recorded. Poor health was certainly not one of them. He was a vigorous forty-six when the Ninth Congress wound up its business and he returned to his home in Charlestown Township. Nor had his interest in politics waned. Family considerations and his marriage problems may have been a factor, but a more likely reason for his not seeking re-election was simply that there was an understanding among politicians of this era that no one should hog the honor of service in the Congress for too long a period. Concerning his ancestor's legislative record, Sutton writes in his *Family History* that Anderson was an ardent Jeffersonian Democrat and that:

> "He supported the Administration in all its measures, and voted in favor of the bill to free all Negroes born in the District of Columbia, and to impose a tax of $10.00 a head upon all importation of slaves, and to limit the time in which all importation of Negroes could be made. His name heads the list of Congressmen who voted for the Louisiana Purchase."

Anderson remained active in public affairs for many years after retiring from Congress. His name was later prominently mentioned as a gubernatorial possibility, and in 1816 he was chosen as a presidential elector. He died on Oct. 27, 1838, at age seventy-eight. One of his daughters married Mathias Pennypacker and was grandmother of Pennsylvania's Gov. Samuel Pennypacker.

CHAPTER 5

CONSTITUTIONAL REPUBLICANS WIN

The Democratic-Republicans were victorious in three elections during the ten years that Chester, Lancaster and Berks counties constituted Pennsylvania's Third Congressional District. In the other two elections the Constitutional Republicans were winners. Of the eleven congressmen chosen by the Third District's voters the best known and most influential was Joseph Hiester, a wealthy Reading businessman who later became governor of Pennsylvania. However, two lesser-known Hiesters elected during this period are of more interest to the Chester County history buff.

Among German family names none was better known by Pennsylvanians of the late eighteenth and early nineteenth century than "Muhlenberg" and "Hiester." History has well preserved the Muhlenberg name, but it has neglected the Hiester name. This is unfortunate, for the Hiesters were patriots of the first order. Fearless of the consequences, they boldly plunged into this nation's struggle for independence and made names for themselves both as military and political leaders. Among the Chester County branch of this distinguished family were John Hiester, a brigadier general in the militia, and his son Daniel. Both of them served in the Congress.

The Hiester (sometimes spelled Heister) family roots were in the Westphalia section of Germany. From the village of Elsoff three brothers journeyed to America in the 1730s and took up residence in Goshenhoppen, now Montgomery County but then a part of Philadelphia County. The two older brothers, John and Joseph, subsequently moved to Berks County where they purchased large tracts. Their younger brother Daniel, a successful tanner and farmer, remained in the Montgomery County area until 1774 when he moved to Reading. Ten years prior to making this move, however, Daniel had bought land along the Schuylkill River in Chester County. His eldest son John settled there and reared a family in Coventry Township.

This John Hiester was in his early thirties when the rebellious colonies declared their independence. Enlisting as an officer in the Chester County militia, he fought in several battles, including the one at the Brandywine. His younger brothers also volunteered. Gabriel, who had been a delegate to the convention that drafted the Pennsylvania Constitution of 1776, served as a field officer in the Berks County militia. Daniel distinguished himself first as a colonel in a Philadelphia militia unit and later as a brigadier general in the

Montgomery County militia. William, the youngest of the immigrant Daniel's four sons, also was enrolled in the militia, but saw limited service since the responsibility of caring for his aged parents fell on his shoulders.

The Hiester brothers held many public offices after the war. John, the Coventry Township farmer-soldier-politician, came to the forefront in county politics at the start of the new century when he unseated state Senator Dennis Whelen, a well known Federalist newspaperman. Gabriel represented Berks County in the state legislature during the 1780s and Daniel served on Pennsylvania's Supreme Executive Council before being elected to the First Congress.

Placing a party label on the Hiesters is difficult. At times they championed Federalist positions and at other times they were strong advocates of the Democratic-Republican viewpoint. They were admirers of President Jefferson, who in his first inaugural address said the two parties were "brethern of the same principle" and "we are all Republicans, we are all Federalists." It is very likely the Hiesters subscribed to this idea.

Local issues divided Jefferson's party when sixty-one-year-old John Hiester campaigned for the seat in the House of Representatives being vacated by his friend Isaac Anderson. As previously noted, the 1805 gubernatorial campaign was a bitter one in which Governor McKean was sharply criticized for nepotism and his stands on judicial and constitutional reforms. Senator Hiester was one of McKean's backers. So were his brothers and cousins, and their influence among German voters was a key factor in McKean's victory. Wounds from this fight had not healed in 1806. Alliances made in the governorship struggle changed the political complexion of the Third Congressional District and it was no longer a case of a heavily-favored Democratic-Republican ticket opposing a weak Federalist ticket. Instead, McKean's supporters (a coalition of conservative Democrats and Federalists) rallied under the Constitutional Republican flag and agreed to back a congressional ticket of Hiester, Lancaster County's Robert Jenkins, and Berks County's Mathias Reichert. The anti-McKean faction, which kept the Democratic-Republican party label, endorsed Congressman Whitehill of Lancaster County, Dr. Roger Davis of Chester County, and William Witman of Berks County.

Unlike earlier elections, the 1806 vote was not determined by the returns from Berks County. The Constitutional Republicans won, but throughout the district the competition was sharp. Less than 1,400 votes separated the highest vote-getter (Hiester) from the lowest. Listed on the next page are the returns:

Candidate	Berks	Lancaster	Chester	Total
Hiester	1627	2695	2387	6709
Reichert	1552	2672	2401	6625
Jenkins	1395	2694	2398	6487
Whitehill	1562	1849	2255	5666
Davis	1446	1823	2276	5545
Witman	1487	1807	2245	5339

WASHINGTON

The nation's capital was hard to reach and was still little more than a backwoods town of fewer than 15,000 persons when Hiester arrived there to begin his congressional duties in 1807. Charles W. Janson, an English writer of this period, described the roads leading to the American seat of government as the worst in the country.

> "In the winter season, during the sitting of Congress, every turn of your waggon wheel (for I must again observe there is no such thing in this country as what we call a stage coach or postchaise) is for many miles attended with danger. The roads are never repaired; deep ruts, rocks, stumps of trees, every minute impede your progress, and often threaten your limbs with dislocation."

Janson found the appearance of the city "grotesque" and observed there was so little activity that quails and other birds were constantly being shot within a hundred yards of the Capitol, "even during the sitting of the houses of congress." Concerning Pennsylvania Avenue, with the President's house situated at the extreme end, the Englishman wrote:

> "This boasted avenue is as much a wilderness as Kentucky, with this disadvantage, that the soil is good for nothing. Some half-starved cattle browsing among the bushes present a melancholy spectacle to a stranger whose expectations has been wound up by the illusive description of speculative writers."

John Hiester's impressions of the embryo city are not recorded. Upon arrival in Washington, though, he undoubtedly found that the Hiester name was well known among the nation's political leaders. Two Hiesters had already preceded him in the Congress. His younger brother Daniel had been at George Washington's first inaugural and had served in the Congress during the eight years the Virginian was president, and his Berks County cousin Joseph Hiester had been a congressman during the ensuing eight years.

Foreign affairs were a major concern of President Jefferson and the Congress when Hiester arrived on the Washington scene. American shipping had long been bothered by illegal blockades and seizures by English and French ships, but it was not until the *Leopard*, a British man-of-war, attacked the *Chesapeake*, an American frigate, in June of 1807—five months before the Tenth Congress convened—that the nation became outraged and demanded redress. Jefferson proposed an embargo on all commerce with the outside world and Congress complied on Dec. 21, 1807, by passing the Embargo Act. It prohibited ships from departing the United States for foreign ports. The legislation was unpopular in many quarters as it completely disrupted the economic life of the country. As the next election approached the embargo was a hot political issue—one the Democratic-Republicans had difficulty defending.

DANIEL HIESTER

When it came time to make a decision on a second term, Congressman Hiester apparently was not interested. His reasons for declining to stand for re-election are not recorded, but being in his sixties he may have been anxious to return to his Chester County farm and a less rigorous life. Or he may have stepped aside so as to give his son Daniel an opportunity to go to Washington as a lawmaker. Daniel was in his early thirties and one of the county leaders in the new Constitutional Republican Party. His political career had gotten off to a promising start some years earlier when the Democratic-Republicans had first elected McKean governor. Federalists at the time occupied nearly all state appointive offices—a situation McKean quickly remedied, and in doing so gained the reputation of being father of the spoils system in Pennsylvania politics. Daniel was the beneficiary of a McKean appointment; he took over the duties of prothonotary and clerk of courts at the courthouse in West Chester on Jan. 6, 1800, and continued to manage these row offices until Governor Snyder (McKean's old foe) replaced him in February of 1809.

As political alliances changed at the state level so did the political alliances in Chester County. Many of the Federalist foes of John Hiester in earlier contests were now his son's supporters as the 1808 election neared and Daniel successfully sought the county congressional nomination on the Constitutional Republican ticket. Except for Daniel replacing his father, the two opposing congressional slates eventually chosen were the same as in 1806; it was again Hiester-Reichert-Jenkins versus Davis-Whitehill-Witman.

The Third District race in 1806 had been fairly close; this one went to the wire as each of the six contenders polled more than 10,000 votes. Only 530 votes separated the top vote-getter (Reichert) and the sixth-place finisher (Witman). The two incumbents and Daniel Hiester won in the district, but Chester County's voters surprisingly indicated a preference for their opponents on the Democratic-Republican ticket—further evidence of the decline of Federalist influence in the county.

The new congressman from Chester County arrived in Washington for the first session of the Eleventh Congress in late May of 1809, less than three months after his father had finished his work as a legislator. The nation had a new leader (James Madison having succeeded Jefferson as president in March), but the same problems that confronted Jefferson and the Tenth Congress now confronted the new administration and the new lawmakers.

British and French naval blockades continued to harass American shipping and the non-intercourse act passed during the closing days of the Tenth Congress proved to be just as ineffective and unsatisfactory a remedy to the problem as the earlier embargo had been. Also confronting government officials was the problem of stiffened Indian resistance on the frontier, where pioneer families lived under the shadow of impending war.

Daniel Hiester did nothing to distinguish himself as a lawmaker, but he did gain a reputation for being an "irregular" in the Pennsylvania delegation because he frequently voted differently from the rest of his Keystone State colleagues. For instance, most members of Pennsylvania's eighteen-member delegation supported President Madison's occupation of Spanish West Florida and voted in favor of legislation authorizing the taking of East Florida as well. Only Hiester and Jenkins voted against the occupation and eventual annexation of the Spanish possessions.

When at home Congressman Hiester worked diligently to build an opposition party to President Madison, Governor Snyder and the Democratic-Republican Party. Reporting on what was described as a large and responsible meeting of "Friends of the Constitution" held in West Chester on May 8, 1810, the *Chester and Delaware Federalist* told how he had presided over the gathering and formed a committee "to correspond with similar committees in other parts of the state . . . and generally superintend and endeavor to advance the success of the Constitutional Ticket." Working with him in this undertaking were such staunch Federalists as Isaac Wayne, Isaac Darlington, Dennis Whelen, Francis Gardner, Jacob Humphrey and John Mennough.

Whelen's *Federalist* became the mouthpiece of the Constitutional Republicans. It strongly endorsed Hiester for re-election and it is reasonable to assume the congressman shared the newspaper's view that President Madison and his party had "disgraced, dishonored and ruined the country, and run the vessel of state up a sandbar." But Hiester and his friends failed miserably in their efforts to build a strong and viable opposition party. The Democratic-Republicans prevailed in 1810 and Hiester was unseated. He continued to take an active role in community and political affairs after leaving the Congress. He was instrumental in establishing the National Bank of Chester County and was its first cashier. From 1815 to 1817 he served as burgess of West Chester and later was appointed the county's register of wills and recorder of deeds after his father's cousin became governor. He afterwards moved to Hagerstown, Md., where he died on March 8, 1834.

The Hiester name remained prominent in Pennsylvania politics for several decades after Chester County's John and Daniel Hiester left the Congress. Joseph Hiester, the Berks County cousin sometimes described as one of the wealthiest men in the state, was one of the mainstays of the Constitutional Republican Party during the period immediately before and after the War of 1812. He served in the Congress during the Monroe administration and then became governor of Pennsylvania. William Hiester, another Berks County relation, and his son Isaac also served in the Congress, as did William's nephew, Hiester Clymer.

CHAPTER 6

DEMOCRATS ELECT DAVIS

President James Madison probably was pleased with the 1810 mid-term election in Chester County that resulted in Congressman Daniel Hiester being unseated by Dr. Roger Davis. Since he had opposed the occupation of Florida and on numerous occasions sided with the minority against administration policies, Hiester could not have been one of the president's favorite congressmen. Dr. Davis, a lifelong resident of Charlestown Township, on the other hand was known to be a staunch party man whose loyalty to the Democratic-Republican cause was unwavering.

The 1810 election marked the third time Dr. Davis had been his party's nominee for Congress. In his previous two outings he had been beaten by the Hiesters, first by the father, then by the son. This time the strengths of the opposing conservative and radical political camps were about equal in both the county and the district and a favorable political wind finally blew his way. Actually, the political winds had begun shifting in favor of the Democratic-Republicans two years earlier when Simon Snyder succeeded Thomas McKean as governor. Dr. Davis had contributed to Snyder's victory and was one of the Democrat leaders responsible for toppling the Federalist or Constitutional Republican hierarchy in Chester County. Along with four other county Democrats he was elected to the Pennsylvania General Assembly in 1809 in an upheaval that saw the defeat of such prominent Federalists as John Bull, Abraham Baily, Nathan Pennypacker and John Menough.

Encouraged by this clean sweep of the state legislator posts, the rejuvenated Democrats set their sights on electing a congressman, state senator, and sheriff in 1810. Dr. Davis was again asked to head the county ticket. Married and the father of thirteen children, he was forty-eight at the time and had been practicing medicine in the county since 1785. As was frequently the case with physicians of this period, his medical education was rather limited by modern standards, having been gained from attending three courses of lectures at the University of Pennsylvania and studying under another physician.

As in the past, leaders of the county's two political factions conferred with their counterparts in Lancaster and Berks counties to select the Third District congressional tickets. Chosen to run with Dr. Davis on the Democratic- Republican slate were Joseph Lefevre, a farmer and party leader in Strasburg Township, Lancaster County, and John M. Hyneman, a courthouse personage favored by the Berks County politicians. Running on the Constitutional Republican ticket with Congressman Hiester were Samuel Bechtel of Lancaster County and Mark J. Biddle, a Berks County lawyer.

For county Democrats the election returns were very gratifying. In addition to electing Davis, Lefevre and Hyneman to the Twelfth Congress, they again won the county contests for assemblymen and elected their man, George Hartman, as sheriff. Only state Senator Isaac Wayne, the staunch Federalist son of the famous Revolutionary War general, handed them a setback—and this was due in part to the fact that his senatorial district extended into Delaware County where the Federalists were still strong. The returns clearly indicated that followers of Jefferson and Madison now had the upper hand in Chester County. Some people were unhappy with this change in the political winds, particularly Dennis Whelen, publisher of the *Chester and Delaware Federalist*, a weekly newspaper established the previous year in West Chester. He once described the Democratic-Republican Party as being made from "the patches and threads of our native population and the worst of our foreign population." The Constitutional Party, according to Whelen, was "made up of Americans almost exclusively, with the exception of a few decent foreigners."

JOURNEY TO WASHINGTON

Dr. Davis' term as congressman officially began on March 4, 1811, but it was not until eight months later that he went to Washington for the opening session of the fateful Twelfth Congress. Dr. Davis did not leave a diary or account of his experiences as a congressman, but his colleague Jonathan Roberts from neighboring Montgomery County provides a fascinating glimpse of an early nineteenth century legislator's life in memoirs written for his children. The trip to Washington for a Pennsylvania lawmaker then was an arduous one, deserving of a momentary digression. Roberts' memoirs, published in the April 1938 edition of the *Pennsylvania Magazine*, vividly describe the travel experience to and from the nation's capital.

As with Dr. Davis, Roberts was a freshman congressman when he left his Norristown home in early November, traveling the first day by stage to the state capital in Lancaster to join Congressman Lefevre, who had suggested they make the trip together by hack via the western route. "I gladly met the offer, as no very eligible public conveyance then existed," Roberts recalled. "The land route from Phila. was bad, and tedious, & the water Packet to me, was worse."

During his layover in Lancaster, Roberts visited with several public officials, including Governor Snyder, whom he found "liv'd at boarding in a style little becoming the salary he receiv'd." On the first leg of their journey from Lancaster the two congressmen made it to a public house in Adams County kept by a Mr. Lauck. Concerning the innkeeper and the accommodations, Roberts recalled:

> "He had been very much distub'd by some disorderly guests, that had recently left him. His house was kept by his youngest daughter. She was about eighteen. . . . A neater house, and kitchen I never saw. . . . She set a supper before us in perfect character, with the neatness of her house. We had a very decent German, as our driver. It became a point of dispute between father & daughter whether the driver should sit with us at the table. The father insisted he should, and the daughter contended it was not according to etiquette. We had no objection either way. . . . They spoke German, a language that was familiar to Lefebvre; & thus it was we came to know the nature of their controversy. In due time we retir'd to bed. The chambers were in good trim, & externally the beds were well enough. On opening them, I felt easiest, not to take off my flannell. This was however no drawback on the merits of the young Lady. She saw little genteel company."

Concerning their journey the next two days and their arrival in Washington, Roberts wrote:

> "We left Mr. Louck's early, without breakfast. . . . We breakfasted at Hanover, & reach'd Frederick at night. We stoppd at the Stage house, but there was no admission. The Court martial were sitting on Gen. Wilkison, & the house was full. One of the young men, very kindly took us to another house. . . . We breakfasted at Clarksburg, din'd at Rockville, & got to Washington a little after night. The taverns were full, & it was not easy to find a place to put down."

Roberts, who was a bachelor at this time, found the seat of government to be "a place of general resort, & presents the occasion of persons meeting from distant places, & assumes something of the character of a Matrimonial mart."

THE WAR HAWKS

Led by Henry Clay, who was elected speaker of the House, the new Congress quickly gained an important place in American history as it moved the nation into another war with Great Britain. Three days after Congress convened Gen. William Henry Harrison defeated Indian attackers at Tippecanoe Creek in the Indiana territory, and in doing so won for himself the warrior accolades that would carry him into the White House thirty years later. Harrison's report that the Indians had been supplied with guns and ammunition by the English angered Clay and the "War Hawks" of the Twelfth Congress. The continued harassment of American ships by British naval blockades was also upsetting to many congressmen.

On June 1, 1812, President Madison delivered a special message to Congress outlining the offending actions of the British. When the final showdown came later in the month Congressman Davis voted with the House majority for a declaration of war. The Federalists, almost to a man, voted against the war measure. The 79-to-49 vote in the House underscored the division in the country.

Returning home after the long and exciting 245-day session, Dr. Davis found himself an unpopular legislator among his district's Quaker constituency. Anti-war sentiment ran high in Chester County and as the October elections approached the Friends of Peace were hard at work trying to replace President Madison and his supporters. Dr. Davis and Montgomery County's Roberts, who had been placed in the same two-member district under a new reapportionment, were severely censured by those opposed to the war as they campaigned for re-election in the new Second Congressional District, comprised of Chester and Montgomery counties. Whelen's *Federalist* was strongly critical of "Mr. Madison's War." Readers were asked in the Sept. 9, 1812, issue:

> "Is there to be no end to this war? or is it to be a war of extermination, as has been proclaimed by the unfortunate General Hull? What end is now to be accomplished by it, and what means of enforcing our demands? So far we have been everywhere unfortunate? But how could it be other wise. The men who misrule our nation are not competent to the task of prosecuting a war with vigour."

A month later in its October 7 edition *The Federalist* charged many attempts had been made to "circumscribe the liberties" of those opposed to the war. Roberts and his "coadjutors" in Congress were blamed for starting this infringement by limiting debate on the war question. In a bitter attack on those supporting Madison, *The Federalist* suggested:

> "Let those who think hard of the friends of peace . . . do something themselves; let them volunteer their services or their purses to retrieve the losses which we have sustained at Detroit and elsewhere. . . . It is the poor that must fight at five dollars a month; it is they, poor fellows must stand the brunt; it is they who must suffer all the privations incident to the war—wounds and even death, whilst the leaders of democracy are sitting quietly at home, drinking their wine and smoaking their segars . . . while the hardy sons of liberty are marching to avenge their injured country."

The American Republican, published in Downingtown by Charles Mowry, supported the president and the war effort. In the October 10 issue his readers were told:

> "Now is the time to show the real principles which actuate you. . . . There are but two sides on the great question before you. You must either take the side of the murdering foe on your frontiers, or you must espouse the cause of your country. You must be either British Tories or American Patriots. There is no time for paltry shufflings of party. You cannot salve your conscience by

> pretensions and professions. There can be but two parties—and one of those parties is now murdering your countrymen."

Sectionalism also divided the country. The South and New England were at odds and both were suspicious of the emerging West. Democratic-Republican leaders in New York resented the way Virginia seemed to be dominating the party. This resentment led to the nomination of New York Gov. DeWitt Clinton as an alternative to Madison, who had been nominated for a second term at a caucus of Democratic-Republicans in the Congress. The Federalists, again without a candidate of their own for president, also came out for Clinton.

With New York and New England supporting Clinton, and with the South and West in back of Madison, Pennsylvania was considered the key to the 1812 election. Although the state was still regarded as a stronghold of the Democratic-Republican Party, the schism in the ranks made the outcome uncertain. Congressman Joseph Lefevre of Lancaster County and other prominent Democrats deserted Madison and began drumming up support for Clinton. Ex-Governor McKean also entered the fray and headed the Clinton electoral ticket.

The presidential election was the main attraction, but the congressional election was also of considerable interest to local politicos. Congressmen Davis and Roberts, supporters of the president, were opposed by Dr. Francis Gardner, of Sadsbury (now Valley) Township, and Montgomery County's Samuel Henderson. The Gardner name was well known in Chester County. Francis was born in 1774 at a time when his father, Dr. Joseph Gardner, was taking an active role in the colonial struggle against the crown. As noted earlier, his father later served in the state legislature and Continental Congress. Undoubtedly, his father's reputation as a patriot helped, but it was his own personality and record that made Dr. Gardner a formidable Federalist candidate in 1812. He was a gifted conversationalist, popular with all classes of people. A former state lawmaker, his credentials also included a military record—a valuable asset for a candidate for public office throughout the nineteenth century. At the age of twenty he had volunteered his services and traveled to western Pennsylvania to help quell the Whiskey Rebellion.

Anti-war demonstrations were common in many parts of the country as the October elections neared. The Friends of Peace were aligned with the Federalists and conservatives of the Democratic-Republican Party—previously referred to as Constitutional Republicans. In this particular election the political foes of President Madison—for whatever reason they opposed him—banded together and called themselves Federal Republicans. Their ticket won high praise from *The Federalist.* Concerning Dr. Gardner and his Montgomery County running mate, the newspaper predicted:

> "Their voice in the national council will be for an honourable and permanent peace. . . . We have received the most favourable

> accounts from Montgomery County. . . . The Germans in that county are withdrawing themselves from the war party daily, and it is confidently believed the warhawks will be in the minority on the day of the election. Is not the hand of Providence in this thing: for these people until very lately either took no papers at all, or read none else but democratic ones; to be sure, lately, some well informed Germans have taken much pains to place their interests and that of their country before them; they will have their reward, for Blessed are the peace makers."

This partisan newspaper prediction proved wrong. Anti-war sentiment prevailed in Chester County, but not in Montgomery County, in Pennsylvania generally, or in the nation. Gardner and Henderson polled nearly 3,300 votes in Chester County, but their pluralities there of slightly over 100 votes were not enough to offset the totals registered by congressmen Davis and Roberts in the other half of the new Second District. In the presidential election that followed later in October the voters of Chester County preferred Clinton (3,109) to Madison (2,789), but these feelings were not representative of the state. President Madison claimed all twenty-five of Pennsylvania's electoral votes. As expected, New York and New England went for Clinton while the South and West voted to keep President Madison in the White House for another four years. The electoral college vote was 128 to 89 in favor of Madison. Pennsylvania was truly the keystone state; had it voted the other way Clinton would have won the presidency by eleven electoral votes.

Years later, in his memoirs, Congressman Roberts recalled the bitter rivalry between the Federalists and Democratic-Republicans:

> "At no time perhaps had party feelings a stronger hold on men's minds, than at the opening of the 12th Congress in 1811. The old federal party after a ten year depression remain'd organiz'd & buoy'd up with the hope of being again seated in power. This party had ever display'd a veneration for British institutions, & a preference for this nation over France. The Republican party on the other hand, felt grateful to France for her aid in achieving the independency of the country."

Congressman Roberts was hurt by the personal attacks made on him during the 1812 campaign as "Mr. Madison's War" was heatedly debated along with other issues such as the country's deteriorating economy and weak frontiers. Especially painful, he wrote, were the attacks made on his record in Congress "by such men as Col. Richard Thomas and Isaac Wayne, my personal friends."

The final two years of service as a congressman were undoubtedly exciting ones for Dr. Davis. Months ahead of the December date when they would normally have convened, members of the Thirteenth Congress were summoned to Washington by President Madison for a summer session to deal with problems arising from the war. This first session lasted seventy-one days.

In 1814, between the second and third sessions of the Thirteenth Congress, the British captured Washington and set fire to government buildings. Dr. Davis did not seek a third term, and he spent his final days as a congressman in a fire-blackened Washington working out of an undamaged patent office building. He died on Nov. 20, 1815—less than nine months after leaving office—in his fifty-fourth year. He is buried in the Great Valley Presbyterian churchyard in Tredyffrin Township.

CHAPTER 7

DARLINGTONS WIN IN CHESMONT

Paraphrasing Lincoln's observation concerning the poor, God must have loved the Darlingtons or he wouldn't have populated Chester County with so many of them. Since four members of this prolific and esteemed Quaker family served in the Congress during the nineteenth century, a brief genealogical digression is perhaps in order before proceeding with an account of the congressional elections during the administrations of Presidents Madison and Monroe. Tradition has it that Abraham Darlington, the man responsible for planting the family tree in Chester County, came to this country from England in 1703 when he was only thirteen. Working first as a saddler, he eventually saved enough money to purchase a farm in Birmingham Township where he and his second wife, Elizabeth Hillborn, reared a family of ten children. Of these, Thomas—the fifth child, born in 1723—is of particular interest to the chronicler of the Quaker seat in the United States House of Representatives since three of his grandsons and a great-grandson became congressmen.

A farmer like his father, Thomas Darlington was married in 1754 to Hannah Brinton, a great-granddaughter of Birmingham Township's first settler—the Quaker William Brinton. Thomas and Hannah had eleven children, and of these Edward, Abraham and Jesse each lived to see one of his sons elected to the Congress. George, a fourth son, was the grandfather of Smedley Darlington, who served in the House towards the end of the nineteenth century.

The almost phenomenal growth of the Darlington clan has been documented in numerous genealogy papers and publications on file at the Chester County Historical Society. One such reference source noted that nearly four hundred of the more than one thousand descendants of the immigrant Abraham Darlington attended the family's sesqui-centennial gathering at Brinton Darlington's East Bradford residence in 1853.

So much for genealogy and back to politics. In 1814 the first of Abraham's great-grandsons was elected to Congress in the midst of stirring events caused by the British invasion of the Chesapeake area and the burning of Washington. As with most of the county's early nineteenth century elections, precious little information has been preserved from which a detailed and accurate account can be reconstructed of this Chesmont congressional campaign. The returns do however indicate the populace was evenly divided on the issues of the day, and the election proved to be one of the closest and most suspenseful in the county's 200-year history of congressional elections.

As already noted, the redistricting legislation which placed Chester and Montgomery counties in the Second Congressional District was drafted by Pennsylvania's lawmakers to favor candidates of the Democratic-Republican political persuasion. Two newcomers—Dr. William Darlington and Dr. John Hahn—replaced Dr. Roger Davis and Jonathan Roberts as the party's nominees for the district's two seats in the Fourteenth Congress. On the Federal Republican side the nominees were Chester County's Isaac Wayne, who had also been nominated for governor, and Montgomery County's Samuel Henderson, an unsuccessful nominee in the previous congressional election.

Coming at a time when British warships were cruising the Chesapeake, there was not much time for politicking in the fall of 1814. Both Darlington and Wayne were soldiering and left the electioneering to their friends. After the burning of the Capitol and other buildings in Washington there was a real fear the British might invade Philadelphia, causing Governor Snyder to issue a call for volunteers to defend the city from the "incendiary incursions of the Enemy." Dr. Darlington, who had earlier been disowned by the Society of Friends for accepting appointment as surgeon for the county militia, wrote in his diary that he and about fifty others "comprising some of the most wealthy and respectable Citizens of Chester County" banded together in a unit called the American Grays. In early September the unit left home and marched from West Chester to Philadelphia to begin a three-month tour of duty with "the satisfaction of believing that we carried with us the good wishes of all those of our acquaintance whose esteem was desirable."

Darlington made no mention in his diary of the upcoming election, but on September 9 (the day after his unit departed) delegates to the Democratic-Republican Party's nominating convention met at John Brinton's place in West Chester and picked him as their candidate for Congress. Ten days after this his diary notes "an Election was held for the purpose of officering the Light Infantry, & Riflemen; which the Governor had arranged into battalions and regiments." Under Pennsylvania military law at this time troops selected their own officers. As a result of this election Darlington was commissioned a major in the Light Infantry. Two other future congressmen—Isaac Wayne and Isaac Darlington—were also elected officers.

The early days of October were uneventful for Major Darlington and his men. His battalion was assigned to Marcus Hook, Pennsylvania's southernmost town on the Delaware, where nearly ten thousand militia were encamped. Being close to home, he was able to now and then get away for a day to see his family and friends in West Chester. His diary gives vivid glimpses of military life.

> "Wednesday Oct 5th was very rainy and disagreeable—& to add to our troubles we obtained no rations until evening—& when they did come, were very indifferent. The Bread was most execrably bad. The men showed some uneasiness, but were pacified by Col. Bache."

Special legislation passed by the General Assembly allowed men in the militia to vote at their camps. Darlington's diary entry on October 11 makes no mention of his congressional candidacy, but he did note the election was conducted "very peaceably and quietly." The next day, however, he wrote with obvious glee:

> "It appears that a very large proportion of the troops in Camp are Democratic—Out of 574 votes from Chester County in service, there are 516 democratic votes, & 58 Federal votes, leaving a majority of 458. Although it was said by some that it was the Feds. only who turned out at the pinch."

At home the election was also conducted without any reported incidents. Approximately 4,000 men cast ballots at Chester County's dozen polling places and once again the Federal Republicans had the better showing and were able to claim nearly all the election prizes. Because of the military vote, however, the count was slow and after two weeks passed the *American Republican* reported "it appears Messrs. Darlington and Wayne, of this county, are elected to the 14th congress." This assumption was incorrect, however, and the next week the newspaper reported Darlington and his running mate on the Democratic-Republican ticket would be the winners if Montgomery County officials allowed twenty-four soldier votes late in arriving to be counted. If not, the *Republican* said Chester County would claim both congressional seats. When all was said and done the two Democrats—Darlington and Hahn—were elected. Only four votes separated the winner Hahn and the loser Wayne. The two-county vote was Darlington 4,781; Hahn 4,779; Wayne 4,775; and Henderson 4,770.

The congressional vote count however was not uppermost in Dr. Darlington's thoughts at this time. Shortly after the election the tranquil routine at Marcus Hook was disrupted when William Duane, a very influential Philadelphia newspaper editor and politician, arrived on the scene. Duane's appointment as adjutant general of the Fourth Military District of the United States was a political one, and when he attempted to reorganize and consolidate the volunteer units he encountered resistance. Colonel Bache (Darlington's commanding officer) refused to go along with Duane's orders on grounds his regiment had been organized under the direction of the Governor of Pennsylvania. Duane viewed this as insubordination and directed Bache to hand over his sword, thereby placing Major Darlington and several other officers in the middle of a federal-state jurisdictional dispute that would eventually lead to their arrests on charges of mutiny and disobedience. According to Darlington's diary:

"Duane then demanded who was next in Command—He was answered by the Adjutant of the Regt. that it was Major Darlington—Duane then turned to me, & directed me to take charge of the Regt.—I replied that I did not conceive myself authorized to do so. My sword was then ordered to be delivered up—Major Pedan was arrested the same way—as were also Captains Schwenck, Nungesser & Ruhe—for refusing to take command as thus newly organized—Duane then desisted; their swords."

To further aggravate an already nasty situation the Pennsylvania troops sided with their elected officers and displayed their feelings in a very demonstrative way. Darlington wrote:

"On Saturday afternoon, Duane struck his tent, & prepared to leave the ground—The Riflemen and Militia shewd a disposition to insult him—although our Regiment observed the greatest decorum. When he mounted to leave Camp I am told he was hooted & Hissed out of the field."

On November 1, Darlington entered this note in his diary:

"This morning the very tedious trial of Col. Bache was concluded, and the Court broke up—The sentence of the Court will of course remain unknown until the General commanding makes it known—I have been attending the Court since Wednesday last, as a witness—but it was decided by the Court that those who were implicated could not be heard—and I therefore expended 10 to 12 dollars in the City to no purpose—The testimony on the Case gave a very honorable account of our Regiment, but it is very uncertain what the sentence of the Court may be."

Eight days later this entry appeared in Darlington's diary:

"We yet remain in ignorance of the sentence of the Court Martial on Col. Bache's case—& can form no idea when the rest of us will know our destinies. The Weather is getting cold to live in these Linen Houses, & the last 5 or 6 days have been very rainy & dull—We however do not expect to be discharged yet awhile, as it is said the British are still hovering on our Coast."

The long awaited sentence was finally announced on November 11. Darlington's diary states Bache was convicted and dismissed from the service "to the astonishment of everyone acquainted with the case." In a long letter to Secretary of the Commonwealth Nathaniel B. Boileau, a close friend of Governor Snyder, the congressman-elect took exception to the Court's finding, claiming state rights were being trampled on and that it was unfair for officers of his "unfortunate" regiment to be "stigmatized as mutinous, disorderly, and disobedient, merely because they claimed the privilege of retaining the organization prescribed by the Laws, and sanctioned by the Governor." He also warned Boileau he was "apprehensive the treatment our Regiment has received will give a death blow to volunteering in this end of the state." A Jeffersonian Democrat and strong believer in states rights, Darlington concluded that "as Pennsylvanians we naturally look to the Governor as our Commander in Chief—to him we tendered our service—and to him we address ourselves as the proper authority to protect us in those few privileges which the rules of Camp leave to the soldier."

The November days in the military for Darlington and his friends were long and unhappy ones, filled with uncertainty and bitterness. At one point he wrote:

> "The Campaign is wearing away, and we arrested officers receive no intelligence of any disposition to try us or re-instate us . . . . It is particularly gratifying to us at this time to know that our Regiment, which has been stigmatized as Colonel Bache's Mob, is Brigadier General Smith's principal dependence for preserving good order in the Camp. Last evening the Militia of Smith's Brigade behaved in a riotous & mutinous manner in consequence of the arrest of two company officers, and the General's staff was reduced to the necessity of calling upon our abused and insulted Regiment to quell the rioters."

Undoubtedly, Major Darlington must have often wondered why Governor Snyder—a political ally—had abandoned him. Finally, he received a letter from Secretary Boileau explaining the Governor's failure to come to his defense. In it Boileau wrote both he and the governor were "astonished and mortified" by the court martial and "nothing but the peculiar & critical situation of our Country" prevented Governor Snyder "from immediately withdrawing the whole of the Volunteers from the service." But such action, Darlington was told, "would no doubt have been immediately communicated to the enemy, and encouraged their approach." Such a decision would also have had political repercussions since the Federalists had been opposed to the war from the start. In defending Governor Snyder's action, or lack of action, Boileau explained:

> "Should he withdraw the Volunteers, his conduct would be misconstrued—those traitors would avail themselves of the occasion to say—Lo, even the Governor of Penn, the most devoted to the General Government has become weary of its tyranny . . . he will no longer support an Administration in the prosecution of their unjust & ruinous war even when the most wealthy & important section of the State is menaced by the Enemy."

Then, in an obvious attempt to encourage the disheartened congressman-elect, Boileau concluded "the Court which I learn has been called to sit for the examination of your conduct will I confidently trust give you an honorable acquittal." However, no trial was held. Darlington was informed near the end of November that his regiment would shortly be dismissed and there would not be sufficient time to hold a trial. In obedience to the directions of the commanding general, the judge advocate informed Darlington he had entered "a nolle prosequi on the charges exhibited against you."

For both Governor Snyder and President Madison a confrontation was avoided. Darlington was not overjoyed by this decision that "lamely and impotently concluded the villanous business." Shortly before the case was dropped he and his regiment marched through "a dreadful storm" back to Philadelphia where on December 2 the troops disbanded "and we all returned to our homes, myself partially disgraced and wholly disgusted." A year later, on Dec. 4, 1815, Chester County's disgusted soldier was in Washington for the opening session of the Fourteenth Congress.

DARLINGTON VERSUS DARLINGTON

Chester County's congressional election in 1816 was a very unusual one—unusual in that it was a Darlington versus Darlington affair involving two of the great-grandsons of the immigrant Abraham Darlington. It pitted Dr. Darlington, the incumbent congressman and choice of the Democratic-Republicans, against his cousin Isaac Darlington, a lawyer and ardent Federalist. Both men were in their mid-thirties. Born a few miles and a few months apart—Isaac in Westtown in December 1781, and William in Birmingham in April 1782—these grandsons of Thomas and Hannah Brinton Darlington each had a Quaker family upbringing. The boyhood days of both were filled with hard work since there was little time for play or school on Chester County farms in the late eighteenth century. Concerning William's boyhood, Washington Townsend wrote in a memorial published in 1863:

> "He was early inured to the severe labors of agricultural life, and when old enough to drive or hold the plow, was kept at work in the summer, and only permitted to go to school in the winter season. The common country schools of that day were lamentably deficient as compared with those of modern times, yet he succeeded in obtaining a plain English education under John Forsythe, an Irish friend, one of the best teachers of that time in the county."

Concerning Isaac, whose father was a blacksmith as well as a farmer, Futhey and Cope wrote in their *History*:

> "Isaac, being the eldest, as soon as he acquired sufficient strength to swing a sledge-hammer, labored continuously with his father in the fields, and was moreover taught to blow and strike in the smith-shop at noon and in the evening. Probably no boy in Chester County was trained to more laborious habits in early life than Isaac Darlington."

Isaac and William each had his fill of farming as a boy and each looked for another way of earning a livelihood upon reaching manhood. William, the eldest son of Edward and Hannah (Townsend) Darlington, pursued a medical career while Isaac, the eldest son of Abraham and Susanna (Chandler) Darlington, took up the study of law. Both had especially keen minds, but family circumstances were such that neither received any formal education as boys beyond the early schooling received from the aforementioned John Forsythe.

Isaac's intellectual attainments were readily recognized and as a teenager he was placed in charge of a country school. Even though younger than some of his students, he reportedly did a creditable job as a teacher. But he had other ambitions, though, and at eighteen he became a law student in the office of Joseph Hemphill, the young West Chester attorney who at the time was a member of the Seventh Congress and one of the county's Federalist Party luminaries. Isaac quickly mastered his legal studies and was admitted to the bar in 1801 shortly before his twentieth birthday.

At about the same time Isaac started his legal apprenticeship, William began studying medicine in the Wilmington office of Dr. John Vaughan. In 1802, during the course of his study, the city was struck with a yellow fever epidemic and he rendered valuable assistance to Dr. Vaughan, the only physician to remain in the city to care for the sick. In 1804, after attending medical lectures during two winter sessions, William became the first Chester Countian to graduate with a doctor of medicine degree from the University of Pennsylvania.

The two cousins had much in common, but they differed on political matters. At an early age William enrolled in the Democratic-Republican ranks where his father was a party leader. Isaac, a Federalist, was elected to the General Assembly in 1807 and 1808, and as with most Federalists was critical of President Madison's foreign policy. But like his cousin William, he too answered Governor Snyder's call for volunteers after the British burned Washington and was among the American Grays who marched out of West Chester in September of 1814 to oppose the British.

History doesn't tell us whether there was any animosity between the two cousins or just why Lawyer Darlington decided to run against Congressman Darlington in 1816. The war was over and there were no major issues dividing the nation as there had been a few years earlier. Newspapers were even beginning to use the "era of good feeling" term to describe the country's political climate. Nor had Dr. Darlington done anything as a freshman congressman to greatly upset his Chesmont constituents. On the contrary, he had received good grades from the folks back home, especially for voting against giving himself a pay increase. Meeting at John Brinton's place in West Chester on April 30, 1816, the county's Democratic Republicans by resolution highly approved of Dr. Darlington's official conduct and political firmness in the national legislature, "and particularly for his vote against the disgraceful Compensation Bill."

Regardless of his motives, Lawyer Darlington's nomination by the Federal Republicans caused confusion and was upsetting to the Democratic-Republicans who immediately charged their opponents with trickery. The *American Republican*, a partisan newspaper, commented:

> "We believe the selection of a candidate with the same sir name as our own shews something more of a design than might at first thought be perceived. It will, however, only be necessary for the Democrats before voting, to examine the tickets, to see if they are headed for congress with the name of Dr. William Darlington . . . as the federalist candidate's name is Isaac Darlington, more generally known by the appellation of Lawyer Darlington."

At the same time party leaders gave approval to Congressman Darlington's performance in Washington by nominating him for a second term, they also adopted a resolution approving "the nomination made by the Republican members of Congress at Washington city, of James Monroe, Esq., as a candidate for President, & Daniel D. Tompkins, Esq., as a candidate for Vice President." Later, at a supper given in Dr. Darlington's honor, toasts were offered praising both Monroe and Tompkins. These toasts, published in the newspapers, stated Monroe's talents and political services "eminently qualify him for the highest office as a gift of the American people," and that Governor Tompkins "has merited and will receive the confidence of the American people."

This toasting by Darlington's friends in the Democratic-Republican Party apparently was premature. The machinery for nominating candidates for the nation's two highest offices at this time left much to be desired. Elsewhere in Pennsylvania other disgruntled politicians were unhappy with the Monroe-Tompkins ticket, claiming they had been betrayed by the legislative caucus in Washington. With the exception of the four years John Adams was the nation's chief executive, the presidency had been occupied by Virginians since 1789. These unhappy Democrats claimed their willingness to support another Virginian had been conditioned upon Governor Snyder being Monroe's running mate. Outraged when New York's Tompkins was picked for the second spot, these disappointed Democrats denounced the Virginia Dynasty and held a special convention at Carlisle in September during which time a set of unpledged presidential electors were picked who favored Dewitt Clinton for president. Chester County's John W. Cunningham, a former state representative and well known politician from New London, was one of the men placed on the independent electoral ticket.

Even though the presidential and congressional elections were held several weeks apart the squabble over presidential electors was divisive and apparently had an adverse effect on the re-election campaign waged by Dr. Darlington and his Second District running mate from Montgomery County. Monroe swept the nation, capturing almost eighty-five percent of the presidential electoral votes, but the Pennsylvania returns clearly showed the depth of the Jeffersonian party split. The Monroe electoral ticket received 25,000 votes and the opposing independent ticket got 17,000. In Chester County the Monroe ticket won by a 1,999 to 1,634 count, indicating there was no great enthusiasm for the Virginian. One can only speculate on the impact the revolt against the "Virginia Dynasty" had on the Chesmont congressional election held earlier in October. But there is little reason to believe Monroe helped any of the district's Democratic-Republicans running for office in 1816.

As in 1814, Dr. Darlington was again paired with Dr. John Hahn of Montgomery County on the Democratic-Republican ticket. Levi Pawling, a Norristown lawyer, and Lawyer Darlington opposed them on the Federal Republican ticket. As in the earlier election when less than a dozen votes separated the winners from losers, the Second District race again went to the wire. As expected, Montgomery County went for the incumbents and Chester County went for their opponents. This time, though, the two-county total put the two Federalist lawyers in the winner column and Isaac unseated his cousin by seven votes. The final tally was reported as follows:

Candidate	Chester	Montgomery	Total
L. Pawling	3,124	1,880	5,004
I. Darlington	3,087	1,849	4,936
W. Darlington	2,867	2,062	4,929
J. Hahn	2,829	1,957	4,786

During Isaac Darlington's tenure as a congressman two new states—Mississippi and Illinois—were added to the union, Florida was purchased from Spain, and General Jackson figured prominently in the news as the country engaged in its first war with the Seminole Indians. But Chester County's lawyer did not find Washington life exciting or appealing enough to seek a second term, returning to West Chester at the conclusion of the Fifteenth Congress and resuming his law practice. He served briefly as deputy attorney general (equivalent of today's district attorney) and in May of 1821 accepted appointment as president judge of the newly-created Fifteenth Judicial District comprised of Chester and Delaware counties. He continued to serve in this capacity until his death on April 27, 1837.

DEMOCRATS RECAPTURE DISTRICT

The year following Lawyer Darlington's election to the United States House of Representatives the voters of Pennsylvania picked a new governor to succeed Simon Snyder. Their choice was State Treasurer William Findlay, a well known Franklin County politician long active in public affairs. The dying Federalist Party was too weak to come up with its own candidate, but Pennsylvania nevertheless had a hotly contested battle for the governorship. Findlay, nominee of the "new school" faction of the Democratic-Republican Party was challenged by the "old school's" Joseph Hiester, longtime political chieftain of Berks County.

Governor Snyder, prohibited by the constitution from seeking a fourth term, supported Findlay as did most party regulars. Joining the more conservative members of the Democratic-Republican Party in backing Hiester, an old Revolutionary War veteran, were the Federalists and Pennsylvania

Germans. Hiester gave Findlay a real battle, losing statewide by approximately 7,000 votes. True to form, the Federalist power structure in Chester County—men such as Lawyer Darlington, Dr. Abraham Baily, Isaac Wayne, ex-Congressman Daniel Hiester and James Kelton—lined up behind Hiester, helping him carry the county by nearly 300 votes.

The 1817 governorship contest emphasized the realignment of the parties that was in the making in Pennsylvania and also set the stage for Chester County's next few congressional election bouts. Findlay's followers remained in one camp and Hiester's in the other. No burning national issues divided the populace as the next election season approached, but the two county political groups held separate conventions and slated candidates for the various offices to be filled. Only the nominations for state senator caused any stir.

Heading the Democratic-Republican ticket again was Dr. Darlington, who for a third time was nominated for congressman. The Federal Republicans turned to James Kelton, a well known political personage from West Grove in his early forties who had served as county treasurer and sheriff and been elected several times to the state legislature. Son of a Scotch-Irish immigrant who had settled on a 500-acre tract in London Grove Township, Kelton was an elder in the New London Presbyterian Church and a director of the National Bank of Chester County.

The vote-getting contest between Dr. Darlington and Kelton was a run of the mill affair, noteworthy perhaps because it was the only election in the county's history in which a congressman previously retired by the voters was able to win back their approval and be returned to Washington. However, even this trivia note needs an asterisk since he owed his success chiefly to the Democrats of Montgomery County, not to any increase in his personal popularity among the voters of his home county. Darlington's running mate in the Second District was Samuel Gross, a Montgomery County farmer-politician in his forties who had previously served in the Pennsylvania House and Senate. Kelton was paired with Congressman Pawling. As in his two previous outings, Dr. Darlington trailed his rivals in his home county, but this time the Montgomery County Democrats came through with healthy majorities to offset the Federal Republican pluralities in Chester County. The district vote total gave Darlington 4,811; Gross 4,729; Pawling 4,178; and Kelton 4,117.

Since the early days of the republic the election returns in Chester County followed a predictable geographic pattern. Growth and development had not changed the 1818 election map (there were still only a dozen polling places in the county's 760 square mile area) nor the voting patterns. The election districts in the north and to the west remained fortresses of the Democratic-Republicans while West Chester, Marshallton and the Quaker townships in the southeastern section of the county continued to be Federalist citadels. As expected, Darlington whipped Kelton 466 to 109 at

Pughtown, 295 to 158 at Brandywine Manor, 304 to 74 at Hood's (Oxford), and 155 to 39 at New London Crossroads. He also came out on top in the voting at Gum Tree and Sloan's (Sadsburyville). Kelton trounced Darlington 474 to 148 at West Chester, 279 to 25 at Marshallton, 351 to 97 at Chatham, and 234 to 74 at New Red Lion (Longwood). He also posted wins at Old Red Lion (Lionville) and Paoli.

Unlike some of the earlier bitterly contested elections, this one was so lacking in issues that some responsible citizens were suggesting political parties be amalgamated. The *Village Record* editor questioned the wisdom of allowing political hard feelings to continue, pointing out that "the narrow minded and factious, who like the pygmy see nothing beyond the first ant hill which bounds their horizon, have not yet unlearned the cry which the days of party rancour taught them." Continuing in this vein, he said "it is time that party feuds and party names, in the manner they have existed, should cease to bear despotic sway in our political concerns." The editor of the rival *American Republican*, commenting on this same topic shortly before the election, said "many of the most moderate and discerning federalists have long regretted the height to which party disputes have been carried, and often have they expressed a wish that party distinctions might be buried in the more important love of country" and concluded "a reconciliation of parties must be wrought out by mutual advances on both sides."

Nothing, of course, came of this talk of amalgamation and reconciliation. Prejudices and personal animosities kept the county divided in two political camps. The divisions dating back to the time of the Revolution (Scotch-Irish Presbyterians on one side and Quakers on the other) and the ratification of the constitution (Federalists in one corner and Antifederalists in the other) remained, thereby insuring the county electorate of some lively political contests during the so-called era of good feeling.

1820 ELECTION

Except for scattered strongholds such as Chester County, the Federalists were almost an extinct species by 1820. President Monroe's popularity was such that no one opposed him when he sought a second term. In Pennsylvania, though, hard feelings rather than good feelings prevailed as Joseph Hiester mobilized his "old school" army to again battle Governor Findlay. For the most part the cast of characters in the county's 1820 election drama was a familiar one. Dr. Darlington was again a candidate for congressman. Running with him on the Democratic-Republican ticket were Isaac Barnard, a military hero and popular political figure; Joshua Evans, owner of the Paoli Inn; Eber Worthington, proprietor of the Turks Head in West Chester; and Colonel David Dickey, of Hopewell. On Hiester's Federal Republican ticket were a number of veteran politicians, including state lawmakers James Kelton, Joshua Hunt, Thomas Ashbridge, and Thomas Baird. But there was also a newcomer—a man who almost overnight became the party's spokesman and whose views were respected by some of nation's top leaders. This newcomer was Charles Miner, who had moved to West Chester three years earlier after purchasing the *Chester and Delaware Federalist.* Miner renamed his newspaper *The Village Record,* but continued to express viewpoints espoused by the county's Federalist hierarchy. Active in politics almost from the moment of his arrival at the county seat, Miner was picked to challenge Dr. Darlington in the congressional race.

While there may not have been significant differences in their political outlook in 1820, the two parties in Pennsylvania apparently whipped up considerable voter enthusiasm. New highs in voter turnout were recorded at both the county and state level as Hiester took the governorship rematch with Findlay by about 1,000 votes. Chester County contributed substantially to this fragile statewide plurality, giving Hiester 3,323 votes and Findlay 2,830. But other than this, there was no cause for celebrating in the Federal Republican camp. Congressmen Darlington and Gross were re-elected; Barnard scored an upset by bettering his opponent for state senator in both Chester and Delaware Counties; and Joshua Evans was elected state representative, ending the Federalist occupancy of all five of the county's seats in the legislature's lower chamber.

Competition for the various offices was keen, however, and there was much suspense as votes in the Second Congressional District were tabulated. Miner and John Henderson, his running mate from Montgomery County, carried Chester County by about 250 votes, but in the hostile territory on the other side of the Schuylkill their Democratic-Republican rivals finished with better pluralities. In the combined tally from the two counties only 121 votes separated the first place winner (Darlington with 5,261) and the fourth place finisher (Henderson with 5,140).

As an election sidelight it might be noted that a thirteenth voting district was created in Chester County in time for the 1820 election. Designated as Downingtown (although the borough had not as yet been established), this new district was comprised of East Caln and East Whiteland Townships, both of which had formerly been linked with Uwchlan and Pikeland in the Old Red Lion district. Surprisingly, not everyone approved of the change and the following year petitions from some inhabitants of the two townships were presented to the General Assembly "praying to be re-annexed" to the Old Red Lion district. The law authorizing the Downingtown district was promptly repealed, touching off a controversy which made for interesting reading in the newspapers. The *American Republican* lambasted those responsible for repeal:

> "But why is all this fuss about re-annexing these two townships to the Old Red Lion district. The hue and cry is expense; the enormous expense of an election district. It is something strange that these expenses were never thought of at the time the petition was presented to the legislature. But stop gentlemen, these

expenses are not the only objections that you have to the new election district. It so happens that a number of democrats, who are the laboring class of men, reside in the upper end of this township, and who seldom, if ever, attend the election when held at the Old Red Lion. Last fall these men did turn out, and the increase of democratic votes in this township sounded the alarm . . . . The increase of 20 votes to the democratic strength in this township has been more alarming than all the expense."

CHAPTER 8

THE MISSOURI COMPROMISE

During the eight years (March 1815 to March 1823) the two Darlingtons occupied the Quaker seat in the United States House of Representatives, the nation expanded from eighteen to twenty-four states. Indiana entered the Union in 1816 during Congressman William Darlington's first term; Mississippi and Illinois were admitted while his cousin Isaac was serving in the Fifteenth Congress; and Alabama, Maine and Missouri gained admittance during William's last two terms as a congressman.

As the frontier continued to push ever westward it was usually just a matter of time for territories to achieve statehood. No big obstacles to statehood were built by Congress during President Washington's administration when Vermont, Kentucky, and Tennessee applied for admission; nor had Ohio, Louisiana, Indiana, Mississippi, Illinois and Alabama encountered any great difficulty joining the Union. With Missouri, though, it was a different story. The debate over its admission was certainly the most memorable and historic happening during William Darlington's career as a congressman.

Missouri first sought admission in 1818, shortly before the second session of the Fifteenth Congress got underway, but Congress was unable to agree on Missouri's admission because some northern lawmakers were determined to prevent slavery from spreading. The matter died with adjournment, only to be reborn when the Sixteenth Congress convened in December 1819. In Chester County, as well as in Washington, there was great interest in the Missouri question. Meeting at the Chester County courthouse several days before the Sixteenth Congress assembled, anti-slavery citizens adopted a resolution setting forth their opinion that "it would be unwise, impolitic, and unjust for Congress to admit the proposed state of Missouri, or any other state, into the Union unless such state shall sufficiently provide by their constitution and frame of government against the introduction of slavery into the same."

Being a talented writer, as well as a dedicated public official, Darlington dutifully kept his constituents informed on developments in Washington that led to the famous Missouri Compromise—a measure he opposed—through weekly letters sent to his friend Charles Mowry, editor of the *American Republican*. These letters not only gave interesting insights regarding the historic legislation, but they also provide the history buff with the congressman's viewpoints on slavery and glimpses of how the nation's business was transacted. Darlington's accounts were also at times quite amusing, as when he told of the arguments involving a proposed Christmas vacation in a letter dated Dec. 22, 1819.

> "A motion was made yesterday to have ten days Christmas frolic—by adjourning from the 24th inst. to the 3d of January—and although it would have not cost the nation more than twenty thousand dollars, yet it failed. The yeas and nays—which are so great a bore to the projectors of such schemes—were ordered upon the question, and it was lost by a vote of 100 to 59. The reasons assigned in favor of adjournment were that the workmen might hang some drapery between the columns, and make some other additions to the Hall to enable the members to hear better. But as the House only sits about three hours in the 24, it was believed there was plenty of time to do the work, if it was properly economized."

The draperies mentioned in this letter were the finishing touch to the renovation work that had been in progress for five years ever since the invasion by British forces in the summer of 1814 had left the Capitol building a smoke-stained ruin. Until the opening of the Sixteenth Congress the nation's lawmakers met in temporary quarters. In an earlier letter dated December 8, Darlington wrote concerning the convening of Congress and the new facilities:

> "The House of Representatives was unusually full for the first day of session—no less than 155 members being present at roll call. Mr. Clay was elected Speaker, almost unanimously. . . . The chambers of the two houses, which are just finished, are probably superior in point of splendor and richness of furniture to any other legislative halls in the world. They are indeed magnificent. . . ."

The Missouri question was uppermost in everyone's mind, but there was no hurry on the part of the legislators to tackle it or any of the other tough problems confronting them. Darlington complained in his December 15 letter, "the proceedings of Congress have as yet been pretty much limited to the organization of committees, the presentation and reference of memorials. . . ." Seven days later he told *American Republican* readers:

> "The principal business of Congress as yet continues to be reference of memorials and the adoption of resolutions. If the number of resolves affords any indication of character, it is certainly a most resolute body."

Reference is made to the Missouri question in his next letter, dated December 29, and a clear indication is given as to where he stood on the slavery restriction issue.

> "On the 15th inst. a committee was appointed in the House of Representatives to inquire into the expediency of prohibiting the extension of slavery in the territories of the United States. It was

> very evident from the composition of the committee (there being several members from slave holding states upon it) that they would never agree upon a report. . . . It is humiliating to know that while the representatives of the slave states present an undivided and serried phalanx on this question, a number of representatives from the free states do not adhere to that side which advocates the restriction of the most awful and menacing evil that hangs over our country."

Darlington's letters during the early months of 1820 were largely devoted to the unsuccessful legislative struggle to prevent the spread of slavery, as the following excerpts indicate:

Jan. 5 "A bill has passed the House of Representatives to admit the province of Maine into the Union as an independent state. Considerable opposition was manifested towards the bill by those who are in favor of extending slavery beyond the Mississippi—not because there was any real objection to the admission of Maine, but with a view to couple Missouri with it, and thereby induce the friends of Maine to pass the Missouri bill without restriction of a rider upon their favorite act. This project, however, failed in the House."

Jan. 12 "Among the subjects recently acted upon in the House of Representatives was a bill to provide for taking the fourth census. . . . It will probably contain provisions for an accurate enumeration not only of free whites and slaves, but also for free blacks in each state; and likewise an account of the three great classes of our population who are engaged in agriculture, manufacturing and commerce."

Jan. 19 "The attention of all persons here has been almost exclusively directed towards the Senate chamber on account of the discussion which is there going on relative to the restriction of slavery in Missouri. The representatives desert their seats by scores to listen to the debates in the Senate, and there will probably be no more business of great importance transacted in the House until the Senate has disposed of that question. The interest which it excites is almost inconceivable by persons at a distance. The galleries are literally crowded. . . ."

Feb. 2 "Yesterday the question was taken in the Senate on Mr. Robert's motion to restrict slavery in Missouri, and was decided in the negative by a majority which the friends of human rights could not have anticipated at this early period of our republic. Mr. Otis, of Mass., as you will perceive by the yeas and nays, has from some cause changed his ground since last year, but the other four New England states were divided and their votes neutralized. . . . Thus you see the virtuous principles of 1787, which were then exerted with effect to stay the spreading of that foul blot upon our national escutcheon, have suffered a lamentable depreciation in the short space of thirty-three years."

Feb. 9 "The attention of the House of Representatives is so exclusively devoted to the question of restricting slavery that there has been no variety in the proceedings since my last letter. Nothing else is done, or can be done, until the subject is disposed of. . . ."

Feb. 16 "The great Missouri question on which our national councils are embarked is still afloat in the ocean of uncertainity, and no one can yet see when or where it is to land. It is buffetted to and fro by the tempest of debate—sometimes close-hauled on the restriction tack, hugging the fresh breezes of argument, and stemming the currents of error—and sometimes bearing away large before the boisterous squalls of declamation, or drifting into danger on the gulf streams of prejudice and infatuation."

Feb. 23 "The contest on the Missouri question has at length assumed a somewhat different shape; or rather, the debate in committee of the whole on the motion to restrict slavery has been superceded for the admission of Maine, with the Missouri bill tacked to it, and a sort of compromise annexed relative to slavery in the remaining territories."

March 1 "It is hoped the long agony respecting the Missouri question in the House of Representatives is almost over. On Monday the House sat from 11 o'clock in the morning until nearly 10 o'clock at night—engaged the whole time in the most ardent discussion, and yesterday morning the contest was renewed with fresh vigor and continued until after eight o'clock in the evening when the bill containing the restriction on Slavery was ordered to be engrossed for a third reading by a majority of nine votes."

Missouri, under the compromise finally reached, was admitted as a slave state and Maine entered the Union as a free state. Slavery was excluded from all states created out of the Louisiana Territory north of 36 degrees, 30 minutes, north latitude. Congressman Darlington was unhappy with this result. At one point during the House debate he spoke for an hour in favor of restricting slavery. Concerning the pressures put on House members to go along with the compromise measure he wrote in his March 3 letter:

> "Then came the trying moment. The most pathetic appeals were made to members—the horrors of disunion were depicted on one hand and the blessings of harmony portrayed on the other. Some wavering friends of restricting slavery disappeared from the House. . . . I am proud, however, to say that notwithstanding the threats, and the appeals to fears and feelings—honest Pennsylvania, faithful Pennsylvania stood firm as a rock."

The Chester County legislator conceded that "Congress possibly averted threatened evils from distempered men of slave holding states" by approving the compromise, but he felt it "humbled the proud character of our republic in the eyes of the world." Several days later he footnoted the Missouri admission saga by telling *American Republican* readers :

> "You will no doubt be glad to hear that the tediously contested bills relative to Maine and Missouri are at length transferred from the tables of Congress to the Statute Book. Disreputable as the result is to the character of the Republic, it is of some relief to be rid of the unpleasant, and—as it at one time threatened to be—almost interminable question."

THE DARLINGTON LEGACY

Both Dr. Darlington and his cousin Isaac Darlington continued their public service careers after leaving the Congress. As a consequence it is for accomplishments completely apart or unrelated to their services in Washington that they have been remembered. Isaac became the first president judge of the Fifteenth Judicial District and it is as a judge, not as a congressman, that he is remembered. William was a man of many talents and interests; his accomplishments were likewise many. When the north wing of the courthouse was built several decades ago it was felt appropriate to inscribe the names of a select group of outstanding persons in the county's history on an outside wall of the new edifice. One of these was "Dr. William Darlington—Physician, Scientist, Banker."

Dr. Darlington helped organize the Chester County Medical Society and became its first president. He published several works on botany and natural science, including one called *Flora Cestrica* that won praise from the worldwide science community. For many years he served as president of the National Bank of Chester County. The descriptive nouns "Physician, Scientist, Banker" are certainly apropos, but conspicuously missing is the word "Politician." He was a man active in party business and well-versed in governmental affairs; omission of "Politician" (on the courthouse wall of all places) in this writer's opinion is regrettable.

Across the street from the courthouse—at 13 North High Street in front of an attractive red brick building now occupied by Fidelity Bank—is another marker commemorating Dr. Darlington's public service. It also avoids the word "politician" in describing him, but by using "congressman" it certainly hints that politics were an important part of his life. The legend on this historical marker reads:

> "Physician, Congressman, began a service of 33 years as president of Bank of Chester County in this building, 1830. Especially noted for his many contributions to the science and study of botany in the early 1800's. He died in 1863."

Perhaps one reason Dr. Darlington's contributions as a congressman and politician have been made to appear secondary to his other endeavors is because his major political achievements occurred during the first half of his life before he began his banking career and gained recognition as a botanist and scientist. He had not yet reached his forty-first birthday when he retired from the Washington scene with three terms as a congressman behind him. Those who wrote his obituary forty years later most likely thought of him as a wealthy elder statesman and had only dim memories or second-hand knowledge of his political struggles and accomplishments.

His was one of the early Chester County voices to speak out in the United States House of Representatives against slavery. Those from Chester County who succeeded him in the Congress during the next four decades—Isaac Wayne, Charles Miner, Joshua Evans, David Potts, Francis James, Abraham McIlvaine, Jesse Dickey, John Morrison, William Everhart and John Hickman—were also quite vocal in their anti-slavery views, thus giving southeastern Pennsylvania's Quaker district a national reputation during the long and divisive debate over slavery and its extension.

Following his defeat in 1822, which was brought about by congressional redistricting, Dr. Darlington continued to have a leading role on both the county and state political stages. His name was mentioned during the 1820s as a possible candidate for both United States senator and governor of Pennsylvania. He left the Congress at a time of great emphasis on internal improvements. The nation had gone on a canal building binge and in Pennsylvania the post of canal commissioner was a highly prized one. Dr. Darlington was appointed canal commissioner in 1825 by Governor Shulze and was involved in this phase of the state's development until May of 1827 when he resigned because he found the duties "incompatible with my professional engagements." With the coming of the railroads he found another hobby or interest. He helped organize and served as the first president of the West Chester Railroad.

The Democratic-Republican Party had a number of prominent men aspiring to succeed President Monroe in the White House when the Seventeenth Congress concluded its business and Darlington said good-bye to his friends in Washington. One of these presidential aspirants was Darlington's friend John Calhoun of South Carolina. A toast to Calhoun offered by Darlington at a political gathering the preceding Fourth of July had received widespread publicity. Commenting on the toast much later the *Village Record* said:

> "Dr. Darlington is the advocate of Mr. Calhoun—he wishes the public to know it; he is anxious to give to that gentleman the weight throughout Pennsylvania of his name and character; he wishes also by this frank and open avowal to let our sister states see who is the choice of the leading men in the great state of Pennsylvania."

Among the masses, though, the most popular Democrat in the country was Gen. Andrew Jackson, the hero of New Orleans. Dr. Darlington, however, was not among the admirers of "Old Hickory." Even after the party's state convention endorsed Jackson for the presidency and Calhoun for the vice-presidency, he couldn't bring himself to support Jackson. Instead, he gave his backing to John Quincy Adams. With both the Jackson and Adams parties united on Calhoun for the vice-presidency, Dr. Darlington's friend from South Carolina was easily elected; he received 182 of the 261 electoral votes. But none of the four candidates for the presidency—Jackson, Adams, Henry Clay and William H. Crawford—came anywhere near having an electoral college majority in the controversial 1824 election. This election was a turning point in Dr. Darlington's life, as it was for many other prominent public men. His decision to back the more conservative Adams, who was eventually elected by the House of Representatives, rather than the popular Jackson, was the beginning of his estrangement from the Democratic-Republican Party.

The 1826 election campaign was the last one in which Dr. Darlington would find himself battling on the side of the Democrats. He was a delegate to the party's state convention that nominated Governor Shulze for a second term. Later, at a county nominating convention, he was chosen as the party's nominee for state senator. Shulze was re-elected, but Darlington lost his race by some 300 votes to the Federal Republican Party's nominee, Joshua Hunt.

Many of his friends and most of his political associates were Jackson enthusiasts, but Darlington stuck with the administration ticket and supported President Adams in 1828. General Jackson won and became not only the dominant political figure on the American scene, but the man generally credited with being responsible for our modern two-party system. As an anti-Jackson man, Darlington eventually became affiliated with the Whig Party which grew out of Jackson's opponents. He was also involved for a time with the Anti-Masonic movement. Newspaper accounts in the 1850s suggest he was a Know-Nothing prior to joining the Republican Party and serving as a delegate at its first national convention in June 1856.

During the forty-year interval between Darlington's retirement from the Congress and his death in 1863, two other Darlingtons figured prominently in local politics. William, the younger brother of Judge Darlington, and also a lawyer, was active in nearly every county political campaign and movement from the mid-1820s until his death in 1879. His cousin Edward Darlington, son of Jesse and Amy Sharpless Darlington, is remembered primarily as a Delaware County politician, but he was a successful candidate for the federal House of Representatives during the 1830s when Chester County was combined with neighboring Delaware and Lancaster counties in a multi-member congressional district.

CHAPTER 9

LAST OF THE FEDERALISTS

Following the census of 1820 the membership of the United States House of Representatives was increased from 186 to 213. Pennsylvania's share of the House seats went from 23 to 26, and once again the lawmakers at Harrisburg drew congressional boundary lines that today are a bit hard to fathom. The apportionment finally approved by the General Assembly on April 2, 1822, resulted in Chester, Lancaster and Delaware counties being combined into a new Fourth District that was entitled to elect three representatives. For Chester County politicians aspiring for a seat in the national legislature this reapportionment made for an entirely new ball game and gave Federalists a much better chance of tasting victory than those of the Democratic-Republican faith. Reviewing the county's "bondage" of the previous twenty years the pro-Federalist *Village Record* told its readers:

> "Be it remembered . . . that Chester county twenty years ago was represented in Congress by Joseph Hemphill, a Federal Republican, the pride and delight of his constituents. The course the Democratic Assembly took to place Chester County in bondage will never be forgotten. In forming Congressional Districts this county was attached to Berks, giving a heavy Democratic majority; Hemphill was thus thrown out, and the county virtually disfranchised. Ten years after this Chester was bound to Montgomery for the purpose of drowning the voice of the Federalists. . . . Ten more years Chester remained in bondage, except in one instance when roused to exertion by a sense of her wrongs, and when Montgomery slept, a Federal Republican was elected to one Congress. So that, for twenty years, Chester County having a majority of Federal Republicans, and containing inhabitants enough to give her a Representative in Congress, has elected only one Federal Republican. Is this right? Is this fair? Is this republicanism, or is it odious tyranny? Last winter an attempt was made again to bind the Federal county of Chester to the chariot wheels of the proud Democracy of Montgomery. . . . Thank heaven all these schemes of iniquity and injustice came to nought."

This new Fourth District with its Federalist majority, however, was an anomaly. Nationally, the two-party system was dead. President Monroe had been re-elected without opposition in 1820 and the Democratic-Republican Party claimed the allegiance of nearly all the nation's top political leaders. To be sure, sectional differences divided both the country and the party, but in this "era of good feeling" there were no longer deep ideological differences such as those that earlier divided the Federalists and the Anti-Federalists when the new nation was launched. In Pennsylvania, though, personal ambitions and longstanding animosities, plus some strange alliances, always made for interesting statewide contests. And in areas such as Chester County where the political rivalry was intense the voters were always presented with at least two tickets from which to make their choices.

Throughout the Fourth District's twenty-year history ticket-makers on both sides always saw to it that each county had a congressional nominee even though the populations of the counties varied greatly. Lancaster County, with a population of over 68,000, was second only to Philadelphia in Pennsylvania's county population standings when the redistricting occurred. Delaware County had fewer than 15,000 inhabitants. Situated between the two with over 44,000 residents was Chester County, the fourth most populous county in the state. Fortunately for Delaware County the conferee method of making nominations worked and there was very little split- ticket voting in the early nineteenth century; on only one occasion was she deprived of her own congressman.

Five men—Isaac Wayne, Charles Miner, Joshua Evans, David Potts, and Francis James—represented Chester County in the Congress during the twenty-year existence of this peculiar apportionment. They served at a time when political party lines were not always easily recognizable and as a group made for a mixed bag reflective of the era. Two were diehard Federalists, the third a staunch Democrat and follower of Andrew Jackson, and the remaining two were supported by Whigs and Anti-Masons. Nine other men from Lancaster and Delaware counties were elected to the United States House of Representatives by the voters of the Fourth District. One of these later became the nation's fifteenth president. A Federalist from Lancaster when first elected to the House, James Buchanan switched his political allegiance to General Jackson during the 1820s—a turning point in his career that led to the United States Senate and eventually the White House. For a time, though, he was regarded by many Chester Countians as "our congressman." From the time he became a supporter of Jackson until his death Buchanan was a popular figure with the rank and file of the Democratic Party in Chester County.

ISAAC WAYNE

Col. Isaac Wayne, son of the Revolutionary War hero, was one of Pennsylvania's more colorful political figures during the early part of the nineteenth century, but as is often the case with sons of famous men he had to live in his father's shadow with the realization that his own political successes were due in large part to the Wayne name. Long before the Revolution the family had been well-known and respected in Chester County. Young Isaac Wayne grew up in "Waynesborough," the family mansion in

Easttown while his father was away fighting the British and gaining a reputation as one of the most courageous military leaders in General Washington's patriot army.

The father-son relationship was not a close one, but young Isaac apparently made the best of a broken home situation. Educated at Dickinson and Princeton, he was admitted to the bar in 1795 and quickly became immersed in county politics. Like his father and grandfather before him, he won a seat in the Pennsylvania General Assembly. An ardent Federalist and supporter of President John Adams, his career as an assemblyman was cut short when the Democratic-Republicans came to power.

The Federalist Party died very slowly; its prolonged life was due to men such as Isaac Wayne. Active on the county political scene for three decades, he was elected to the Pennsylvania Senate in 1806 and re-elected four years later. With the War of 1812 he abandoned his career as a legislator and served for a time in the military with a cavalry unit. Against his wishes, leaders of the Federalist Party in Philadelphia belatedly nominated him for governor in 1814. The Democratic-Republican Party was divided; many of its members were unhappy with Simon Snyder and wanted to deny him a third term as governor. When the Philadelphia Federalists refused to accede to Wayne's request that his name be withdrawn, a number of "old school" Democrats decided to support him rather than the Governor. Non-candidate Wayne carried Philadelphia, Chester, Delaware, Lancaster and Adams counties and statewide polled 29,566 votes. But it was not really a contest and Snyder was elected with 51,099 votes.

As noted in an earlier chapter, Colonel Wayne had been his party's nominee for Congress in 1814. Had he received five more votes in that election he would have served in the Fourteenth Congress. With the redrawing of congressional boundary lines he had no difficulty winning election to the Eighteenth Congress. Running with him on the Federalist ticket in the new three-county Fourth District were two incumbents—Lancaster County's Buchanan and Delaware County's Samuel Edwards. Their opponents on the Democratic-Republican ticket were Dr. Darlington, the Chester County incumbent; Jacob Hibsman, a Lancaster County farmer and major general in the Pennsylvania militia; and William Anderson, a Chester hotel manager and former officer on the staff of the Marquis de Lafayette. His race with Darlington eight years earlier had been neck-and-neck, but Wayne won this time by more than 1,100 votes. His lawyer running mates on the Federalist ticket were also victorious.

As an 1822 election sidelight it might be noted that the number of election districts in the county had increased to nineteen. A polling place was established again in Downingtown along with new voting places in East Vincent, East Nantmeal, East Fallowfield, West Nantmeal and West Caln.

Congressman Wayne did not seek a second term. When the Federal Republican leaders assembled in Downingtown on Sept. 11, 1824, to pick a ticket they were given a letter from Wayne stating: "I decline the honour of a nomination for the Nineteenth Congress, and avail myself of the occasion to state that bodily indisposition alone has induced me to withhold in this instance the use of a name which many of my fellow citizens have repeatedly delighted to honour in the person of my deceased ancestor, and that of his son." He apparently recovered from whatever ailment he was suffering and lived another twenty-eight years, frequently becoming involved in political activities. He died on Oct. 25, 1852, in his eighty-second year.

CHARLES MINER

Except for John Hiester, all of Chester County's early congressmen were born in the county. Some had family roots here that went back to the days of William Penn or thereabouts. Not so with Charles Miner, the tenth Chester County congressman to occupy a seat in the United States House of Representatives. He was not even a native of Pennsylvania, and his stay in Chester County was a relatively short seventeen years—from 1817 to 1834. Yet on the national political stage he may have been the most influential of the county's early nineteenth century legislators.

Born in Norwich, Connecticut, on Feb. 1, 1780, Miner's family roots in America ran much deeper than those of his Quaker associates in Chester County. His ancestors had emigrated from England to Massachusetts almost sixty years before Penn founded his colony. The youngest of four children, Miner displayed an early talent for writing. About 1799 he joined his brother Asher in Pennsylvania's Wyoming Valley where together they published a newspaper called the *Luzerne Federalist.* It was here in the Wilkes-Barre region that Miner quickly made a name for himself as both a newspaperman and a politician. It was also here in January of 1804 that he married Letitia Wright, a fifteen-year-old Wilkes-Barre girl who gave birth in October of that year to the first of their ten children.

Miner dissolved business connections with his brother and became sole proprietor of the *Luzerne Federalist* shortly after his marriage. The newspaper was a useful promoter of the political party which gave it its name, and it wasn't long before Miner was embroiled in the politics of Luzerne County. In 1807 he was sent to Lancaster, then the state capital, to serve in the General Assembly. Although only in his twenties and a freshman legislator, Miner had no qualms about speaking out on the issues. To a friend back home he wrote:

> "I must tell you that Governor Simon (Snyder) is very polite to me. I could not wish him to be more so and I must confess I wonder at it for I am sometimes rather saucy in my language in the House. I have two or three times been called to order for lashing the Democratic Party."

A believer in Federalist principles, Miner undoubtedly found many readers in Chester County who shared his views when he moved to West Chester in 1817 to take over *The Chester and Delaware Federalist,* the weekly political journal that had been established eight years earlier by Dennis Whelen. Miner renamed the small sheet (18 by 24 inches) *The Village Record* and soon he was well on his way to becoming one of the state's most original and influential newspaper editors even though he espoused a minority viewpoint. *The Village Record* was published every Wednesday morning; subscriptions cost two dollars a year, plus an additional twenty-five cents if sent by post. Miner, who was able to boast a weekly circulation of over 1,800 by 1819, assured his readers in one of the early editions that "the politics of the paper are decidedly Federal Republican," but he also promised them that political discussions would be "carefully excluded from the literary page."

Miner's political debut in Chester County came in 1820—the year of the gubernatorial rematch between William Findlay and Joseph Hiester—when the Federal Republicans picked him to go against the incumbent Darlington in the Second District congressional race. Running with him on the Federalist ticket were well known Chester Countians such as Joshua Hunt and James Kelton. Had the balloting been confined to the Chester County side of the Schuylkill River, Miner would have been a winner even though he was a political newcomer. However, in the Montgomery County half of the Second District he and his running mate encountered stiff opposition. Their 200 vote pluralities in Chester County were wiped out and the Democratic-Republican nominees were elected by approximately 100 votes.

Politics continued to fascinate Miner and occupy much of his time, even to the detriment of his business. Appealing to delinquent advertisers and subscribers to pay their bills, Miner confessed in the Oct. 22, 1823, edition:

> "We have devoted ourselves for the last six months so entirely to the Governor's election that business was sadly neglected. Our paper maker, journeymen and other accounts have accumulated, and we must make an effort to put things in order again. To this end we make an appeal to our good patrons for their aid. . . ."

A few months after making this appeal Miner threw his hat in the ring a second time when Congressman Wayne removed himself as a candidate for re-election. This time he did not have to worry about strong opposition from the Democrats in Montgomery County, but instead could anticipate friendly receptions in Lancaster and Delaware counties. The campaign, however, was a rough-and-tumble one typical of the early nineteenth century. In his home county Miner was bitterly attack by the *American Republican*, a rival newspaper and the mouthpiece of the local Democratic-Republican Party. Some of the abuse he suffered may have been tit for tat, resulting from items of a disparaging nature pertaining to Darlington that had appeared in the *Village Record*. Miner was accused of heaping "twenty broad columns of obloquy and slander" on the former congressman and in retaliation the *American Republican* said:

> "It has been the study of Mr. Miner to exhibit himself before the

> Society of Friends, on whom he has been lavishing the most disgusting flattery, as a persecuted man; and he has generally represented our worthy citizen Dr. Darlington as the principal agent in the persecution; but whether Chester county merit or yankee intrigue will triumph when judged at the bar of an enlightened community, all-trying time will determine."

As this passage suggests, the rival newspaper found it repugnant that the Federal Republicans stooped to pick a transplanted New Englander as their congressional nominee. The following appeared in the August 25 *American Republican*:

> "None of the Natives are worthy of Congressional honors—they are better calculated to be voters to elect a Yankee than to represent the people of Chester county in the National Legislature. There are a number of respectable federalists in Chester county, as for instance Mr. Kelton, Mr. Menough, Mr. Pusey, Dr. Bailey, Mr. Lindlay, Mr. Ashbridge, Dr. Fairlamb, Mr. Potts, and Mr. Hunt; all respectable for talents and goodness of character; and in soundness of judgement any of them exceed the editor of the Record. The only reason that can be assigned by their party, why they should not take precedence of Mr. Miner, is that they have not been employed the last seven years in fawning upon and daubing the respectable families, and every thing in connection with them, with hypocritical adulation. This is their sin."

Efforts of the rival newspaper to discredit Miner apparently failed. He polled 2,720 votes in the county to 2,512 for his county opponent, Isaac Barnard. The Federal Republican trio of James Buchanan, Samuel Edwards and Miner came out on top in the voting in all three counties of the Fourth District to register wins with pluralities ranging from 700 to 1,000 over Democrats Barnard, William Anderson, and Samuel Houston.

THE 1824 ELECTION

Shortly after Miner's election triumph the voters of Pennsylvania went to the polls again and registered their choices for president. This election was unlike any other for the nation's highest office. The two-party system was virtually dead as far as national politics were concerned; nearly all of the country's top statesmen considered themselves Democratic-Republicans of one brand or another. Within this "umbrella party" Andrew Jackson, John Quincy Adams, William H. Crawford, Henry Clay, Daniel Webster, and John C. Calhoun all hoped to achieve the presidency. Four of these famous American statesmen, each representing a different party faction or section of the country, campaigned for the office in 1824.

General Jackson, the backwoodsman from Tennessee, found considerable support in Chester County. On Election Day he received 1,471 votes—far more than the other candidates. It was a contest of individuals rather than parties. Clay, the "war hawk" from Kentucky who was largely responsible for the War of 1812, finished a poor second in the county with only 344 votes. Ironically, even though his position a dozen years earlier had been anathema to the Federalists, Clay was supported by Miner who boasted that his newspaper was the only one in the state to back the Kentucky congressman. Adams, son of the Revolutionary War patriot and the nation's second president, polled only 165 votes in the county, followed by Georgia's Crawford with 90.

Nationwide, Jackson was high man in both the popular and electoral vote count, but the final result did not give "Old Hickory" a majority in the electoral college. For a second time the House of Representatives was called upon to make the decision. Clay, who finished fourth in the Electoral College, threw his support behind Adams, who was subsequently elected by the House. Clay came in for a great deal of criticism after this maneuver. Although not involved in the decision made by the outgoing Eighteenth Congress, Miner wholeheartedly supported it in his newspaper. His efforts to legitimize the election of Adams, however, had little influence on most Chester Countians who believed Jackson rightfully deserved the nation's highest office. Two weeks after the House rendered its verdict the *Village Record* editor assured his readers all was well.

> "The public mind seems settling down under the election of Mr. Adams more calmly than could have been expected so soon. The noble conduct of Gen. Jackson has had an effect to produce this result; and to himself immortal honour. He met Mr. Adams at the President's house immediately after the choice was made and taking Mr. Adams by the hand congratulated him on his success. This also shows that the General must be satisfied there could have been no corrupt or unworthy conduct on the part of Mr. A. to obtain the election; and consequently none on the part of Mr. Clay."

But all was not well, and it is doubtful that many Chester Countians bought Miner's story. The subsequent appointment of Clay as secretary of state rankled many Democratic-Republicans. The new administration was branded with a "bargain and corruption" label that would not wear off. Three years later, when the friends of Jackson were gearing up for the 1828 campaign, endless resolutions were adopted at political meetings condemning the manner in which Adams had been elevated to the presidency.

Congressman Miner was a friend and supporter of both President Adams and Secretary Clay during his four years in Washington. New alliances were formed at the national, state and county levels during this period, however, and the Fourth District's three congressmen began to move in different directions. Congressman Buchanan was among the first Pennsylvanians to jump on Jackson's bandwagon, and in doing so he brought about an estrangement with many of his former Federalist friends. Miner and Buchanan, although in different political camps at Washington, remained on friendly terms and, strange as it may seem, found themselves on the same ticket again in 1826. Concerned about the support he would receive in Lancaster County, Miner wrote to Buchanan in the summer of 1826 regarding the upcoming election. Buchanan responded in a letter dated Sept. 26:

> "In my opinion there neither is nor will be any foundation for the suggestion that Lancaster County should throw you off for being a friend of the Administration. There is, without doubt, in the county a very great majority of both parties in favor of the election of Gen. Jackson, but the Federalists believe, and believe correctly, that they could not with propriety oppose the candidate selected for Congress by the party of Chester County, and thus violate the implied faith existing between the two counties, merely because he differed from them concerning the comparative claims of Mr. Adams and Gen. Jackson. They have no other objection against you; on the contrary they feel grateful to you for the able, persevering support which you have always given to the cause. It is possible, nay probable, that a few of the warm Jackson men may not vote for you, as there will be a few warm Adams men who will not vote for me; but these scattering votes, if there should be such, will be lost in the general result."

Buchanan's assessment proved correct. He and Miner were re-elected. Samuel Anderson, their Delaware County running mate, was also successful. Their victory margins remained about the same as in 1824; Buchanan was high man for the winners with 5,930 votes and Miner was low man with 5,670. Their opponents—Joshua Evans, George G. Leiper and John McCamant—received nearly 5,000 votes.

If a listing was made of the legislators who led the fight against slavery from the time of the Missouri Compromise in 1820 until the outbreak of the Civil War forty years later, Miner's name most certainly would be found near the top. Frequently speaking out against slavery while in the House, he caused quite a stir in 1826 by offering a series of resolutions calling for the gradual abolition of slavery within the District of Columbia and immediate elimination of slave trade there. His friend Daniel Webster is reported to have approached him afterwards and said, "Mr. Miner, you have kindled a torch that will set fire to the whole world." These efforts in Washington won praise for Miner in abolitionist circles throughout the country. One such resolution of thanks that received widespread publicity was from the New York Society for Promoting the Manumission of Slaves. On New Year's Day, 1828, Miner wrote to a friend in Wilkes-Barre:

> "I am employed in gathering information respecting slavery and the slave trade in this District. It has increased more than any other business since you were here, and is now carried on at wholesale. Besides hundreds in the prisons brought in and confined here for sale, there are houses kept for their reception where pens are made and the southern traders hold their headquarters."

In their book *Charles Miner—A Pennsylvania Pioneer,* Charles and Elizabeth Richardson attribute Miner's decision to not seek a third term to his increasing deafness and his wife's unhappiness. Letitia's years in West Chester had been marked with the loss of three children. Francis, born in 1818, died in 1820; Emily, born in 1821, died in 1822; and her tenth baby Charles, born in 1823, died the next year. Writing to her husband in Washington in early 1828, Letitia made her feelings perfectly clear: "you must not be a candidate at the next election; I am tired of keeping house alone, now the farm requires so much attention and you know I have neither the health nor taste for farming; so you must stay at home."

Whether he bowed to his wife's wishes or whether he perceived defeat at the polls is not known, but Miner was not a candidate in 1828. His friend Buchanan made a complete break with the Federalists that year and led the Democratic-Republican congressional candidates to victory. Whether Miner would have earned a prominent place in American history had he remained in Congress is a matter of conjecture; one thing is certain though, his voice would have been heard. Miner left West Chester and returned to his beloved Wyoming Valley in the early 1830s. An item in the *Village Record* on April 15, 1834, announced that the newspaper had been transferred to Henry S. Evans, "a young man of promising talents and much industry." Miner lived to be eighty-five and saw slavery abolished. He died on Oct. 26, 1865, six months after Lee surrendered to Grant at Appomattox Courthouse. Concerning this early anti-slavery congressman from Chester County the historian Futhey wrote:

> "Mr. Miner was the associate of the great men of his day. Intelligent and social, he was attractive, and the ease and brilliancy with which he expressed his thoughts on paper made him useful as well as ornamental in advancing the doctrines of his party, and in furthering the objects of the mighty leaders who wielded the baton of power. Henry Clay, at the time Secretary of State, recognized at once the abilities and usefulness of the member from Pennsylvania, made him his friend personally, as he knew him to be politically, and looked to him more than any other gentlemen of the House to carry out his views upon the subject of internal improvements, the tariff, and a United States bank."

CHAPTER 10

BARNARD NAMED SENATOR

Since the establishment of our federal government two hundred years ago Chester County has elected twenty-five of its leaders to the House of Representatives, but only once has it had one of its leaders occupy a seat in the United States Senate. Ironically, the man on whom this honor was bestowed was a House also-ran—a candidate rejected at the polls by the voters of the Fourth Congressional District. For the resilient General Isaac Dutton Barnard, though, his loss to newspaperman Charles Miner in the 1824 congressional race was but a small setback, one he quickly brushed aside as he took on other challenges.

A talented attorney and perhaps the county's most prominent Democrat when Andrew Jackson achieved the presidency, Barnard was certainly one of the most interesting public figures on the county scene during the 1820s. His political influence extended well beyond the borders of Chester County. One of Pennsylvania's top Democrats, his forte was state politics, not national affairs, and had it not been for some quarreling within the party ranks in his home county he would in all likelihood have been elected to the state's highest office. Gov. Andrew Shulze, a close friend, made him secretary of the commonwealth in 1826, and the following year Pennsylvania's legislators elected him to the United States Senate. Elevation to the Senate was the pinnacle of his relatively short but meteoric political career.

Born in Aston Township in Delaware County on March 21, 1791, Isaac Barnard grew up in a home where politics was very likely a main topic of conversation. His father served at various times as the county's sheriff and prothonotary. When he was only fourteen Isaac began working at the courthouse in Chester as a clerk in the prothonotary's office. Here he became acquainted with lawyers and politicians and made his decision to pursue a legal career. The War of 1812, however, interrupted his law studies.

Seeing the war clouds gather, Barnard enlisted a few days before his twenty-first birthday. On March 12, 1812, three months before war against Great Britain was declared, he received his commission and was assigned the task of recruiting men. Even though many in Chester County disapproved of "Mr. Madison's war," the manner in which young Barnard conducted himself received favorable comment in the *Chester and Delaware Federalist*. An item on June 22 (four days after war was declared) stated:

"Captain Barnard has enlisted 70 men since he commenced

> recruiting. Industry, good quarters, lenient and gentlemanly treatment of the soldiery, have all had their share in crowning his labors with success. There has been no flogging or whipping, or disposition to inflict so ignominous a punishment if it was within his power; whipping being forbid by an act of Congress."

Sent to the Canadian frontier, Barnard distinguished himself as a fighter and leader. He came home an authentic war hero. Concerning the young officer's war experience the *American Republican* had this to say on Sept. 26, 1820:

> "During the last brilliant campaign, he was with Izard's army at Plattsburgh, where in consequence of the death and captivity of superior officers, he had the command of his corps, and received the marked approbation of the commander in chief, for its fine appearance and excellent discipline. He arrived upon the Niagra frontier, however, in time for the affair at Lyon's Creek, in which he particularly distinguished himself by his good conduct before the enemy. In the general orders of brigadier general Bissel, subsequent to that affair, he says Major Barnard led his regiment to the charge in most gallant and soldier-like style. It is a matter of historical fact that the marquis of Tweedale was routed upon the occasion by an inferior force."

Barnard's bravery and leadership were recognized even by his foes. The historians Futhey and Cope said when the Marquis of Tweedale visited Philadelphia some years later he was anxious "to make the acquaintance of the young gentleman, Barnard, who had so gallantly driven him from his position at Lyon's Creek." Barnard's military career continued on a parttime basis after the war's end. He organized the Republican Artillerists of Chester County, a military group which undertook and completed the task of erecting a commemorative monument to the Revolutionary soldiers who had perished in the Paoli massacre. During the administration of Gov. Joseph Hiester he was commissioned major-general of the Chester-Delaware County militia division, and in 1825 he had the honor of commanding the troops assigned to meet and escort General Lafayette on his return visit to the Brandywine battlefield. But soldiering by then was an avocation for Barnard and it was on the political battlefield that he made his mark during the 1820s.

Settling in West Chester after the war, Barnard resumed his law studies and was admitted to the bar on May 7, 1816. Seven months later he was commissioned deputy attorney general for the county, a post he held for nearly three years. During this period he married Harriet Darlington, the eldest daughter of ex-congressman Isaac Darlington. Although the evidence seems to indicate Barnard's political views differed somewhat from those of his father-in-law, the marriage to a daughter of such a prominent member of the bar certainly helped, rather than hindered, the young war hero's professional and political advancement.

As noted in an earlier chapter, the two-party system was virtually dead as far as national politics were concerned in 1820 when Barnard was elected to the Pennsylvania Senate. President Monroe went unopposed and on the national scene nearly everyone considered himself a member of the Democratic-Republican Party. In the state, though, there were bitter rivalries and many of the contests for state office were intense. Highlighting the election card was the gubernatorial rematch between the incumbent Findlay and challenger Hiester. Barnard was a supporter of the Governor and ran locally on the Findlay ticket along with two other prominent Democrats—Dr. William Darlington and Joshua Evans. Although Findlay was defeated, Barnard was successful in his first vote-getting venture. He edged out Thomas Smith, the state senator nominee of the Hiester faction, by 298 votes in the Chester-Delaware County district.

Barnard made many friends during his term as state senator. He also became one of his party's most respected leaders during these four years at Harrisburg. But in his home bailiwick the alliance of conservative Democrats and former Federalists, who were calling themselves Federal Republicans, remained strong and as a consequence Barnard suffered defeat when he went against the tide in 1824 and tried to capture one of the Fourth District congressional seats. He polled more than 6,100 votes in Chester, Delaware and Lancaster counties, but they were not enough; Charles Miner, his county opponent on the rival Federal Republican ticket, collected 6,700 and was elected along with James Buchanan and Samuel Edwards.

Barnard was a strong supporter of Andrew Jackson in the 1824 campaign and his efforts on behalf of "Old Hickory" did not go unnoticed. Had he wanted, Barnard could have been president judge of the Lancaster-Dauphin County Judicial District. Governor Shulze offered him the appointment, but he turned it down. When Shulze made a second offer—the secretary of the commonwealth cabinet post—Barnard accepted. He received his commission on Jan. 2, 1826, and served until Nov. 28, 1827. It was while holding this important state post that his lawmaker friends within the Democratic Party elevated him to the United States Senate. Under the election methods employed at this time, senators were picked by the General Assembly in joint session from nominations previously made in the two houses. Both bodies habitually came up with many nominees and as a result many ballots were usually required before a majority vote could be obtained for one of the nominees. This was not the case though when Pennsylvania's 128 legislators gathered on Dec. 12, 1826, and chose the thirty-five-year-old cabinet secretary from Chester County. Barnard received 55 votes on the first ballot (ten shy of a majority) and 108 on the second. His chief rival for the nomination was a Philadelphian named Samuel D. Ingram—a man who would later thwart his gubernatorial ambitions. Two others considered for the post by the Pennsylvania lawmakers were Congressman James Buchanan, the future president, and Joseph Hemphill, Chester County's congressman during the

Jefferson administration.

General Barnard served in the Twentieth Congress during the latter half of the Adams administration and in the Twenty-first Congress under President Jackson until poor health forced him to resign. During his short stay in Washington all evidence seems to indicate his performance as a lawmaker was a most creditable one. A protectionist interested in shielding Pennsylvania's fledgling iron industry from overseas competition, he delivered a widely publicized speech on the floor of the Senate in the spring of 1828 opposing the importation of duty-free iron and machinery for the Baltimore & Ohio Co. and other railroads. Recognized as an authority on the military, he was on occasion involved in naval affairs debates. In March of 1830 he introduced a series of resolutions calling upon the secretary of the Navy to furnish Congress with specific information relating to naval operations and the training of seamen. Some New York newspapers felt his record merited an appointment to Jackson's cabinet. Had he been able to remain in the Senate, Barnard might have won a place in the history books along side Webster, Clay and Calhoun.

Being a Jackson enthusiast, Senator Barnard worked hard for the sixty-one-year-old war hero from Tennessee during the 1828 presidential campaign. Undoubtedly, he was very pleased with the results. A winner in fifteen of the twenty-four states, Jackson bettered Adams this time in the electoral college, 178 to 83. As had been the case four years earlier, Jackson was extremely popular in Pennsylvania, polling 101,652 to Adams' 50,848. Even in conservative Chester County he was a winner by 300 votes. But the returns did not reveal the hostility within the Democratic-Republican ranks in the Keystone State. In one camp were "Original Jackson Men." Barnard was one of the most prominent members of the "Original" faction, having been a Jackson supporter in 1824, but some of his associates had once been Federalists. For this reason his faction was sometimes disparagingly called the "Amalgamation" group. Heading the other wing of the party was the previously mentioned Samuel Ingram, who later became secretary of treasury in Jackson's cabinet. Ingram and his followers stuck with South Carolina's John C. Calhoun as long as he remained in the field for the presidency and then made a last minute switch to General Jackson. For this they were dubbed "Eleventh Hour Men" by the Barnard faction.

The power struggle between the two hostile camps climaxed early in 1829 when delegates from throughout the commonwealth gathered at a Democratic-Republican Party convention to select a nominee for governor. Senator Barnard was the choice of the "Amalgamation Men" and George Wolf, of Northampton County, was backed by the Ingram crowd. There were other candidates, but Barnard and Wolf were the principal contenders. Unfortunately for Barnard there was a newspaper war going on at this time in his home county. Since its establishment twenty years earlier the *American Republican* had been recognized as the organ of the Democratic-Republican

Party in Chester County. Its editor, Simon Siegfried, was a friend and booster of Barnard. However, in August of 1827 the *Independent Journal* was established in Downingtown. Its owners, Dr. George Fairlamb and George Plitt, were vigorous supporters of General Jackson and claimed their publication was the party's mouthpiece. If not responsible for the split within the county's Democratic-Republican ranks, the two newspapers certainly fanned the flames of disunity.

The *Journal* turned on Senator Barnard early in 1829 after he was endorsed for the governorship at a party gathering in West Chester presided over by Congressman-elect Joshua Evans. It reported matter-of-factly "Barnard is not the choice of Chester County" and contended his endorsement came at a meeting which had been illegally called. Delegates to the party's state convention had been chosen at this meeting and throughout the months of January and February the two newspapers and two party factions argued over the legality of the election of these delegates. Finally, the faction opposed to Barnard met at Joseph Thornbury's house in Gallagherville on February 23 and picked other delegates who wished to see George Wolf become governor.

The sending of two competing sets of delegates from Chester County to the state convention was embarrassing for Barnard. More importantly, he was the loser in a nasty fight over the seating of these delegates. The convention decision to seat the pro-Wolf delegates picked at the Gallagherville meeting ultimately cost Barnard the nomination and the governorship. At the state convention the senator led on the early ballots. He was ahead of Wolf by a 49-to-34 count on the twelfth ballot, but with four men in the race he was unable to muster a winning majority. Eventually the voting swung the other way and Wolf was nominated and subsequently elected. The *Journal*, of course was ecstatic, having been a Wolf booster from the beginning. Its March 31 edition reported:

> "The nomination of Mr. Wolf as the Democratic Republican candidate seems to be well received throughout the state. Already fifty English democratic journals and fourteen German papers have come out openly in favor of Mr. Wolf as the democratic Jackson candidate."

The *American Republican*, on the other hand, felt Wolf got the nomination dishonestly and commented:

> "It was a fraud to eject the democratic delegates of Chester County and admit those chosen by the federalists and malcontents, the fag end of faction, and the remnants of the old Snyder democratic party."

Barnard was only thirty-eight when he made this bid for the governorship, but it was his last try for public office. He continued to serve in the United States Senate until Dec. 6, 1831, when poor health forced him to resign. Internal improvements were one of his main concerns as a Washington lawmaker. Even opposition newspapers at home gave him high marks for his votes favoring turnpike and canal construction. An 1830 item in the *Village Record* reported:

> "It is understood that the retention and consequent rejection of the Light House bill was mainly in consequence of an appropriation, introduced on the motion of General Barnard, and nobly sustained by him, of $40,000 to perfect the navigation of Back Creek so as to make the navigation through the Chesapeake and Delaware Canal easy, safe and complete. We regard the motion of General Barnard as in strict accordance with the policy long sanctioned by the General Government and approved by Pennsylvania. His course merited and received almost undivided approbation."

One of the most memorable debates in the Senate's history—the Webster-Hayne debate—took place while Barnard was a senator. It began in January of 1830, shortly after the opening of the Twenty-first Congress, when South Carolina's Robert Y. Hayne delivered a brilliant defense of the doctrine of state sovereignty and nullification. New England's Daniel Webster countered with an eloquent plea for the American union.

Senator Barnard died on Feb. 18, 1834—a month before his forty-third birthday.

CHAPTER 11

CONGRESSMAN FROM PAOLI

If they had a mind to, some imaginative and enterprising movie or television producers could make a documentary dealing with the life and times of Congressman Joshua Evans Jr. and his Welsh forebears that would be enjoyable watching as well as a profitable American history lesson. Such a film might begin with a 1719 setting in Merionethshire, Wales, as forty-two first cousins bid farewell to loved ones and then board the same ship to make the long voyage to America. Another film sequence might follow the ship up the Delaware and show the arrival of these Welsh settlers at the colonial ports of New Castle and Philadelphia. Next, the filmmakers might want to zero in on one of the Evans cousins—the congressman's grandfather William Evans—as he journeys inland renewing old friendships with Welsh kinfolk, most of them Quakers, already living in Merion, Haverford, and Radnor before making his decision to buy five hundred acres in Tredyffrin—the township in the Great Valley of eastern Chester County.

Next, the script might call for a boyhood episode or two in the Great Valley involving Joshua Evans, the congressman's father, depicting eighteenth century life in the Quaker colony before the French and Indian War. Other scenes might record Joshua's courtship of Mary Malin and the opening in 1769 of his public house—soon to be known far and wide as the "Paoli." It was here that Anthony Wayne and other patriot leaders met and discussed grievances that were the seeds of the American Revolution. The script, of course, would clearly show that Joshua Evans not only provided a meeting place for the patriots, but that he himself was a Committee of Safety leader frequently chosen to go with Wayne, Richard Thomas and others to meetings in Philadelphia and Chester to confer with other radicals on the course of action to be pursued by the colony. Once war came, the portrayal would depict the congressman's father as a staunch supporter of the Revolution.

Little did Joshua Evans Sr. realize when he hung a sign board bearing the equestrian figure of Gen. Pasquale di Paoli in front of his inn that the name would stick and become indelibly inscribed in the nation's history. Paoli, a celebrated Corsican general living in exile in England, was looked upon by Evans and his radical patrons as the ideal patriot and champion of liberty. Legend has it that Evans christened his tavern in honor of the Corsican rebel after a night of heavy drinking during which time endless toasts were offered by Wayne and his friends in praise of General Paoli. Regardless, the tavern's environs gradually became known as Paoli, and Wayne himself thereafter gave his address as being "at the sign of the Paoli tavern."

It was against this background that Joshua Evans Jr., the Chesco congressman of the Jacksonian era, was born on January 29, 1777, at a time when patriot spirits in Chester County were buoyed by Washington's recent victories over the British at Trenton and Princeton. Before the year was out, though, the tide turned; the Continental Army was beaten at the Battle of the Brandywine and Washington's ragged troops were encamped at Valley Forge enduring frigid weather, hunger and hardship. Historical records do not show what losses Evans' father suffered when the county was overrun by British and Hessian soldiers in the fall of 1777, but his tavern gave the name to the surprise attack that took place one and a half miles to the southwest on the night of Sept. 20, 1777. The routing of Wayne and his troops by the British went down in the history books as the "Paoli Massacre."

Little has been recorded about Joshua's youth in Tredyffrin Township, but with the Paoli Tavern as a backdrop the film makers would certainly have an easy time showing the boy's keen interest in politics as some of the nation's most important political personages stopped at his father's famous hostelry for a meal or a night's lodging. Another scenario might have veterans of the Revolutionary War engaged in a political debate at the tavern in 1800, the year young Joshua lined up with the Anti-Federalists in support of Thomas Jefferson.

The inn, which Joshua took over from his father in 1814, was no ordinary early nineteenth century hostelry. It was one of the best and it took a good businessman to operate it. Business had been thriving since the Lancaster Turnpike, the first turnpike in the United States, was built past the tavern's door in 1794. A traveler recorded this picture of the Evans establishment in 1813:

> "At dusk when we stopped at the Paoli to water the horses and brandy the gentlemen the busy scene around the inn by the roadside, with several great four-horse stages pouring forth their cargoes by the dozens, would have furnished many a page in the sketch book. A scene of bustle unprecedented by anything I had ever met before presented itself till midnight, supper was spread three times for twenty people, and as the chambers were not very numerous we were under the necessity of agreeing amongst ourselves for bed fellows."

Colorful scenes such as this one would certainly be entertaining and necessary in portraying Evans the hosteler, but he was a man of many interests. Other episodes might have Joshua enlisting in the state militia, fighting in the War of 1812, becoming a brigadier general in the militia, and offering a toast to the Marquis de Lafayette on the famous Frenchman's return to Chester County in 1825. Interspersed, of course, would be the romance that culminated in 1808 when he married Lydia Davis, daughter of Dr. John

Davis, the surgeon in charge of the Pennsylvania forces at the Battle of Long Island. Also, it would be necessary to record the sadness accompanying the death of Lydia in 1818, leaving Joshua a widower with six small children to care for.

It was shortly after his wife's death that Evans moved from the wings to center stage in the Chester County political theater. His party (Democratic-Republican) and the opposition party (Federal Republican) were evenly matched in the county when he made his political debut in 1819. By 127 votes he missed capturing one of the county's five seats in the Pennsylvania House of Representatives. He tried again the next year, polled 3,030 votes, and was declared a winner by nineteen votes. The only Democrat elected to the House from Chester County that year, Evans' stay in Harrisburg was a brief one. He was unseated by 156 votes in 1821 when the Federal Republicans made a clean sweep of all the legislative contests.

Evans ran again in 1824 and 1825 for assemblyman. On both occasions he made a good showing, but the conservative opposition continued to hold the upper hand. Described by historians Futhey and Cope as an uncompromising Democrat and a man "of singular good sense and judgement," Evans was beginning to exercise great power in both the county and state by the mid-1820s. The inn, which had prospered under his father, continued to do well and provided Evans with the financial wherewithal to devote considerable time to politics. The strategic location of the Paoli Tavern on the Lancaster Turnpike also placed him in the hub of community life in the eastern end of the county. Not only was his inn at one time the voting place for residents of five townships, as well as a gathering place for gossip and the holding of political meetings, but it housed the community's post office. Evans was named Paoli's first postmaster in 1826.

The Federalist Party was defunct in both the state and nation when Evans tried for a seat in the United States Congress in 1826, but the party had not yet given up the ghost in the Fourth District. Party loyalty was so deeply rooted that most Federalists voted their party ticket and overlooked the fact their nominees were traveling different roads. (Congressman Miner was supporting President Adams and Congressman Buchanan was pledged to General Jackson). Evans and his running mates for the district's three congressional seats polled almost 5,000 votes in the three-county area, but came up about 700 votes short of upsetting their Federalist opponents.

Two years later when he was again a congressional candidate the situation had changed somewhat. The Adams-Clay wing of the Democratic-Republican Party, with which Federalists such as Isaac Wayne and Charles Miner aligned themselves, in some areas was being referred to as the National Republican Party. But in many parts of the country, including Chester County, party labels were forgotten in 1828 and candidates for public office were presented to the electorate on either a "Jackson Ticket" or an "Adams Ticket." Evans ran for Congress this time on the "Jackson Ticket" against

Townsend Haines, a well known West Chester lawyer who wanted to return President Adams to the White House for a second term. The old saw that politics makes strange bedfellows was most certainly true in this election. George Leiper, who had run unsuccessfully with Evans on the Democratic-Republican ticket in 1826, was again Delaware County's congressional choice on the "Jackson Ticket," but the third member of the "Jackson Ticket" congressional team was Lancaster County's Buchanan, the Federalist foe of both Evans and Leiper in the earlier election. Haines, a Mason who in years past had voted with the Democrats, was teamed up with William Hiester, a leader in the Anti-Masonic movement in Lancaster County, and Congressman Anderson of Delaware County.

The close balance between the two sides made for an exciting election in 1828. Congressman Buchanan was top vote-getter in Chester County with 3,813 votes, but his victory margin over the sixth place finisher was only seventy-eight votes and he was the only member of the "Jackson" team preferred by the county's voters. Elsewhere in the district, though, the "Jackson Ticket" prevailed and both Evans and Leiper were sent to Washington along with Buchanan to serve in the Twenty-first Congress. The editor of Downingtown's *Independent Journal* found the returns very gratifying.

> "It is an honest trait in our nature to rejoice at success, particularly when we have been contending with an active and vigilant enemy. After the most strenuous exertions of the administrative party to defeat Hon. James Buchanan, he has been elected (together with his colleagues) by an overwhelming majority. This is a victory indeed! A triumph of principle!"

Two weeks after this election the voters of Chester County again went to the polls and cast their ballots for president. "Old Hickory" was a winner. Returns from the county's twenty-six voting districts gave Jackson 3,835 votes and Adams 3,535.

Evans served two terms in the House of Representatives. His four years in Congress paralleled Jackson's first term in the White House and were eventful ones, highlighted by the Webster-Hayne debate and the President's fight with Congress over the renewal of the charter of the Bank of the United States. No clue could be found in the archives to explain why Evans did not seek a third term. Perhaps he tired of Washington's political intrigue and social whirl. Perhaps he reasoned the Anti-Masonic climate in the Fourth District was too unfavorable and not worth exerting a great deal of effort on a longshot election campaign. Perhaps he felt his presence was needed fulltime at his inn.

At about the same time Evans was beginning his congressional career, plans were being developed for the construction of a railroad from Philadelphia to Columbia, a Lancaster County borough on the Susquehanna River. Initial surveys of the path for the proposed railroad took a route far from

The Paoli. Evans feared the railroad would have an adverse effect on his business, but through his political influence he was able to reroute the line so as to pass his tavern. Legend has it that he invited the engineers and officials to his house, wined and dined them, and then convinced them they were wrong in their surveys.

During his last year in the Congress—on Oct. 18, 1832—the first railroad car stopped at The Paoli. A four-wheeled affair modeled after a stage coach and drawn by horses, it carried mail and thirty passengers. As Evans had suspected, the railroad ruined many inns along the turnpike. But business boomed at The Paoli. With the arrival of the railroad his establishment became the terminus for the Pittsburgh stages; passengers were taken from this point into Philadelphia by horse cars over the railroad's single track.

It was not until 1836 that steam began to supplant horse power. With an eye for business, and to keep up with this change, Evans established a wood yard for the convenience of the railroad. When the trains stopped for wood and water their passengers were able to refresh themselves at his inn. By 1840 locomotives were being used exclusively along the line, and by 1846, shortly before his death, business had increased so greatly at The Paoli that a separate bar and lunch room was erected for the travelers.

During these busy years Evans continued to be active in public affairs. From 1836 to 1846 he served as president of the Tredyffrin School Board. He remained an influential member of the Democratic Party and on two occasions was persuaded to run for Congress. When he died on Oct. 2, 1846, at age seventy-two the *American Republican* said:

> "As a public man he had the full confidence of his party, retaining at the same time the regard of his political opponents. While a representative in Congress he gained the esteem and friendship of many of the first men of the Country, and their respect for his virtues, and unassuming character, followed and remained with him in his retirement."

CHAPTER 12

COUNTY ELECTS TWO CONGRESSMEN

The 1830 congressional election in Chester County was unique. The campaign was both confusing and exciting, but other congressional campaigns have matched it on these counts. There was bargaining and conniving, but wheeling and dealing have always been regarded as commonplace in politics. It was the results that made this election unique. Only once in its long history has Chester County elected two men to serve at the same time in the federal House of Representatives. This was in 1830 when incumbent Joshua Evans Jr. of Tredyffrin, running as a Jacksonian Democrat, was elected to the Twenty-second Congress along with David Potts Jr., an ironmaster from East Nantmeal who wore an Anti-Masonic Party badge.

Chester County was one of Pennsylvania's most populous counties (fourth behind Philadelphia, Lancaster and Berks), but its population of almost 51,000 did not entitle it to send two congressmen to Washington. Under the existing apportionment Pennsylvania's Fourth District comprised three counties and there were no restrictions or rules in regard to residence; congressmen were chosen in an at-large election by the voters of Chester, Lancaster and Delaware counties. But while there were no statutory requirements pertaining to residence, party leaders had heretofore always managed to arrange it so each county had one representative. That they were unable to guarantee Delaware County a congressman in 1830, however, is not surprising; the political situation in the district was one of unrestrained bigotry and utter confusion. Men took their politics seriously then and for many devotion to party was almost a religion. But the old Federalist Party was dead and the Democratic-Republican Party of Thomas Jefferson had been split asunder during the 1820s. The two party system that soon would pit Democrat against Whig had not yet crystallized, and in 1830 the men of Chester County, like men throughout the country, were searching for a new party to offer their allegiance. Two months before the election the *Village Record* reported:

> "At Home, here in Chester county, the political elements are all in commotion. Never was there such a complete disorganization and wreck of old parties; and we do not doubt but good will grow out of it. On all sides we are led to look to principles."

At the root of the chaotic political situation was the Anti-Masonic movement, a strange phenomenon that mushroomed in the late 1820s. It began as a protest over a murder in western New York and quickly evolved into a defense of republican institutions from the secrecy and power of the Masonic fraternity. The movement took a strong hold in some areas of Pennsylvania. One of these areas was Chester County where almost overnight the Anti-Masonic Party became a viable political force. The attack on the secrecy and power of the Masonic fraternity struck a responsive chord among farmers and mechanics, particularly those of German and Scotch-Irish extraction. Meetings were held throughout the county in 1828 and 1829 condemning secret societies and blaming Masons for corrupting the government. At one such meeting held in Willistown at the public house of George Davis a resolution was adopted and publicized urging voters "not to support any person as a candidate for any office . . . who is known to be a mason, provided an anti-masonic candidate of equal worth and capacity is in nomination."

Efforts to stem the Anti-Masonic tide by men such as John Cunningham, a Scotch-Irish politician from New London, failed. Pleading for tolerance, Cunningham and his associates held meetings and passed resolutions to combat the hysteria that some historians have likened to the witch trials in Salem. One such resolution stated:

> "We disapprove of the attempts made in this County to create injurious political excitement against the Society of Masons . . . . We cannot condemn and proscribe a numerous body of freemen, among whom are, and have been asociated, the greatest benefactors of our race, without any proof of guilt in them."

At this particular time there were half a dozen Masonic lodges in Chester County, the first lodge having been established in East Whiteland in 1790. In the eyes of some county residents the Masons appeared to hold a monopoly upon the professions and public offices. This resentment first had its impact in 1829 when the Anti-Masons scrutinized the tickets of both the Democratic-Republicans and Federal Republicans and then took candidates from each and placed them on their own Anti-Masonic ticket. The candidates so blessed were winners. The *American Republican* commented afterwards that the outcome was "more favorable than usual" for the Democratic-Republicans.

Just how deeply Evans and Potts were involved in the controversy over masonry is difficult to ascertain. The masonry issue inflamed prejudices and was the campaign's most widely debated topic, but both candidates seemed to have downplayed it. Since it was neither a presidential nor gubernatorial year one might have expected the congressional contest to draw the most attention, but this was not the case. The focus was on party organization and principles, not candidates, and the men who held center stage in 1830 were the organizers of the various political factions and those attempting to form alliances and bring about reconciliations.

Potts and Evans stood fairly close on the major national issues—internal improvements and the tariff. Potts, a manufacturer and former Federalist, favored a protective tariff and the spending of federal funds for internal improvements. Congressman Evans, in spite of his Jacksonian Democrat label, held similar views and had so demonstrated by his voting record in the Twenty-first Congress. At the outset of the election season one group of Democratic-Republicans resolved:

> "that the improvement of our country by means of national roads, canals, and other public works to facilitate internal commerce and intercourse, from the revenue of the union, is required by sound policy and the best interests of the nation; and that we approve of the conduct of our Representative in Congress at the last session, in favor of this national policy."

That there seemed to be general agreement amongst the county's citizens on the matter of internal improvements is understandable. Aside from realizing the importance of being able to expeditiously market agricultural products, they were fascinated by a project of major significance taking place within the county's boundaries: the Philadelphia to Columbia railroad, which was then under construction. On other political questions, however, there seemed to be little or no agreement. The Democratic Party, officially known as the American Democracy, was in power in both Washington and Harrisburg in 1830; its national leader, Andrew Jackson, was not only an immensely popular president, but a strong chief executive who commanded respect. Early that year he had stopped dead a movement in the South toward secession. The manner in which he served notice on southern leaders that he would not tolerate nullification—a theory that suggested states had the right to decide whether an act of Congress was constitutional—became part of the nation's folklore. His toast ("Our federal Union—it must be preserved!") delivered at a Jefferson Day dinner at the Indian Queen Hotel in Washington left no doubt in anyone's mind as to where "Old Hickory" stood.

Enroute to his 1828 presidential victory, Jackson registered a tremendous majority in Pennsylvania. The next year his party won the governorship in the Keystone State, but by a greatly reduced plurality. The convention fight between Isaac Barnard and George Wolf in 1829 left the party divided. Furthermore, the gubernatorial election made it clear that a new and strong Anti-Masonic Party had arisen in Pennsylvania. Joseph Ritner, the party's unsuccessful nominee for governor, came out on top in the voting in seventeen counties, including Chester County where he bettered Wolf by 73 votes.

It was against this setting that the 1830 election campaign began with a flurry of resolutions being published, debated and commented upon in the county's newspapers. First shots of the campaign were fired by the Democratic-Republican Committee of Correspondence, headed by James Monaghan, at a meeting June 15 in Ann Mason's tavern in West Chester where resolutions were adopted giving approval to "the firm, honest, intelligent and patriotic administration of Andrew Jackson," and favoring internal improvements and a tariff system "by which the productive industry and manufactures of the country may be effectually encouraged and protected, and be thereby rendered wholly independent of foreign powers." These positions on the tariff and internal improvements were significant in that they differed from those of the president and were much the same as those advocated by the county's anti-Jackson leaders. The *Village Record,* at this time still owned by ex-Congressman Miner, continued to have a Federalist bias and was quick to point out some of the ambiguities and inconsistencies contained in the resolutions passed by Monaghan's group. It took exception to the accolades given President Jackson, stating it was "compelled by a regard to truth and candor to say . . . we see no ground for confidence, but much for apprehension and alarm, and we have reason to think that many who supported him have seen his course with pain and regret."

Continuing, the *Record* claimed, "the leading measures of his Administration . . . and the decided stand taken against Internal Improvements . . . are in variance with the sentiments of a majority of Pennsylvanians, as shown in the vote of her Representatives in both Houses of Congress." Barnard's record was cited as an example of the inconsistency in the thinking of the Democratic- Republican Committee of Correspondence. In conclusion Miner's newspaper maintained:

> "We cannot favor a National System of Internal Improvements and at the same time approve of the conduct of those who arrest the system. It is morally impossible. The lines are drawn by the Administration, and Pennsylvania is forced to the point to give up her principles and policy—for the sake of a man—or to let principles rule and to support those men who will sustain her system of measures."

Shortly after this newspaper article appeared another group of political leaders met at Sansom Babb's tavern in West Chester and adopted a series of resolutions, some of which were quite similar in content to those passed earlier by Monaghan's Democrats. But this second group of politicians, many of whom were former Federalists or supporters of the Adams-Clay wing of the old Democratic-Republican Party, had no inclination to unite with the supporters of Andrew Jackson to battle the new Anti-Masonic Party. These politicians who gathered at Babb's tavern called themselves "friends of the American System" and their meeting is of some historical significance in that it marked the beginning of the National Republican Party (which later evolved into the Whig Party) in Chester County.

Ironically, the preamble to the resolutions adopted by the "friends of the American System" at Babb's tavern was a plea for unification very similar to the proposal of Monaghan's Democrats. It noted "the lines of political division which for many years have subsisted among our fellow citizens . . .

no longer mark distinction of principle, or even of opinion" and suggested it might be desirable to act together rather than remain in separate and hostile camps. But in the weeks that followed nothing happened to bring about a reconciliation of the Jackson Democrats and the friends of the American System.

As showdown time for nominating candidates approached it was obvious each of the political factions within the county was bent on going its own way; principles gave way to personalities. Two groups of Democrats, each claiming to speak for the party, held conventions on the same day—August 26—one at Major Kerlin's in Brandywine Township and the other at Gallagher's tavern in Caln Township. Both groups endorsed Congressman Evans for a second term, but came up with opposing slates for the state legislature. The group at Kerlin's, headed by Cromwell Pearce, nominated Thomas S. Bell, the son-in-law of ex-Congressman Isaac Darlington, for state senator; the Gallagherville convention, chaired by James Ralston, named Col. David Dickey of Oxford as its nominee for state senator. The *American Republican* gave its blessing to the ticket formed at Kerlin's, pointing out the nominees selected were well known throughout the county.

> "They are not the upstart politicians of yesterday; but men whose ability to serve the public have [sic] been tested by the experience of years—whose attachment to republican principles has become matured as their country presented new proofs that the people were capable of self government."

In contrast with this ticket the *American Republican* claimed any man who called himself a Jackson or Wolf Democrat would be "mortified when the ticket formed at Gallagherville is presented for his support." Fraud and corruption were stamped on it, the *Republican* said, and some of the candidates were "notoriously among the most violent and open-mouth'd abusers of Gen. Jackson there are in the county, while others make no secret of their opposition to Governor Wolf."

Much of the criticism of the Gallagherville ticket centered upon Col. Dickey, heretofore a highly regarded member of the Democratic-Republican Party. A Mason and one of the early directors of the National Bank of Chester County, Dickey was Oxford's postmaster and a prominent public figure. Eager to become state senator, he unsuccessfully sought the nomination at the Kerlin meeting. Losing there to Bell, and after reportedly promising to support the ticket, he left this convention and went to Gallagherville where he accepted the senatorial nomination of Ralston's faction. The incident caused a great hullabaloo and aggravated the already strained relations within the Democratic Party. Furthermore, this rift over the state senator nomination also had an impact on the Fourth District congressional race. Chester and Delaware counties were united in one state senatorial district at this time and it was necessary for party conferees to meet and agree upon a nominee for senator just as was necessary for conferees from Chester, Delaware and Lancaster counties to meet and decide on the party choices for congressmen. When Delaware County's Democrats chose to recognize the Gallagherville conferees and subsequently announced their endorsement of Dickey for state senator the Chester County Democrats who met at Kerlin's retaliated. Instead of conferring, they unilaterally nominated John Edwards of Delaware County for one of the three congressional nominations rather than endorse Archibald T. Dick, the choice of the Delaware County Democratic convention. As a result of all this politicking one group of Democrats in the county supported Lancaster County's Samuel Boyd, Joshua Evans, and Dick for the Fourth Congressional District's three seats while the other group backed Boyd, Evans and Edwards.

The nominating decisions clearly illustrated the Jackson party disarray in Chester County, but the embryonic county chapter of the new National Republican Party was unable to take advantage of the situation. These followers of Henry Clay, the party's best known leader at the national level, could not agree on how their new opposition party should be organized and operated. At their September 11 convention at the Swan Tavern in Downingtown divided opinion resulted in some of the delegates walking out and conducting business at Isaac Downing's nearby tavern. In explaining the walkout the *Village Record* reported:

> "When it was seen that a number of distinguished Masons were active in urging the formation of a ticket with the manifest intention to array the National Republicans against Anti-Masons, the course was exceedingly regretted not only by the great body of those who were opposed to making a nomination, but especially by many who were Masons. . . . Disapproving of making Anti-Masonry political—they were not less opposed to Masonry mingling with politics; as a matter wrong in itself—as giving color to the charges made against the institution, and furnishing ground for the invectives—as calculated to keep up the excitement which otherwise must in nature of things decline—as mistaken in point of policy because nine-tenths of the Anti-Masonic party accord entirely with the National Republicans on all questions of National policy, and if not pitted against each other by an impolitic course, there seemed no reason to doubt but they would act together in the coming struggle."

This reasoning—however valid—did not prevail. Those who remained at the Swan Tavern named a ticket. Congressman Evans was endorsed for a second term, and for state senator an endorsement was given to David Dickey, the Mason from Oxford slated by the Gallagherville Democrats. Nor did the National Republicans pick any new faces for the four county seats in the Pennsylvania House of Representatives. Instead, they nominated former Congressman Miner's son-in-law Joseph Lewis and Josiah Phillips, both of whom had already been endorsed at the Democratic convention at Gallagher's, and Dr. Samuel McLean and John Morgan, two of the nominees on the ticket picked at Kerlin's. In another strange move about a week later these National Republican ticket-makers conferred with political associates in neighboring counties and agreed to support a Democrat from Delaware County and an Anti-Mason from Lancaster County for the second and third spots on their congressional ticket. Beneficiaries of these hard to fathom endorsements were Lancaster County's William Hiester and Delaware County's John Edwards.

The dissenting National Republicans who left the Swan Tavern and adjourned to Downing's establishment were headed by David Townsend, a Quaker in his mid- forties who was cashier (manager) of the National Bank of Chester County and one of West Chester's most prominent citizens. He had served a term as county commissioner and had also at one time been county treasurer. Unlike so many of the politicians of his day, Townsend was issue-oriented and a long range planner. A supporter of President Adams in the 1828 campaign, he was of the opinion that for a new anti-Jackson party to be successful it should stay out of the 1830 imbroglio insofar as endorsing candidates was concerned. One of the resolutions adopted by his group explained:

> "We do not consider the formation of a ticket on this occasion required by existing circumstances, and it is not our disposition to interfere with the present local division and arrangement of parties, but it is our earnest desire to prepare in due season for the contest that is approaching, on great national principles, involving questions of paramount importance and of deep interest to the whole community."

Believing "the future prosperity of the country to depend upon the system of Internal Improvement and protection of Domestic Industry," the National Republicans in Townsend's group viewed "with anxiety and alarm" policies of the Jackson administration. Looking towards the next presidential election, Townsend's group praised Henry Clay and Daniel Webster in the following resolutions:

> "That this meeting regard the Hon. Henry Clay as among our most distinguished, highly gifted, and patriotic statesmen, whose temperate views upon the subject of slavery, and whose course upon the great national questions of Domestic Industry and Internal Improvements, entitle him to our fullest confidence and warmest gratitude.
>
> "That the late able exposition in the Senate of the United States of the true principles of our political compact, and the powerful and statesman like defence of the Union against the new broached doctrines of nullification, give to Daniel Webster, Senator from Massachusetts, a claim to the highest consideration and best thanks of every true friend of his country."

Meanwhile, the Anti-Masons met at Coatesville and picked their candidates. In 1829 they had been satisfied to take suitable nominees from other tickets and adopt them as their own. This time they made selections from within their own ranks. David Potts, an ironmaster from Warwick Township, and William Jackson Jr., a Quaker farmer in his early forties from London Grove Township, headed their ticket. Potts was chosen for the congressman spot and Jackson was slated for state senator. Unlike the other political groups or factions in the county, the Anti-Masons appear to have worked together amicably throughout the year and appear to have entered the campaign strongly united.

Almost six thousand men from Chester County's forty-two townships and one lone borough went to the polls on Oct. 12, 1830. Some voted their principles, but most voted their prejudices. If some were confused, it is little wonder. They had four tickets to choose from and the names of some candidates appeared on more than one ticket. Joshua Evans, who was supported by everyone but the Anti-Masons, came out on top in the county balloting for congressmen; David Potts finished fourth. But the three-county district count was a different story. William Hiester, leader of Lancaster County's Anti-Masons, was the top vote-getter with 8,471 and Evans was runner-up with 8,150. The third winner was also a Chester Countian. Potts finished twelve votes ahead of Darlington, his Delaware County running mate on the Anti-Masonic ticket, thus depriving Delaware County of a seat in the House of Representatives. The vote tally was reported as follows:

	Lancaster	Chester	Delaware	Total
Hiester	4,815	2,926	730	8,471
Potts	4,805	2,677	451	7,933
Darlington	4,806	2,570	542	7,918
Evans	3,800	3,264	1,086	8,150
Boyd	3,801	2,938	904	7,643
Dick	3,752	1,364	878	5,994
Edwards	——	1,952	451	2,402

CHAPTER 13

WARWICK IRONMASTER CHOSEN

The story of Warwick Furnace is a familiar one to most Chester County history buffs. Founded in 1736 by Rebecca Nutt, widow of the early ironmaster Samuel Nutt, the furnace along French Creek was the place where hundreds of cannons and cannon balls were cast for George Washington's Continental Army. The patriot in charge of this early and famous ironworks at the time of the Revolution was Samuel Potts, grandfather of Congressman David Potts Jr., the first lawmaker from Chester County to serve more than three terms in the United States House of Representatives. Considering the political climate of the 1830s and the absence of a single overpowering party in the county, the winning of four congressional elections was no mean accomplishment. It is as an ironmaster, not as a politician, however, that Potts is usually remembered.

Few families contributed more to Pennsylvania's early industrial supremacy than did the Pottses. The family's success story has many chapters; Congressman Potts' reign of almost fifty years as head of operations at Warwick Furnace was one of these, but it has not been publicized as much as ones concerning his illustrious ancestors. The saga of the great fortunes amassed by the Potts family had its beginnings about 1690 when Thomas Potts, a ten-year-old orphan from Wales, arrived in Philadelphia with a determination to make his mark in the new world. When he died forty years later his sons and daughters (eight in all) were married and deeply involved in Pennsylvania's fledgling iron business.

The establishment of early ironworks such as the one at Warwick required a large amount of capital and mechanical know-how. The young emigrant from Wales lacked the former, but his abilities and qualities as a worker were recognized by the colony's early iron industry entrepreneurs—Thomas Rutter, Samuel Savage and Samuel Nutt. They made him their agent at their Colebrookdale operation in modern Berks County. Shortly before undertaking this responsibility the youthful Potts had married Martha Keurlis at a Quaker meeting in May of 1699. She was a member of one of the dozen families who had accompanied the German Quaker Francis Pastorius to America to help William Penn found his colony.

Potts moved out into the wilderness to begin the Colebrookdale operation. The ironworks, located along Ironstone Creek south of present day Boyertown, made money for Potts and the others involved in the venture.

Other furnaces were later built in the vicinity along the creeks and strong streams that afforded constant water power. Warwick Furnace, situated in the midst of a thickly wooded territory that furnished an inexhaustible supply of charcoal, was one of these.

Only one hundred years separated the death of the immigrant Thomas Potts from the election of his great- great-grandson to the Twenty-second Congress, but one almost needs to be an experienced genealogist to trace the family from Potts the progenitor to Potts the congressman. As was the case with many families of this era the Pottses were prolific; they also frequently married cousins. During the first hundred years or so of Pennsylvania's iron industry there developed intricate relationships and intermarriages between the Potts, Nutt, Savage and Rutter clans. In the case of the congressman, his parents were first cousins as were his mother's parents; all were directly descended from the immigrant Thomas Potts.

John Potts, the son of Thomas and Martha Potts, and grandfather of the congressman, is remembered primarily for being the founder of Pottstown. When he died in 1768 he was one of the wealthiest men in Pennsylvania. His marriage to Ruth Savage, daughter of Samuel Savage and granddaughter of Thomas Rutter, reportedly was a major social event in the colony and the alliance undoubtedly placed him in a position of leadership in the iron industry at an early age. This marriage produced thirteen children, eleven of whom married and had families.

For historians of the American Revolution the sons of John Potts have provided numerous historical footnotes. The home of Isaac Potts was used by General Washington for his headquarters at Valley Forge. It was also Isaac who observed Washington on his knees at prayer in the woods at Valley Forge, and presumably he is responsible for this facet of Washington's life being enshrined in our history. His brother Samuel labored hard at Warwick Furnace casting cannons and cannon balls for the patriot army while brother Thomas on several occasions entertained Washington at his Pottsgrove mansion, one of the finest in colonial Pennsylvania. It was at the Potts mansion, according to one account, that Baron Steuben, Lafayette, General Green, General Knox, Lord Sterling and General McIntosh conferred with Washington a few weeks after the Battle of the Brandywine and formulated plans for the tired and ill-clad American army's winter encampment.

The entrance of David Potts Jr. onto Chester County's political stage in the early 1820s probably surprised no one. Members of his family had been involved in Pennsylvania politics for over a century, representing Philadelphia, Berks and Chester counties in the Provincial or General Assembly from as far back as 1720. David was nearing his twenty-ninth birthday when he was elected state representative on the Federal Republican ticket. Re-elected in 1824 and 1825, he served with three other prominent Chester County Federalists—Joshua Hunt, John Chandler and William Thompson. He then suddenly retired to the sidelines and stopped being a lawmaker.

Just what role Potts played, if any, on the county political stage during the decade's closing years can only be a matter for speculation since little was recorded concerning his activities during this period. His business at Warwick Furnace may have been such that he did not feel he could spare the time to be a legislator. Perhaps he was disenchanted with politics. The Federal Republicans with whom he identified were so weak statewide they were unable to run anyone against Governor Shulze in 1826, and because of the way John Quincy Adams ascended to the presidency many persons were turned off by the new National Republican Party.

By 1830, though, Potts was back in the political arena running for Congress on the Anti-Masonic ticket. Just why he aligned himself with the Anti-Masons is unclear. Family background may have had something to do with his decision. Many Quakers and Germans embraced the new party because of their dislike for the oath-taking and ritual observances of the order. Emerging a winner by a dozen votes from the political bedlam of the Fourth District's strange and confusing congressional contest, Potts joined his political rival and fellow Chester Countian Joshua Evans in Washington as a representative in the Twenty-second Congress. The victory catapulted him to a place of prominence and throughout the 1830s he remained a major figure in every election campaign.

The Anti-Masonic Party had a relatively short life, but won a place in American history books for holding the first national political convention -at the Athenaeum in Baltimore in September 1831. The convention picked William Wirt of Maryland as the party's presidential nominee. A few months later both the Democrats and National Republicans held conventions and chose President Jackson and Henry Clay as their respective standard-bearers.

For the anti-Jackson politicos the Clay and Wirt nominations created a problem. They realized a divided opposition bettered Jackson's re-election chances, but leaders of the National Republican and Anti-Masonic parties were unable to resolve their differences and unite behind one candidate. Clay, who had a national reputation and was much better known than Wirt, was a Mason and unacceptable to most men who had pledged allegiance to the Anti-Masonic Party. County leaders of the two anti-Jackson parties, however, were able to submerge their differences and still preserve their integrity. They devised a scheme whereby supporters of both Wirt and Clay would vote for the same presidential elector, one Nathan Pennypacker. This maneuver, which the National Republicans thought would ultimately benefit Clay, also worked to Potts' advantage since as part of the deal the National Republican chieftains promised to support the legislative nominees on the Anti-Masonic ticket. "Every consideration of patriotism and virtue require that we use our strenuous exertions to change the administration of general government," prominent National Republican leaders such as Townsend Haines and David Townsend told their followers. For some Masons this endorsement was bitter medicine to swallow. In a full page advertisement in the *Village Record* the

Jackson foes appealed to Masons to go along with their proposal, stating "to those who love their Country better than Masonry, it cannot be a matter of doubt."

Anti-Jackson sentiment prevailed in the county, but Pennypacker never had an opportunity to cast an electoral vote for president. This honor went to Sheriff Oliver Alison of London Grove, a staunch Jackson man, when Pennsylvania again went for "Old Hickory." Jackson's victory proved to be decisive; he won in sixteen states and claimed 219 of the electoral college's 286 votes.

For Congressman Potts, running again on the Anti- Masonic ticket in 1832 with Congressman William Hiester of Lancaster County and Delaware County's Edward Darlington, the Jackson animosity in the National Republican camp was a boon to his campaign. There was still a schism within the Democratic Party, but it had no bearing this time on the congressional election. The *American Republican* explained to its readers all factions were joined in support of President Jackson while "the friends and opponents of Governor Wolf will each pursue their separate course on this dividing and irreconcilable question without lessening in any degree the united and zealous support of the whole party in favor of the ticket for county officers."

Heading the county Democratic ticket as a candidate for Congress was John Morgan, a carpenter from Charlestown Township and son of a Revolutionary War soldier. As with Potts and Evans, he was of Welsh extraction. Born in Radnor Township in 1786, Morgan moved to Charlestown in 1808 and opened a store at the Fountain Inn. He became involved in politics shortly thereafter and gradually emerged as the leading Democrat from the Phoenixville area. Elected to the state legislature on the Jackson ticket in 1828, he had been unseated the following year by the Anti-Masons. Although they were able to agree on a ticket, the Democrats lacked the muscle to win in 1832. Morgan and his congressional running mates, Frederick Hambright and Col. Henry Myers, were beaten by about 1,000 votes in the county, and by an even greater margin in the district. Governor Wolf was re-elected, but he took a shellacking in the county where he received only 2,374 votes to 4,301 given to Joseph Ritner, the perennial Anti-Masonic candidate for that post.

The Anti-Masons continued to have the upper hand in Chester County in 1834 even though their party remained an enigma to many. Its lack of fixed political principles baffled county newspaper editors who wondered how party members in one county could support Jackson while party members in another county could be anti-Jackson. As far as the congressional election was concerned, it was a repeat of 1832 with Potts being the nominee of the Anti-Masons and Morgan being the candidate of the Democrats. The results were the same. Potts was returned to Washington for a third term along with his running mates Hiester and Darlington.

By this time the National Republican Party was about out of business and most of its members were now calling themselves Whigs, a name inspired by their Revolutionary forebears of that label who battled King George III. The new party, however, was slow in taking hold in Chester County and bringing all the anti-Jackson elements under its wings. This was due partly to the fluke that resulted in the Anti-Mason Joseph Ritner winning the governorship in 1835.

Leaders of the new Whig Party in the county were successful however in arranging for a joint county convention with the Anti-Masons in 1836 so as to present a united front in the upcoming presidential election battle with the Democrats. Isaac Wayne, the ex-congressman, was picked to preside at this joint convention. Forty years earlier William Henry Harrison, who was being boomed for the presidency, had served as an aide to Wayne's father in a frontier campaign against the Indians. Now the younger Wayne was one of Harrison's backers. How much influence he had at the county convention is not recorded, but the two anti-Jackson groups gave their endorsement to the old Indian fighter. They also nominated Potts for a fourth term.

At their convention the Democrats nominated John Cunningham, a Scotch-Irish Presbyterian from New London, for congressman. Eight years earlier he had been a Jackson presidential elector. In his late fifties, Cunningham had long been active in the Democratic Party, having served as a state legislator in 1809 and more recently as the county's prothonotary. Although united and stronger than they had been for years, the Democrats were unable to win in the Fourth District. Potts was elected a fourth time. His running mates—Congressman Darlington and Lancaster County's Edward Davies—were also victorious.

The Democrats, however, won the big prize in 1836. Their presidential nominee—Martin Van Buren—was elected. Sectional rivalry reared its ugly hydra head, keeping the Whigs from getting behind one candidate, and as a result the election turned into a kind of free-for-all with four Whigs in the field against Van Buren. Chester County gave Harrison a plurality of only 634 votes, an indication of the close balance existing between the two rival political camps.

During his eight years in the House Potts served with three congressmen—James K. Polk, Millard Fillmore and Franklin Pierce—who would later become president. Polk was the speaker during Potts' last two terms. Arkansas and Michigan were admitted as states, a Texas petition for annexation was refused, and the Iowa territorial government was authorized while he was a congressman.

When the Twenty-fifth Congress finished its business in March 1839 Potts retired from the Washington scene and returned to Chester County where he remained active in public life for another twenty-five years. In the late 1840s when the Free Soil Party was established he became one of its leaders at both the county and state level. His was one of the outspoken voices against slavery in the years preceding the Civil War. Potts died on June 1,

1863, at age sixty-nine. A Philadelphia newspaper had this to say at the time of his death:

> "The great features of his character were soundness of judgement, decision, firmness, with integrity in all affairs, public or private. His high reputation for the most scrupulous honesty and honorableness in all transactions might well be aimed at by anyone."

CHAPTER 14

CONGRESSMAN FRANCIS JAMES

Affixing a party label to Francis James, a West Chester lawyer and two-term congressman, is almost as difficult as describing the color of a chameleon. His party affiliation changed with the times. As was the case with many of his contemporaries in the Chester County political arena, James began his political career as a Federalist and concluded it as a Republican. Sandwiched in between, as the nation's two-party system took shape during the second quarter of the nineteenth century, James figured prominently in the Anti-Masonic movement and Whig Party affairs. He was also at times accused by his enemies of being an Abolitionist. The last of the five Chester Countians to be elected to the federal House of Representatives from Pennsylvania's Fourth District, he was backed by both Anti-Masons and Whigs in the 1838 and 1840 election campaigns.

When he died in 1886, three months before his eighty-seventh birthday, James was eulogized by both Republican and Democrat attorneys for his public service, but when he was running for Congress in the 1830s he was painted as a political opportunist by his foes. The abolitionists and their cause were not popular in many circles at this time. James readily admitted being sympathetic to some of the objectives espoused by the abolitionists, but denied being one himself. However, the *American Republican*, took him to task for his anti-slavery views, declaring in one of its diatribes:

> "It has been proclaimed by us, and we now reiterate that he is an abolitionist. . . . That he was nominated by abolition influence remains uncontradicted, and will so remain, unless he shall venture to deny that Whittier and other abolitionists were electioneering in several townships for his nomination. . . . Those who know him know that his language, both private and public, on all abolition questions is that of an abolitionist.
>
> "It is no doubt recollected by all who know this gentleman's course at the commencement of anti-masonry that he was very backward about taking hold of it politically. He was no political anti-mason—yea could deny being one—in the earlier and unprofitable days of the excitement, but when it gained strength and began to afford a prospect of profit and political advancement, a change appeared over his mind, and by the time it had acquired the desired ascendancy, he was first and foremost among the political antimasons of Chester County."

Even after James left Congress the *American Republican* continued to heap abuse upon him, questioning his credentials as a Whig. In an 1843 issue it stated:

> "Francis James is just out of Congress. How—by what political influence—he got there is generally known. Certain it is—it was not Clayism or Whigism. He was also in the State Senate. Neither was it Clayism or Whigism that sent him there. These are the two isms—pretty much synonymous—with which Mr. James has made an acquaintance but very recently, if at all."

This, of course, was biased newspaper reporting. A letter dated March 5, 1840, written by Congressman James from Washington to Uriah V. Pennypacker in West Chester indicates he was an enthusiastic supporter of Clay and a loyal Whig. Commenting on political activities at the capital, James wrote:

> "Henry Clay did attend the meeting at Richmond, and was received with acclamation by an unprecedently large political assembly. It is said that his speech on that occasion has rarely (if ever) been surpassed by his best efforts. The enthusiasm exhibited at the meeting was of the highest order, and gave glorious promise of a rich harvest. . . . Old Virginia it is believed will go for Harrison & Tyler Electors. . . . I am sorry to hear that you have no hope of Penna. Can it be possible that under the existing state of affairs brought about by the miserable policy of this administration, and while the Keystone State is reeling from the effects of blows aimed at her prosperity by the minions of Van Burenism, that her hardy sons will again bow at the footstool of power and sacrifice their best interests on the altar of party? I hope not, and I am not yet ready to believe it."

Unlike David Potts, his predecessor in the Congress, James did not come from a wealthy family. Of Welsh ancestry, he was born in Thornbury Township on April 4, 1799, and grew up in East Goshen Township. His first business venture was a partnership with Jesse Kern to open a store overlooking Strode's Mill in East Bradford Township. This was in 1820. He quickly tired of storekeeping and moved to West Chester where he attended a school operated by Jonathan Gause, one of the county's most respected educators. Next, he studied law under attorney John Duer and was admitted to the bar in 1825.

James moved to the center of the county political stage in 1834 when the Anti-Masons nominated him for state senator. He waged a successful campaign, defeating his Democrat opponent, Joshua Hunt, by some 500 votes in the county. His victory coincided with Joseph Ritner's gubernatorial triumph, thus placing him in a position to exert considerable influence at both the county and state level. Newspaper accounts do not give a clue as to what prompted James to run for Congress in 1838. Congressman Potts was rounding out his fourth term and apparently some politicians were under the impression he didn't want a fifth term. They may have used this as an excuse to coax James into running. Or he may have had a falling out with Potts and decided on his own that the time was ripe to make his move from the state to national political arena. Regardless, by one vote the Anti-Masons picked him over Potts to be their congressional nominee when they gathered at Albert Way's place in Coatesville for a ticket-making session. In passing, it is interesting to note that two former congressmen—Isaac Wayne and William Darlington—were in attendance at this meeting. The presence of these two leaders who in years past had squared off against one another in congressional contests clearly illustrates not only how diverse was the composition of the Anti-Masonic Party, but how strong was its leadership in Chester County.

The 1838 campaign was a very nasty one. Politicians of various persuasions were all looking toward the 1840 presidential campaign and as a consequence the policies and personality of President Martin Van Buren were a main consideration in the congressional race. James and his congressional running mates (John Edwards and Edward Davies) ran on a ticket frequently referred to as the Anti-Van Buren Party ticket. They were successful in the Fourth District, but in Chester County the vote was close. Joshua Evans, the ex-congressman and Democratic Party warhorse, made a good showing and lost to James by only 244 votes. The featured election attraction in 1838, however, was for the governorship, and in this contest the Democratic Party's David R. Porter toppled Governor Ritner statewide by 5,500 votes to end the Anti-Masonic era in Pennsylvania politics. Editorializing on the Ritner loss, the *Village Record* solaced its readers by stating:

> "The labors of the Anti-Van Buren party are not lost; they have gained much, and even if they have not the majority in the Senate, with their talent and number, Gov. Porter, if tempted to do evil, would stand in awe of their power."

****

Sarah James accompanied her husband to Washington for the first session of the Twenty-sixth Congress, a session that ran from Dec. 2, 1839, until the following July 21. Mrs. James kept a dairy (now held by the Chester County Historical Society) while in Washington, but her daily entries were routinely only a half-dozen or so words, usually about the weather, and the researcher is hard pressed to find material pertaining to her husband's legislative activities or Washington social life. Nevertheless, the diary is worthy of a brief digression for several of her entries give an interesting insight into early nineteenth century life at the nation's capital. Her first entry states:

> "Left home November 25th, remained in Philadelphia until the morning of the 29th, left for Washington and arrived the same evening. . . . Found our boarding house (Elizabeth Jenney's) with but little difficulty. Next day being very pleasant, we took a walk to the Capitol. We found it to surpass our expectations in magnificence. It's [sic] situation is an elevated one. It is west of the

city. The grounds are beautiful."

Although she wrote nothing about her husband's work or the hours he kept, she did note on December 12 that "Congress did not adjourn until 12 o'clock at night." Her entry four days later read: "Very cold. Congress elected a speaker." For the trivia collector, it might be noted that the man chosen for this post was a Virginian, Robert Mercer Taliaferro Hunter, who at thirty years and seven months was the youngest man ever to be elected Speaker of the House.

Later in the month, Mrs. James wrote that Washington had experienced "one of the severest storms ever known here." Snow began falling on the evening of the 21st, she wrote, and continued through the night and all the next day, accumulating to six or eight inches, causing a train from Baltimore to become stranded. It was the beginning of a long, cold, and probably lonely winter for the congressman's wife. The following are a sampling of her 1840 diary entries:

> Jan. 16—Blew up very cold in the night and this morning is said to be the most cutting we have had this season.
>
> Feb. 1—Commenced snowing in the night and continued to snow until noon. It is 6 or 8 in. deep. It will be five weeks tomorrow since the first snow fell. It was good sleighing until a few days ago.
>
> Feb. 10—This morning the sun came out beautiful, but is now clouded over. Last night the ice in the Potomac broke up and carried off the Virginia side of the bridge.
>
> March 1—Morning damp. Afternoon fine. Dined at Phineas Jenneys.
>
> March 8—Wind blew but little in the morning as we went to meeting, but on our return there was a cold southeast wind.

Less than 34,000 persons resided at the capital then, and Mrs. James' diary seems to indicate there was very little happening in the way of entertainment for a congressman's wife—or, being a Quaker, she may have avoided such entertainment, if there were any. Viewing the Congress while in session was one of the most important and liveliest diversions of the day, but her diary indicates it was not until the spring and nice weather that she ventured out and took advantage of the opportunity to hear some of the country's most gifted public speakers. No clue is given as to her opinion of the speakers, but she apparently was impressed by Henry Clay since she mentioned hearing him speak several times.

> March 9—Morning pleasant. Went to the Capitol to the exhibition of the blind. Sprinkled rain about 12 o'clock; cleared off beautiful in the afternoon.
>
> April 8—Clear and cold. Went to Senate chamber to witness the funeral ceremony of Thaddeus Betts.
>
> April 21—Cool. Heard Henry Clay make a speech in opposition to

the Pre-emption law.

May 7—Cool. City filled with strangers from Baltimore convention.

May 13—At the Capitol heard Mr. Crittenden on the bankrupt law. Jas. Everhart called. Had cucumber for dinner.

May 15—Took a walk to the long bridge over the Potomac. Warm after ten o'clock. Had cherries.

May 18—Warm. Heard Daniel Webster on the bankrupt law.

May 31—Warm. Heard the Rev. Mr. Bates deliver a discourse on moral education.

June 13—Very warm. Apples in market brought from Florida.

June 21—Pleasant. Walked to Friends meeting.

One can only conjecture as to what Mrs. James felt to be the highlight of her sojourn in Washington, but it may have occurred on the evening of May 30. "Called at John Quincy Adams in the evening," was all her diary tells of this visit with the former president and his wife. Apparently all went well, though, for two days later the wife of the Chester County congressman wrote that in the company of two other women she "rode in John Q. Adams carriage to the Capitol."

****

As with his predecessors, Congressman James corresponded a great deal with friends back home while in Washington. In one of these letters dated March 4, 1840, he wrote West Chester banker David Townsend that "in the opinion of the best informed men of this country the political days of Martin Van Buren are numbered" and "hope springs high in the heart of the opposition everywhere, and the administration party is trembling in every fibre." In the same letter he sang the praises of Henry Clay, saying "the true causes of the present calamitous state of affairs are so clearly laid down by Mr. Clay as to force conviction in the mind of every individual of ordinary intelligence."

Disappointed that Clay was passed over, James nevertheless became deeply involved in the presidential campaign as well as his own re-election campaign when he returned home following the adjournment of Congress. The Whigs and Anti-Masons again joined forces in the 1840 campaign (the last one in which the voters of Chester, Delaware and Lancaster counties picked three congressmen) and backed Jeremiah Brown, a newcomer from Little Britain Township in Lancaster County, and incumbents James and Edwards. Joshua Evans was again the choice of Chester County's Democrats. His running mates from the neighboring counties were Isaac Winters and William Gray. Although the two sides were fairly evenly matched in Chester County, the Democratic hopefuls were again trounced in the district. Lancaster County—still an Anti- Masonic stronghold—furnished James, Brown and Edwards with fat majorities, enabling them to win in the Fourth by about 5,000 votes.

For the Democrats these losses were only a small part of the 1840 election disaster. President Van Buren was defeated in his second term bid by William Henry Harrison. Using log cabins, coonskin hats, and hard cider, the Whigs pictured their standard-bearer as a homespun war hero and sold the nation on "Tippecanoe and Tyler Too." Not everyone appreciated the political hocus-pocus that characterized the successful Whig campaign. The *American Republican*, which backed Van Buren, told its readers on September 8:

> "The principal log cabin politicians in West Nantmeal, living in splendid mansions and faring sumptuously every day, have erected a log cabin upon wheels, which they parade at all hard cider gatherings, not out of regard for the tenants of real log cabins, but to catch votes for Federalism and its candidate—Harrison."

Chester County, which now had forty voting districts as compared to fourteen in 1820, had a large voter turnout on Election Day. Over 10,500 votes were cast, but Harrison's plurality was only 761. Statewide over 287,000 votes were cast and Harrison came out on top with a slim victory margin of less than 400 votes. Chester County's Whigs jubilantly took credit for placing Pennsylvania in the Harrison column. Gloating over the victory and boasting of having "done our duty to the Whig Party," the *Village Record* confessed:

> "We cannot indulge the belief that during the late highly excited political campaign we have not said and published things, perhaps many, which may have been indiscreet. What political editor can avoid such things? But we will say in justice to ourselves, that no one entered the contest with a greater determination to deal fairly with our political adversaries. . . ."

Needless to say, the *American Republican* was unhappy with the 1840 returns and looked for excuses.

> "Men were brought to the polls on Tuesday last who had not been out for years. . . . The aged, the blind, the sick, all were brought forth; and those of them who ever have been known for rigid attachment to Federalism and its principles, voted the entire Harrison ticket. But the defeated, the Democrats of Chester County are not subdued."

The sessions James attended during his four years in the House were not especially noteworthy, but he did have the distinction of being Chester County's first congressman to serve under more than two presidents. During his first term Van Buren was in the White House; during his second term President Harrison died shortly after taking office and was succeeded by John Tyler, the first vice president elevated to the nation's top office due to the death of a president. While in Congress James was personally acquainted with John Quincy Adams, Henry Clay, Daniel Webster, Thaddeus Stevens and other prominent national figures.

Returning to West Chester after his second term, James devoted most of his time to his law practice and played a less conspicuous part on the county political stage. An advertisement in the *American Republican* in January 1846 announced that he and J. Smith Futhey had "associated themselves together as partners in the practice of law" and that "any business entrusted to them will be promptly attended to." He was elected burgess of West Chester in 1850.

His last years of life were marked with much pain and suffering, but he continued to take an interest in public affairs until the very end. He took pride in going to the polls at every election and on Election Day in 1885, two months before his death, the *Local* reported he was conveyed to the polls in a carriage and had to be assisted to the polling place window "where he deposited the straight Republican ticket." James died at his residence on North High Street on Jan. 4, 1886, three months before his eighty-seventh birthday. At a memorial service conducted by Judge Futhey, his former law partner, it was noted that James was the oldest member of the county bar and the "last link connecting the bar association with the eighteenth century."

CHAPTER 15

OUR OWN DISTRICT

Since the establishment of the federal government in 1789 until the present day there has been only one brief interlude during which the voters of Chester County have been able to go to the polls and exclusively elect their own congressman. This was in the 1840s following the decennial census. After every other census Chester County was always linked in one way or another with one or more adjoining counties in the congressional districting.

Pennsylvania's membership in the federal House of Representatives was reduced from 28 to 24 following the 1840 census, but Chester County was not adversely affected. Quite the contrary; its political subdivisions alone were designated as the new Seventh Congressional District even though the county's population fell 13,000 short of the Pennsylvania ratio of one congressman per 70,680 residents. With the creation of this new district there followed five lively and close contests between Whig and Democrat aspirants for the county seat in the House. The Whigs won four of these bouts. They first elected Abraham Robinson McIlvaine to the Twenty-eighth Congress. He was re-elected twice and then succeeded by Jesse C. Dickey, a one-term Whig, and Dr. John A. Morrison, a one-term Democrat.

During the tenure of these three lawmakers the nation saw its greatest expansion. Florida, the twenty-seventh state, was admitted in 1845, followed by Texas, Iowa, Wisconsin and California. Not everyone enthusiastically supported this expansion. Congressman McIlvaine was among those opposed to the Texas annexation and the war with Mexico that followed. Futhey and Cope state in their *History* "he stood among the earliest and most constant opponents of the annexation of Texas" and "opposed appropriations for the prosecution of the war" because he felt it was "wrong and wicked."

During this period the nation also experienced more changes in its presidential leadership than in any other comparable time. From Washington's first inauguration in 1789 until the end of the Van Buren administration in 1841, a span of fifty-two years, the nation had had eight presidents. During the next twelve years it had five, beginning with William Henry Harrison, the first president to die in office. John Tyler—a Virginian, slaveholder, and former Democrat placed on the Whig ticket to attract southern votes—completed Harrison's term, but was rejected at the 1844 Whig convention when he sought to be their presidential standard-bearer. James Polk, a Democrat and the country's first "dark horse" candidate, was the next White House occupant. One term was enough for him. The Whigs scored their second and last presidential triumph in 1848 when they put up another military hero, Gen. Zachary Taylor, a Louisiana sugar planter who had gained fame at the Battle of Buena Vista during the Mexican War. He died in 1850, sixteen months after taking office, and was succeeded by Millard Fillmore, a longtime New York politician who was also later rejected by the Whigs when he sought his party's presidential nomination.

Closely linked with the expansion question and presidential politics during the period when McIlvaine, Dickey and Morrison served in the House was the slavery issue. Although it was not paramount among the problems confronting Congress in the early 1840s, slavery became more bothersome toward the end of the decade. Initially, it was not so much the institution of slavery itself that divided legislators from the North and South. Rather, division came over the question of whether slavery should be permitted in new territories.

ABRAHAM McILVAINE

Abraham McIlvaine, a well-to-do Scotch-Irish farmer from West Nantmeal (now Wallace) Township, was forty years old when he was picked by the county electorate to serve in the Congress. Since the congressional apportionment in Pennsylvania was not decided until the spring of 1843, the first election in the Seventh District was a year later than it normally would have been. However, since the first session of the Twenty-eighth Congress didn't begin until December 1843, the redistricting tardiness on the part of the state legislators caused no serious harm; McIlvaine and his Pennsylvania colleagues had ample time to get to Washington for the opening session.

Grandson of James McIlvaine, who had emigrated from the north of Ireland in 1740, McIlvaine was born in Ridley Township, Delaware County, on Aug. 14, 1803. There he received a basic education while growing up on his father's farm. Described in Futhey and Cope's *History* as a "systematic and thorough farmer," McIlvaine became involved in Chester County politics during the 1830s after coming into possession of Springton Manor, the beautiful estate that is now part of the county's park system. After twice being elected to the lower chamber of the General Assembly, he was encouraged by friends to run for state senator in 1838. However, he refused to try for a seat in the upper chamber, thus avoiding a conspicuous role in the acrimonious battle waged that year between the Democrats and Anti-Masons. Two years later he was one of the state's electors who helped choose General Harrison as the nation's ninth president.

Some Whigs were unimpressed with McIlvaine's credentials when he expressed an interest in going to Washington. They felt the honor of representing them in Congress should go to Townsend Haines. No one in Chester County had labored longer or harder for the Whigs than Haines, a

West Chester attorney in his early fifties. The Whig Party in the county was an offshoot of the National Republican Party started in the 1820s during the Adams administration, but it was not until after the dethroning of Governor Ritner and the Anti-Masons in 1838 that Whiggery captured a position of preeminence on the county political stage. As long as Anti-Masonry was popular, the county's anti-Jackson leaders such as Haines had no chance for political advancement. For this reason a goodly number of veteran rank-and-file Whigs, tired from so long playing second fiddle to the Anti-Masons, were disappointed when McIlvaine was made the party's congressional nominee.

Long before McIlvaine had settled in the county Haines had been battling the Democrats. He had served in the General Assembly in the 1820s and was a candidate for Congress on the Adams ticket in 1828. His political career had appeared promising until the advent of the Anti-Masonic movement. Being a Mason and not one to quietly retire to the sidelines when a controversy arose, even if it meant defending an unpopular position or cause, Haines countered the personal attacks being made on Masons and refuted the irresponsible charges made against his brotherhood by writing a number of articles defending the order. In doing so he made enemies. Both the Anti-Masons and the National Republicans in Chester County were opposed to the policies of President Jackson, but Haines felt it necessary to present the National Republican point of view, as distinct and apart from that of the Anti-Masonic Party. To accomplish this he purchased the *American Star* newspaper and for a short period during the 1830s was its editor.

Even though Haines and his friends had no real or distinctive county party organization during the early 1830s, they denounced Jackson's policies and championed those of Kentucky's Henry Clay, presidential nominee of the National Republicans in 1832. In doing so they kept an opposition party, albeit a very weak one, alive in the county during the brief reign of the Anti-Masons. Faced with two painful alternatives, going with the Anti-Masons or going with the Democrats at election time, most National Republicans opted for the Anti-Mason ticket. Haines, however, could not bring himself to support Ritner, the perennial Anti-Mason gubernatorial candidate. This, along with his opposition to Anti-Masonry, was held against him by some Anti-Masons as their party faded into oblivion and they became affiliated with the new Whig Party that emerged as the Democrats' primary opposition during President Jackson's second term. Some of them were among the Whig delegates who assembled at Marshallton on Sept. 5, 1843, to pick a congressional nominee. By one vote, much to the surprise of most political observers, the nomination went to McIlvaine on the third ballot.

The *American Republican*, a Democratic newspaper, said "our party knew him to be a true Clay man" and claimed "it was the general opinion among the Whigs in every section of the county that Mr. Haines would and ought to receive the nomination." The *Village Record*, mouthpiece of the Whig Party, gave no indication of a struggle for the nomination in its columns; its convention report indicated everyone was pleased with the ticket selected and everything was copacetic. In extolling the party's nominee for congressman it pointed out that first and foremost he was "a practical farmer, and his house, barn, crops and the general condition of the farm indicate that he not only labors with foresight and industry, but with a profound knowledge of the rules and principles which have elevated his profession among the sciences."

Having beaten Chester County's most influential Whig for the nomination, McIlvaine again proved himself to be a competent vote-getter at the October election when he outdistanced his Democrat opponent Oliver Alison by 285 votes. Both parties were strong during this period and elections could, and did, go either way. In this match McIlvaine polled 4,391 votes and Alison, a former sheriff and assemblyman from London Grove, received 4,106. *The Jeffersonian* observed afterwards it took an eleventh-hour endorsement from Haines to put McIlvaine across, claiming in its October 17 issue that Haines was induced on the election's "very eve to issue an address to his fellow citizens in order to reconcile that portion of his party who desired his nomination to Congress."

One of the campaign's interesting sidelights was the activity of the Chester County Anti-Slavery Society. At a convention held at the courthouse in the early summer its members resolved:

> "That American Slavery is a system of such unmixed and unmitigated atrocity, so at war with every principle of religion and every dictate of humanity, that no plea of expediency can justify its continuance for a day, or can avail any man or class of men, as an excuse from faithfully laboring for its overthrow.
> "That inasmuch as the people of Pennsylvania and the other northern States are practical slaveholders through the aid which they give as members of the Union in the arrest and return of fugitive slaves, it is therefore their imperative duty to investigate the nature and justice, or injustice of the system; and, if they find it wrong, then to exercise all their influence, moral and political, for its overthrow; or at least, for the removal of their own participation in it."

In various newspaper articles the Society said it was interested in knowing the views of the candidates on the slavery issue, but it is unlikely these views were a deciding factor in the outcome of the election. The abolitionists received much publicity, but did not command a great deal of respect in Chester County. The *American Republican* called them modern reformers who "do not hesitate to set themselves up as the only true standards of Christianity and patriotism, and denounce and proscribe all who do not concur with their peculiar views." While the question of how much influence the abolitionists had on the election outcome is a moot one, the election of

McIlvaine probably met with the approval of the Anti-Slavery Society. He was opposed to slavery and made his views known during his stay in Washington. But other issues—the tariff and the war—tended to overshadow the slavery question while McIlvaine was in Congress.

As with other county congressmen during this era, McIlvaine corresponded with numerous friends back home and a goodly number of these letters have been preserved in the Chester County Historical Society's archives. Among other things, these letters indicate McIlvaine was an ardent supporter of Henry Clay as were his Whig friends in Chester County. In a letter dated Feb. 3, 1844, McIlvaine was updated on the county political situation by Ferdinand E. Hayes, who wrote:

> "First let me inform you that the Whig party of the County is more thoroughly organized than the same has been within my knowledge. I am inclined to think we can give the Whig ticket next fall some 1200 majority. You can have no idea of the excitement there is. Why our Clay clubs are now more numerously attended than the Tippecanoe Clubs in 1840 on the eve of the Election. We are being well organized and our Township meetings are attended by hundreds."

Then, a little further along in his letter, Hayes told McIlvaine he wanted nothing for himself, but. . . .

> "In case of the election of Mr. Clay, which no one doubts, I wish . . . to have Townsend Haines appointed solicitor of the Treasury of the United States. . . . I think Mr. Haines is wishing something, perhaps not so high, but in my opinion he is eminently well qualified for the place, and I know you will take pleasure in advancing him."

As had been the case in his first run for Congress, McIlvaine faced stiff opposition when he sought re-election in 1844. His opponent was John Hickman, a man who would soon become the most influential and controversial politico in Chester County. Both McIlvaine and Hickman campaigned vigorously, but their Seventh District race was overshadowed by the presidential race and Pennsylvania's governorship contest. Henry Clay, unsuccessful in three previous bids for the presidency, headed the Whig ticket; James Knox Polk of Tennessee was the Democratic Party's standard-bearer. The governorship contest pitted Francis R. Shunk, an experienced Democrat politician from Allegheny County, against Joseph Markle, a warrior-farmer in the mold of General Harrison who had fought the British and Indians in the Northwest Territory.

Many of the nineteenth century political campaigns were ugly. This one was no exception. Bloody riots occurred in Philadelphia when the smoldering resentment between native American Protestants and Catholic foreigners erupted during the course of the campaign. Clay's efforts to avoid sectional issues and to sidestep the Texas annexation question cost him votes. Texas and the boundary dispute with Britain over Oregon ("Fifty-four forty or fight") on the other hand were Polk's chief campaign issues. They caught the imagination of the people and the Democrats won.

The Chester County voter turnout in 1844 was exceptionally large, but as has been frequently the case from colonial times down to the present day the county results differed from the national and state results. The Whig ticket prevailed, but not by the majority predicted by Ferdinand Hayes. The victory margin was slim for Clay (520 votes), Markle (644 votes), and McIlvaine (519 votes). In passing it might be noted that Haines did get an important job with the Treasury of the United States, but his appointment came a few years later and was made not by Mr. Clay nor on a recommendation from Congressman McIlvaine.

During McIlvaine's second term as a congressman Texas was admitted to the union and war against Mexico was declared. He was among the minority opposed to both the annexation and the war. In a speech delivered before the House on June 18, 1846, a month after he declined to vote for the declaration of war against Mexico, McIlvaine expressed his belief that the war was "unnecessarily and unjustly forced upon the country" by President Polk "without the authority of law." This view was later shared by a freshman congressman from Illinois with whom McIlvaine became friendly during his third term in the House. Commenting on the propriety of Polk's military action, McIlvaine's friend Abraham Lincoln was quoted as saying "the war with Mexico was unnecessary and unconstitutionally commenced by the President."

McIlvaine's Democrat rival in 1846 was John Rutter, a West Chester attorney. The voter turnout was down considerably—only 6,750—but the Seventh District race was again fairly close. McIlvaine won a third term by fewer than 400 votes. Statewide, though, the Whigs picked up five congressional seats for a majority of sixteen out of twenty-four. The stand taken by the Democrats against the protective tariff, which was championed by Whigs such as McIlvaine during the previous session of Congress, was cited as one of the reasons for the Democratic Party setback. But the chief reason the Whigs won control of the House in the Thirtieth Congress was the war's unpopularity.

The war, now in its eighteenth month, was McIlvaine's major concern upon returning to Washington in late 1847. In a letter to William Darlington dated December 7, he wrote:

> "It will now become the duty of Whigs to decide whether they will vote men and money to compel Mexico to give up more territory. . . . The idea that war is popular seems in some cases more controlling than the fact that a unnecessary war is wrong and should therefore be abandoned."

Seven days after this letter was written President Polk's message to

Congress filled the columns of the *Village Record*. The message was not one Whigs of McIlvaine's ilk were willing to accept. The *Record's* editor wrote:

> "We had an intense desire to see it, in the hope that after so much fighting, bloodshed and expense, the president would be able to hold up to us the prospect of peace—of a return to the halcyon days of constitutional government. But the hope was in vain. The message contains a series of facts and arguments why, in his opinion, the war was just and necessary—of battles and deeds of bravery—but affords not the most distinct glimmer of peace."

The first session of the Thirtieth Congress was a lengthy one—from Dec. 6, 1847, until Aug. 14, 1848—and it is unlikely McIlvaine had much time at home for fence-mending during the months preceding the county Whig convention. He hoped to win a fourth term, but other Whigs felt they were deserving of a turn and his bid for renomination failed. Returning to Springton Manor, McIlvaine turned his attention to agricultural pursuits and for a number of years he was president of the Agricultural Society of Chester and Delaware Counties. He was elected president of the Pennsylvania Agricultural Society in 1855. His interest in politics continued, though, and during the 1860 election campaign he corresponded with candidate Lincoln, his Whig colleague in the Thirtieth Congress. In a letter dated October 19, sent to McIlvaine at Brandywine Manor, Lincoln wrote:

> "Yours of the 10th (day after your election) was duly received, and for which I am much obliged to you. The prospects for the general election really look very cheering. If we go through clear, then for the difficulties of the administration."

On March 2, 1861, McIlvaine headed the community's welcoming committee when the train carrying Lincoln to Washington for his inauguration stopped at Downingtown. What counsel, if any, McIlvaine may have given Lincoln after the election can only be a matter for speculation. From many sources it is known that one of Lincoln's first major headaches in office was finding ways to reward Pennsylvania's political bosses for their help in boosting him to the Republican nomination, so it's not inconceivable that Abe Lincoln may have turned to his old friend Abe McIlvaine for advice. Still, one reads with skepticism in the Futhey and Cope *History*:

> "When President Lincoln was about to form his cabinet, he wrote to Mr. McIlvaine, asking who would best please Pennsylvania, and the name of Cameron was given. After the appointment the latter wrote to Mr. McIlvaine, thanking him for his letter to Lincoln, who told him he owed it to Abe."

McIlvaine, who was five years older than Lincoln, did not live to see the conclusion of the war between the North and South. He died on Aug. 22, 1863.

THE 1848 ELECTION

The Whigs won their second and last national election in 1848. Considering their party's disarray six months before the election, this feat was somewhat remarkable. From its birth when opponents of "king" Andrew Jackson banded together and dubbed themselves Whigs, just as King George's enemies in the colonies had called themselves Whigs before the Revolution, the party always found it easier and safer to define what it opposed rather than what it supported. This held true early in 1848 when the party's two great statesmen—Henry Clay and Daniel Webster—and two popular generals—Zachary Taylor and Winfield Scott—entertained thoughts of replacing President Polk in the White House.

Writing from Washington in January of 1848, Congressman McIlvaine urged that the delegate chosen to attend the party's national convention from his district be a man of principle "who could and would resist stoutly . . . any attempt to force upon the party a man unknown and unpledged to our principles." In his view the nomination and election of General Taylor would be a calamity. "He is not the choice of our state," McIlvaine wrote, adding that New York, Ohio, Indiana and every northeast state was against him. But five months later at their national convention held in Philadelphia the Whig delegates nominated Taylor. For those party members with strong anti-slavery views the choice was not a particular pleasing one. Taylor came from the South and was a slave owner. Other Whigs who had vigorously opposed the war with Mexico found it ironic that their presidential nominee was one who had become a hero vigorously prosecuting Mr. Polk's war. There were also those who questioned Taylor's credentials as a Whig. He had not voted for forty years, but his supporters were satisfied with his explanation that had he cast a ballot in 1844 it would have been for Henry Clay.

Chester County's Quakers, many of whom were affiliated with the Whig Party, came under attack in Democrat newspapers for supporting Taylor. An article in the *Pennsylvania Freeman*, which was reprinted in county newspapers, struck especially hard at the Quakers.

> "While they exalt the slave-owner and slave- buyer to the highest political honors, and bestow the richest rewards upon military exploits, of what worth are their sermons and testimonies and queries?"

For many voters the slavery question was the only issue that mattered. Since David Wilmot, an anti-slavery Democrat, introduced a resolution in the House that would have prohibited slavery in territory (Texas, New Mexico and California) acquired from Mexico, the slavery issue had become a volatile one. The "Wilmot Proviso," as it came universally to be called, had been offered by the Pennsylvania congressman in August 1846 after President Polk asked Congress to appropriate two million dollars to be used in purchasing the territory from Mexico. After heated debate the House approved the resolution, but the Senate refused to concur.

As the 1848 presidential campaign got underway not all of the county's Whigs were in Taylor's corner. Along with some anti-slavery Democrats these "conscience" Whigs held a Free Soil rally in West Chester and lambasted Taylor for being an "extensive slaveholder" and Lewis Cass, the Democratic Party's standard-bearer, for his "shameful desertion of the principles of the Wilmot Proviso." Led by David Potts, the ex-congressman, the county's anti-slavery protesters resolved not to back any candidates for public office whose views on the slavery question were found to be unacceptable. Potts and several other county men were sent as delegates to a Free Soil convention in Buffalo. Here they nominated Martin Van Buren for president and Charles Francis Adams, son of John Quincy Adams, for vice president. Other than the noise they made, though, the Free Soilers had little impact on the election results in Chester County. The former president received only 507 votes.

It was against this background that the battle for the congressional seat in Pennsylvania's Seventh District was fought. Chester County has always prided itself in conducting honest elections during the nearly two hundred years it has been electing representatives to serve in the United States Congress. The results in some of these contests were very close, but they were never challenged with charges of ballot box stuffing or other voting irregularities as often happened in other places. On more than one occasion, though, the nominating process preceding these elections has been tainted with hanky-panky charges of one sort or another. This was the case in 1848.

JESSE DICKEY

Jesse Dickey, a Whig from the village of Hopewell in Lower Oxford Township, was nominated for the congressional seat reluctantly being vacated by Abraham McIlvaine. His Democrat opponent was Joseph Hemphill, a West Chester attorney who was the nephew and namesake of the Federalist elected in 1800 to the Seventh Congress. Although Dickey was the clear-cut winner by a vote of 5,786 to 5,160 at the general election, a cloud of suspicion hovered about his nomination, and throughout his short congressional career (one term) reference was repeatedly made in the newspapers to the "fraudulent" way in which he became a congressman.

Starting as a poor farm boy, Dickey gained an education through his own efforts and advanced himself politically to the point where he was able to secure a Whig nomination for state representative in 1842. A winner that year, he was twice re-elected. Yet many claimed surprise when this forty-year-old farmer and educator from the county's southwestern hinterlands "stole" the Whig congressional nomination. Concerning his 38-to-36 vote victory over Robert Parke at the party's nominating convention, one West Chester newspaperman wrote that the result struck many Whigs with astonishment and "many will doubtless be anxious to know how it was brought about." Continuing, this writer charged that during the pre-convention maneuvering

Dickey passed himself off "as all sorts of a Whig to all kinds of Whigs—peddling out some of his legislature speeches wherever he thought they would take—and professing friendship for this and that candidate for other offices." Dickey couldn't really be faulted for this, but he was also accused of stealing two votes from Parke.

The "nominated by fraud" charge originated in London Grove after it became known that the township's two convention delegates ignored the wishes of their constituents and voted for Dickey. The township's Whigs had expressed a preference for William K. Correy, another aspirant for McIlvaine's seat. Parke, a Sadsbury Township Whig who had served in the General Assembly, was the second choice of the seventy men attending the township caucus. Dickey received only two votes at the caucus. At the county convention, however, the two London Grove delegates gave their votes to Dickey, rather than Parke, after Correy was no longer in the running, and this was the basis of the fraud charge.

As the campaign progressed (and again in 1850 when he sought re-election) the fraud story was repeated and magnified many times. It is unlikely that Dickey was quite the villain the Democratic press made him out to be as character assassination by the newspapers was commonplace during campaigns then. Dickey was a longtime admirer of Henry Clay and had no problem running on a ticket claiming to be "Friends of a Tariff, Free Soil, Good Wages and Home Industry." His anti-slavery views were well known, and like other Whigs who opposed slavery he was sometimes branded a "Wooly Head." It is very likely that his anti-slavery stance and views on other issues were the real reason for the Democratic press making such an issue out of how he won the Whig nomination. The *American Republican* professed shock in its September 19 issue when Dickey did not heed its suggestion that he decline the nomination.

> "We understand that he is determined to hold on and thus add outrage upon outrage, and insult upon insult, to the party to which he professes to belong. Having by unfair means secured a nomination which he hopes will send him to Congress, he is afraid to throw the matter again into the hands of his own party . . . . That Mr. Dickey's nomination was fraudulent, is generally known . . . . There is a principle of morality involved in Mr. Dickey's position and conduct. A wrong has been perpetrated, and he knows it. He has it in his power to right it, but he refuses to do so."

Dickey weathered the storm. His party sustained him and in its campaign advertisements in the *Village Record* warned: "Whigs Beware of Slanders against the Whig Candidates." In a special plea to farmers to back the party ticket the Whig campaign strategists advised:

> "Farmers—ye who want a market for your produce, support the Whig Ticket, for Free Trade is the bane of the farmer. Turn out and vote for your own interests, and against the party that would break

down your home market, and build up the labor of Europe."

At the time of his election the Dickey family name was well known throughout the southern part of Chester County. His home village of Hopewell, not far from Oxford, was a thriving community. Samuel Dickey had established a cotton factory there in 1822, and from then until the Civil War the community grew and prospered. His family reportedly owned not only mills, but "just about everything" between Oxford and the Octorara Creek. Congressman Dickey's membership in this prosperous branch of the Dickey clan, though, was through marriage to Col. David Dickey's daughter Margaret, not by birth. His own Scotch-Irish ancestors had settled in the New London area during the first half of the eighteenth century, but he had been born in New Castle, Lawrence County, on Feb. 27, 1808, several years after his father sold the family farm and homestead in Chester County and moved to western Pennsylvania for business reasons. The move proved to be an unwise one and when Jesse was only four his father moved the family back to Chester County. Concerning his early life, Futhey and Cope wrote in their *History*:

> "At the early age of eleven, Jesse became a farmer's boy, and continued working in the summer and attending school in the winter until twenty-one years of age, when he began teaching. For six years he taught and attended school alternately. He was very ambitious and anxious to advance in scholarship, and pushed forward with untiring energy towards the acquirement of an education. A share in the New London Library furnished him with excellent reading, and contributed largely in storing his mind with valuable knowledge."

HOPEWELL ACADEMY

By the mid-1840s his financial circumstances were such that Dickey was able to consider establishing his own school. After purchasing the residence of his father-in-law and making improvements, he opened the Hopewell Academy. According to Futhey and Cope's *History*:

> "A liberal patronage made this work a success. Many young men came hither to secure an academical education, and no young man proving himself worthy of aid was ever denied a home and advantages of instruction."

On Oct. 5, 1847, the year before he made his first run for Congress, Dickey the schoolmaster placed this advertisement in the *American Republican*:

> "The Winter Session of this Institution will commence on the 1st Tuesday of November next. The subscriber would refer to his past success, as an inducement to a continuance of public favor. The course of instruction includes all the branches of a superior English and Classical Education. The Terms for Boarding, Washing, Tuition, Etc., during the Winter Session are $55. Hopewell

Academy is beautifully located within two miles of the Borough of Oxford, Chester County, Pa."

As a legislator Dickey's performance was both praised and criticized by the press, depending upon the political viewpoint of the newspaper. He served in the Thirty-first Congress—one of the best-remembered ones in American history because of Clay's Compromise of 1850 providing for admission of California as a free state, the drastic fugitive slave law, the abolition of slave trade in the District of Columbia, and the formation of the New Mexico and Utah territories. Democrats outnumbered Whigs 116 to 111 in the House, but party lines were not clearly drawn. Within the national legislature were southern or Taylor Democrats, northern Democrats, Free-Soilers, Native Americans or Know-Nothings, and Whigs of the northern and southern variety.

Congressman Dickey found the slavery issue to be on the mind of everyone when he arrived in Washington for the opening session of the national legislature in December 1849. Because the speaker had the power to make committee assignments, and because membership on the committees dealing with territories was so crucial to the slavery debate, a great battle developed over the selection of a speaker in the House—one that took three weeks and sixty-three ballots to decide. The session was a long one (302 days) and the *American Republican* would later charge that Dickey was absent from the House for weeks at a time. This may or may not have been true, and if it was there may have been extenuating reasons for Dickey's taking time off. Regardless, there is evidence that he took a strong anti- slavery stand when he was in Washington. *The Philadelphia North American* gave him high marks, saying "his speech on the admission of California was an excellent one, and among the soundest of the session."

Congressman Dickey was nominated for a second term by the Whigs, defeating Robert Parke on the first ballot at the party's 1850 county nominating convention. However, the Democratic newspapers continued to harp on the 1848 convention, claiming he "stole" his party's nomination from Parke. Undoubtedly, these attacks and Whig defections benefited his opponent. By a paper-thin margin of seventy votes Dickey failed in his re-election bid. The *Village Record* called the results "disastrous" and predicted the voters would regret electing a "Free Trade, Locofoco member of Congress."

> "The best interest of the country required the wisdom and councils of a good, sound, reliable, clear-headed Whig. . . . Had Mr. Dickey been defeated by the enemy, we could like it better. But upon examining the returns, it will be found that it was not the potency of locofocism, but the disaffection of members of the Whig party."

Dickey continued to dabble in politics for a number of years after leaving the House of Representatives, but he was never again elected to high public office. As a member of the newly-organized Republican Party, he was a supporter of President Lincoln and held a responsible position in the Union Army during the Civil War. Various newspaper accounts report he distributed over five million dollars to army personnel while serving as a paymaster in the southern states of Mississippi, Tennessee, Georgia, Louisiana and Florida. Dickey died in 1890 shortly before his eighty-second birthday. In their *History of Chester County*, published in 1881, Futhey and Cope wrote:

> "Since the war Mr. Dickey has been actively engaged in farming, taking always a deep interest in the growing skill and intelligence of the agriculturist. To the laboring class of the community he has ever been a fast and efficient friend, advocating their cause both in public and private. The passing years have touched him lightly, his physical nature being still strong and vigorous."

DEMOCRATS ELECT MORRISON

In 1850, after a dry spell of twenty years, the Democrats of Chester County finally elected one of their own, Dr. John Morrison of Cochranville, to serve in the House of Representatives. By and large, the year was a good one for Pennsylvania Democrats; they bounced back from the 1848 fiasco and captured fifteen of the state's twenty-four congressional seats, a gain of six, and retained control of the state legislature.

Morrison was thirty-six and had been active in his party for about thirteen years when elected to Congress. As already noted, it was probably not a shifting of public opinion towards Democratic Party policies that helped him achieve what other Democrats had been unable to do. Rather it was disenchantment in the Whig ranks stemming from the manner in which his opponent had been nominated in 1848. Accusations of "fraud" were constantly hurled at Congressman Dickey during the campaign and a sizeable number of Whigs reportedly bolted, enabling Morrison to squeeze out a 4,671 to 4,601 win in the Seventh District balloting. Concerning his political involvement, Morrison some years later recalled:

> "In 1837 I commenced taking an active part in politics, supporting the Democratic ticket from that year to the present time without interruption. My name was before State Conventions of the party for Canal Commissioner and Surveyor-General, but I failed each time in securing the nomination, perhaps for lack of interest on my part and an unwillingness to bargain for spoils. I was nominated for Congress in 1850 without any solicitation whatever on my part."

As had been the case with his Seventh District predecessors, Morrison's ancestry was Scotch-Irish, his great-grandfather Gabriel Morrison having emigrated from Ireland about 1735 and settled in southern Lancaster County. It was here in Lancaster County that Morrison was born on Jan. 31, 1814. At an early age his parents moved to Chester County and settled in Sadsbury Township where he attended neighborhood schools before enrolling at Jefferson College in Philadelphia to study medicine. After the Democrats asked Morrison to run for Congress at their fall nominating convention in 1850, the *American Republican* commented in its September 10 edition:

> "For most of the offices there were but few candidates named . . . . Where there was competition, of course there was a difference of opinion—each man preferring and urging the nomination of his favorite. This is natural; it is democratic and proper, and no exception can be taken to it. All, however, after the ticket had been selected, appeared so far as we had opportunities of seeing, to be satisfied that the successful candidates were good men and true, worthy of the confidence of every man professing to be of the democratic party. Dr. Morrison who received the nomination for Congress, is a gentleman of fine talents and education, a good public speaker, a man of high moral character, and well informed on questions of State and National policy."

Directly above this account of the county convention appeared a short news item headlined "From Washington."

> "The bills settling the boundary between Texas and New Mexico, and providing a Territorial Government for New Mexico passed the House on Friday, in an Omnibus, by a vote of 108 to 97—the members from Texas voting in the affirmative. Saturday, the Utah bill passed, 97 Ayes to 85 Nays; and the California bill, by 150 Ayes to 57 Nays. This is really good news."

For months the main political question confronting the nation had to do with the admission of California into the Union. Among the resolutions adopted by the Democrats at a county committee meeting in July was one stating California "ought to be recognized by Congress as a free and independent state." Another resolution urged Congress "to provide without delay governments for New Mexico and Utah" and a third blasted President Fillmore and his Cabinet for being "devoted to all the obnoxious measures of Federalism by which the principles of popular government are invaded and the rights of the people curtailed."

California was admitted as the thirty-first state in September, removing it as a political issue during the closing weeks of the campaign. The decade's most volatile issue—the slavery question—appears to have received scant attention during the campaign. Morrison's party had earlier adopted a "hands off" policy regarding the subject and the county's Whigs apparently were not ready to challenge the Democratic Party's position on slavery. A resolution approved by county Democrats at their spring convention in 1850 recognized the rights of individual states and concluded that "any interference by the people of non-slaveholding states" should be regarded as being "in direct opposition to the spirit in which our national union was formed, and deserving of the condemnation of all patriotic citizens."

Although those who followed him would grapple with the problem, Morrison's stay in Washington was relatively serene and he was not involved in the deep conflict that characterized other legislative sessions during the 1850s. Nor were his contributions as a lawmaker during the presidency of Millard Fillmore especially noteworthy. Reminiscing about the Thirty-second Congress many years later, Morrison recalled:

> "Hon. Linn Boyd, of Kentucky, was Speaker of the House while I was a member, and John W. Forney was clerk. . . . No great issues were at that time involved. The Wilmot Proviso (or Free Soil) element was creating some dissension in the old parties. Practical economy was the order in legislation. It was a notable Congress in some particulars. The Senate and House numbered some very able men, among those of the former being Clay, Webster, Cass, Douglas, Seward, Sumner and Chase, and of the House Stevens of Pennsylvania, Stephens of Georgia, and Joseph R. Chandler of Pennsylvania. It was while I was a member of Congress that the hand of death removed Clay and Webster."

With reapportionment and the addition of Delaware County to his congressional district, Morrison decided against seeking a second term, reasoning the Whig majority would be too great to overcome. He continued to be an active Democrat for many years, however, and was a frequent delegate to his party's state and national conventions. After leaving the Congress he spent eight years in the United States Appraiser's store in Philadelphia, five as drug examiner and three as head of the department. Morrison resumed his practice of medicine at Cochranville when the war broke out and took an active part in the peace movement. Active in the Masonic fraternity, he was also an elder and clerk of sessions at the Faggs Manor Presbyterian Church for a number of years. With the establishment of the Parkesburg National Bank in 1880, he became one of its directors and served on its board until his death on July 26, 1904, at age ninety.

Dr. William Darlington served three terms in the U.S. House of Representatives under Presidents Madison and Monroe. CCHS Photo Archives

Isaac Darlington, A Federalist, was a member of the Fifteenth Congress. He later became Chester County's first president judge. CCHS Photo Archives

Abraham R. McIlvaine, a well-to-do Quaker farmer, was elected three times to Congress on the Whig ticket during the 1840s. CCHS Photo Archives

Francis James, onetime state senator and burgess of West Chester, was elected to the first of his two terms in Congress during the presidency of Martin Van Buren. CCHS Photo Archives

John Hickman, a West Chester attorney, earned a national reputation while in Congress for his opposition to slavery. He was elected to the first of his four terms in the national legislature as a Democrat in 1856. CCHS Photo Archives

William Everhart, a prominent West Chester builder, served in the Thirty-third Congress under President Franklin Pierce. CCHS Photo Archives

Washington Townsend, a banker and attorney, represented Chester and Delaware Counties in the national legislature during the years after the Civil War when Ulysses S. Grant was president. CCHS Photo Archives

Thomas S. Butler had the longest tenure of any Chester County congressman, serving in the U.S. House of Representatives from 1897 until his death in 1928. CCHS Photo Archives

Paul B. Dague, of Downingtown, represented Chester and Lancaster Counties in the U.S. House of Representatives from January 1947 to January 1967. CCHS Photo Archives

Congressman John H. Ware, 3rd of Oxford was elected to the House in 1970 and served two terms. Courtesy John H. Ware, 3rd.

Congressman Ware greeting his former House colleague, President Gerald R. Ford in 1974. Courtesy John H. Ware, 3rd.

Congressman Edwin D. Eshleman (left) and his staff assistant Robert S. Walker, who succeeded his mentor in the U.S. House of Representatives, are pictured above in 1974 when their book, *Congress, The Pennsylvania Dutch Representatives* was published. Chester County municipalities assigned to the Sixteenth Congressional District have been represented by Eshleman and Walker since January 1973. Courtesy Robert S. Walker

Robert S. Walker, of Lancaster County, was first elected to Congress by voters of the Sixteenth District in 1976. With redistricting in 1992 sixty-one of Chester County's seventy-three municipalities have been placed in the Sixteenth District. Courtesy Robert S. Walker

On July 4, 1976 in Valley Forge, President Gerald Ford presented Congressman Dick Schulze with the pen used in signing the bill creating the Valley Forge National Historical Park. Having legislation enacted to guarantee preservation of one of the nation's most historic landmarks was a major accomplishment and rewarding experience for Chester County's freshman legislator in the Ninety-fourth Congress. Courtesy Richard T. Schulze

CHAPTER 16

THE DELCHESTER DISTRICT

Congressional redistricting following the national census in 1850 resulted in Chester County being combined with Delaware County to form Pennsylvania's new Sixth District. It was an arrangement that would continue for eighty years and one to which Whig and Democrat politicians in the two counties adjusted easily. For years the respective party organizations in the two counties had designated "conferees" to select nominees for the office of state senator. Over the years the conferees had developed a close and amicable working relationship; usually they were able to reach agreement on senatorial nominees acceptable to the rank-and-file of their respective parties on both sides of the Delchester line.

Chester County was larger than its neighbor in population as well as size. Its population in 1850 was recorded at 66,438; Delaware County's was 24,679. With the increase in Pennsylvania's membership in the federal House of Representatives to twenty-five the mathematics of the apportionment produced a ratio of one congressman for every 93,423 persons in the Commonwealth. The Sixth District had a population of slightly over 91,000 persons. This was about as close to this ratio as anyone could hope for, and the "congressional marriage" was certainly more equitable than some of the apportionment solutions contrived in the past. Aside from this, the two counties shared a common heritage and generally thought and voted alike.

WILLIAM EVERHART

The first of the ten congressmen to be elected from the Delchester district was William Everhart, a wealthy West Chester businessman credited with erecting over one hundred brick buildings in the county seat. One of these was the historic Mansion House, which stood on the southeast corner of Church and Market streets for many years. In helping to develop the community he was also responsible for laying out of a number of streets, including four he named for former members of Congress—his friends Isaac Wayne, Charles Miner, and Dr. William Darlington, who served in the House, and Isaac Barnard, who was elected to the Senate in the late 1820s.

As with others who preceded him in the congressional line from Chester County, Everhart's roots in the county were deep, dating back almost fifty years before the American Revolution to the time when his grandfather Frederick Eberhart emigrated from Germany and settled in West Vincent Township. Frederick's son James, father of the congressman, dropped the "b" and substituted a "v" in the family name. At eighteen James enlisted and fought in the Revolution. He later became proprietor of a furnace in Schuylkill County and served in the General Assembly.

William Everhart was born on May 17, 1785, in West Vincent Township where he obtained sufficient education in geometry and mathematics to enable him to work as a surveyor before he was eighteen. By the time he was twenty-one, though, Everhart was engaged in a mercantile business in Tredyffrin Township. Next, he had a business at Pughtown and bought a farm in West Whiteland Township. It was not until he was in his late twenties, after his marriage to the granddaughter of Isaiah Matlack that the county seat became his home. Old Isaiah had been owner of most of the land on the north side of West Chester. The ninety-nine acres of land Everhart purchased now comprise the southeast part of the heart of the borough.

Everhart's life was not the humdrum one of the ordinary small town merchant. During the War of 1812 he raised a rifle company of eighty volunteers and offered their services to the government in the event they were needed. Sailing to England on a business trip in 1822 aboard the packet ship *Albion*, he was one of the survivors when the ship wrecked off the coast of Ireland. While engaged in his various business enterprises and rearing eight children (one of whom would follow in his footsteps and become a congressman), Everhart took an interest in borough politics, serving as a justice of the peace for many years and as chief burgess for a period during the 1830s.

The first of the long series of battles for the Delchester seat in the House of Representatives is noteworthy not only because it was the last time the Whigs were victorious, but because of the insight it furnishes as to how party politicos controlled nominating procedures. The Democrats, at a meeting in July, endorsed Congressman Morrison for a second term, but he subsequently wrote a letter to the county committee stating he would not be a candidate again. Later, at the county convention, the nomination went to Dr. Andrew Murphy of Sadsbury Township. Delaware County's Democrats went along with this choice. The Whigs conferees, however, had a sticky problem to resolve when they met. At their convention Whig delegates from Chester County nominated Everhart; their counterparts in Delaware County nominated John M. Broomall. There was much wheeling and dealing, but the conferees could not agree on a candidate and for a time both Everhart and Broomall considered remaining in the Sixth District race. In a letter expressing regrets for the disagreement between the conferees of the two counties, William Butler, chairman of the Whig correspondence committee in Chester County, wrote to William Eyre, his counterpart in Delaware County:

> "Leaving altogether out of view, for the present, our opinions of the superior claims of this county to the candidate, we desire to meet you in a friendly and liberal spirit, and avoid, if possible, the misfortune that otherwise awaits this District. The Committee

instructs me to say to you that Mr. Everhart will not be a candidate for re-election, and that, so far as this Committee has authority in the premises, the next nomination will be conceded to Delaware county. Can you not, in view of all the circumstances, say aye to this proposition? We hold out the olive branch, and all good Whigs here will rejoice if you can accept it."

Butler's letter to Eyre was published in newspapers of both counties. His proposal was accepted; Broomall stepped aside and Everhart promised to withdraw after one term if elected. The letter is also of interest because of the way in which Butler promoted Everhart and made a not very subtle bid for the Irish vote in the new district.

"While we will receive the united support of the Whig party, we will, we are confident, gain a large accession of strength from two classes of those who have usually opposed us. Years ago, it is known to you, Mr. Everhart was shipwrecked, and cast ashore upon the Irish coast; was taken up by the generous inhabitants, nourished, his necessities supplied, and was treated with that true humanity that distinguishes and enobles Irishmen. Mr. Everhart in the day of his prosperity has never forgotten the generous friends who came to him and staid by him in the dark hour of his adversity. No Irishman since that day has called upon him for aid, and been turned away without it. In consequence of these circumstances, relations, the warmest and kindest, have grown up between him and our adopted citizens of Irish birth, and they will stand by him at the polls almost to the man. With the German population of this county, Mr. Everhart is identified, and will receive its cordial support."

Everhart and the Whigs prevailed in 1852, but the returns from both the congressional election in October and the presidential election in November revealed the two parties were of about equal strength in Chester County. Over 10,500 men voted in October; Everhart polled only about 600 more votes than Murphy in Chester County. In the following month's presidential election Gen. Winfield Scott, the unsuccessful Whig standard-bearer, had a county plurality of under 200 votes.

Everhart was sixty-seven, considerably older than his predecessors, when elected in 1852 to serve in the Thirty-third Congress. Not since 1806 when John Hiester was chosen had Chester County voters picked a man in his sixties to represent them at the national capital. A goodly number of the former representatives (Joseph Hemphill, Daniel Hiester, the two Darlingtons, David Potts, Francis James, Abraham McIlvaine, and John Morrison) were in their thirties when first elected, but Everhart's status as the oldest in the Chester County cavalcade of seventeen congressmen was of no consequence when he went to Washington. His health was good and he enjoyed his legislative experience.

The Kansas-Nebraska Act permitting state option on slavery was enacted while Everhart served in the House. He opposed the measure and spoke out against it. Futhey and Cope wrote in their *History*:

> "He delivered a most able, forcible and comprehensive speech in Congress on May 19, 1854, on the Kansas and Nebraska bill of Senator Douglas repealing the Missouri Compromise, which speech showed with prophetic eye the dire results that would follow its passage, and that its authors would reap a tornado."

Returning home after one term in the House, Everhart continued to be an active businessman and community leader. When he died in 1868 at age eighty-three it was said that in his life he had done "more to contribute to the wealth and prosperity of West Chester than any other one of its citizens."

CHAPTER 17

THE CONGRESSMAN WHO CHANGED PARTIES

The first session of the Thirty-fourth Congress began on Dec. 3, 1855—over a year after John Hickman was chosen by the voters of Chester and Delaware counties to represent them in the federal legislature. A few days before he left for Washington to assume his new duties the *American Republican* commented:

> "Mr. Hickman is an independent thinker, and those who expect to put a hook in his nose and lead him about wheresoever they will, will find themselves mightily mistaken."

Truer words were never written in the *Republican*, a West Chester weekly with a strong bias for the Democratic Party. Hickman's independent thinking and outspoken criticism of administration policies made him one of the nation's most controversial legislators during the tumultuous years preceding the Civil War. He was elected four times and served during the presidencies of Franklin Pierce, James Buchanan and Abraham Lincoln. David Potts, an earlier Chester County congressman, was elected to four terms, but Hickman's string of congressional election triumphs was unusual because he seemed to have a different group of supporters in each campaign. Beginning his congressional career as a zealous Democrat, he owed his 1854 victory, at least in part, to the Know-Nothings. Two years later he was still in good standing with the rank and file of the Democratic Party and was returned to Washington on the Buchanan bandwagon. Neither party wanted him in 1858, but with help from independents and friends of various political persuasions he was successful in his third term bid. Finally, in his last try for the Delchester seat Hickman had the endorsement of the Republican Party and ran on a ticket headed by Lincoln, Hamlin and Curtin.

Congressman Hickman has the distinction of being Chester County's last Democrat and first Republican elected to the national legislature, but he can not be described as an opportunistic political chameleon. Rather, he personified the political realignment taking place throughout the country as men everywhere grappled for a solution to the slavery problem that divided the nation. Although he played it coy by remaining silent during the 1854 campaign, once he got to Washington there was no mistaking where Hickman stood on major issues confronting the country. His stand and leadership in the bitter fight over Kansas statehood made him a national figure and won for him the admiration of Abraham Lincoln, who proposed "three cheers for the gallant Hickman of Pennsylvania" while delivering a speech in Columbus, Ohio, a year before his election to the presidency.

Later, reflecting on that speech and the events leading up to the Civil War, President Lincoln told a writer for *Lipincott* magazine that of all the Democrats who opposed the pro-slavery Lecompton government in Kansas and who had been brought to his attention, only Hickman "had the true, genuine ring of metal." Lincoln said that when he spoke at Columbus he "desired to get down to the temper of the people and to test the depth of the anti-Lecompton feeling, which boded no good to the Democracy," and that when he proposed three cheers for Hickman, "the whole audience arose and cheered lustily my sentiment."

As an untiring opponent of slavery, Hickman earned a national reputation. His views were well known. But he was also a skillful politician, clever and witty, and on occasion he could juggle a hot potato as well as any practitioner of the trade. Such was the case when a delegation of temperance men endeavored to find out his position and that of his opponent on the drinking of alcoholic beverages. His rival told the temperance people he didn't drink, but he had no objection to anyone else doing so. Hickman answered he was on the fence on the question. When pressed to explain he admitted that he himself would drink, but he was utterly opposed to anyone else so doing, and was willing to do all in his power to put a stop to it. Although puzzled by Hickman's reply, the temperance men reportedly decided his was the better position of the two and therefore deserving of their support.

Born on a farm in West Bradford (now Pocopson) Township on Sept. 11, 1810, Hickman was a precocious child whose parents endeavored to secure for him the best education they could afford. For a time he was a pupil at the West Chester Academy run by Jonathan Gause, the noted Chester County educator. He later studied medicine, but abandoned this pursuit due to ill health and entered the law office of Townsend Haines to prepare for a career more to his liking. Admitted to the bar in April 1833, he was soon recognized as one of the county's leading attorneys.

Commenting on Hickman's courtroom skills, Washington Townsend, a congressman during Grant's administration, said "through his able and stirring pleadings, verdicts were gained which possibly were not in harmony with their merits." This observation was made after Hickman's death, but it was one with which he would not have argued. For it was, after all, this same Hickman whose irreverence shocked some barristers when today's historic courthouse at West Chester was being constructed. Those in charge of the project sought an appropriate motto for the new edifice. Hickman flippantly proposed: "Justice is damned uncertain here." Needless to say his suggestion was not accepted. In his book *Sidelights On The Bar And Bench Of Chester County,* Wilmer W. MacElree recounts another Hickman saying which survived long after his death and became a courthouse folklore tidbit. Asked why he preferred the Episcopal Church, Hickman reportedly replied "because it interferes neither with a man's politics nor his religion."

DEMOCRAT LEADER

Hickman's involvement in Democratic Party politics began shortly after his admission to the bar. His first try for a seat in Congress came eleven years later—in 1844—and was an unsuccessful one. He made a strong showing against Congressman McIlvaine, the Whig incumbent, but lost by 529 votes. He was also a delegate to his party's national convention that year. According to the *American Republican*, county Democrats held him in high esteem because of "his character and talents, and the bold and decided stand taken by him in support of the principles and men of the party, and in opposition to Federal Whiggery—never hesitating to vindicate the former and expose the latter in all its various attitudes of duplicity and error."

Hickman remained in the public eye during the interval between his 1844 defeat and his successful run for Congress ten years later. He served as deputy attorney general (an appointed post equivalent to today's elected district attorney) for a short time, but figured in the news mostly as a party leader. After representing the county Democratic organization on numerous occasions at state level meetings and conventions, he was chosen chairman of the Democratic State Central Committee in 1850. In presenting the Democratic ticket to its readers in 1854 the *American Republican* recalled Hickman's contributions to the party since 1844, stating:

> "During that canvass he appeared before the citizens of this County, and addressed them at more than a hundred different meetings. In every Presidential campaign since, he has thrown his whole energy into the struggle, and friend and foe have freely admitted his great ability, not only as an effective orator, but also as a close and logical reasoner. Indeed we have heard it admitted by gentlemen with ample opportunities of judging that his superior on the political hustings was not to be found in the state. Mr. Hickman is every where known as a democrat of the most radical school. On all the great questions that so long furnished controversy for the two parties he occupied the boldest positions. . . . His political position at this time is not a matter of his own choosing, but he occupies it at the earnest solicitation of many friends, against every wish and desire of his own."

Changing attitudes on slavery and its expansion were largely responsible for the political party realignment which occurred throughout the nation during the 1850s. Contrary to the popular notion that Chester County was an abolitionist hotbed prior to the Civil War, only a few county politicos spoke out forcefully against slavery during the early part of the decade. Abolitionists were regarded as radicals and troublemakers. Their views were unacceptable in most quarters and office seekers avoided the "abolitionist" label like the plague. Hickman was no exception. He mirrored the views of the great majority of Chester Countians who recognized slavery as an evil, but who were inclined against any action which might precipitate trouble with their neighbors in the South. Like others in the North he hoped the evil could be contained in the South and gradually extinguished.

POPULAR SOVEREIGNTY

The slavery issue was paramount in mid-September of 1854 when the Democratic Party made Hickman its congressional nominee. Earlier in the year Sen. Stephen Douglas of Illinois had introduced and pushed through Congress a bill for the organization of the Nebraska Territory. This controversial legislation incorporated the principle of popular sovereignty—the right of the people of any new state to decide for or against slavery in that state. By implication the bill repealed the sacred Missouri Compromise of 1820. Two new territories, Kansas on the south and Nebraska on the north, were created under the Douglas bill with the question of whether each would be free or slave left for the voters of the territories to decide.

Douglas was well aware of the controversy his bill would cause when he presented it and predicted it would "raise a hell of a storm." He was denounced throughout the North by Whigs, abolitionists and Free-Soilers. Even some prominent and longtime Democrats spoke out against his Nebraska Bill. But in Chester County the Democratic Party supported the Douglas legislation, saying it was "wise and eminently proper because the right to form a republican constitution and to pass laws consistent therewith is guaranteed to the people when they emerge from territorial governments and seek admission into the community of States that form our glorious Union."

Although the Nebraska Bill was a major topic of conversation at their county nominating convention, the Democrat delegates surprisingly seemed to be of one accord in 1854 when they adopted resolutions backing President Pierce and endorsing the legislation passed by the Thirty-third Congress relative to the organization of the Kansas and Nebraska territories. There is no evidence to suggest that Hickman at this time rejected the popular sovereignty principle and its corollary of non-intervention by Congress with respect to slavery in states and territories. Having announced when nominated that he would not address public meetings or solicit votes, Hickman was able to sidestep the controversial issue. It was an unusual strategy for a man running for Congress, but a wise one. By keeping quiet he offended no one. Since he had not solicited the Democratic nomination, Hickman explained in a letter to a lawyer friend that he did not feel obligated to campaign for the congressional seat being vacated by Rep. William Everhart.

> "When I consented to submit to the wishes of my friends, I resolved to do no act which could be construed by any fair man into electioneering. As I have been placed in nomination by the

> voluntary action of my fellow-citizens, my election, if it comes at all, must come in the same way. I desire no person to yield his vote to me whose unbiased judgement does not approve this act. As I prize my own self-respect above official position, so I am resolved not to lose it by cringing subserviency or servile adulation."

The Whigs at their convention branded the Douglas legislation as "a high-handed attempt to force slavery into a vast new territory now free from it by law." Hickman's Whig opponent, John M. Broomall, a well known lawyer from Chester, followed the party line on the campaign hustings by condemning the Nebraska Bill. But there were other controversial issues besides slavery in 1854. Among many of the so-called native Americans there were strong prejudices against the new wave of immigrants pouring into the country. American workmen complained of losing jobs to foreigners, and Protestants viewed with alarm the country's growing Roman Catholic population. Secret societies (whose members used the phrase "I Don't Know" as their password) sprang up around the country to combat the "alien menace." Chester County unfortunately was not immune from this bigotry and the Know-Nothings became a powerful political force.

Some observers credited Hickman's victory to the Know-Nothings. The Futhey & Cope *History* states matter-of-factly "through some influences which have never been satisfactorily explained, Mr. Hickman secured the vote of the order and was elected by a majority of 2,656 in the district." During the campaign, however, the *American Republican*, a staunch supporter of the Democratic Party and its candidates, endeavored to paint Hickman as a political paragon who would not stoop to inject religion into a campaign. It claimed:

> "Mr. Hickman has not gone out to solicit the foreign or any other vote in the present campaign. . . . He has made no appeal to Protestant or Catholic, but has left the election to the people of the district, without any other pledge than the history of his past political life."

From a distance of more than one hundred years a judgment of Hickman's involvement with the Know- Nothings is difficult to make since the newspaper reporting then was extremely biased. Hickman was undoubtedly considered a "native American" by the county electorate since his Hickman forebears, as well as his Jefferis ancestors on his mother's side, had settled in the county during William Penn's time. Very likely he benefited from the anti-Catholic and anti-foreign bigotry prevalent then while Know-Nothingism was at its height, but that he himself appealed to the baser emotions of the voters seems highly unlikely. A more likely reason for the Know-Nothing support was given by the *Washington Union*, mouthpiece of the Pierce administration, when it reported:

> "Hon. John Hickman, who is elected to Congress from the heavy whig district composed of Chester and Delaware counties, was

> doubtless chosen by aid of the secret society of Know- Nothings. This resulted not from his identity with that order in the slightest degree, but from the position of his whig opponent who first joined and then deserted the society."

Hickman's victory received press attention throughout the state. The *Star of the North*, a Democratic journal published in Bloomsburg, said:

> "The darkest cloud has its silver lining, and in the disastrous results of the late election we can find a few cheering spots like the election of John Hickman to Congress from the Chester and Delaware district. . . . There is hardly a man in the State who can command a dignity like that on Hickman's brow, and he is truly one of nature's noblemen. He was the head and front of the Pennsylvania delegation in the national convention that nominated Mr. Polk for the Presidency; and we mistake much if the pride of the South can in Congress match his gallant and chivalrous bearing."

The *Washington Union* described Hickman as being "the most consistent and active democrat in his district for many years" and predicted he would be "one of the soundest and most reliable democrats in the Thirty-fourth Congress." At home, though, readers of county newspapers were probably confused as to where Hickman stood on the issues. The *Jeffersonian* stated:

> "He received the united support of the Democratic party—and also of the Irish and Know Nothings. His election is claimed as an Anti-Nebraska victory. We cannot see on what grounds. He was nominated by the Democratic Party, but not on that issue. Having accepted the nomination of the party, he stands morally bound to advocate its principles, and we believe he will not flinch from his duty."

The *Village Record*, a Whig organ, was equally puzzled as to why Hickman's success was being interpreted throughout the state as an anti-Nebraska victory. It pointed out Broomall was the avowed, openly declared anti-Nebraska candidate while Hickman had "concealed his opinions on this question and all others" and had as yet "not publicly or privately, that we know of, declared his hostility to the Kansas Nebraska Bill." It further pointed out he "was nominated and supported by a party which had endorsed the Nebraska Bill and all the iniquities of the present Administration."

But the *Independent Herald*, the county's Free-Soil newspaper, interpreted Hickman's victory differently.

> "Mr. Hickman's position was just such as was calculated to conciliate votes. . . . He was nominated in spite of stringent efforts put forth by the satellites of the post office and the priesthood to prevent it; he had expressed himself uniformly in terms of energetic reprobation of the Nebraska inequity, and his election was thought on all hands to be the bitterest pill that the

> people of the district could administer to the manikin politicians and pigmy statesmen at Washington. . . . He for these reasons was sustained cordially by Whigs and Democrats, foreigners and Know-Nothings, who desired to see the general administration practically rebuked."

Hickman arrived on the Washington scene when the overriding issue confronting the nation was whether the territory of Kansas should be admitted to the Union as a free or slave state. Because the speaker of the House made committee appointments, particularly the crucial committee to be appointed to investigate the Kansas situation, the speakership selection once again took on great significance when the 234 members of the House of Representatives gathered for their first session in December of 1855. The two main political groups were now the Democratic and Republican parties, but neither had a majority in the House. The Republicans had 108 congressmen; the Democrats 83. Another 43 members, most of whom had been elected on the American or Know-Nothing ticket, held the balance of power in the speakership contest. On the first vote for speaker there were twenty-one candidates. Northern anti-Nebraska men in the various parties outnumbered southern Democrats, but they were unable to unite behind a single candidate. As a result the struggle for the speakership lasted two months and it was not until Feb. 3, 1856, on their 133rd try that members of the Thirty-fourth Congress finally elected Nathaniel P. Banks, a former Free-Soiler and Know-Nothing from Massachusetts, as their speaker.

As a freshman member of the House, Hickman was not the least bit bashful in expressing his views. He took an active part in the speakership fight and proved the *American Republican* correct when it said he was an independent thinker who could not be led about with a hook in his nose. The inability of the House to organize resulted in much newspaper criticism, and a good share of the blame for the deadlock was placed on the shoulders of Hickman and a few others described by the *New York Times* as "the miserable handful known as the 'scattering' who have baffled and postponed the result" by not voting for Banks "while steadily avowing a preference for any other Northern man." Finally, after it was decided that the speaker could be elected by a plurality rather than a majority vote, Banks was chosen with 103 votes over South Carolina's William Aiken, who received 100. When the speakership fight was over the *Times* reporter wrote:

> "There is a glowing poetry in this result. The workingman of the Old Bay state, gifted by nature and accomplished through self-culture, was pitted against the prince of Southern chivalry—the wealthiest slaveholder in the universe—a gifted and accomplished son of South Carolina—and the former has won the hard contested race. It was the representative of the industrial masses, against one of the brightest gems of American aristocracy. . . ."

In Chester County, though, not everyone appreciated the glowing poetry in the result. Editor John Hodgson took Hickman to task in the *Jeffersonian* for not voting with the Democrats.

> "Hickman and Barclay, professing Democrats, threw away their votes. These two votes would have elected the Democratic candidate and defeated Banks. Hickman's friends claim that he controls Barclay. By this treachery of Hickman and his man, Banks is made Speaker, and the House of Representatives given over to the Black Republican crew of Giddings, Grow, Dunn, Dodd and others who convert it into a political machine for the elevation of John C. Fremont to the Presidency."

The Kansas question continued to be debated among Washington's legislators throughout the long first session of the Thirty-fourth Congress. Hickman took an active part in the debate. In a speech given on the floor of the House in early March, Hickman outlined his opposition to the Kansas-Nebraska bill, stating he would have voted against it had he been a congressman when it was presented. At the same time he indicated he would vote against restoration of the Missouri Compromise because "it has gone into the arms of debauchee" and "has been deflowered, dishonored, polluted and cannot be restored to its original sanctity." This speech received wide publicity throughout the country and put Hickman on the side of the Republicans on the slavery question. Later, he voted with the anti- slavery majority in the House to admit Kansas as a free state, but the pro-slavery majority in the Senate blocked the admission. When Congress adjourned in August the question of Kansas was still unsettled.

Returning home, Hickman's attention was focused on the upcoming fall elections. Both the state and county Democratic organizations were solidly behind James Buchanan, the party's presidential standard-bearer.

As one of the party's luminaries, albeit a controversial one, Hickman campaigned hard on behalf of the Buchanan-Breckinridge ticket. In his book *The Disruption of the Pennsylvania Democracy*, John F. Coleman singles out Hickman as one of the top speakers who with "scores of lesser Democrats crisscrossed the state and, at innumerable mass meetings, spread the party gospel."

Renominated for a second term in Congress by the Democrats, Hickman enjoyed the backing of both the *Jeffersonian* and *American Republican* newspapers. This was unusual as editors Hodgson and George W. Pearce seldom saw eye to eye on political matters. Pearce, a close friend of the congressman, wrote in mid-September:

> "Even those who have failed to approve of every act in his short Congressional career ought to feel a pride in having a representative who has done us all so much honor. His own party with entire unanimity places him before the people of the district for re-election. . . . It remains to be seen what appreciation our

people have for the services of a man whose political and moral integrity is above and beyond suspicion, and whose talents are unquestioned."

Hodgson was first and foremost a party man. In August he wrote that he "opposed Hickman from a conviction of duty as the editor of a Democratic paper" and lashed out at the congressman for voting "with the Black Republicans and against his party" on the Kansas question. In October, though, *The Jeffersonian* editor swallowed hard and gave his blessing, saying:

> "When we consider censure due, we give it, and where praise is due, it is our duty not to withhold it. Mr. Hickman is undoubtedly a man of talents, and as a public speaker, is not easily surpassed. . . . As a man of integrity and correct business qualifications he is the equal of the best. . . . Both as to talents and fitness for the office he is incomparably superior to the candidate nominated on the Republican ticket."

CLOSE RACE

The 1856 election is of some county historical significance in that it was the first time the Republicans fielded a team of candidates for public office. After Hickman's 1854 encounter with John M. Broomall the Whig Party faded into political oblivion and most of its members allied themselves with the Free Soilers, Know-Nothings, and abolitionists who made up the new Republican Party. John S. Bowen, a West Chester lawyer, was the first Chester Countian to run for Congress under the Republican banner. Since he had been elected to the state legislature on two earlier occasions, Bowen was a familiar figure in the county political arena. But the new party was neither well liked nor well organized and there was dissension in the ranks, all of which worked against Bowen and to Hickman's advantage. The partisan press, most noticeably the *American Republican*, was also especially hard on the new party's nominee.

> "It is Mr. Bowen's misfortune that the people—men of all parties in both counties—know him, and having known him in various public positions from all of which he retired without credit to himself. . . . The character and interests of the District demand that he should not be elected to Congress. . . . Democrats cannot vote for Mr. Bowen; the friends of Clay and Webster will not; the supporters of Mr. Fillmore will not; and Republicans themselves who desire Chester and Delaware counties to have a representative in Congress who can ably, creditably, and successfully represent the District will not vote for John S. Bowen."

Although not conclusive, evidence seems to indicate Hickman did not have the support of the Know-Nothings in 1856. Some of the order's most prominent members were associated with the new Republican Party. When ex- Congressman McIlvaine and William Butler, the party's county chairman, were named as delegates to the national Republican convention in Philadelphia, one newspaperman said he was unable to say positively whether both were Know-Nothings, but "one of them certainly is, and many old line Whigs assert they both are."

The new party's association with the Know-Nothing movement was hammered home repeatedly by newspaper editors such as Pearce in an obvious attempt to keep the foreign vote, particularly the Irish, in the Democratic column. It charged Bowen was a leading Know-Nothing, but said his organization had entered the fray "pretending to love the Irishman." Since the abolitionist viewpoint continued to be anathema to many Chester Countians, the Democratic newspapers overlooked Hickman's record on that issue while claiming Bowen enjoyed the support of antislavery radicals. "Why is it," the *American Republican* asked, "the abolitionists are moving heaven and earth to secure the election of Mr. Bowen?"

In addition to the damage from these newspaper attacks, which were commonplace in campaigns of this period, Bowen lacked enthusiastic party backing in Delaware County where some Republican politicians remained disgruntled because their man Broomall had been muscled out of the congressional picture by the Republican leadership in Chester County. But in spite of the dissension, bad press, and other obstacles, Bowen made a surprisingly strong showing. Almost 15,900 votes were cast in the district and he lost by only 173. For Chester County Republicans, though, the loss to Hickman was offset by other victories in the October election. They unseated three Democrat legislators in the Pennsylvania General Assembly and elected William Butler, their popular young leader, as district attorney. Results of the presidential election that followed in November were also encouraging for the new party even though the Buchanan-Breckinridge ticket of the Democrats prevailed in the nation, state, and county. Running against the ex-congressman from Lancaster County on the Republican ticket was the explorer John C. Fremont, who campaigned with the slogan "Free Speech, Free Press, Free Soil, Free Men, Fremont and Victory." Also in the race was ex-President Millard Fillmore, the nominee of the Know-Nothings. Buchanan defeated Fremont by better than a thousand votes (6,332 to 5,308) in the county, but had Fillmore not polled some 1,400 votes it is quite likely the Buchanan-Fremont race would have been much closer.

BUCHANAN ELECTED

Buchanan was an ideal compromise candidate for the Democrats. He had friends in both the northern and southern wings of his party. His long years of public service and two earlier bids for his party's presidential nomination gave him name recognition throughout the nation. More importantly, he had been out of the country serving as ambassador to the Court of St. James when President Pierce, Senator Douglas and most party leaders were alienating one constituency or another with their votes or stands on the Kansas question.

Shortly after his nomination Buchanan was visited at his Wheatland home by Congressman Hickman and a delegation from Chester County who wanted to know if rumors were true that he favored extension of slavery into the territories. He reportedly answered he was opposed to the extension of slavery and Hickman returned from Lancaster County ready to go on the stump for "Old Buck." In his inaugural address, though, President Buchanan emphatically endorsed the application of popular sovereignty to resolve the status of slavery in the territories generally, and especially in Kansas where the partisans of slavery and its opponents were engaged in a fierce and sometimes bloody struggle. Later, on Dec. 8, 1857, the day after the Thirty-fifth Congress convened for its first session, Buchanan asked the lawmakers to accept a constitution for Kansas that had been drawn up by a small, rigged pro-slavery convention at a little town in the territory called Lecompton. Since an overwhelming majority of the Kansas settlers were believed to favor a free state, and since the Lecompton constitution protected slavery, Congressman Hickman and others pointed to the Lecompton constitution as a travesty of the principle of popular sovereignty.

It was a turning point in Hickman's political career. He was branded a renegade and no longer regarded as a loyal Democrat. Democratic newspapers called him a "Black Republican." In his home town *The Jeffersonian* blasted him for abusing the president and dividing the Democratic Party. "The inconsistency of the man is so gross, glaring and reckless," it fumed, "the honest right-thinking men of all parties are sure to condemn it." But by taking a stand that put him at loggerheads with the administration, and by breaking with his party's congressional leadership on the slavery question, Hickman became a national figure and a hero among the Republican Party's former Free-Soilers and abolitionists.

The Senate voted to accept the Lecompton Constitution, but in the House (which had a membership of 131 Democrats, 92 Republicans, and 14 Know-Nothings) it was rejected. Hickman's role in defeating the measure gained him further notoriety. Kansas was eventually admitted as a free state and Abraham Lincoln would later say it was the anti-Lecompton fight that made him president. As a leader of the anti-Lecompton Democrats, Hickman was despised by legislators from the South as well as those from the North who were loyal to the president. At home he became the county's most controversial political figure, causing the Democratic Party to divide into two factions—Lecompton or administration Democrats and anti-Lecompton Democrats. Pearce's *American Republican* strongly supported Congressman Hickman; Hodgson's *Jeffersonian* staunchly backed the president and had no time for the turncoat congressman.

When the Democratic Party prepared for a county meeting in February of 1858 *The Jeffersonian* called upon party members to "stand fast by President Buchanan and shield him from all assaults, direct and indirect." It also fired a potshot at Pearce's newspaper, stating:

"The *Republican*, in its anxiety to sustain Mr. Hickman's Black Republican declaration of war upon President Buchanan and the National Democracy, is becoming quite desperate and manifests a disposition to assail all Democrats who will not lend themselves to the effort to abolitionize the democratic party of Chester county. . . . If Mr. Hickman chooses to take Black Republican grounds against President Buchanan, and the *Republican* chooses to follow and sustain him, they can do so, but they must not expect Democrats who would maintain the party in its integrity and nationality, to endorse or approve their conduct. The motto of every true democrat is and should be—one country and one democratic party. The motto of Mr. Hickman's speech as fairly construed is—Sectionalism, Slavery agitation, and disruption of the democratic party and of the Union."

Further attacks on Hickman and the *American Republican* editor were made in a group of letters from irate Democrats published in *The Jeffersonian* on February 20. One writer lamented:

"The *Republican*, which in times past has been one of the anchors of our hopes in Chester county, maintaining the rights of the Democratic party and the people against all factions and cliques . . . has gone over to the enemy and is now arrayed side by side with the Black Republican prints against the principles and policy of the Democratic Party. . . . The editor of the *Republican* not only opposes Mr. Buchanan's policy on the question of admitting Kansas as a State into the Union, but he continues to denounce every Democrat in the County and elsewhere who will not unite with him in his heresy. It appears to me that his object now is to alienate a portion of the party from the principles of Democracy and attach them to the car of Black Republicanism in order to effectually pave the way for the success of a sectional candidate for the Presidency in 1860."

Another Democrat voiced support for Buchanan and lambasted editor Pearce and his newspaper, saying:

"We are a solid body for Old Buck. He is honest; these West Chester trimmers are not. . . . I say again we are opposed to Know-Nothings, Black Republicans, and the *American Republican* while it remains an advocate of the Black Republican Party. . . . We go for sustaining Old Buck as the President of the Union, and the choice of the great National Democratic Party. You shall hear from me again."

THE 1858 CAMPAIGN

The summer of 1858 was a difficult time for Congressman Hickman when he returned home after the lengthy first session of the Thirty-fifth Congress and began preparing for the upcoming election. Highly regarded by many in the North for his stand against President Buchanan over the admission of Kansas, at home he was a man without a party. Most rank-and-file Democrats were loyal to the president, and those in the Anti-Lecompton faction who admired their congressman lacked the votes to nominate him for a third term. Hickman's spellbinding orations once drew raves in partisan newspapers, but now when he traveled about the county speaking out on the issues he was maligned by nearly all the newspapers. The *Jeffersonian* said he was "on the stump, not for the Democratic party, but for himself," and that he had lost all hope of reconciling Democrats because of his repeated treachery to the party and open war on Buchanan. It maintained his only chance for re-election was with the Republicans and Know-Nothings, and for this reason he was making "sectionalism his prominent theme" and laboring to excite sectional feeling in the North against the South.

By convention time in late August the Democratic Party's bigwigs in Chester and Delaware counties had decided to make Charles Manley, a former state legislator from Delaware County, their nominee for Congress from the Sixth District. Hickman and his friends attended the convention held at the courthouse in West Chester, but withdrew before the nominating began since it was obvious they did not have the delegate votes to win. The *Jeffersonian* claimed his appearance at the meeting was a disruptive one and reported "there was an open attempt upon the part of Hickman, his satellites, and certain Black Republicans and Abolitionists to gain the ascendancy in the organization of the meeting, and failing in that step, they openly and recklessly began a disorganizing movement." It also blamed the congressman and his lieutenants for inviting intruders.

> "They came not only from Chester County but Delaware also, and some even from Brandywine Hundred in the State of Delaware. Their collusion with the Hickman disorganizers was at once apparent at the meeting. They were in gangs, distributed over the Court House, ready to shout down the Democracy who thought President Buchanan and his Administration should be endorsed fully and without reserve. Their conduct was such that a gentleman rose and read the Acts of Assembly inflicting penalties for the disturbance of any public meeting, religious, political or social. This warning was received by hooting, hissing, stamping of feet, yells, clapping of hands, and cries of Hickman, Hickman."

That Congressman Hickman was no longer a member in good standing in the Democratic Party was understandable; his highly publicized speech the previous January against Buchanan's policies, and other uncomplimentary remarks about the president that found their way into print, had many Democrats seething. That he had voted with the Republicans during the last session of Congress was also unforgivable. But his stand on slavery and the manner in which he had conducted himself while in Washington had gained him new friends and admirers, including some of the county's most prominent citizens and political leaders. Judge Townsend Haines, the former

Whig chieftain and onetime secretary of the commonwealth under Governor Johnston, was now in Hickman's corner. So was West Chester attorney William Darlington, the younger brother of the late Judge Isaac Darlington. Other supporters included ex-Congressman James, and two future congressmen—Washington Townsend and Smedley Darlington. Wayne MacVeagh, the county lawyer who would later serve in the cabinets of presidents Garfield and Arthur, was a Hickman booster, and so was Joseph Lewis, the West Chester attorney who would earn a place in history for writing the first biography of Abraham Lincoln.

Outside the congressional district some of the most powerful and influential political leaders in the North began speaking out on Hickman's behalf. Pennsylvania Senator Simon Cameron, state chieftain of the People's (Republican) Party and one of the country's most skillful political manipulators, wanted Hickman returned to the Congress. So did Horace Greeley, the famous New York journalist who praised Chester County's congressman in his *Weekly Tribune*. Their endorsements, however, failed to sway Hickman's old enemies in command of the new People's Party county organization. These former Whigs, Anti-Masons and Know-Nothings were not yet ready to welcome Hickman into their midst and make him their candidate for Congress.

So diverse were the views of those who comprised this new party that some wags joked it was one in which every man carried a plank to make his own platform. As had been the case with the Democrat convention, the People's Party gathering was an unruly one from start to finish. Hickman's followers were again very vocal, but so were those who wanted the congressional nomination to go to Delaware County's John M. Broomall, the made-over Whig who had been beaten four years earlier by Hickman. Broomall had a goodly number of friends in Chester County. More importantly, he had the backing of William Butler, leader of the new party, and two West Chester newspapers—the *Village Record* and the *Register & Examiner*. Also among his backers were ex-Congressman Dickey, Schuylkill Township's Mathias J. Pennypacker, and West Chester attorney J. Smith Futhey.

Hickman's friends and foes were almost evenly matched among the county delegates, and the outcome of the contest was in doubt when eighty-nine delegates to the People's Party convention assembled at the courthouse. Hickman's managers were optimistic. The first test of strength came on a vote for convention chairman. The Hickmanites proposed the name of Thomas W. Parker of Pocopson. When he lost by four votes to Dr. Pennypacker, choice of the Broomall men, attorney Joseph Wilson, leader of the Hickman forces, resorted to a filibuster in an effort to postpone the nomination until a later date. His strategy "to speak the convention out" was finally detected when weary and suspicious Broomall delegates grew tired of having resolutions introduced and then discussed at great length by Wilson and company. According to *The Jeffersonian*:

> "Efforts were made by the Broomall delegates to get a vote without further delay on these resolutions, but the shouting, stamping and noise of hundreds of outsiders completely drowned their calls for a vote, as well as the address of Wilson. The pounding of the floor with feet and heavy canes, and the wild yells, were heard a square distant."

When a vote was finally taken on these resolutions the Hickmanites suffered a second setback. Their delaying tactic having failed, Hickman's delegates retired to the grand jury room for a conference. After a protracted absence, they returned and announced their determination to secede from the convention. Thirty-three delegates then walked out in a body, attended by their outside crowd of co-workers, reportedly some four hundred in number. The remaining delegates then proceeded quietly with the business of the day and by acclamation nominated Broomall as their candidate for Congress.

Later, the seceders held a rump convention open to all those "opposed to the National Administration, in favor of protection to American Industry, and friendly to the re- election of John Hickman for Congress." The presence of President Judge Townsend Haines among the seceders did not go unnoticed since he carried considerable weight in Chester County. Although criticized by most newspapers for becoming a stump speaker, the judge's comments made sense to his listeners. Speaking at this independent People's Party convention, Haines said a new party was being organized out of old elements, but this had been forgotten by Broomall's supporters at the earlier convention when they abandoned the People's Party and went back to the old Whig Party with issues of by-gone days. He argued that Hickman, his former law student, was "out of the pale of both parties" and urged his audience "to take him as he is; don't ask him to change; he stands on our platform." As expected, Hickman accepted the nomination of the seceders, giving a speech in which he took a strong stand for a free Kansas and a protective tariff. *The Jeffersonian* delighted in reporting on the split in the opposition ranks and the embarrassment Hickman was causing.

> "The Republicans will not own John Hickman as one of their party, and persist in declaring him a Democrat. Why is this? Having been openly repudiated by the Democratic party—and having openly voted the Republican ticket, is he not to all intents one of them? Why not acknowledge him then?"

The ensuing campaign was a spirited one. In addition to the slavery question ("Shall the territories be preserved for the free homes of free laboring men?"), the protective tariff issue ("Shall our labor be protected against the pauper labor of Europe?") was debated from one end of the county to the other. The *Village Record* contended both Hickman and Manley were cut from the same cloth.

> "The two democratic candidates have been consistent free trade men all their lives. Mr. Hickman's free trade speeches have been his boast—abuse of Henry Clay, the father of the Protective System, and opposition to the system itself were the staples of his numerous speeches in 1844; and the same is true of Mr. Manley, the other democratic candidate. John M. Broomall stands squarely upon the doctrine of Protection for Protection's Sake."

Political meetings were held almost every night of the week. Handbills distributed by the Democrats advertised meetings in Cochranville, Kemblesville, Steamboat in West Whiteland, Humphreyville in East Fallowfield, Radcliff's store in West Pikeland, Coatesville, Oxford, Phoenixville, West Chester and Downingtown. Other meetings were scheduled at the Eagle, at Hause's store in East Nantmeal, at the Seven Stars in East Vincent, at Buck Tavern in South Coventry, and the Birch Run school house. Featured speakers at these gatherings included nearly all the party's luminaries—Judge Thomas S. Bell, John H. Brinton, Joseph Hemphill, John Rutter, Dr. Edmund C. Evans, Robert E. Monaghan, and William Wheeler.

Similarly, the backers of the other two candidates in the three-cornered fight held scores of meetings and rallies throughout the district. Few congressional campaigns, if any, were dirtier than this one. The barbarous clangor of American politics in the 1850s is hard to imagine today. Newspapers used any means to elect their favorite candidates. *The Jeffersonian* was especially crude in its effort to discredit Hickman. Its bigotry is best illustrated by its "All The Niggers For Hickman" headline in its Oct. 9 issue. The story that followed began:

> "The colored 'Brudders' about town are becoming very much enlisted in favor of Mr. Hickman. A person seldom passes a squad of them without hearing one expressing a wish that Mr. Hickman could be elected."

Although it was in general agreement with Congressman Hickman's views on slavery, the *Village Record* dug back in the past to fault him for giving himself a pay raise when he voted with the majority for the Compensation Act of 1855, which raised the pay of congressmen from eight dollars per day to $3,000 per year. Less vicious than *The Jeffersonian* in its criticism of Hickman, the *Record* nonetheless stressed party unity and chided the Hickman seceders for failing to abide by the majority rule principle. Only the *American Republican* stuck with Hickman in his independent bid.

On Election Day (October 12) Chester County's voters gave Hickman handsome pluralities over his two Delaware County opponents. He was top vote-getter in over half of the county's fifty-seven election districts, polling 5,765 votes to Manley's 4,021 and Broomall's 2,388. In Delaware County it was a different story; he finished third with 1,021 votes behind Broomall

(2,288) and Manley (1,164). His overall vote total, however, made him an undisputed winner—but not in the eyes of *The Jeffersonian.* It suggested he decline his election because he failed to obtain a majority of the votes cast. Needless to say, this suggestion was ignored. Unable to accept defeat gracefully, the West Chester newspaper attributed Hickman's victory to "lying, deceit, whiskey and money." The headline over its election story read: "The Mongrel Victors." The account explained:

> "The parties or rather factions that triumphed at the election in this county on Tuesday last were Black Republicans, Know-Nothings, and Sectional Abolitionists. All these factions were brought into union in support of John Hickman, and in opposition to the Democracy and with the aid of political ingrates and renegades from the Democratic organization, they were successful."

Hickman's victory was a remarkable feat considering the verbal abuse heaped upon him by the partisan newspapers and considering his independent campaign, waged at a time when most men voted the straight party ticket. Running without party backing and winning is a feat that has never yet been duplicated in the long history of congressional elections in Chester County. Without question, the 1858 victory was Hickman's most noteworthy vote-getting triumph, but one he was unable to savor due to the great personal loss he suffered election night when his wife died. In writing of the sudden death of Eunice Phelps Hickman, a native of Vermont and daughter of a prominent lawyer there, the *American Republican* said:

> "A friend informs us that she partook of dinner as usual, and retired to her chamber to rest, when she was attacked with hemorrhage of the lungs. She arose and walked to her husband's library, where he then was, and died shortly afterwards. Thus, at the very moment when the people of the Sixth District were preparing to reward Mr. Hickman for his adherence to the right, and to vindicate him against the assaults of his enemies, God called from his side the noble woman who had been his stay and his comforter for many years past."

Elsewhere, the 1858 election was a disaster for the Democratic Party in Pennsylvania. It was credited with winning only four of the state's twenty-five congressional races. Ironically, Hickman was officially recorded as being one of the Democrat winners even though he had separated from the Buchanan administration and beaten the party-endorsed congressional candidate.

Left with five small daughters to care for, Hickman must have found it difficult to return to Washington for the opening session of the Thirty-sixth Congress. Arriving there he found the city beset with controversy. On Dec. 2, 1859, three days before Congress convened, John Brown was hanged for his ill-fated raid on Harper's Ferry. Hickman's presence at the capital did nothing to ameliorate the ill will which existed between House members from the

North and South. His criticism of the Buchanan administration and caustic remarks about slavery irritated lawmakers from the North as well as the South. His party affiliation, or lack of it, also annoyed some legislators, especially since neither the Republicans nor the Democrats had a majority in the House. Once again the House had a difficult time getting organized; it took two months and forty-four ballots to elect a speaker. During this prolonged period of frustration Hickman was a central figure. Although he still regarded himself as a Democrat, his views on slavery were diametrically opposed to the vast majority of the party's congressmen. Stating his position on the floor of the House during the speaker debate shortly after the session got underway, Hickman told his colleagues:

> "I prefer the election of a sound Democrat. By that I mean a Democrat opposed to the Administration—an Anti-Lecompton Democrat. I have endeavored for a week to elect such a man, but I am beginning to fear that I shall be unable to consummate that work. I believe that either a friend of the Administration or a Republican is ultimately to be elected Speaker. I am frank to say, in that event, I have decided on the choice of the latter."

In addition to the 109 Republicans and 101 Democrats, the House membership included a Whig and twenty-six Know-Nothings. Not all of the Anti-Lecompton Democrats followed Hickman in joining with the Republicans in an effort to organize the House, and for a time it appeared as though the legislators from the South would be successful in preventing the election of a speaker. From the outset the Democrats from the South and those loyal to the administration wanted the speakership to go to John Bocock of Virginia. The Republicans favored John Sherman of Ohio, who on several occasions during the long ordeal came within three to five votes of winning. Not only did Hickman switch his support to Sherman, but he became one of his most ardent boosters during the bitter speakership fight. Recalling Hickman's role in the memorable contest, Robert Styles wrote in his book entitled *Four Years Under Marse Robert*:

> "The Democrats, seeing there was no possibility of electing their original candidate, Thomas S. Bocock of Virginia, had put up William H. H. Smith of North Carolina, an old line Whig or Southern American, and it seemed certain they would elect him. . . . It was then openly proposed to withdraw Sherman . . . John Hickman of Pennsylvania then took the floor to resist what he characterized as cowardice and treachery. Hickman had not voted for Sherman until the crisis was reached, but had openly been charged on the floor of the House with secretly desiring and plotting to elect him. Pryor of Virginia, and Klitt of South Carolina, and other hot-headed Southerners had attacked Hickman fiercely, and leading Northern Democrats had upbraided him for his desertion. Under these taunts and threats he had become the bitterest man upon the floor.

> "In the gloom which seemed to overshadow the House, Hickman as he rose looked pale, repellant, ghastly, almost ghostly. Repeatedly during his harangue, which really was one of great power, he walked from his seat in the back part of the House, down the narrow aisle toward the Clerk's desk, his right arm lifted high above his head, his fist clinched and his whole frame trembling with passion, and as he reached the open space in front of the desk, he would shriek out the climax of a paragraph, simultaneously smashing his fist wildly down upon a table that stood there.
> "The speech produced a profound, almost awful impression. . . . He shouted on his last stride down the aisle, glaring around upon his Republican associates, 'I know not and care not what others may do, but as for me and my house, we intend to vote for John Sherman until Gabriel's last trump, the crack of doom, and day of judgement.' "

Hickman's effort to elect Sherman failed. Reporting on the speakership fight as it reached its final round, the *New York Times* on January 30 said "almost the entire population of the District, including thousands of strangers, flocked to the Capitol this morning to witness, as they had hoped, the election of a Speaker." Sherman had withdrawn and the Republicans were pushing for William Pennington, a freshman lawmaker from New Jersey. By two votes, though, they failed to put him across. It was not until February 1 that the deadlock was broken and Pennington was elected. Hickman voted with the majority for Pennington. Long before the fight was over other Democrats loyal to Buchanan had written Hickman out of the party. During one debate an Illinois congressman branded him "a recreant, a traitor to the Democratic Party" and said his insolence was unbearable.

It was also at about this time that Hickman incurred the wrath of the South for boasting on the floor that should secession occur, eighteen million northern men would have no great trouble in bringing to subjection the six million men in the South, burdened as they were with four million slaves. The remark received press attention throughout the country, heightened tensions and inflamed the passions of sectional conflict. Not everyone in the North agreed with Hickman's estimate of northern superiority. His hometown newspaper, *The Jeffersonian*, commented:

> "We had not thought John Hickman so foolish to make such a threat. Bring the South to subjection, aye! Why twice eighteen million couldn't do it. But John Hickman ought to know that if a civil war was brought about by the fanatics, the northern states, and not the southern, would be the theatre in which its atrocities would be committed. No northern army would penetrate the South."

The exchange of harsh words and insults between House members from the North and South continued after the speakership fight, escalating occasionally to physical violence. In his *History of the U.S. House of*

Representatives, George B. Galloway wrote that members of the Thirty-sixth Congress "came armed with revolvers and bowie knives and it looked as if the Civil War might begin in the House itself." One incident in mid-February involving Congressman Hickman received much publicity (favorable and sympathetic) in northern newspapers. It took place at night on a Washington street when the Chester County congressman was accosted by an angry House member—Henry A. Edmundson of Virginia. Heated remarks were exchanged, after which Edmundson picked up a stick or switch and struck Hickman across the face. The two lawmakers grappled briefly before Vice President Breckinridge and others were able to pull them apart and break up the fight. Threats to his physical well-being did not deter Hickman; he continued to speak out against slavery and on the problems he felt were created by southern sectionalism.

CHAPTER 18

REPUBLICANS BACK HICKMAN

The fledgling Republican Party, or People's Party as it was called in Pennsylvania, was still a coalition of rival factions in Chester County as the long and crucial 1860 election season got underway. Its leaders came from widely separated backgrounds; some had been Whigs, others Know-Nothings, and a few had been Jacksonians. In its midst were high-minded idealists, protective tariff advocates, haters of the South, abolitionists, and politicos on the make. But even though there were divisions within the party, the animosity was not as deep-seated as it had been two years earlier when the supporters of Congressman John Hickman and Delaware County's John Broomall went their separate ways. Publicity emanating from Washington since then had enhanced Hickman's political standing at home; he was now acceptable to all factions. His speeches and leadership role in the Congress had given him new stature in the Sixth District and those in the People's Party who once reviled him now praised his efforts. When some 1,200 persons gathered at Horticultural Hall for a party gathering in February a resolution was adopted extolling him for his "courageous, independent and statesman-like position . . . in resisting disunion sentiments, in endeavoring in every parliamentary way to procure an early organization of the House of Representatives, and on every other subject that has been agitated there."

The acceptance of John Hickman, once a bright star in the Democratic Party galaxy, by county Republicans was significant, but equally significant was the organization's leadership change. Control of the People's Party had shifted from the Broomall supporters of 1858—men such as Henry S. Evans and William Butler—to the Hickman seceders—men such as Judge Haines, Washington Townsend, Wayne MacVeagh and Joseph J. Lewis. Paramount in everyone's mind at the start of the year was the upcoming Republican National Convention in Chicago, and there were differing opinions as to whom the county delegates should be and whether they should be selected by appointment or by election. A decision was finally made in favor of having the delegates elected at a county convention, and eventually Townsend and Lewis were chosen in a spirited vote-getting battle with Butler, Uriah V. Pennypacker and Robert Parke.

LINCOLN BOOSTERS

Much has been written by Chester County historians concerning the county's role in the nomination and election of Abraham Lincoln as the nation's sixteenth president. The story of Lincoln's first biography is a familiar one, but a brief digression is perhaps in order concerning the historical marker on Market Street in West Chester in front of an old double-chimneyed office building opposite the courthouse that tells those passing by: "The first published biography of Abraham Lincoln was printed in this building on February 11, 1860. It was prepared from Lincoln's own notes, and served to introduce him to the public as a potential presidential candidate."

In capsule form, the story of this biography involves four natives of Chester County, two of whom moved to Illinois and became close personal friends of the future president. Jesse Fell, an attorney and one of Lincoln's campaign managers, was born in New Garden Township and is credited with persuading Lincoln to write a short autobiography that could be used to introduce him to the voters in the East. The other transplanted Chester Countian supporting Lincoln was Edward Lewis, a Bloomington, Ill., newspaper editor. Born in Westtown Township, he was the son of the abolitionist Enoch Lewis, a Westtown School mathematics instructor. Through the efforts of these two Illinois men, Lewis's brother Joseph back in West Chester became impressed with Lincoln. It was to Joseph Lewis that Fell sent the material Lincoln prepared, and on February 11, 1860, the first published biography of Lincoln appeared in Samuel R. Downing's *Chester County Times*. In introducing Lincoln to his readers, Downing wrote:

> "Among the distinguished men who, by their patriotism and eloquence, have assisted to create and sustain the party of constitutional freedom which now predominates in most of the free states, there is no one who has a firmer hold on the confidence and affections of the people of the Great West, or is more an object of their enthusiastic admiration than Abraham Lincoln of Springfield, Illinois."

Prior to printing the biography, the *Times* copied and endorsed an article from an Illinois newspaper suggesting Lincoln for president. It was on the basis of this endorsement that Downing would later boast:

> "On the 29th of October last, the *Chester County Times* brought forward the name of Abraham Lincoln as a candidate for President of the United States. It was his first nomination by any paper in Pennsylvania, and, we believe not more than second to any paper in the United States."

At the time Downing and Lewis were booming Lincoln, the front-runner for the Republican presidential nomination was Sen. William Seward of New York, a former governor and leader of numerous Republican factions in the East. He had the best organization, the most money, and the greatest prestige. Others in the running were Salmon Chase of Ohio, Edward Bates of Missouri, and the favorite son candidate of Pennsylvania—Sen. Simon Cameron. At this particular time—February of 1860—there was also great interest in the selection of Pennsylvania's next governor. The names of both Judge Haines and Henry Evans, the *Village Record* publisher, were proposed at the county convention of the People's Party, but nothing came of these suggestions. The Haines faction being in control elected its delegates to the state convention and gave the judge five votes for the gubernatorial nomination. The winner and overwhelming choice of the Pennsylvania People's Party, however, was Andrew Gregg Curtin of Bellefonte, Centre County. In addition to nominating Curtin, the state convention adopted a resolution instructing its delegates to the national convention to vote for Senator Cameron as long as he remained a candidate for the presidency.

By convention time in May, Cameron was out of the running. He was given no chance of securing the 233 delegate votes necessary for nomination and on the first ballot trailed Seward (173) and Lincoln (102) with only 50 votes. After this the Pennsylvania delegation abandoned Cameron and plumped for Lincoln, who was nominated on the third ballot. Chester County's delegates—Joseph Lewis and Washington Townsend—not only were Lincoln supporters from the start, but worked hard throughout the convention securing other delegate votes for their man.

Meanwhile, Congressman Hickman's name was frequently mentioned in connection with the vice- presidency. Two weeks before the convention he delivered a major speech on the floor of the House that received widespread newspaper attention. Whether he was attempting at this time to advance himself as a candidate for the vice presidential nomination is a speculative subject. The Chester Countian was most certainly a nationally known political figure, admired by many in the North, but the sketchy bits of information that have been written regarding Hickman and the number two spot on the 1860 Republican ticket leave serious doubts as to whether he earnestly sought the nomination. What contact Hickman had with the two county delegates during the months preceeding the Chicago convention is not known. Since Townsend and Lewis had been two of his principal backers in the 1858 congressional campaign, it is very likely he had some correspondence with them on the issues of the day as well as political matters, perhaps including the Republican Party's vice president nomination. George B. Pearce, editor of the *American Republican,* wrote a month after the convention that his friend Hickman "continually shunned," rather than sought the vice president nomination. "The country is altogether familiar with the fact that his name was constantly mentioned in connection with the position," Pearce said, "and I think the written record will show that he steadily declared he would not give the snap of his fingers to secure the place."

Since Hickman's name was placed in nomination a few words are perhaps in order about the selection of Lincoln's running mate. Among the delegates assembled at the Wigwam in Chicago were many who felt the nomination should go to Cassius Clay of Kentucky, an out-and-out radical on the slavery issue. The other principal contender for the number two spot was Sen. Hannibal Hamlin of Maine, a friend of Seward and a moderate.

Hickman's name was placed in nomination by a delegate from Kansas, not one of the county's delegates. He received fifty-eight votes on the first ballot, but then lost ground as New England's delegates created a bandwagon for the Maine senator and put him across on the second ballot. Hickman's support, it should be noted, came not just from his home state. Pennsylvania's delegates gave him seven votes on the first ballot; the other fifty-one votes came from delegates of twelve other states.

1860 CAMPAIGN

Throughout the divided nation there was much political activity during the summer of 1860. "It was like no campaign ever waged before—except possibly the log-cabin-and-hard-cider monstrosity of 1840," Bruce Catton observed in *The Coming Fury*, a book dealing with the crucial events leading to the Civil War. "The nervous unease that lay across all sections of the country drove men to sudden displays of wild enthusiasm, as if in the flare of torches and the excitement of moving parades some reassurance about the future might be found."

For the Republicans of Chester County this enthusiasm reached its crescendo towards the end of July with what was billed as "A Grand Demonstration" in West Chester for Lincoln, Hamlin and Curtin. Held on a Friday and reportedly attended by some ten thousand persons, the demonstration featured parades and a great deal of speechmaking, including addresses by the Republican gubernatorial nominee Andrew Curtin and Congressman Hickman. In describing the event, the *Village Record* reported that the town put on its gayest attire and extended flags across the streets at nearly every corner. A cannon brought from Phoenixville for the occasion began early in the morning "booming forth its terrific peals, fairly shaking the earth and waking up the whole town." Heavy showers during the night "cooled the air and laid the dust," making the day "most propitious." From early morning until noon, "every avenue leading to West Chester was thronged with people on foot, on horseback, in carriages, and in big teams."

As was the case throughout the North, the county had a number of Wide-Awake clubs (organizations of Young Republican enthusiasts) that generated much of the fervor for the event. The West Chester Wide-Awakes—some 120 in number wearing drab-colored glazed capes and light-colored caps—took charge of organizing the procession that marched through town in the early afternoon to the railroad to welcome Curtin and escort him back along Gay, Church and Miner streets to Everhart's Grove where the speechmaking took place. The Wide-Awakes, carrying a banner proclaiming "Labor is King—not Cotton," were followed by Taylor's Cornet Band and other bands and delegations from throughout the county. In describing the parade the *Village Record* reported:

> "Then came the cannon, drawn by two stout bays, decorated with flags. Then followed a wagon filled with 'Small Fisted Farmers' . . .

followed by 'Rail Splitters' who were engaged in good earnest splitting up a number of fine logs as they passed along. Then came a wagon load of 'Greasy Mechanics' and a five horse team drawing a full load of 'Northern Mud Sills' and the Marshallton Brass Band. Then followed the delegation from the Bradfords. . . . This delegation was large. On one of their wagons was a fine likeness of Lincoln, placed on the end of a heavy fence rail. . . . This delegation was followed by the Coatesville Sax Horn Band in a gay uniform, riding in an elegantly constructed band wagon drawn by four beautiful bays."

The Coatesville, Downingtown, East Fallowfield, Charlestown, Phoenixville and Willistown delegations followed in the line of march with bands from Charlestown and Phoenixville. The Charlestown marchers carried a "Protection to American Industry" banner, and those from Phoenixville had one which promised "Good for 200 Majority." The *Record* reported a marcher from Unionville carried a rail on his shoulder the entire parade distance and a number of delegations carried mauls, wedges and other implements used in rail-splitting.

Hickman's address that afternoon at Everhart's Grove was given a big play in the *Record*. Those who heard it could have no doubts as to where he stood on the slavery question. Unlike Lincoln and moderates in the new party, his goal went far beyond preservation of the Union and beyond containing slavery in the South. In his speech that July afternoon Hickman contended all men should be free, just as the writers of the Declaration of Independence had intended them to be.

"It was Thomas Jefferson who declared all men were created free. It was he who declared that men had the right not only to control the Government as it existed at the time, but that he had a right to alter and even abolish Governments when they became subversive of the ends of human justice. This man, long reverenced and held up as the Father of the Democratic Party, proclaimed the sentiments of the world, and I call the attention of this audience to the fact that it was not John Brown, or William Lloyd Garrison, or Wendell Philips who declared that all men were created free and endowed with the inalienable right of self-government. . . . What Democrat of the present day dare utter these sentiments of Thomas Jefferson and stay within the ranks of his party? . . . It was lawful for the father of Democracy to denounce it as a crime against God and Nature, but no man of the present day dare say it."

Hickman's address was the serious part of the day's program. With his address and the other campaign oratory out of the way the Wide-Awakes took over and staged the evening's festivities, a torch-light parade and fireworks. According to the *Record*, "the night's procession, with its accompaniments, was one of the grandest displays ever witnessed in Chester county."

HICKMAN WINS FOURTH TERM

Assembling again in September as the People's Party, the county's Republicans endorsed Hickman for a fourth term. Unlike the convention in 1858, this gathering was a tame affair with very few contests. Hickman, who in a few days would observe his fiftieth birthday, was the only person nominated for the congressional post. However, he again faced two challengers at the October election, the principal one being John Brinton, an uncompromising Jeffersonian-Jacksonian Democrat who had once been his political ally. Son of Maj. Thomas Brinton, he was admitted to the bar in 1832, a year before Hickman, and succeeded Hickman as deputy attorney general. As with Hickman, he supported Buchanan in the last presidential campaign and had the honor of being one of the state's presidential electors. The congressional race's third candidate was P. Frazer Smith, also an attorney. A supporter of Stephen A. Douglas for president, Smith was among the small group of stubborn anti-Lecompton Democrats who remained behind and refused to follow Hickman into the new People's Party.

On Election Day, October 9, Chester County went Republican, as did Pennsylvania, and a new era in county and state politics began. Hickman was re-elected and Andrew Gregg Curtin won the governorship. In the Chester County portion of the Sixth District the congressman polled 7,192 votes. With a large segment of the county's population sympathetic to the South and hostile to blacks and abolitionists, Brinton received 5,670 votes. Smith, who was never really in the running, garnered only 256 votes.

With the presidential election five weeks away, these October triumphs were encouraging signs for Lincoln and his campaign managers. But the conjoined issues of slavery and race, with their implications for Chester County, were emphasized and exaggerated repeatedly by *The Jeffersonian* in its usual bigoted way during the closing weeks of the second campaign. On November 3 (three days before the election) the West Chester newspaper prophesied dire consequences should the Republicans win.

> "In the general stampede of southern negroes that would follow the extinction of slavery, Pennsylvania would be overrun. She would get off well if she escaped with fewer than five hundred thousand of them. . . . We object to having our places usurped by liberated slaves. Therefore we oppose the election of Lincoln whose programme embraces the abolition of slavery and the spread of free negroes over the northern states. . . . In the event of Lincoln's election to the Presidency, a dissolution of the Union will follow . . . such a victory will not only be an intentional insult to the South, but will be regarded as a declaration of war."

Many Chester Countians shared these fears and prejudices. In both the county and state the Democratic Party was pro-southern. At a party gathering earlier in the year the county organization went on record as favoring the elevation of Vice President John C. Breckinridge to the presidency. A newsman covering the state convention at Reading reported "when the name of Breckinridge was proposed it was received with thunders of applause." But Pennsylvania's enthusiasm for the Kentuckian was not shared by Democrats from other northern states. When the Democratic National Convention assembled in Charleston, South Carolina, to adopt a platform and pick a presidential standard-bearer the delegates became embroiled in bitter arguments over the platform's slavery plank. The dispute was so divisive the convention adjourned without a candidate and with the party in disarray. The northern wing, which identified itself as the National Democratic Party, met later at Baltimore and nominated Stephen Douglas, the "Little Giant" from Illinois, as its presidential candidate. But county Democrats, by and large, stuck with Breckinridge, who was chosen by the Southern Democracy to carry the colors of the Constitutional Democratic Party.

Over 13,000 Chester Countians went to the polls on November 13. As was the case in the nation and state, Lincoln was a winner. He received 7,771 votes to runner-up Breckinridge's 5,008. Senator Douglas, who was endorsed by the *American Republican*, polled a paltry 263 votes. John Bell, an old-time leader of the Tennessee Whigs running as the nominee of the Constitutional Union Party, finished a poor fourth with only 202 votes.

Hickman departed for Washington shortly after the election for the brief, but fateful, second session of the Thirty-sixth Congress. To a friend in West Chester he wrote on December 8 that "the day of compromises has passed and the issues between the South and North, or rather between Slavery and Liberty, is flatly joined." Efforts to preserve the Union proved futile. South Carolina seceded on December 20. Six other Dixie states followed her in early 1861. With lawmakers from these states departed, Hickman and others who led the anti-Lecompton fight had little difficulty having Kansas admitted to the Union as a free state on Jan. 29, 1861. But within a week the Confederacy was organized and it was just a matter of time until the fighting began.

Congress adjourned on March 3. The next day Lincoln became president of the divided nation. Four more states—Virginia, North Carolina, Arkansas and Tennessee—seceded during the spring of 1861 as Lincoln issued a call for volunteers and prepared for war. On July 4, just seventeen days before the first battle of Bull Run, the Thirty-Seventh Congress began its first session rather than wait until early December, the usual beginning time.

Hickman's relationship with the new president during this time is not clear. Some biographical sketches of the congressman found in the Chester County Historical Society files indicate he was a close friend of Lincoln, but his speeches and newspaper stories seem to indicate otherwise. Hickman was a radical, an outspoken one, and from the start of the rebellion he was at odds with the president and the conservatives in Congress over the purpose of the war. Restoration of the Union was Lincoln's sole objective; the faction within the Republican Party to which Hickman belonged wanted to see an end of slavery. These radicals were determined to see to it that the southern states did not return to the Union with slaveholders as political leaders and with the institution of slavery intact. During one debate over "subjugating" the South, Hickman startled some House members when he suggested it might be necessary "to leave the track of chariot wheels of war so deep on southern soil that a century may not obliterate it."

For President Lincoln and the Republican Party the summer of 1861 was not a pleasant one. Those who felt the Confederacy could be crushed with relative ease learned a grim lesson in July at Manassas Junction, near Bull Run creek, thirty-five miles southwest of Washington, when the Union Army was soundly beaten. News of the South's victory at Bull Run was neither received nor reported in the same manner by the various newspapers back in Chester County where there continued to be sharp differences of opinion as to the rightness of the Union cause.

The biased news reporting in *The Jeffersonian*, which gained a national reputation for being one of the North's most critical copperhead newspapers, infuriated the Chester County congressman. Other persons apparently shared his view that *The Jeffersonian* was a danger to the war effort and its editor a traitor. On a Monday night in mid-August an enraged mob broke into the office, tossed the press out the window, and literally wrecked the place. The *Village Record* reported that "the office presented a desolute looking spectacle." Shortly after this raid deputies of the United States marshal shut down the newspaper on an order for its suppression issued by the district attorney. The courts, however, restored the privilege of publication and editor Hodgson continued his attacks on the administration. His readership was reduced, though, when Postmaster General Blair denied him the use of the mails. Concerning West Chester's copperhead newspaper, Dr. Roy H. Abrams wrote in an article for the *Pennsylvania Magazine* that "ample circumstantial evidence" pointed to Hickman as being the person "ultimately responsible for the seizure of the *Jeffersonian* and its being barred from the mails."

As chairman of the House Judiciary Committee, Hickman's role was an important one during the sessions of the Thirty-Seventh Congress. Although slavery was abolished in the District of Columbia in April of 1862, Hickman and other radicals were never satisfied with Lincoln's emancipation plans or war effort. Along with others he questioned the loyalty of Mrs. Lincoln, who had three half-brothers and three brothers-in-law in the Confederate service. From a distance of over one hundred years, Hickman appears to have been almost paranoid on the subject of loyalty. Speaking at what was billed a "Great Union Meeting" in West Chester during the summer of 1862, he declared "the time is coming when this will not be a contest between the North and South, but a contest between the loyal and disloyal in every community." Striking out at the president in this speech, he said:

> "I am not satisfied with the way the Administration has managed the war. . . . It is idle to lay the blame upon General McClellan, or any officer in the army. . . . The fault is we have a weak

> Administration. . . . We have failed in the war up to this time because Mr. Lincoln has failed in his policy. . . . He has been surrounded by Southern influence, the same that controlled Mr. Buchanan. Southern men have urged him to pursue a conciliatory course. He has done so and his policy has failed."

For health reasons, Hickman did not seek a fifth term. Had he continued to serve in the House he no doubt would have been closely allied with Thaddeus Stevens and other radicals bent on punishing the South and advocating civil rights for the former slaves. Hickman remained in the Republican Party, but it is questionable as to whether this once ardent Democrat was ever really happy there. *The Jeffersonian* said, "Hickman was opposed to Lincoln in '64; not only refused to vote for him, but denounced him as unfit and unworthy to be President."

After the war, Hickman was elected to the state Legislature. While there he continued to battle for civil rights, much to the consternation of the editor of *The Jeffersonian*, who reported on February 9, 1868:

> "The Hon. John Hickman has been urging his peculiar views on the Representatives at Harrisburg with his accustomed pertinacity. He proposed an amendment to the Constitution of Pennsylvania striking out of that instrument the word 'white.' He was also strongly in favor of allowing all colors to vote on school matters. . . ."

Disgusted with the Grant administration, Hickman was one of the political luminaries from Pennsylvania who traveled to Cincinnati to take part in the Liberal Republican revolt of 1872. At the time of his death at his home in West Chester on March 23, 1875, in his sixty-fifth year, Hickman was known everywhere as an uncompromising advocate of universal suffrage and equal rights for men of all races.

In a eulogy delivered at a Bar Association gathering, James B. Everhart, who some years later would be elected to Congress, stated:

> "He was one who impressed his individuality upon his generation, modified the direction of contemporaneous history, formulated current sentiment into a policy, resolved some of the gravest problems of the insurrectionary crisis. It was he who stood forward, if not foremost, to assert the exhausted forbearance and belligerent defiance of the North. It was he who sounded the slogan through the land, calling, like a clarion, the free States to their guns. His self-reliance, his decisiveness, his indomitable will, his inspiring manner, and intellectual alertness fitted him to be a leader."

****

In addition to Hickman, another of Chester County's native sons served in the House of Representatives during the Civil War years. Joseph Baily was born in Pennsbury Township on March 18, 1810, a son of Jacob and Elizabeth Parker Baily. During the early 1840s he represented Chester County in the

Pennsylvania House and Senate before moving to Perry County where he engaged in the manufacture of iron. A Democrat, he was returned to the Pennsylvania Senate by the voters of Perry and Juniata counties in 1850 and later chosen state treasurer by the Legislature. In 1860 he was elected to the first of two terms as congressmen from the Fifteenth District composed of Perry, Cumberland and York Counties. He died on Aug. 26, 1885.

CHAPTER 19

RECONSTRUCTION REPRESENTATIVES

During the eighty year (1853-1933) congressional district marriage of Chester and Delaware counties ten men were sent to Washington to represent the southeastern Pennsylvania district in the federal House of Representatives. The third of these legislators was John Martin Broomall, a Delaware County attorney, whose election in 1862 came shortly after the bloody Battle of Antietam. Since there was still considerable southern sentiment in some areas of Chester County, loyalty to the Union was a major campaign issue in this first Civil War election.

A former Whig and one of the organizers of the Republican Party in his home county, Broomall had been trying for years to capture the Delchester seat in Congress. Twice he lost at the polls to John Hickman. On two other occasions he had been an unsuccessful contender for his party's nomination. With Hickman out of the picture Broomall's political ambition was fulfilled in 1862 with relative ease after he was endorsed by acclamation at a convention of Union Party delegates held at West Chester's Horticultural Hall.

Born in Upper Chichester Township, Delaware County, Broomall was of English Quaker descent, his immigrant ancestor John Broomall having settled in Pennsylvania shortly after Penn founded his colony. Although he had a Quaker upbringing and had been educated in schools operated by the Society of Friends, Broomall was disowned by the Friends when he married Elizabeth Booth "out of meeting" in 1841. She died several years later, leaving him with two small children.

Prior to being admitted to the bar in 1840 and establishing a legal practice in Chester, Broomall had been a teacher. He had served two years in the General Assembly at Harrisburg during the early 1850s and had moved to the forefront in Delaware County politics when the Whigs there recommended him for Congress at their 1852 convention. As already noted, though, Whig conferees from Chester County wouldn't go along with this recommendation and muscled him out of the race. Undaunted, Broomall continued to labor hard for the Whigs, and later for the new Republican Party. By 1862, when his hour finally arrived, he was one of the best-known politicians in southeastern Pennsylvania. Unlike Hickman, an independent-minded Johnny-come-lately to the Republican Party, the forty-six-year-old Broomall was a strong party man. Like Hickman, though, he was an outspoken critic of slavery.

His 1862 Democrat opponent—George Archibald McCall—was somewhat of a hero in the Sixth District. A West Point graduate, class of 1822, he had resigned his commission in the early 1850s and retired to a farm in West Goshen Township where he was living when Governor Curtin asked him at the outbreak of hostilities to organize the Pennsylvania Reserve Corps. Captured in the early Civil War fighting, McCall had just recently been released in a prisoner exchange when the Democrats made him their nominee for congressman. With his record of service to his country, McCall could never personally be attacked for being disloyal, but Republican newspapers charged he was being manipulated and used by Democrats who were not supporting the war effort.

While the disloyalty issue may have been overblown in the newspapers and campaign oratory, there were undoubtedly some shreds of truth to the accusation that some Democrats were interfering with the war's prosecution. Congressman Hickman, addressing a political gathering in August, declared "there can be no peace here in Chester County until we decide that either Southern sympathizers shall control us or we shall subdue them." Among the county's chief backers of McCall was John Brinton, a Breckinridge Democrat who maintained the abolitionists were the county's real disunionists. Brinton, who lost to Hickman in the 1860 congressional race, opposed the war and continued to advocate peace and compromise. Another of McCall's backers was John Hodgson, publisher of *The Jeffersonian.*

Over 12,000 Chester Countians went to the polls in October 1862. Broomall carried the county (7,137 to 4,975) and was an easy winner in the district. If the returns were indeed a reflection of the county's loyalty to President Lincoln, the Union, and the war effort, it is debatable as to whether fifty-nine percent of the vote was anything to brag about. Yet the *Village Record* interpreted the returns as "a noble testimony to the loyalty of the citizens of Chester County" and claimed "the candidates upon the Union ticket were elected by unprecedented, and indeed, unexpected majorities."

The Thirty-eighth Congress assembled in December of 1863, fourteen months after the election. Arriving in Washington the new Delchester congressman was regarded as a friend of the president. At his party's national convention in Chicago he was one of three Pennsylvania delegates who from the beginning had cast their votes for Lincoln, rather than for Simon Cameron, the state's favorite son candidate. He had also been a presidential elector in 1860. Upon entering the Washington arena and assuming his legislative duties, though, Broomall's views on the war and slavery soon placed him in the radical Republican camp headed by Congressman Thaddeus Stevens. Unlike Lincoln, who always felt the purpose of the war was to save the Union, the radicals viewed it as a crusade against slavery. It was not until the end of the war was in sight, and after his re-election was accomplished, that Lincoln asked the Thirty-eighth Congress to pass the Thirteenth Amendment prohibiting slavery.

During his first term Congressman Broomall donned a military uniform to assist in the fighting, serving as a captain in the Twenty-ninth Regiment of the Pennsylvania Emergency Militia. The national spotlight did not focus on him as it had on his predecessor from the Delchester district, but his constituents were apparently satisfied with his performance in the national legislature. When election time rolled around in 1864, and again in 1866, Broomall was returned to Washington. In the first of these outings he defeated Springfield Township Democrat William Beatty, and in the second he won over Nathaniel Pratt, another Delaware County Democrat.

The Democratic Party was very weak then and neither of these opponents gave Broomall much of a battle. Rather than be branded as "copperheads," many Democrats retired to the sidelines and sat out the wartime elections. The *American Republican*, commenting on the inactivity of West Chester's top Democrats, sarcastically noted after the party's 1864 county convention that "the leading candidates at former conventions from the Borough such as Brinton, Hodgson, Monaghan, Hemphill, Rutter and Strickland took care to keep off the ticket this year, as they wanted their county friends to have all the honors." Broomall bettered Beatty, 6,415 to 1,483, in Chester County and other Democrats "honored" with nominations in 1864 were rewarded with similar drubbings. Two years later the party's fortunes improved somewhat; Pratt's loss was by only about 2,000 votes in the county.

The Thirty-eighth Congress concluded its work on March 3, 1865, the day before President Lincoln's second inaugural. During the next few eventful weeks Richmond, the Confederate capital, was evacuated, General Lee surrendered at Appomattox Courthouse, the crazed actor John Wilkes Booth assassinated President Lincoln, and Andrew Johnson was elevated to the presidency.

A former Democrat who in 1860 had voted for John C. Breckinridge for president, Johnson had been fiercely loyal to the union from the war's outset and had served as military governor of Tennessee during Lincoln's first term. To strengthen his position in the border states, Lincoln dumped Vice President Hamlin in 1864 and gave Johnson the second place on the Republican ticket. Whether Congressman Broomall approved of this political strategy is uncertain, but throughout his final four years of service in the House he was numbered among President Johnson's severest critics. He favored unconditional Negro suffrage and joined with other radicals in the Congress in attempting to punish the South by making political reconstruction as slow and as difficult as possible. President Johnson, following the lines laid down by Lincoln, took the position that suffrage was a matter for the states to decide and favored a speedy reconstruction.

Johnson did not see the need for calling the nation's lawmakers back to Washington for a special or early session after assuming the presidency. Consequently, it was not until the regular assembling time in December of

1865 (seven months after Johnson moved into the White House) that Broomall and his colleagues in the Thirty-ninth Congress were able to effectively deal with the problems of reconstruction. By then the country was in a bitter mood. One of the first things the radicals did was block the seating of senators and representatives from the eleven states that had seceded and formed the Confederacy, thus preventing recognition of the state governments Johnson had approved earlier. This action was followed by another rebuff in the form of an announcement that no legislator from a southern state would be seated until both houses of Congress had declared his state was entitled to representation.

Later, a civil rights bill that precluded states from discriminating on grounds of color or race was passed by Congress. Vetoed by Johnson, it was overridden by his opponents in the national legislature. The tug of war between President Johnson and Congress continued when the Fourteenth Amendment was proposed to the state legislatures by the Thirty-ninth Congress. In spite of Johnson's denouncements and urgings that it not be approved, the amendment conferring citizenship on all persons born or naturalized in the United States was ratified. This far-reaching legislation forbad states from depriving any person of life, liberty, or property without due process of law.

This working at cross purposes and hostility between the Congress and the president eventually resulted in the historic Johnson impeachment trial. Congressman Broomall was recorded among the majority (126 to 47) of House members who voted on Feb. 24, 1868, that the president "be impeached of high crimes and misdemeanors in office." President Johnson survived the impeachment ordeal, but he was an ineffectual leader. However, with vindictive partisans such as Charles Sumner, Thad Stevens and Ben Butler in the Congress and William H. Seward in the Cabinet calling the shots, Broomall had the opportunity to vote on some of the nation's most significant and far-reaching legislation. In addition to voting for the Thirteenth and Fourteenth Amendments, both of which were ratified during his tenure as a congressman, he voted for the third of the so-called Civil War amendments while a member of the Fortieth Congress. This Fifteenth Amendment, which wasn't ratified until 1870, prohibited states from denying a citizen the right to vote because of race, color or previous condition of servitude. Broomall also voted for the admission of three states—West Virginia, Nevada and Nebraska—and was a member of the legislative body that haggled over the price of Alaska after Secretary of State Seward signed a treaty taking title to the 586,400 square mile "icebox" from Russia for $7,200,000. The Senate approved the purchase treaty, but the House claimed its right to withhold the necessary appropriation and for more than a year delayed voting the necessary funds.

Among members of Broomall's freshman class in the Thirty-eighth Congress with whom he became friendly, and who later figured prominently on the national political scene, were James G. Garfield of Ohio and James G. Blaine of Maine. Broomall's political career was confined to Delaware County after leaving the Congress. For a short period during the 1870s he served as judge by appointment. He died on June 3, 1894, at age seventy-eight.

GRANT ELECTED

The presidential election of 1868 pitted Civil War hero Ulysses S. Grant against Horatio Seymour, a former governor of New York. Nominated on the first ballot by the Republicans at their national convention in Chicago, General Grant had no difficulty defeating Democrat Seymour. He was a winner in 26 of the nation's 34 states and received 214 of 294 electoral votes to become the country's eighteenth president. Republican politicians in Chester County were glad to be rid of Johnson and expected great things from their new leader. Meeting at Horticultural Hall in West Chester several weeks after Grant's inauguration, the Republican County Committee unanimously adopted a series of resolutions, the first two being:

> "We hail with gratitude the delivery of our country from the misrule of Andrew Johnson, that has delayed the settlement of the issues of the war, and retarded the loyal men of the nation in their efforts to reconstruct the seceding States on a permanent basis, and on the enduring principles of humanity and justice.
>
> "We welcome the administration of Ulysses S. Grant and feel assured that with his hand at the helm of state, the nation will make rapid progress in material wealth, in social and moral advancement, and in political freedom."

Historians have branded Grant's administration as corrupt, scandalous and incompetent, but the voters liked their president and returned him to the White House for a second term. Grant won in 29 of 35 states in 1872, amassing 286 electoral votes to newspaperman Horace Greeley's 66. Chester County again gave the Republican leader a sizeable plurality.

WASHINGTON TOWNSEND

The Delchester district in the Congress was represented during the Grant years by Washington Townsend, a supporter of the president. Townsend, a banker-lawyer from West Chester, was one of Chester County's most influential political leaders during the second half of the nineteenth century. Like Broomall, he was also a member of one of Pennsylvania's oldest Quaker families. Richard Townsend had come over on the "Welcome" with William Penn; his nephew Joseph Townsend, from whom the congressman was descended, had immigrated to the colony about 1711 and shortly thereafter purchased an 800-acre tract in Bradford Township near the present site of West Chester.

For several generations farming was the principal occupation of the Townsends, but David Townsend, the congressman's father, chose a career of politics and banking. In 1810, David Townsend accepted a position at the courthouse as clerk in the combined office of the register of wills and recorder of deeds. From there his political advancement was swift. He was elected county commissioner in 1813 (the year his son Washington was born) and later served as county treasurer and prothonotary. It was in the banking field, though, that David Townsend is remembered. In 1817, three years after the National Bank of Chester County was established, he took over management of the bank and was its cashier for nearly a third of the century. It was during his tenure in the mid-1830s that the noted architect Thomas U. Walter erected the handsome bank edifice that still stands on High Street opposite the courthouse.

Washington Townsend emulated his father in many ways and in due time succeeded him as the bank's cashier. Starting out as a clerk when he was only fourteen, he became the bank's second teller when he was eighteen. Five years later he was named first teller. While pursuing his banking career young Washington Townsend took up the study of law in the West Chester office of William Darlington. In 1844, at the age of thirty-one, he was admitted to the bar. For a short period in the late 1840s he served as the county's prosecuting attorney, but banking rather than the law appears to have been his first love. When his father stepped down as cashier in the spring of 1849, Washington took his place.

Politically, Washington Townsend was very active during the years leading up to the Civil War. He was a delegate to the 1852 Whig convention in Baltimore, participating in the lengthy proceedings (fifty-three ballots) which resulted in Winfield Scott being nominated for the presidency. Later, he helped organize the Republican Party in Chester County and went to Chicago as a delegate to the national convention that nominated Lincoln. By 1868, when it was Chester County's turn to pick a congressman, Townsend was one of the county's most influential Republicans.

Three other well known Republicans were also desirous of replacing Broomall in the Congress. One of these was Dr. David Wilson Hutchison, a former Whig whose political involvement in the county dated back to 1840 when he had campaigned for William Henry Harrison. Born on a farm in Nottingham, he had a strong following in the Oxford area. Another aspirant for the Delchester seat was Henry Evans, the West Chester newspaperman and former state senator. Apprenticed when he was thirteen to Charles Miner, the Federalist congressman and newspaper publisher, Evans had learned the printing trade and had taken over the *Village Record* when he was only twenty-one. A dyed-in-the-wool Whig, he had twice been elected to the General Assembly and in 1854 had been an unsuccessful candidate for his party's gubernatorial nomination. Evans also had family connections; he was married to the daughter of Dr. William Darlington, the noted botanist, banker and congressman.

Townsend, Hutchison and Evans were all in their fifties. At thirty-five,

Wayne MacVeagh was the youngest of the contenders for Broomall's seat. An attorney, he had been born in West Vincent Township. His Irish-born father had for years been a Democratic Party leader. His mother was a Lincoln, being of the family of Mordecai Lincoln, great-great-grandfather of the president. A graduate of Yale, MacVeagh was serving as district attorney at the outbreak of the rebellion. Enlisting as a militia private, he later became captain of a militia infantry. He was active in community affairs after the war and was elected burgess of West Chester. He was one of the men instrumental in establishing a normal school in the borough. He also had family connections; his father-in-law at this time was Joseph J. Lewis, a prominent member of the county bar who had served as commissioner of internal revenue under President Lincoln.

Because of the personalities involved the Republican convention in the fall of 1868 was one of the party's more interesting gatherings. Townsend led on the balloting for congressman from the start, but it was not until the fourteenth roll call that he was able to muster the fifty-seven votes necessary for nomination. On the first ballot he received 47, Evans had 25, Hutchison 21, and MacVeagh 19. There was little change through the next twelve ballots and it was not until Evans withdrew that Townsend clinched the nomination.

The political campaign that followed may have been the cleanest, most sensible, and most enlightening congressional election campaign ever waged in Chester County. The nominee of the Democratic Party was Robert Emmet Monaghan, a West Chester attorney. At forty-six, Monaghan was a familiar figure in the county political arena, having engaged MacVeagh in a spirited contest for district attorney before the war and having once been elected to the General Assembly on the Democratic ticket. His views, particularly those relating to the tariff, national debt and government financing, differed sharply from those of Townsend. But the two nominees were good friends and as a consequence the campaign was waged strictly on the issues of the day and was completely devoid of personal mud-slinging. Since the two candidates stumped the county together the electorate had the unusual opportunity of hearing both sides of an issue, not just one party line. Reporting on one of their "discussions" at Oxford, a county newsman estimated the audience at from 1,500 to 2,000 people, "entirely too many to be accommodated in the hall, and consequently the speeches were made in the open air."

As was the case with many Democrats, Monaghan had not supported Lincoln's war policies. He described himself as a "State Liner" and as such was connected with a company of militia willing to defend Pennsylvania, but unwilling to fight in the South. Despite this unpopular stance, Monaghan made a respectable showing at the polls when he went up against Townsend. The county vote—8,761 to 6,736 in favor of Townsend—indicated that the Democratic Party, although still in the minority, was greatly revitalized and showing signs of recovering from the "copperhead" stigma attached to it during the war years.

Townsend's second congressional election campaign was marred by racial bigotry. The Fifteenth Amendment to the Constitution, ratified in the spring of 1870, touched off considerable debate in the county. It prohibited states from denying citizens the right to vote because of race, color or previous condition of servitude. The *Jeffersonian* (now run by John Hodgson's son, William) felt the amendment to be a monumental mistake and printed so many articles against the Negro that a modern observer might have thought the West Chester weekly was a Ku Klux Klan publication. When county Republicans passed a resolution congratulating the nation on final adoption of the amendment the *Jeffersonian* reported that "amalgamationists have control of the Republican Party." Hodgson was especially harsh on Townsend. In one diatribe aimed at stirring up whites to vote against the congressman the *Jeffersonian* said:

> "Washington Townsend is in favor of putting the negro into the Jury.
> "Washington Townsend is in favor of having the negro take his seat at the Hotel table by the side of white guests.
> "Washington Townsend is in favor of allowing the negro to walk into any of the pews of our Churches, and take his seat by the side of the white occupants.
> "Washington Townsend and his radical Colleagues in Congress have a bill on file which they intend to enact into law, the provisions of which will force these odious measures upon the people. It therefore becomes the duty of all white freemen who do not desire to see the success of this movement to vote against Washington Townsend on Tuesday next, and for Henry Askin, who is known to be opposed to it, and who is publicly committed against it."

In accepting the Democratic nomination for congressman of the Seventh District, Askin, a Radnor businessman, acknowledged the "gentlemanly bearing" and "undoubted ability" of his opponent and expressed a desire that "the present canvass should be conducted as between gentlemen, solely on principle, and without indulging in any personalities, harsh words or insulting language." Although he himself appears to have campaigned on the issues, taking Townsend to task for supporting the income tax and denouncing Congress for voting thousands of acres of the public domain to land grabbers, the Democratic press attempted to win him support by fanning racial prejudice. The *Jeffersonian,* for example, introduced the Democratic ticket to its readers with a caption which read "The White Man's Ticket." The story under this caption began:

> "The following is the Democratic or White Man's Ticket, and every man on it is worthy of the confidence and support of every white freeman in the County of Chester."

Another *Jeffersonian* article began:

"On the second Tuesday in October the people of this County and State will witness the unusual spectacle of negroes at the ballot-box. The Democratic party washes its hands of any responsibility in this desecration of the ballot, for it opposed, from first to last, political equality between the white man and the negro. All the credit of this movement, if any, belongs to the Radical party, and we yield to them every negro vote in the county."

As a result of the bigotry injected into the campaign, by newspapers such as *The Jeffersonian,* the landmark 1870 election was not the pleasant experience it might have been for black voters. There were slightly over one thousand black voters in the county and very likely most of those who went to the polls cast their ballots for Townsend and the other candidates on the Republican ticket. Townsend again won in both counties of the Seventh District, defeating Askin by nearly 2,200 votes.

As with others who served in the House before and after him, the achievements of Townsend as a legislator are hard to discern. Historians have not given the lawmakers of his time high marks for any legislation they put on the books, but correspondence that has been saved by the Chester County Historical Society seems to indicate that much of Townsend's time was devoted to looking after the interests or peculiar needs of his friends back home. Short and to the point, his letters do not provide much of an insight into Washington life during the Grant era. In a letter dated March 14, 1871, to West Chester lawyer William Darlington, though, he was more communicative than usual.

"Yours of 12th received this morning. There will be no opportunity to pass the bill you speak of at this Session as there will be no committees appointed and very little legislation. The House has become very restive and want to go home. Every day we stay seems to me a disadvantage to the Country. The Senate today laid on the table our motion to adjourn tomorrow. I will see Col. Pleasants concerning your view of the case, but I do not expect it will be satisfactory. The deposition of Sumner creates much feeling here against Grant and is looked upon as an unwarrantable interference with the privileges of the Senate. Its effect on the party will be unfortunate."

The third session of the Forty-first Congress, which began in early December, concluded on March 3, and the opening session of the Forty-second Congress began the following day—which explains the restive spirit Townsend described. Charles Sumner, who led the Senate fight against President Grant's proposal to annex Santo Domingo, was ultimately deposed from the chairmanship of Senate Committee on Foreign Affairs.

The spoils system flourished during Grant's first term and as the 1872 election season approached there was dissension within the Republican Party. Anti-Grant Republicans, rebelling against the carpetbag governments in the South, were calling for a civil service to end the corruption of patronage and the spoils system in the federal government. These opponents of the Grant administration organized the Liberal Republican Party and nominated Horace Greeley, founder of the *New York Tribune,* for president. This opposition to Grant, however, did not seriously hurt Congressman Townsend. He remained popular among rank and file Republicans and at the 1872 county convention was nominated by acclamation for a third term.

Dr. Franklin Taylor, editor and founder of Kennett Square's first newspaper, the *Kennett Square Free Press,* was Congressman Townsend's opponent in 1872. In an effort to consolidate opposition to the regular Republican organization, the county's Liberal Republicans and Democrats held a joint convention in West Chester's Horticultural Hall in mid-September and agreed to support the same ticket. As might be expected, the *Jeffersonian* applauded this action. Heralding the convention's action as "a new era in Chester County politics," it editorialized:

> "Men differing widely in their political views, and without any renunciation of their political faith, united in the formation of a County Ticket solely upon the ground that they desired to do all in their power to bring about an honest, faithful and efficient administration of our government, believing such to be essential to the preservation of our institutions."

The re-election of President Grant and the election of John F. Hartranft as governor, both of whom were backed by Simon Cameron's powerful Pennsylvania GOP machine, dealt a death blow to the Liberal Republican movement. Townsend was returned to the House for a third term, whipping Taylor by a resounding 14,011 to 8,819 vote in the October election. The Republican organization victory in November was also impressive; Grant defeated Greeley in the county by more than 5,400 votes enroute to his landslide national win.

A member of the House Committee on Public Lands since becoming a congressman, Townsend became the committee's chairman when the Forty-Third Congress convened. According to the *Western Land Owner,* a Washington, D.C. publication which gave him high marks for his leadership, Townsend "from the first evinced an industry that has made him conversant with every detail of our complicated land system." An article appearing in its September 1874 issue reported:

> "He well deserves the honorable position of chairman of the committee that in a great measure is responsible for the disposition of the public lands. He entered Congress shortly after the Western States had obtained large grants in aid of canals and railroads, and now that a network of iron has been spread over the country he favors a policy that will secure the remainder of the public domain

for educational and homestead purposes."

According to the writer of the article, the people of the West had the Chester County lawmaker to thank for securing passage in the House of a proposed homestead law and "few Congressmen have so many warm friends among their fellow members, or have so thoroughly established themselves in the confidence of the Executive Departments, as Mr. Townsend."

In his fourth and final congressional race Townsend's opponent was Dr. J. Larkin Forwood, a Civil War veteran who four times was elected mayor of the City of Chester. The Democratic Party nominee was well-known in the West Chester area, having been born at the county seat in 1834. After graduating from the University of Pennsylvania, Dr. Forwood settled in Chester and established his medical practice there. A depression and a series of unsavory revelations involving all branches of government in Washington during Grant's second term, along with Liberal Republican defections, combined to give the Democratic Party a victory in the 1874 congressional elections for the first time since the Civil War. But Townsend weathered the storm and was elected to a fourth term. His Chester County plurality, however, was reduced to slightly more than 1,600 votes.

Townsend would like to have continued serving in the House, but Delaware County's politicians felt four terms was enough. Rather than engage in a battle for the nomination, he stepped aside in 1876 and resumed his banking career. He became president of the National Bank of Chester County in 1879 and continued to serve in that capacity until his death in 1894 at age eighty-one.

CHAPTER 20

CENTENNIAL YEAR ELECTION

In the view of some it was a time of crisis; there was unemployment and poverty throughout the land, corruption in government was widespread, and there were numerous signs of moral decay. But most Americans were in a festive mood on Jan. 1, 1876, as they brought in the new year and prepared for the centennial celebration of the birth of their nation. They were a patriotic people, intensely proud of what they had accomplished. The thirteen little colonies along the Atlantic seaboard, with a population of under four million in 1776, were now thirty-seven states stretching from the Atlantic to the Pacific. The nation's population stood at forty million. Before the end of the year another star would be added to the flag when Colorado achieved statehood. The country had survived four wars and numerous economic and political crises. Centennial optimists were confident the problems of 1876 would in time also be resolved.

Chester County had also changed drastically by 1876. With about 80,000 citizens it was among the eight most populous counties in Pennsylvania. It now had eleven boroughs—West Chester, Coatesville, Phoenixville, Downingtown, Parkesburg, Spring City, Kennett Square, Malvern, Oxford, Hopewell and Atglen—and all but one (West Sadsbury) of today's fifty-seven townships had been organized. As with many other areas, Chester County was moving into the industrial era. Although still regarded as a rural district, the county boasted a number of thriving industries, two of the principal ones being the Lukens Rolling Mills in Coatesville and the Phoenix Iron Works in Phoenixville.

Philadelphia, the nation's second largest city, was the focal point of the country's one hundredth anniversary celebration. From May to November upwards of eight million persons visited Fairmount Park to view the centennial exhibits and participate in the festivities. The great fair dominated the national scene, but there were moments when attention was diverted elsewhere to exciting political conventions and a closely contested presidential election.

President Grant occupied the White House during the centennial year, but from a political standpoint it was not a happy year for him or his party. His performance as the nation's chief executive had been a poor one and he no longer enjoyed the popularity that had been his when he led the Union Army to victory. Administration scandals had hurt the Republican Party and at the last election the Democrats captured the House of Representatives for the first time since the beginning of the Civil War, transforming a Republican majority of 110 into a Democratic majority of sixty.

In addition to outnumbering the Republicans in the House, the Democrats in the Forty-fourth Congress had the added pleasure of sitting back and watching their opponents squabble amongst themselves. The GOP was divided in three factions during Grant's last year in the White House. Those loyal to the President were called Stalwarts; the anti-Grant reformers headed by former Treasury Secretary Benjamin Bristow were called Mugwumps; and a middle ground group led by Maine Congressman James G. Blaine were known as Half-Breeds. Taking advantage of their superior numbers and the Republican unhappiness with Grant, one of the first things the House Democrats did after convening in December 1875 was to introduce a resolution condemning third terms for presidents as being "unwise, unpatriotic, and fraught with peril to our free institutions." The resolution passed by a 234-to-18 vote—bad news for the small but determined group of Stalwarts in high places advocating a third term for Grant.

Prior to the party's sixth national convention in Cincinnati there was a fierce battle for delegates as several prominent Republicans vied for the GOP presidential nomination. Chester County's J. Smith Futhey went to the convention as a supporter of Blaine and reportedly created a furor there by refusing to bow to the wishes of Pennsylvania party chief Don Cameron, who insisted the state delegation vote as a bloc for favorite son Gov. John F. Hartranft until he and other Stalwart bosses came up with a suitable candidate.

In addition to Blaine, Bristow, and Hartranft, the field of candidates included prominent Republicans such as New York's Roscoe Conkling, Indiana's Oliver Morton, and Gov. Rutherford B. Hayes of Ohio. None of these had corralled enough delegate votes to clinch the nomination before the balloting began and there was uncertainty as to whom eventually would emerge the winner. Blaine led on the early ballots, coming within 71 votes of receiving the nomination, but the prize went to Hayes, a viable compromise choice who had not alienated any of the party factions. Meeting later, the Democrats picked New York Governor Samuel J. Tilden as their standard-bearer.

Having selected their nominees, politicians from both parties recessed to celebrate the hundredth birthday of the republic. Highlighting the Fourth of July activities in Philadelphia was a program at Independence Hall featuring music, speech-making and the reading of the Declaration of Independence. Not on the program was an "invasion" by Susan Anthony and several suffragists who crashed the birthday party to present their Declaration of Independence for Women. Miss Anthony's struggle to win the vote for women would continue for many more years.

News traveled slowly in 1876, and perhaps it was just as well for those celebrating the Fourth of July in the East. A damper would have been thrown on their celebration had they known what had happened at the Little Big Horn Creek in Montana on June 25. It was not until July 7 that a one column headline on the front page of the *Daily Local News* told its readers "General Custer Killed." The sub-heading over perhaps the centennial year's most historic event read "Another Battle Fought With The Sioux, Resulting In The Slaughter Of The Brave Young Cavalry Officer And Over Three Hundred Of His Men."

Not until late summer did county politicians begin to earnestly consider the other nominees to be placed on the Hayes and Tilden tickets. Since Congressman Townsend was expected to be a candidate again, interest in the Republican camp was focused on the selection of the state senator nominee. Being the centennial year one letter writer to the *Local* thought it would be appropriate to give the nomination to Capt. William Wayne of Willistown, a Civil War veteran and "only living descendant" of the Revolutionary War hero. But Wayne was not interested and the honor went to James B. Everhart, who was subsequently elected.

Congressman Townsend hoped to return to Washington for a fifth term and Chester County Republicans obligingly nominated him by acclamation at their convention in September. But those at the GOP convention in Delaware County felt it was time for a change. Accordingly, the Delaware Countians nominated William Ward, a Chester attorney, for the Delchester seat in the House. The so-called conference method employed by the political parties for selecting congressional nominees was a generally accepted practice, but it had its shortcomings and sometimes caused hard feelings. Under this setup three conferees selected by each county convention were given the responsibility of meeting and picking the nominee. Since they were in the minority and had little chance of electing a congressman, the Democrats had no reason to squabble over which county was awarded the nomination. For the Republicans, though, it was a different story. For nearly three decades the conference method and the rotating of the "congressional plum" was a source of contention and misunderstanding.

Townsend and Ward each received three votes when the six Delchester district conferees met at the Bingham House in Philadelphia on September 30, but a nasty situation was avoided when the Chester County conferees withdrew Townsend's name and agreed to go with Ward. Then, after agreeing on the nomination, the conferees adopted a resolution urging that "a better method than the present conference system be adopted for selecting candidates for Congress." Unfortunately, no action was taken by party leaders and the resolution gathered dust. Several years later a similar situation arose that was not handled as expeditiously and amicably.

Ward was approaching his fortieth birthday and held a place of prominence within the Republican hierarchy of Delaware County when he made his bid to replace Townsend in the Congress. Born in Philadelphia and educated at the Stephen Girard College, he had learned the printing trade at the *Delaware County Republican* before taking up the study of law in John M. Broomall's office. Admitted to the bar in 1859, he was actively connected with various land enterprises and public improvements in the Chester area. For a time he served as a councilman and solicitor for the City of Chester.

His Democrat opponent in the 1876 race was Dr. William D. Hartman, a West Chester physician and member of a well known Chester County family. Both Hartman's great-grandfather and grandfather had fought at the Battle of the Brandywine. His father, Gen. George Hartman, was an officer in the Pennsylvania militia for many years. In addition to having earned distinguished records as military men, the Hartmans were active in county politics. Dr. Hartman's grandfather served as sheriff and his father had been elected recorder of deeds. The Hartman name, however, was not enough to win the Delchester seat in the Congress. Ward bettered the West Chester physician at the polls by 5,503 votes.

By a 9,715 to 6,621 vote count, Republican Hayes beat Democrat Tilden in Chester County. Elsewhere, though, the outcome was not as clear-cut, resulting in the centennial presidential sweepstakes being entered in the history books as the nation's most controversial election—one in which the candidate who received the most votes was the loser. To win the presidency 185 electoral votes were needed. Unlike today, the *Local* did not splash big headlines over its news stories in 1876, and one has to almost search its front page on November 8, the day after the election, to learn "Samuel J. Tilden and Thomas A. Hendricks have probably received a majority of the Electoral votes."

Contradictory claims of Republicans and Democrats were reported daily in the weeks that followed as twenty electoral votes from three southern states with "carpetbag" governments remained in dispute until March 3, 1877, the day before Rutherford B. Hayes was sworn in as the nation's nineteenth president. Returning to Washington in early December for the last session of the Forty-fourth Congress, Washington Townsend found the city rife with rumors of insurrectionary movements. For the county's lame-duck representative this historic and dramatic session had to have been the most exciting and intriguing of his eight years in the House.

The Constitution provided that the electoral votes should be counted in the presence of both houses of Congress, but with the Senate controlled by Republicans and the House by Democrats there was no agreement as to how the disputed votes should be counted. To end the deadlock Congress finally set up an Electoral Commission composed of five representatives, five senators, and five Supreme Court justices. Some of Townsend's Republican colleagues suggested he be made a member of this commission, but he was passed over and the two House Republicans chosen were James A. Garfield and George F. Hoar. Newspaper accounts contain little of Townsend's activities during this tumultuous period, but very likely he was involved in the compromises made to avert violence.

Undoubtedly, the nation's citizens must have been bewildered and confused by the news from Washington as the duel for the presidency and political power dragged on and on. There were even some doubts as to whether the Electoral Commission would be able to reach a decision. On February 27 the *Local* reported "the Committee on Privileges in the House agreed yesterday to report the bill for the filling of a vacancy in the Presidential office in the event of there being no Constitutional declaration of an election before the commencement of the regular term." Several days later when House members opposed to the completion of the electoral count began a filibuster the *Local* reported the session was "one of the most turbulent ever held by that body." Voting on partisan lines, eight to seven, the Electoral Commission voted to count the disputed electoral votes for Hayes. At 4:05 on Saturday morning, March 3, the Senate came into the House and announcement was made that Hayes was the "duly elected" president.

Returning as a private citizen to West Chester "after eight years of most efficient public service," the *Local* commented in its March 5 edition, "Mr. Townsend has not shown intemperance or the snarlishness of constant objection, but has been a credit to his district and an honor to himself by a clean, pure career, which neither belies his Quaker ancestry nor his homespun training. He also enjoyed the confidence of his colleagues, and upon the first ballot for member of the Electoral Commission received a vote equal to that of Mr. Hoar."

Congressman Townsend's successor, William Ward, was twice re-elected and served in the House under presidents Hayes, Garfield and Arthur. He had a relatively easy time of it in both the 1878 and 1880 elections, turning back Democrat challengers Bethel Custer and R. Jones Monaghan. When he sought a fourth term, however, he was muscled out of the picture by Chester County's Republican leadership and forced to retire. Ward died on Feb. 27, 1895, at age fifty-eight.

CHAPTER 21

THE GREAT RIVALRY

At no time in the history of Chester County has the rivalry for high political office been as intense and far-reaching as it was in the 1880s, when three Republicans of considerable wealth and stature battled for the honor of representing the Delchester district in the United States Congress. Money went on political campaigning like it never had before. One observer said this extravagant spending introduced "a new epoch in the politics of Chester County, since which time boodle has played a most conspicuous part."

In all likelihood there was some bribing of delegates, but other aspects of this great rivalry made it one of the county's most intriguing political dramas of the nineteenth century. The brass bands, the oratory, the campaign clubs and the torchlight parades all added to the excitement, but the high point of all this electioneering hoopla were the county conventions. Over the years the county's Republicans have had numerous noteworthy and enthusiastic conventions, but it is doubtful if any had the prolonged suspense of the September gatherings in 1882 and 1884 at West Chester's Horticultural Hall (now the Chester County Historical Society) where on ballot after ballot the party's loyal, but stubborn, delegates split their votes amongst Everhart, Darlington and Waddell.

James Bowen Everhart, whose father had served in the Thirty-third Congress, and William Bell Waddell, a nephew of Judge Thomas Bell, were West Chester attorneys. Princeton was the alma mater of both. Everhart graduated with honors in 1842 and continued his education at Harvard and in Philadelphia before being admitted to the county bar in 1845. Before settling down to work, though, the scholarly Everhart went abroad and studied at the universities of Berlin and Edinburgh. He also took extended tours through Europe and parts of Asia and Africa. Waddell, a member of the Princeton class of '49, was admitted to the bar in 1853 after having studied law at the county seat under Joseph Hemphill.

The third principal contender for the Delchester congressional seat was Smedley Darlington, another descendant of the patriarch Abraham Darlington who had settled in the county in 1690. Three of Abraham's progeny—William, Isaac and Edward—had already been sent to Congress by the voters of Chester and Delaware counties. Unlike his rivals, Smedley Darlington was neither a Princeton man nor a lawyer. Nor did his family's finances permit him to study abroad and leisurely tour foreign countries for two years. Darlington went to work as a teacher after graduating from Friends' High School in Philadelphia and later became a shorthand reporter for a Philadelphia newspaper. Returning to Chester County in 1851, he established a school for girls at Ercildoun in East Fallowfield Township. He successfully managed his school for a number of years, but when oil was discovered in western Pennsylvania the adventuresome Darlington saw an opportunity to make money. He sold his school, converted his other possessions into hard cash, and in 1862 departed for the oil fields. The venture paid off handsomely. Returning to the county several years later, he bought a home in East Bradford Township and turned his attention to banking and the buying and selling of securities. Success followed him in the brokerage business; he speedily gained a large clientele and was soon recognized as one of the county's wealthiest men.

Politically, the three rivals for the Republican congressional nomination traveled different paths to prominence within their party. Until the Civil War, Waddell had been a Democrat, which was not surprising since his uncle (Judge Bell) for many years was one of Chester County's most prominent Democrats. A backer of Stephen Douglas for president in 1860, Waddell afterwards supported the war effort and drifted into the Republican camp. He was elected in 1865 to the first of three terms in the Pennsylvania House of Representatives. Here he quickly assumed a leadership role and was a candidate for the speakership in 1867. Later, following the death of state Senator Henry Evans, he was elected to complete the senator's unexpired term. Selected as a delegate to the stormy 1880 Republican National Convention in Chicago, Waddell was one of the dissidents in the Pennsylvania delegation who helped block ex-President Grant's bid for a third term.

Like his father, Everhart was a Republican from the time of the party's inception. Although not in the political limelight during the years immediately before and after the Civil War, Everhart was always a loyal party man. When he did decide to enter the political arena the Everhart name and a distinguished war record (he had served as a major in the Pennsylvania militia during two emergencies) made him a formidable candidate. He was elected to the Pennsylvania Senate in 1876 and 1880.

Darlington's affiliation with the Republican Party also dated back to its organizational days in 1855. He was a delegate from East Fallowfield that year at the party's first county convention. Some years later, though, he deviated from the straight and narrow Republican path—a sin for which some party purists never forgave him. This indiscretion occurred in 1872 when he sided with the Liberal Republicans and stumped the county for Horace Greeley against President Grant. The ignominious failure of the Greeley movement taught Darlington a lesson; he remained a GOP stalwart afterwards and had nothing but contempt for those who cut the party ticket. After allowing time for memories of his prominence in the Greeley movement to fade, Darlington again became involved in politics during the 1880s when the GOP was transforming itself into the party of big business. Moving to the forefront again as a leader in the 1880 campaign to elect James A. Garfield as president, he organized political clubs, made substantial financial contributions, and campaigned vigorously for the Republican standard-bearer.

Canvassing for the Delchester congressional seat began early in 1882. As early as January the names of Everhart, Waddell and Darlington were being mentioned in the newspapers as possible replacements for Congressman Ward. Interest in the fight for the GOP nomination mounted with each passing month and spread beyond the borders of Chester and Delaware counties. By August newspapers in other counties were giving the contest coverage in their news columns. The *Pottstown Chronicle* regarded Waddell and Everhart as the principal contenders. It described Waddell as "a first-rate lawyer, enjoying one of the best clientages of the bar," and a man whose "whole life has been a training for just such a position." Everhart, according to the *Chronicle,* was "a young man of fine scholastic abilities" who has "excellent literary qualifications" and has "written some very good poetry and makes very pleasant speeches." (Actually, Everhart was a bachelor in his early sixties and older than Waddell and Darlington, both of whom were in their mid-fifties.) But the Pottstown paper was probably on target when it observed in its pre-convention analysis that Darlington's "method of campaigning does not suit the old Quakers of Chester County, and he seems to have fallen far behind."

The pre-convention fight for delegates was described as being exceedingly acrimonious, especially between the followers of Waddell and Darlington. The "personal abuse and vituperation" reportedly reached a deplorable stage during the closing days of the campaign when a circular was distributed, the authorship unknown, which made a scurrilous attack on Darlington. Finally, the big day—the first Tuesday in September—arrived. Hundreds of spectators flocked to West Chester for the showdown at Horticultural Hall. *The Phoenixville Messenger* reported "the body of the hall was full, the galleries were full, and the platform contained a fair sprinkling of newspapermen, ready with pencil and paper to note the passing events." The gathering, it said, was the "most important and exciting Republican convention that ever assembled in Chester County."

There were other hats in the ring in addition to those of Everhart, Waddell and Darlington. One belonged to ex-Congressman Jesse Dickey, who had served in the House during the Taylor and Fillmore administrations. Robert L. McClellan, a Cochranville dentist and brother-in-law of Judge J. Smith Futhey, also was interested in the nomination. So was Dr. Nathan A. Pennypacker, a Schuylkill Township physician. Both had served in the Pennsylvania legislature and had backers among the 151 delegates.

Republican Chairman Thomas W. Pierce knew he was in for a long day when the first roll call was taken. Seventy-six votes were needed for the nomination. None of the six candidates came near this magic number. Everhart led the pack with 41 votes, followed by Waddell with 40, Darlington with 28, Pennypacker with 26, Dickey with 11, and McClellan with 5.

On the eighth ballot Waddell took the lead with 44 votes; Everhart was given 43. At one o'clock, after two hours of voting and little change in results, Chairman Pierce called a timeout for lunch with the hope something could be accomplished during the recess to break the deadlock. Nothing happened, though. Everhart regained the lead with 47 votes on the eleventh ballot, but was unable to make any significant gain during the early afternoon roll calls. He had only 53 votes—twenty-three shy of the magic number—on the eighteenth ballot. Finally, Darlington withdrew and threw his support to Everhart. On the twenty-fifth ballot the deadlock was broken; Everhart captured the endorsement of the Chester County Republican Party with 78 votes. Waddell received 70 votes on this final ballot, and three diehard Dickey delegates cast their votes for the ex-congressman.

The victory at Horticultural Hall, however, was not the end of the nomination struggle for Everhart. He still needed endorsement from the Republicans of Delaware County. Normally, this would have been no problem. Acquiescence was the key to making the Republican conferee system work in the Delchester district. When it was Chester County's turn to pick a congressional nominee the conferees from Delaware County usually went along with the selection made at the neighboring county convention. Similarly, Chester County's conferees abided by the desire of their counterparts when it was Delaware County's turn to choose. The six conferees of the Delchester district had heretofore always come up with a unanimous endorsement of the party's congressional nominee.

In 1882, though, there was no acquiescence, even though the *Chester Evening News* described Everhart as "an able lawyer, a sound statesman, and above all an honorable gentleman." The Delaware County newspaper further commented that Everhart's nomination "was an eminently fitting and proper recognition of his high character, sterling integrity and pure unsullied Republicanism." But Congressman Ward wanted a fourth term and Delaware County's GOP leaders insisted he was entitled to the nomination. Their position was that since the establishment of the district in 1852 the congressional district had been occupied for eighteen years by Chester Countians and only twelve years by Delaware Countians. Their mathematics were correct. Everhart's father served one term and both John Hickman and Washington Townsend served four terms to give Chester County eighteen years; John M. Broomall and Ward, each with three terms, accounted for the twelve Delaware County years.

Chester County's Republicans pointed out that Hickman was not a Republican three of the four times he was elected. They further argued that the Whigs and Republicans of Delaware County had been given the opportunity to pick the congressional nominee eight times out of fifteen.

Their mathematics were also correct since Broomall had been a nominee five times and Ward three times.

The conferees from the two party organizations met first in Chester County and then in Delaware County. The result was the same at both meetings—three votes for Everhart and three votes for Ward. Next, there were meetings on neutral turf—the Bingham House in Philadelphia. Following the second of these meetings a September 25 news item noted the conferees voted eleven times "without any definite result being reached." As the days and weeks passed the Republican Party's top brass in Pennsylvania became fidgety over the impasse. A gubernatorial campaign was in progress and it was feared the dispute would injure the state ticket. Ward and Everhart were summoned to a meeting at the Union League in Philadelphia. No announcement was made concerning the decisions reached at this mid-October powwow, but shortly thereafter Congressman Ward pulled out of the race and Everhart was endorsed by the Delaware County Republican Committee.

Meanwhile, the Democrats also had a problem settling on a congressional candidate. William P. Schell, of West Chester, was nominated at the Chester County convention and J. Edward Clyde was nominated by the Delaware County Democrats. In this case, though, the Democrats from Chester County acquiesced and Clyde, a retired businessman whose family was well known for its European steamship line, became the party's choice.

The two counties again went Republican and Everhart was elected to the Forty-eighth Congress by a comfortable margin of nearly 5,000 votes. But it was not a good year for the party in Pennsylvania. Taking advantage of dissension within the Republican ranks, the Democrats elected Robert E. Pattison as governor.

ROUND TWO

An incumbent usually has an easy time winning his party's nomination, but such was not the case when Congressman Everhart sought re-election in 1884. He was again opposed by Waddell and Darlington at his party's county nominating convention—a convention similar in many respects to the one held two years earlier. Again, seventy-six votes were needed to gain endorsement. Again, there was much suspense and excitement at Horticultural Hall as the balloting stretched from the morning into the afternoon. Again, Everhart needed more than twenty ballots to claim victory. There was however one significant difference; the positions of Waddell and Darlington were reversed.

Everhart led on the first ballot with 65 votes, followed by Darlington with 48 and Waddell with 38. The count changed only slightly as roll call after roll call was taken during the morning session. After lunch when results of the eleventh ballot were announced Everhart remained in the lead, but was fourteen votes shy of clinching the convention's endorsement. Throughout the afternoon Darlington's managers wooed over several delegates and at the conclusion of the twenty-first ballot Everhart had only a 62-to-57 advantage over Darlington. But on the next ballot Waddell withdrew and Everhart went over the top with 85 votes for his second convention win.

This time the Republican leadership in Delaware County accepted Everhart without a fuss. The Democrats gave their nomination to Dr. Frederick W. Heckel Jr. of Spring City. It was not the first time the two faced one another in a political contest. A surgeon with a Pennsylvania Cavalry regiment during the Civil War, Dr. Heckel competed unsuccessfully with Everhart for a seat in the Pennsylvania Senate in 1880. In this second meeting he was again defeated, losing in the district by a vote count of 18,593 to 11,551.

Among Democrats all over the country, though, there was tremendous elation. After twenty-four years they had elected a president. The year had been one of economic troubles and businessmen were uneasy about the future. This worked against James G. Blaine, as did a Protestant clergyman's bigoted remark at a Blaine rally characterizing the opposition party's antecedents as "rum, Romanism and rebellion." New York Gov. Grover Cleveland finished ahead of Blaine in the voting in twenty states to register a 219-to-182 victory in the electoral college.

From a distance of over one hundred years it is difficult to measure Everhart's effectiveness as a legislator. Following his re-election in 1884 some Pennsylvania newspapers such as the *Shenango Valley News* were saying Everhart "would make a good U. S. Senator for his State." It described him as "a man of broad culture and fine literary attainments, and at the same time a practical statesman in the proper sense." The *North American,* of Philadelphia, in speaking of the senatorship, likewise felt he "would make a satisfactory Senator." Nothing came of this, but two years later in January 1886 the *Washington Post* commented after Everhart's delivery of a speech before the Princeton Alumni Association that he enjoyed "the reputation of being one of the most scholarly men in Congress."

Everhart was also a practical politician. Letters of his, kept at the Chester County Historical Society, indicate he devoted considerable time to looking after needs or problems of his constituents, particularly those of postmasters such as Marsh's Jesse Hause. Postmasters in the nineteenth century were deeply involved in politics, and being federal appointees they frequently served as a congressman's aide or lieutenant back home. Among Everhart's letters from Washington on House stationery to the Marsh postmaster were the following that give a flavoring of the congressman's modus operandi.

> Dec. 17, 1883—"Would you be so kind as to furnish me with as full a list as convenient of the regular patrons of your office together with their occupations and politics. Your early reply will be appreciated and considered a favor."
>
> Jan. 19, 1884—"I had been posting myself in regards to Postmasters back pay sometime before the receipt of your letter and the matter

> is just now tied up pending an opinion of the Attorney General, but if you will write me again concerning the same in about six weeks I shall take pleasure in seeing what can be done."
>
> July 15, 1884—"In referring to our former correspondence of last session I take pleasure in forwarding you the enclosed circular lately issued by the Post Office Department relative to the back pay of Postmasters. If you will furnish me with the information desired on the form indicated I will endeavor to see that it is given due consideration by the officials here."

Returning home to West Chester on a Saturday evening in August 1886 after completion of the first session of the Forty-ninth Congress, Everhart received a warm welcome from his friends and neighbors. According to the *Village Record:*

> "He went to Washington last December when the session of Congress first opened and remained at his post until the session closed, devoting himself to the interests of his constituents and the duties of his office. No member of Congress has a better record of close attention to duties than the member from Chester County."

Even the *Local* had kind words:

> "Congressman Everhart and his friends must have felt proud at the large assembly of people of this borough and vicinity who tendered him a welcome home from the national capital. The occasion spoke volumes in favor of his course in the councils of the nation, and the social qualities of the reception were refreshing to witness."

The Republican Party's nominating convention was only a few weeks away and Everhart had little time to prepare for it. As far as the *Kennett Advance* was concerned no preparations were really needed. It reported on August 14 he "was so far ahead in the Congressional race that his nomination is a foregone conclusion." It reasoned by common decency he was entitled to another term because of his "untiring devotion to the duties of his station." But Smedley Darlington had other ideas and had been untiring in his devotion to politics while Everhart was away. By convention time he had built a strong and effective organization of his own within the Republican Party. Lawyer Waddell, however, no longer entertained ambitions of becoming a congressman since plans were underway (reportedly engineered by Darlington) to create a second judgeship for the county that would go to him.

So instead of a three-cornered fight for the GOP congressional nomination in 1886, it was a two-man fight with Everhart the incumbent in one corner and Darlington the challenger in the other. Newspapermen reported that the battle for delegates during the late summer was one of the most desperately fought contests in the history of the county. Waddell came out publicly in support of Darlington at a campaign rally in Lionville, giving substance to the charge that he had been told to back Darlington if he wanted the judgeship.

DARLINGTON'S TURN

Unlike the previous GOP nominating conventions, it took only one ballot to reach a decision on the congressional endorsement in 1886. Darlington was the winner—by one controversial vote which left the party divided. Charges and countercharges were exchanged and in the ensuing struggle nearly all of the party's influential personages lined up in back of either Darlington or Everhart. The losers maintained the nomination had been gained illegally since the judge of elections in Westtown Township had refused to allow two of Everhart's supporters to participate in the election of delegates to the party's nominating convention. They argued that had these two men been permitted to participate in the township caucus an Everhart delegate would have been chosen and Everhart would then have been the winner by one vote at the convention.

Feeling that the nomination rightfully belonged to him, Congressman Everhart took his case to the people and ran as an independent at the general election. Concerning the controversial Westtown incident, he explained in a letter:

> "At their delegate election two electors' votes . . . were rejected. These electors were qualified in every respect, as was abundantly proven. They were natives and residents of the neighborhood, gentlemen of character, lifelong members of the Republican Party, and except for casting a ballot for Cleveland generally voted the Republican ticket, and this year promised to support it—a promise which gives even a Democrat the right to vote in the organization."

Supporting Everhart in this move were a number of prominent Republicans, including Thomas Pierce, the party chairman, ex-Congressman Washington Townsend, and Dr. Nathan A. Pennypacker. The split in the Republican ranks hurt Darlington in Chester County, but the Republicans of Delaware County were unsympathetic to Everhart's "foul play" charge. The *Chester News* said his past victories were "not because he was a proper representative of the working people of Chester County, but because he bore an honorable name, was a gentleman of culture, and an aristocratic representative of the blue blood of the district."

The Democratic Party's O. B. Dickinson was unable to capitalize on the Republican rift, however, and Darlington was elected to the Fiftieth Congress. He polled 11,841 votes in the district to Dickinson's 10,529. Everhart finished a poor third, collecting 4,239 votes in his home county and only 727 in Delaware County. Another 1,270 votes went to Prohibitionist Ellis P. Marshall of Concord.

For the Republicans of Chester County there was no love feast following the election. Some of Everhart's friends published a lengthy letter in the newspapers charging Darlington with demoralizing the party and expressing the hope that party leaders and future candidates "will see the dangers ahead and will return to the cleaner methods of electioneering that have heretofore prevailed amongst us."

In contrast to the bachelor Everhart, who did not cut much of a figure in Washington society, Smedley Darlington's presence at the nation's capital attracted attention. He had money and made no effort to conceal his wealth. When he first went to Washington to lease a residence the *Philadelphia Times* correctly predicted he would be "a great acquisition to the representation from Pennsylvania from a social point of view." It noted:

> "With his family of seven daughters, two married and five in society, he will create a stir in fashionable life at the capital. Mr. Darlington is a portly gentleman, with a large, kind face, and a jovial tendency in manner and conversation. Mrs. Darlington in her maiden days was the belle of Chester County. . . . Mr. Darlington, who is a man of liberal means, proposes to live well and entertain in a manner that becomes the rich and prosperous counties of Chester and Delaware."

Another Philadelphia newspaper article that appeared shortly after the opening of the first session of the Fiftieth Congress reported:

> "The Darlingtons by ancestral conviction and present belief are followers of the religious tenets of Fox. Their Quaker doctrines, however, do not savor of that ancient orthodox austerity of the early days of the sect in England and Pennsylvania. They enjoy the innocent relaxations of life."

Readers were told the Darlington ladies had "six carriages and four blooded Delaware county horses, with liveried groom and footman to match, at their disposal." The article also reported:

> "Their residence in Washington . . . is a spacious towered and bay-windowed brick edifice, looking down Massachusetts avenue upon the mounted bronze effigy of Scott. . . . The interior is rich in tanned fur mats of the Wild West, rugs of the Orient, bric-a-brac from the shops of both continents and paintings by known artists."

Years later after Darlington had departed from the Washington scene the *Philadelphia Record* reminisced:

> "While in Congress, Mr. Darlington acquired the finest establishment ever before or since attempted by a Representative from the Sixth District. He leased the palatial residence of ex-Senator Van Wyck, of Nebraska, in an exclusive part of the city, at a rental of $5,000 per session, and lived in the most lavish style, his accomplished family cutting a wide swath in social circles. His stable of horses and carriages was eclipsed by none at the national capital, and as he drove along the magnificent avenues he was frequently pointed out as the man who could foreclose a mortgage

on half the State of Kansas at any time."

The entertaining that the Darlingtons did in Washington, of course, won them no votes in Chester and Delaware counties. At home Darlington had his enemies; the Everhart wing of the Republican Party was determined to block his bid for a second term. In July of 1888 the *Local* reported:

> "The Congressional squabble is going to be enacted over again—and the Everhart forces are marshaled early in the campaign. They have organized an executive committee in every township, and are making a systematic movement upon the Darlington stronghold."

But another convention fight involving the two archrivals never materialized. A few days before the primary Everhart was stricken with a malignant attack of dysentery from which he never rallied. He died on August 23 at the age of sixty-seven. For the anti-Darlington forces his death could not have come at a more inopportune moment. Although there was little time to regroup, Darlington's foes were determined not to allow him to have the nomination by default. On August 28 the *Local* reported:

> "Immediately after the mortal remains of Honorable James B. Everhart, late candidate for Congress from this district, had been laid away to rest at Oakland yesterday afternoon, there was a large and enthusiastic meeting of the deceased's warm political friends and ardent supporters held at Everhart headquarters on Market street. The rooms were filled to overflowing by members of the Republican Party from all sections of the county."

Efforts to persuade ex-Congressman Townsend to become a candidate failed. Horace Beale, the Parkesburg ironmaster, also refused to stand for office. But as the *Local* observed, "the spirit with which the followers of Mr. Everhart were animated was not to be buried with the remains of their dead leader." Captain Robert T. Cornwell, a Civil War hero, was induced to become a candidate and a last-minute whirlwind campaign was conducted in which Cornwell's war record was emphasized. (He had raised a company of volunteers, suffered in a Rebel prison camp, regained his health after being exchanged, and returned to duty and fought under General Sheridan.) But against the Darlington machine, Cornwell was no match. He received only 42 votes at the GOP convention; Darlington was renominated with 100 votes.

Against Samuel Greenwood, his Democrat opponent, Congressman Darlington had a relatively easy time of it, winning over the Valley Township woolen manufacturer by some 6,500 votes in November. With Benjamin Harrison heading their ticket, the Republicans also recaptured the White House. President Cleveland actually had upwards of100,000 votes more than Harrison, but the vote distribution was such that the electoral vote went against him 233 to 168.

It was Darlington's last campaign. He did not seek re-election. "I am now sixty-three years of age," he told a *Local* reporter in May 1890 as the election season approached, "and this gives me only a margin of seven years to live if I am to accept the regular schedule as laid down for my ancestors, which I cheerfully do, and I tell you that I am arranging to spend those seven years in a good time for myself and family." He lived another nine years and remained politically active until shortly before his death on June 24, 1899. Just how much money Darlington spent to satisfy his congressional ambitions was the subject of much speculation. A figure of $100,000 was a popular and frequently quoted estimate. The *Philadelphia Record* used this figure in one of its stories describing how "Uncle Smedley" frequently would "call in one of his lieutenants into his office on a Saturday during the progress of a campaign, hand him a roll of bills and tell him to take the boys on an excursion to the seashore, where they would revel until Monday morning on the fat of the land." The *Local* said he "made contributions for political purposes of thousands of dollars, and conducted perhaps the greatest campaigns ever seen in this county."

Newspaper articles in the early 1890s seem to indicate Darlington's crowning achievement as a congressman was getting a public building for the City of Chester. For his efforts in guiding an appropriations bill through Congress that made possible this public building the townspeople there honored him with a banquet in February 1891. Concerning this affair the *Local* reported:

> "It was a memorable occasion, for there was assembled there the old and the young, elegantly attired, and all bent upon one mission—that of doing honor to him that had done so much for them. . . . Other Congressmen equally renowned for their sagacity and learning had fought the good fight, but came back home with the sombre drapings of defeat upon their ermine, so that it remained at last for a Chester countian to carry off the honor of the long and bitter struggle."

Darlington told the townspeople he was proud that his children and his children's children might one day pass their fine new edifice and see in it a memorable result of his efforts while in Congress. The establishment of over a dozen post offices in his district was another achievement in which he took pride. At the time of his death the *Local* said:

> "He served two terms in Congress, during which time his family became prominently identified in social circles at the National Capital. He made a good Representative, improved the postal service of the district, and secured for the city of Chester a $100,000 appropriation for a public building."

CHAPTER 22

DELAWARE COUNTY'S TURN

After almost a decade of Republican infighting in Chester County over the party's congressional nomination the scene of battle shifted to Delaware County in 1890. Months before Smedley Darlington announced his plan to retire from the House of Representatives a number of would-be congressmen in the neighboring county began actively campaigning for his job. James Everhart and Darlington had occupied the Sixth District seat for four terms and it was generally understood within the Republican Party that it was Delaware County's turn to pick a congressman. The infighting for the party's endorsement went on for months in Delaware County, but when the smoke finally cleared in September the nomination belonged to John Buchanan Robinson, owner of the *Media Ledger*.

Born in 1846, Robinson had been just a teen-ager when he joined the Union Army toward the end of the Civil War. He later enlisted in the Navy and went to the United States Naval Academy. Graduating in 1868, he pursued a naval career for seven years and then took up the study of law. His political career was launched shortly after he moved to Media from Philadelphia in 1878 to practice law and edit the *Delaware County Gazette*. Elected to the Pennsylvania General Assembly in 1884, he quickly advanced himself to a position of leadership within the Republican Party of his adopted county.

Initially, Robinson had reservations about running for Congress. As a state senator from one of the more populous counties he carried considerable weight in Harrisburg. Because it was rotated between the two counties, the office of congressman had its drawbacks for a politically ambitious man in his forties. The *Philadelphia Press*, commenting on this situation in January as Robinson was weighing the pros and cons, reported:

> "One thing which makes Mr. Robinson hesitant about beginning a canvass in the Sixth District is the uncertainty which surrounds the tenure of the Congressional office. The rotation system, where two or more counties compose a district, has caused no end of trouble in the past, and caused the needless defeat of talented and representative men just at a time when they were attaining recognition in Washington and getting in a position to do some good for their constituency upon the floor of the House and in the departments."

Once he made the decision to run, Robinson had the inside track for the

Delchester congressional seat. His endorsement by the Delaware County Republican Committee, however, was not received enthusiastically by the "anti-machine" Republicans of Chester County. They were opposed to the way Col. Matthew S. Quay and his lieutenants were running the Republican Party in Pennsylvania, and rightly or wrongly, Robinson was tagged as being one of Boss Quay's boys. But in spite of the grumblings, the top brass of the Republican organization in Chester County fulfilled its obligation and blessed the Robinson candidacy.

Owner of a farm in West Brandywine Township, but never regarded as a Chester Countian, Quay served a long apprenticeship in the amoral politics of Pennsylvania before becoming a United States senator in 1887 and taking over management of the Cameron machine. Ranked as one of the nation's most powerful political bosses, Quay was a central issue in the Sixth District congressional campaign, placing Robinson in an awkward situation. Wherever he went and whenever he spoke, Robinson tried to put as much distance as possible between himself and Quay without offending the party's stalwarts. Addressing a Republican rally in West Grove, he assured the independents and reformers in his audience that he was "under no obligation to Mr. Quay in any way, shape or form" and that in neither his senatorial nor congressional canvasses did Quay "raise his finger to assist me."

Just as Quay had the reputation for running a corrupt political machine statewide, Congressman Darlington was regarded by some as a political tyrant in the Sixth District. To counter charges he was Darlington's pawn, and at the same time endeavoring not to offend the congressman's friends, Robinson lauded Darlington as an effective legislator while assuring audiences such as the one in West Grove that he himself had never been helped by Darlington. Quayism and Darlingtonism were touchy subjects. Explaining his relationship with Darlington at one GOP gathering, Robinson said he originally had been an Everhart supporter, but he felt that Darlington had made a very creditable representation.

> "He secured us a public building in the City of Chester and was always prompt, courteous, and industrious in the performance of his duties at Washington. I will say this much for Mr. Darlington, although he will tell you and every other politician in the two counties will tell you, that he never appointed a single Federal officer at my request in Delaware county, or even paid any attention to my political requests whatsoever. He consulted with my opponents in the distribution of patronage in our county, and all the postmasters and tide-waiters and appointees of Mr. Darlington in the late primary contest were arrayed against me."

Overshadowing the congressional race and all other contests in 1890 was the gubernatorial election. The Republican nominee was George W. Delamater of Crawford County, labeled by most newspapers as Senator Quay's candidate. At a special election in June held for the purpose of selecting convention delegates the Republican voters of Chester County rejected Delamater by an almost two-to-one margin. They preferred Gen. Daniel H. Hastings, the anti-machine candidate.

It was against this background that the Democratic Party leaders in the Delchester district mapped their strategy. They realized the chances of a Democrat being elected to Congress were very slim, but they were anxious to have as strong a candidate as possible to go against Robinson and add strength to the state ticket. Running for governor and heading their ticket was Robert E. Pattison of Philadelphia, a popular political figure and a proven vote-getter. Once before, in 1882, Pattison had been elected governor and things were again looking up for the Democratic Party at the time county leaders—men such as Col. Archibald M. Holding, Robert E. Monaghan and J. Frank E. Hause—pondered over selections for the county ticket during the summer of 1890. With the Republican Party divided and many independents decrying Quay's boss rule, they anticipated a close gubernatorial race. To strengthen the ticket for Pattison in the Sixth Congressional District the party pros from the two counties turned to Thomas W. Pierce, a West Chester attorney, for help. Eight years earlier he had been chairman of the Chester County Republican Committee when Pattison upset James A. Beaver in the governorship contest. Now, eight years later, he was a member of the Pennsylvania Committee of Independent Republicans backing Pattison. The Democrat strategists proposed he be made the party's nominee for congressman to go against Robinson.

For many Democrats the proposal to endorse a Republican, albeit an anti-machine one and a Pattison supporter, was hard to swallow. At a three-hour session in late September at the Girard House in Philadelphia the conferees from the two counties were unable to decide whether to back a "straight out Democrat" or go with Pierce. Later, however, after convincing themselves a Pierce nomination wouldn't boomerang, the conferees met again in Media in early October and announced that Pierce, the independent Republican, would be the Democratic Party's nominee for congressman.

Although the district was blessed with a short campaign of only about a month duration, it was a dirty, hard-hitting affair from start to finish. A resolution adopted by the Democrat conferees at their Media meeting set the tone. It began by setting forth that Robinson's nomination was secured "by the improper use of money and the introduction of other elements of debauchery into the politics of Delaware County." It further stated that the tactics employed by Robinson to gain the nomination "have done much to demoralize and corrupt this county as similar methods introduced by Smedley Darlington did to demoralize and corrupt Chester County."

As already noted, Pierce's disenchantment with the Republican Party began at the 1886 county convention when Darlington defeated Everhart for the party's congressional nomination. He had supported Everhart's unsuccessful independent bid for re-election that year and three years later supported

Democrat Joseph Hemphill in a bitterly contested judgeship fight against Darlington's son-in-law, Judge Thomas S. Butler. These and other positions taken by Pierce after stepping down as the county GOP chairman, of course, did not endear him to the Republican regulars, who now branded him a traitor.

The attacks made by Robinson and Pierce on one another were quite vicious and received a big play in the newspapers. Accounts of various political rallies seem to indicate both candidates traveled a low road rather than a high one in making their canvasses for votes. The newspaper treatment of the campaign was such that readers at times may have thought the Robinson-Pierce bout was a prizefight rather than a political contest. Both men were lawyers and talented stump speakers. Each challenged the other to debate and each accused the other of cowardice. Answering a Pierce taunt, Robinson told one partisan gathering: "Why should I be afraid to debate? He is not very big physically, morally, politically, or intellectually." Finally, arrangements were made for the two antagonists to debate at Horticultural Hall in West Chester. Describing the event, which took place on the evening of October 21, the *Daily Local News* reported:

> "Long before the doors were opened hundreds of men from all over Chester and Delaware counties were clamoring for admittance, for it was in that building that 'Fighting Jack' Robinson and 'Fighting Tom' Pierce . . . were in a few minutes to address them on the issues of the campaign and other kindred subjects. When the doors were opened a grand rush was made, and it was as much as the whole police force of the town could do to keep the people from breaking down the doors. The hall was filled in five minutes and hundreds were unable to get near enough either to hear the speakers, much less see them."

The protective tariff was the main issue discussed by candidates Robinson and Pierce. According to the *Local*:

> "People of all shades of political color, with free trade, anti-protection, protection, tariff-for-revenue only, and all other kinds of tariff views packed together irrespective of what their individual opinions were or their personal preferences for candidate or party. . . . The scene and wordy battle was one long to be remembered. . . . Happily all passed off pleasantly.

There was no winner at Horticultural Hall, but at the polls a few days later the verdict went to Robinson. He received 17,447 votes in the Sixth District to Pierce's 13,342. It was not a good year, though, for the Republican Party in Pennsylvania. In a gubernatorial election which drew over 900,000 men to the polls, Democrat Pattison was victorious with a plurality of under 17,000 votes. Whether Pierce added strength to the state ticket is difficult to say, but rock-ribbed Republican Chester County gave Delamater a plurality of slightly over 1,000 votes. Elsewhere in the nation the party suffered many reversals and lost more than eighty seats in the United States House of Representatives.

Dissension within the Republican Party at the county, state and national levels persisted throughout the 1890s. Congressman Robinson skillfully avoided becoming a central figure in the clashes between the rival factions and was twice able to get re-elected with relative ease. On both occasions the congressional contest was largely obscured in the news columns by coverage given to the main events—the 1892 presidential rematch between Benjamin Harrison and Grover Cleveland (won by Cleveland and the Democrats) and the 1894 gubernatorial race won by Republican Daniel Hastings. Robinson's Democrat opponents were Garrett E. Smedley of Delaware County in 1892 and Dr. Thomas Edge Parke, the chief burgess of Downingtown, in 1894.

Pennsylvania was entitled to two additional congressmen as the result of the 1890 census, but the state's lawmakers made no new apportionment. Congressional district lines remained the same for the twenty-eight existing districts. This left the party bosses with the power to pick nominees for the two at-large representatives to be elected by the voters of the entire commonwealth. For the Delchester district the decision not to draw up new boundary lines was of little consequence since the combined population of the two counties was slightly over 164,000—about 11,000 under the state ratio of one congressman per 175,000 residents. The new population figures, however, were scrutinized very closely by politicians of the two counties since they clearly indicated Delaware County would soon be the larger of the two. Forty years earlier when the district had been created slightly over 91,000 persons had resided in the two counties, but better than seventy percent of them had lived in Chester County, thus giving Republican politicians there a much larger voice in candidate selections. The new figures showed that Delaware County's population had tripled and that better than forty-five percent of the district's 164,000 residents were now Delaware Countians.

The change in the Sixth District's population distribution was cited by Delaware County's Republican leaders in 1896 when Congressman Robinson sought a fourth term, but their counterparts in Chester County wouldn't listen, claiming it was their turn to pick a candidate. A bitter fight within the Republican ranks ensued and Robinson was the eventual loser. He was also a loser two years later when he tried to recapture the Sixth District seat.

As president of the League of Republican Clubs of Pennsylvania for six years (1891-97), Robinson was well known beyond the limits of the Delchester district. Throughout the 1890s and early years of the twentieth century he continued to be active politically, serving as a delegate to three national conventions (1892, 1896 and 1908) and as a United States marshal for the eastern district of Pennsylvania from 1900 until his retirement in 1914. He died on Jan. 20, 1933, at age eighty-seven.

CHAPTER 23

THE NAVY'S "FIGHTING QUAKER"

During the 1890s West Chester's *Daily Local News* ran a column of gossipy political tid-bits under the heading "Home Political Glints." These glints were sometimes amusing and usually informative, but they could never be accepted as gospel. For example, on Oct. 18, 1894, the column contained this tid-bit:

> "Ex-Judge Thomas S. Butler, in the most emphatic manner at his command, declared yesterday he was not a candidate for Congress, nor was he for Judge, and that he never, never would be a candidate for anything while he lived. He says that he is entirely out of politics, and that all his ambitions are centered in his law practice."

Adverbs used by politicians sometimes have a nebulous meaning. For Butler "never" meant a brief period; in less than two years he became a candidate—a successful one—and the remainder of his life was spent deeply involved in politics and running for public office.

Thomas Stalker Butler's service in the United States House of Representatives spanned thirty-one years—from March 4, 1897, when he was sworn in as a freshman member of the Fifty-fifth Congress, until his death on May 26, 1928, at age seventy-three. Butler served in the Congress during the administrations of six presidents—William McKinley, Theodore Roosevelt, William H. Taft, Woodrow Wilson, Warren Harding and Calvin Coolidge. During the two hundred year history of the United States Congress only a few congressmen, and none from Chester County, have been able to match Butler's long tenure. At the time of his death he was the oldest member of the House in continuous years of service and the holder of the longest continuous record of service for all time.

Butler's first political campaign had not been a pleasant experience so he may have been sincere in 1894 when he said he was out of politics. Admitted to the bar in 1877, he had quickly gained a reputation as a skilled lawyer. Courthouse personages marked him as a comer and predicted he would follow in the footsteps of his esteemed uncle, William Butler, and become a judge. They were right; in 1889, when he was only thirty-two, Butler was appointed as an additional law judge by Gov. James Beaver to fill a vacancy on the county bench occasioned by the death of Judge J. Smith Futhey.

In addition to talent, Butler had some other things going for him at this time. As a young lawyer entering the political arena he enjoyed a special advantage over others aspiring for a judgeship or high office since he was the son of Samuel Butler and son-in-law of Smedley Darlington—two of the county's most influential (and affluent) Republicans during the post-Civil War era. As noted elsewhere his father-in-law was a controversial political figure who was twice elected congressman from the Delchester district. His father, an abolitionist who ignored the rigid rules of the Society of Friends and left his farm to become a soldier during the Civil War, was not as flamboyant or as controversial a politician as Darlington, but he was an extremely effective one. Elected state representative in 1876, Samuel Butler quickly earned the respect of his colleagues. During his second term the Republican state convention unanimously nominated him for state treasurer on the first ballot. He was subsequently elected with an overwhelming 58,000 vote majority.

Family influence undoubtedly helped secure for Thomas Butler the judgeship appointment, but his career on the bench was short-lived. Nominated for a ten-year term by the Republican Party in the fall of 1889, he was rejected by the electorate in the first of several interesting judgeship contests in which the bipartisan bench issue was hotly debated. The fact that Butler was of the same political persuasion as the county's other judge, William Bell Waddell, did not sit well with some Chester Countians; they reasoned that as long as the county was to have two judges it might be wise for one of them to be a Democrat. Joseph Hemphill, a Democrat, tossed his hat in the ring, captured his party's nomination, campaigned quietly and effectively, and emerged the winner by the narrow margin of thirty-two votes.

Butler was only thirty-four when he stepped down from the bench. He and his wife Maud, the eldest of Smedley Darlington's seven daughters, had been married for eleven years and resided in West Chester in a large and attractive brick house at 228 W. Miner St. The couple had two sons, Smedley, and Samuel, named for their grandfathers. Returning to the private practice of law in a partnership with William S. Windle and his cousin William Butler Jr., Thomas Butler had no financial worries. The firm was one of the county's leading legal establishments and had among its clients the Farmer's National Bank of West Chester, which had been organized in 1882 by Butler's father, father-in-law, and a few others.

Newspaper accounts do not indicate whether ex-Judge Butler actively sought the Republican nomination for the Delchester congressional seat in 1896 or whether he was drafted by the party's ruling elders. One thing is certain, though; the political bigwigs were determined a Chester Countian should serve in the Fifty-fifth Congress. Similarly, the Republican leadership in Delaware County was bent on returning "Jack" Robinson to Washington for a fourth term. Undoubtedly, Chester County's leaders knew well in advance of Robinson's intentions to seek re-election, and realizing there would be a fight, perhaps they deemed it advisable to have a strong candidate—someone with widespread name recognition such as Thomas S. Butler.

Regardless, Butler was nominated at a convention held on August 18 during which time a resolution was adopted that stated "it is the sense of this convention that Chester County is entitled to, and must insist upon, naming the Republican candidate for Congress from this district." When conferees from the two counties met later in the month at the Charter House in Media no one was in the mood to compromise. Each side reviewed the history of the district and reached a different conclusion as to which county was entitled to name the candidate. T. Lawrence Eyre, the Republican boss of Chester County, claimed an agreement had been reached some years back whereby Delaware County was to have the congressional seat for six years and then Chester County was to have it for eight years. But the County of Delaware had grown tremendously since the district had been established in the early 1850s, and Republicans there maintained that such an arrangement was no longer equitable. District Attorney W. I. Schaffer, chief spokesman for the neighboring county's conferees, said in the past Delaware County had "bowed in acquiescence to every demand Chester County has ever made in the matter of this congressional situation," but this time there would be no acquiescence.

In an effort to break the deadlock a second meeting was held in West Chester on September 7. The same arguments were repeated. Neither side would budge. A reporter for the *Local* said "the flights of oratory which were heard before the session today were entirely useless, having no more effect upon the members than the breezes which wafted the fumes from their fragrant Havanas from the building." Unable to resolve their differences, each Republican organization prepared its own ticket. Butler was on one ticket and Robinson was on the other.

A third contender for the Delchester congressional seat was William H. Berry of Chester, who two years earlier had campaigned for the post as a Prohibitionist. This time he was the Democratic Party's nominee. The three-cornered fight generated much interest and some newspaper accounts said there was more interest in it than in the 1896 election card's main bout—McKinley versus William Jennings Bryan. The voter turnout on Election Day hit a new high and at press time the following day there was still uncertainty as to whether Robinson or Butler was the winner. "Both Sides Claim Victory On A Close Vote" was the *Local's* headline. When the dust settled, though, Butler had unseated Congressman Robinson by some 1,600 votes. As expected, each was top vote-getter in his own county; Butler bettered Robinson 9,826 to 4,254 in Chester County, and Robinson topped Butler 8,917 to 5,285 in Delaware County. Berry was unable to capitalize on the Republican split and finished third with a total vote count of 9,288.

The currency issue was a dominant one throughout the campaign. The Democratic Party platform called for "free and unlimited coinage of silver and gold" and its presidential nominee, Bryan—the boy orator of the Platte—won a place in American history at the party's national convention in Chicago for a mesmerizing speech and one oft quoted line—"You shall not press down upon the brow of labor this crown of thorns, you shall not crucify mankind upon a cross of gold." Bryan was nominated for the presidency on the fifth ballot, but he received nary a vote from Pennsylvania's sixty-four delegates, who supported favorite son ex-Governor Robert E. Pattison until the bitter end. The Pennsylvanians were also among the minority who favored a gold standard plank in the party's platform.

Ohio Gov. William McKinley had the Republican nomination sewed up before the rap of the opening gavel at the GOP convention in St. Louis, but the currency plank in the party's platform caused a bit of commotion. When a resolution favoring unlimited coinage of silver and gold was voted down, two dozen silver delegates from Colorado, Idaho, South Dakota and Utah walked out of the convention in protest. Arguments on the currency issue continued from convention time to Election Day when McKinley garnered 271 electoral votes from twenty-three states (including the big electoral vote states of New York, Pennsylvania, Ohio and Illinois) to win. Bryan carried twenty-two states in the South and West, but received only 176 electoral votes.

Some historians have viewed the election of McKinley as the beginning of modern party politics in the United States. The Civil War and Reconstruction were largely forgotten, the Democratic Party was no longer regarded as the "party of treason" in the North, and the winds of political change were blowing throughout the land when Thomas S. Butler traveled to Washington in March 1897—just six years after his father-in-law's departure—to occupy his seat in the Fifty-fifth Congress. The frontier was closed and urban America was replacing rural America as the dominant force in the nation's politics. A new generation of political leaders in both the North and South was replacing the war veterans who had run the country for thirty years. The tariff most certainly was still a hot and divisive issue, just as it always had been, but new subjects were being discussed such as the eight-hour work day, votes for women, popular election of senators, interstate commerce, child labor, and the regulating of the nation's giant industrial corporations. The "Progressive Era" had commenced and Butler would have to wrestle with and vote upon legislation dealing with economic, social and political reforms of one type or another during most of his long stay in Congress.

Inaugurations of presidents still took place on March 4, not January 20, in McKinley's time. It was also still customary for Congress to convene for its first session in December of the year following the congressional elections, but after taking the oath of office, McKinley expressed a desire for the lawmakers to meet immediately to tackle certain financial problems confronting the country. "The best way for the Government to maintain its credit is to pay as it goes," he said in his inaugural speech, "not by resorting to loans, but by keeping out of debt—through an adequate income secured by a system of taxation, external or internal, or both." He favored a high protective tariff, and during Butler's first term a new law known as the Dingley Tariff was passed by the Republican majority. The freshman House member from Chester County voted with his party, but more importantly he did his homework and gained the respect of business leaders in the Sixth District. Several years later the *Chester Times* recalled:

> "When the Dingley Tariff bill was made, and before the schedules were adopted, he met the manufacturers of our city and county to get their views, and while with so many diverse interests the adjustment of a tariff schedule is a difficult one, we believe our manufacturers were satisfied with the measure, and certainly content with Mr. Butler's efforts on their behalf. After a hard fight, both before the committee and in the House, he secured a satisfactory schedule on gypsum rock. . . . Another knotty problem was that of duty on trees and shrubbery, and the nurserymen of this and Chester county appreciate the efforts of Mr. Butler in this matter."

The new tariff legislation was the chief accomplishment of this special session. For the Chester County congressman, however, an assignment (one probably made with little thought or consideration) by Speaker of the House Thomas B. Reed of Maine, was to change Butler's interests for the remainder of his life. Butler's predecessor from the Delchester district had been an Annapolis graduate, a man with an understandable interest in the Navy. Naming Robinson to the House Naval Affairs Committee made sense. Placing Butler, who grew up on a farm and had little knowledge of the sea or ships, on the committee simply because he was Robinson's replacement in the Congress made no sense at all. Butler, however, accepted the assignment, mastered it, and grew to like it. It might be noted that Butler's arrival on the Washington scene was coincidental with the return of the controversial Theodore Roosevelt to the nation's capital as assistant secretary of the Navy in the new administration. Roosevelt was an ardent expansionist; he wanted to turn Spain out of Cuba and favored an immediate, rapid build-up of the American Navy. With Cuba and Hawaii being the issues of the hour, and with Roosevelt pushing for a navy that could compete with those of Britain, Germany, Spain and Japan, the committee assignment given Chester County's freshman lawmaker soon took on added importance.

On the home front a significant political development occurred shortly after Butler's return from Washington that would also have an important effect on his life. Republican leaders from Delaware and Chester Counties met and ironed out their differences on the congressional nominee selection process. Commenting on these negotiations on August 15, the *Philadelphia Times* reported:

> "The meeting of the conferees of the two counties composing the

> Sixth Congressional District this week was one full of business and apparently satisfied all the factions. It took what is considered the concluding step towards wiping out the old moss-covered system of selecting a congressional nominee by the conferee plan and substituting a district convention. . . . This is a pet measure of the Delaware county leaders and has been advocated by them for years while Chester county's statesmen turned a cold shoulder to it. This new political vaccination is to take effect in 1900 and West Chester is to have the first convention."

The Delaware Countians, according to the *Times*, were satisfied with Butler's performance and indicated he would not be hurt by the change. One of them was quoted as saying Butler "had a great deal more cause to keep his fences in repair in Chester county than he had to dread anything unfair from Delaware county." Aside from politics, another happening in 1897 had a bearing on Congressman Butler's future. His cousin and law partner, William Butler Jr., was elected to join President Judge Joseph Hemphill as the county's additional law judge, a vacancy on the bench having been created by the death of Judge Waddell. Fortunately, the congressman did not have to look far for a replacement law partner to look after his interests when he was in Washington. His sister-in-law, Isabel Darlington, who had graduated cum laude from the University of Pennsylvania Law School, became his new partner. Her admission to the bar on Oct. 4, 1897, is noteworthy since it marked the first time a woman was admitted to the bar of Chester County.

During the second session of the Fifty-fifth Congress, which got underway on Dec. 6, 1897, the Naval Affairs Committee figured prominently in the news. In mid-February the battleship Maine exploded and sank in Havana harbor. American relations with Spain had been strained for a number of years, and many in the United States were quick to blame Spain for the mysterious disaster that claimed the lives of 250 sailors. Platforms of both the Republicans and Democrats in the past had expressed sympathy for Cuban independence, and it was no secret that arms and money from this country were being sent to Cuban insurrectionists. Hearst newspapers and others in the yellow press, seeing an opportunity to increase circulation with screaming headlines, called for retaliation. President McKinley, however, reserved judgment and sought to learn the truth before fixing responsibility for the tragedy.

The country blazed with patriotic emotion. "Remember the Maine" became a national slogan as the war fever spread. Returning home to West Chester five weeks after the tragedy, Butler was quoted in the *Local* as saying: "Yes, it looks very much like war. . . . A very strong war spirit prevails in Washington at the present time. . . . Unless Spain yields a conflict will surely come. . . . The American people are thoroughly aroused to the situation in Cuba." The enemy attack theory for the disaster advanced by the newspapers was much more popular and acceptable than the accident theory presented by more knowledgeable persons. Finally, on April 25, war was declared against Spain. Among those caught up in the patriotic fervor was the congressman's teen-age son, Smedley Darlington Butler. He joined the Marines and was soon off to Cuba while he was still four months shy of seventeen. To meet the age requirement of eighteen, Smedley lied about his age, telling the recruiter he had been born on April 20, 1880. His Quaker parents apparently were willing to overlook Smedley's lie. Years later, after he became famous, "Old Gimlet Eye" told the writer Lowell Thomas that his father's reaction to the enlistment was: "All right. If thee is determined to go, thee shall go, but don't add another year to thy age, my son. Thy mother and I weren't married until 1879." As with many of Smedley's exploits, the story was no doubt embellished somewhat and grew better with the telling.

Exhilarating news accounts, beginning with Commodore Dewey's smashing defeat of the Spanish fleet at Manila Bay in the Philippines, filled the front pages of the nation's newspapers during the weeks following the declaration of war. Hawaii was annexed to the United States by an act of Congress on July 7, 1898, and by the end of the year when the Treaty of Paris was signed the United States was a world power, having enabled Cuba to gain her independence and having acquired Puerto Rico, Guam and the Philippines from Spain.

Congressman Butler was preoccupied with political affairs in the Sixth District, not foreign affairs, during the late summer and fall of 1898. He wanted to be returned to Washington for a second term, but he had an image problem. Philadelphia newspapers were depicting him as an unsavory politician, one of Boss Matt Quay's puppets. His problem stemmed from the conferee method of choosing a congressional nominee. The Republican politicians from Delaware and Chester counties had earlier agreed this was to be the last time the conferee method would be used, but this was no consolation to Butler as he struggled to win re-election. Republican delegates to the party's summer nominating convention in Chester County readily endorsed him for a second term, but their counterparts in the other half of the Sixth Congressional District were of the opinion the nomination should go to a deserving Delaware Countian.

Former Congressman Robinson, who served as the neighboring county's convention chairman, was empowered to select the Delaware County conferees with the understanding that they would support either Robinson himself or some other Delaware Countian for the congressional nomination. One of the conferees picked by Robinson was Prothonotary Billy Matheus, chairman of the Delaware County Republican Committee. Without first giving public notice that a meeting was to be held, Matheus and another Delaware County conferee got together in Philadelphia with Chester County's three conferees—Larry Eyre, State Senator William Snyder, and Dr. J. K. Evans—and made Congressman Butler the GOP nominee. As might be expected, Robinson was furious. The nomination story received a big play in the newspapers and was cited as another instance of Matt Quay's corrupt machine politics.

Taking Matheus to task for his treachery, the *Philadelphia Times* claimed it was "an open secret that he perfidiously bargained with Representative Butler to give him the selection of a number of important Federal appointments in consideration of which Mr. Matheus would betray his people and vote to renominate Mr. Butler." The newspaper concluded "these facts are known to every voter of Delaware County, and in no way can Mr. Matheus pretend to justify or even excuse his action."

In an effort to undo what had been done, Robinson chose three new conferees and sent them to West Chester to meet with the Chester County conferees. Eyre and Company declined to recognize Robinson's new appointees. As far as Eyre was concerned, Butler was the party's nominee and there was no need for another meeting. The matter was then referred to a judge in Dauphin County after both Butler and Robinson filed nominating certificates at Harrisburg claiming to be the Sixth District's Republican nominee. Testimony was heard in mid-October and a decision was handed down adjudging Butler's petition as invalid. This in effect made Robinson the legal Republican nominee.

Robinson's court victory was a hollow one. Two weeks later the voters of the Sixth District went to the polls and gave their verdict to Butler. As in 1896, the congressional race involved Butler, Robinson and Berry. This time Butler won big with a majority of over 8,700 votes. The help received from the party organizations led by Eyre and Matheus can't be minimized, but Butler's victory was also a personal triumph. It was a gubernatorial year and the Republican Party in the district and throughout the state was divided—Quay Republicans on one side and anti-Quay Republicans on the other. The anti-Quay reformers in Chester County were quite strong and the fact they chose not to oppose Butler is certainly an indication that little credence was placed in the newspaper stories implying that Quay had the Chester County congressman in his hip pocket. It should also be noted that the Democrats and the reform wing of the county GOP came up with a "fusion ticket" in 1898 and elected four anti-Quay legislators to the General Assembly. For the Republican organization this was a staggering blow. State legislators at this time chose the United States Senators and the county winners would later contribute to the unseating of Senator Quay himself. In the gubernatorial race, though, Quay's organization prevailed. Unable to prevent William H. Stone, the Quay choice, from being nominated for the governorship at the state GOP convention, many reformers within the Republican Party threw their support to the Rev. Silas Swallow, nominee on the Prohibitionist, People's, Liberty and Honest Government tickets. The Democrats, however, declined to join in a statewide fusion effort; they supported George A. Jenks. With the opposition divided, Stone won by a substantial plurality.

1900 ELECTION

Congressman Butler had his fences mended and in good repair throughout the Sixth District when it came time for him to run for re-election in 1900. Organization Republicans in both counties were behind him and so were the independents. Employing for the first time their new rules and procedures for selecting the party's congressional nominee, Republican delegates (202 from Chester County and 196 from Delaware County) gathered at the Opera House in West Chester on a warm Saturday afternoon in late June and unanimously nominated the forty-four-year-old Butler for a third term. From all accounts the replacement of the conferee nominating procedure with a district convention was well received. Newspaper stories indicated the convention was a fun time for both the delegates and the overflow crowd of spectators. In describing the event the *Local* reported:

> "Today there is sort of a reunion—or a love feast, it might be called—of the Republicans of the Sixth Congressional District. . . . The occasion is the first Congressional Convention held in the history of the Sixth District, and harmony the like of which is rarely seen at a political convention pervades the very atmosphere. Everybody is for McKinley & Roosevelt and for Hon. Thomas S. Butler for Congressman."

Butler's name was placed in nomination by Col. H. H. Gilkyson, the Phoenixville publisher and one of Chester County's most prominent independent Republicans, who told the convention he stood with a flag of truce in one hand and the flag of McKinley in the other. He praised Butler for his attention to duties, unflinching zeal and devotion to the Republican Party. Another speaker was Butler's old rival, ex-Congressman Robinson, now a United States marshal, who suggested "burying the old hatchet in the sea of oblivion." Noting that all reforms move slowly, Robinson placed his stamp of approval on the convention, saying he was happy to see the conferee system abandoned.

With all this unity within the Republican Party, Butler's election in November was a cakewalk. He polled more than 26,000 votes; his Democrat opponent, Nathaniel M. Ellis, received only 10,098. As the new twentieth century approached, though, the election victory was probably quickly forgotten by Butler as his thoughts turned to the homecoming of his son Smedley, a young Marine hero whose military travels had taken him to Cuba, the Philippines and China. Both the congressman and Mrs. Butler traveled across the country to San Francisco to be on hand to meet the transport *Grant* when it arrived from the Far East carrying their nineteen-year-old son who had been cited for bravery by President McKinley. Being the son of a congressman and a member of perhaps the county's most prominent Republican family, young Captain Butler's return to West Chester rated more than just a run-of-the-mill small town parade. Under headline captions which read "Glad Welcome Home For Captain Butler" and "The Gallant Young Man May Arrive In Town Tomorrow," the *Local* reported that "residents of the Sixth District of Pennsylvania, which the gallant young officer's father so ably represents in Congress, are anxious to see and extend a welcome to Captain Butler, for the reason they have watched his career with great interest, and are proud of a lad who can achieve such distinction."

The Butlers arrived home on Friday evening, January 10. The next night the townspeople of West Chester turned out to honor Smedley at a ceremony sponsored by the McCall GAR Post in the town's Assembly Building. Although Secretary of the Navy John D. Long was unable to attend (as had been announced earlier in the week), the platform was crowded with dignitaries, including Gov. William A. Stone, who gave the principal address, and State Treasurer James E. Barnett. Being the center of attention was a new experience for the young Marine, but it would not be his last. During the next forty years Smedley Darlington Butler would figure prominently in the news, occasionally capturing the national spotlight.

Congressman Butler continued to have an easy time winning elections during the early 1900s. He brushed aside Franklin H. Rhoades by 10,000 votes in 1902, trounced Col. Archibald M. Holding by 20,000 votes in 1904, defeated John J. Buckley by more than 11,000 votes in 1906, and won by 16,000 votes over D.P. Hibberd in 1908. These victories reenforce the popular impression that the Republican Party has had little difficulty dominating the Chester County political stage since Civil War days. This impression, however, is not borne out by some of the other campaign struggles and election results during this period. Butler's victories were an exception, not the rule in Chester County. The new century's first decade was a time of intense and bitter fighting within the ranks of the Republican Party and for a while it was Butler's good fortune to be able to stay out of the crossfire.

In 1910, as a result of the division within the party over state and national issues, Butler's easy coasting days ended and he came up against a sturdy rival in the person of Eugene Bonniwell, a Philadelphia lawyer who resided in Wayne. Before the Republicans and Democrats held state conventions to pick gubernatorial nominees, Butler had no inkling that stormy days were in the offing. Through his efforts, President Taft paid a visit to West Chester on a Saturday afternoon in June. Chester Countians turned out en masse to get a glimpse of the president. A reporter for the *Coatesville Times* wrote that "shouting crowds, young and old, sang patriotic songs, waved flags and cheered until they were hoarse, the only President of the United States who ever visited Chester County while holding office." The visit—held the same day the Republican County Committee was meeting in West Chester—was a brief one, but nevertheless a feather in Butler's hat. It began with a short reception at the Villa Maria Convent grounds and was followed by a motorcade into West Chester where President Taft told the crowd of well-wishers:

> "It's all owing to your Congressman Butler that I am here today. You know what kind of a man he is. He asks you to do one small thing, and before you are out of it you have done twenty. He is a man of energy, and I commend him to you. We like him in Washington, and hope you will continue to send him there."

Then, after briefly addressing the crowd, President Taft was whisked off to the train station where he departed for Lincoln University to deliver a commencement address and award diplomas. Still, as the *Times* observed, "it was a big day for West Chester, a big day for the County Committee, and a big day for Congressman Butler and all his friends." Within weeks after the president's visit, though, Butler was in trouble. A new political party known as the Keystone Party was organized. Its members endorsed Bonniwell, the Democratic Party's nominee for congressman, and slated William H. Berry for the governorship. The Keystoners attracted many Republicans as they campaigned aggressively against boss rule and corruption. This time, Butler was caught in the crossfire.

Berry—the Delaware Countian whom Butler had twice defeated in congressional contests—came out on top in the Chester County voting for governor, but statewide the gubernatorial race was won by Republican John K. Tener. Along with others on the Republican ticket, Butler felt the campaign backlash of the reformers. For the first time since losing the judgeship in 1889, Butler was beaten in his home county; Bonniwell received 5,697 Keystone and 1,781 Democrat votes to edge out Butler by a 7,478 to 7,307 count. A strong Republican vote in Delaware County, however, more than offset the 171-vote deficit and Butler was returned to Washington for an eighth term in the House of Representatives.

During the first decade of the new century a number of significant changes were made in Pennsylvania's election procedures. Among these reforms was a uniform primary law that resulted in candidates for public office being nominated directly by the voters rather than by delegates at party conventions. With this legislation the responsibility for conducting the primaries was transferred from the political parties to county government. For the Republican politicians of Chester and Delaware counties, who had quarreled for nearly half a century over the method of choosing a congressional nominee, it may have seemed ironic that corrective legislation was adopted so shortly after they themselves had finally worked out what they considered a satisfactory solution to their bothersome congressional nominating problem.

For Butler the new primary law presented no problem; he enjoyed a good rapport with the Republican sachems in Delaware County and had no worries about their running someone against him. Leaders of the party establishment in both counties had come to realize that the frequent rotation of the office between the counties was not in their best interest and that it was advantageous for the district to have someone with seniority serving in the

House. Nor were the reformers or independents out to get Butler; they frequently supported anti-organization candidates for state and county offices at the primaries, but they did not put up anyone to go against their incumbent congressman.

Newspaper articles indicate Butler was very responsive to the needs and desires of his Sixth District constituency. He was one of six congressmen who worked out arrangements for the funding of what became known as rural mail delivery on an experimental basis. His efforts in this field won him many accolades from the home folks . . . and he himself enjoyed talking to newsmen and promoting this pet project. After helping to draft a postal appropriation bill in 1901 he enthusiastically told a *Local* reporter:

> "Already the sum of $3,500,000 has been assured for the rural mail, which grows more and more popular. I believe in a short time our whole district will be covered by the service if the people want it. The Senate is as favorably disposed towards it as the House, as everywhere that it has been introduced it seems to be a success. The most favorable showing of all is in West Chester, as the increase in patronage here has been so remarkable that there is nothing like it anywhere. It is difficult to make the people at Washington fully appreciate what has been done here. An order has been issued to go into effect at Brandywine Summit and Boothwyn, Delaware County, in a short time. I am expecting that soon an order will be issued establishing the service at Malvern, where routes have been laid out."

The phrases "if the people want it" and "difficult to make the people at Washington fully appreciate" have a familiar ring. Butler was a true politician. He was also a strong party man and made it a point to let his interviewer know that his friend Perry S. Heath, the "father of rural delivery," was now secretary of the Republican National Committee.

Following the assassination of President McKinley by the foreign-born anarchist Leon Czolgosz in 1901, Butler gained considerable recognition as a "law and order" lawmaker when he urged that legislation be passed making an attempt on the life of a president punishable by death. He also recommended that Congress enact more stringent immigration laws and proposed a number of frightening ideas which smack of a police state. A Washington newspaper said he was "enthusiastic in denouncing anarchy" and felt "for a person to be present at an anarchist meeting should be a crime punishable with a long term of imprisonment." It was also reported that the Delchester congressman wanted to see newspaper reporters made a part of the government's secret service to obtain information that could be used to break up "organizations of individuals whose aim was inimical to the good of society." Fortunately, these ideas did not blossom and the paranoia about anarchists was short-lived.

ELECTION OF 1912

The new election laws passed in the early 1900s with respect to the primaries did not result in a rash of would-be congressmen throwing their derbies in the Delchester political ring. Butler went unopposed at the 1908 and 1910 primaries, but in 1912 he was challenged for the Republican nomination by William Ward Jr., the mayor of Chester and a son of one of the district's former congressmen. As would be the case with other challengers, Ward's efforts to capture the GOP congressional nomination were for naught.

Bonniwell was chosen again by the Democrats at their primary and for a while it appeared the November election would feature a Butler-Bonniwell rematch. The Republican Party's national convention in Chicago had an impact on the local contest, however, and the Seventh Congressional District (Chester and Delaware counties became the Seventh District under the new apportionment) had a three-cornered fight reminiscent of the earlier Butler-Robinson-Berry bouts. Unhappy with the nomination of President Taft for a second term, supporters of ex-President Roosevelt seceded from the Republican Party and held their own Progressive Party convention and made Roosevelt their standard-bearer. In Pennsylvania these Roosevelt followers organized the Washington Party and slated their own ticket. Butler, a Taft man, was not included on it. For the Seventh District congressional seat the Washingtonians endorsed a young Delaware Countian named Frederick A. Howard.

Realizing many Republicans would be supporting Roosevelt rather than Taft, the congressman's backers organized the "Butler League" and carried on an extensive advertising campaign on his behalf. Voters of all political complexions were invited to join the Butler League regardless of whether they were for Taft, Roosevelt or Gov. Woodrow Wilson of New Jersey, the Democratic Party's nominee for the presidency. Taking on the role of peacemaker, Butler made a number of attempts to get Roosevelt's supporters to back all the local Republican nominees, but without success. Speaking at one meeting, he said:

> "While we clash and dispute over the nominations at Chicago . . . no exception whatever can be taken to the exact honesty of our local nominations. . . . Republicans agree upon nearly every issue found in either platform made at Chicago. Our differences grow out of our views upon candidates for the Presidency. Men of strong convictions are upon either side of the dispute. Men who have always stood together for the country's good, now decline to make common cause. They are all for protection to American industries, and for this reason alone if no other could be found, they are all Republicans although found under different names."

Knowing the Chester County voter's penchant for voting a straight party ticket, and realizing that Roosevelt's popularity exceeded President Taft's in the county, Butler and his strategists had cause for concern. In the previous congressional election Bonniwell had received approximately forty-six percent of the votes cast. Fearful that the Republican Party split might allow Bonniwell to score an upset, Prothonotary Howard S. Conner, a friend of Butler's and a Roosevelt enthusiast, came up with a slick but controversial plan designed to siphon off votes of the Roosevelt supporters for Butler. Conner, a Modena storekeeper, and some of his friends preempted the name of "Bull Moose Party" and slated a ticket identical to that of the Republican Party's with the exception of the nominees for president and vice president.

Candidate Howard and his Washington Party friends were furious. They rightly viewed Conner's stratagem as being deceptive and claimed the nomination papers for Butler and the Bull Moose candidates had been fraudulently filed. Taking his complaint to the Court of Common Pleas of Dauphin County, Howard maintained that the "Bull Moose" name was commonly applied to the party supporting Roosevelt. He argued that those filing the nominating papers were "exerting all their powers to defeat Theodore Roosevelt" and therefore not entitled to file nomination papers under such a party name. He further charged the nominating papers were filed with the intent of deceiving electors by inducing them to believe that Butler was a follower and supporter of Theodore Roosevelt, thus hoping to secure their votes, while if they knew Butler's true position they would vote against him. Conner, of course, said Howard's allegations were false. He told the *Local*:

> "I will appear with several others shortly at Harrisburg and will be ready to produce all the necessary proof that the Bull Moose Party is just what it claimed to be. How anybody can say that I am not for Teddy is more than I can understand. The ticket we presented is a good one and we are all for it, and that is all there is to it."

Howard's effort to have the Court rule out Conner's Bull Moose Party failed. In the meantime, the Butler League concentrated its fire on Bonniwell, who was employed by the City of Philadelphia, making him out to be a city slicker with little interest in rural Chester County. In its final salvo—an advertisement in the *Local* on October 30—it asked: "Why vote for an obscure outsider, who states he lives in our district, and swears monthly that he lives in Philadelphia to receive his salary from that city?"

Bonniwell responded by threatening W. H. Hodgson, president of the *Daily Local News*, with arrest for criminal libel. Saying he would not tolerate "calumny or defamation," Bonniwell demanded a retraction. He claimed the statement was "deliberately, wantonly and maliciously false" and a "gross breach of the libel laws of Pennsylvania," since no assistant solicitor of Philadelphia took an oath either as to residence or service. The Butler League insisted, however, a Philadelphia ordinance required its employees to be bona fide residents of the city and that the interests of the Democratic Party's congressional nominee were in Philadelphia.

In addition to the Republican, Democratic, Washington and Bull Moose parties four other political parties were involved in the Seventh District's 1912 congressional contest. The demise of the Keystone Party had not yet come about. Its Chester County chieftain, I. Franklin Chandler, urged the true-hearted to keep the Keystone faith even though most of the Republican reformers and independents who earlier had swelled his party's ranks were now supporting Roosevelt. In trying to hold his organization together and win support for Bonniwell, the choice of the Keystoners, Chandler maintained the Washington Party's nominations showed that it had "no quarrel with bossism." Also in the congressional race, but generally overlooked in news accounts, were Edwin P. Sellew, the Prohibition Party's nominee, and Walter N. Lodge, the Socialist candidate. The eighth party listed on the ballot was called "Roosevelt Progressive." Like the Bull Moose Party it listed Butler as its nominee for Congress. Commenting on the 1912 election ballot, the *Local* said:

> "It will be much larger in dimension than usual owing to the multiplicity of regular and pre-empted party designations. There will be nine columns of usual width in which Presidential electors will be printed, and one column entirely blank in which names can be written. This will make the ballot about 27 x 27 inches in size or a trifle smaller than two pages of the *Local News*. It will be bulky to handle in the small election booths by those who desire to skip about in different columns."

With the Republican Party divided, Wilson and the Democrats scored a great triumph in 1912. The New Jersey governor captured 435 of the nation's 531 electoral votes; Roosevelt was a winner in only six states (including Pennsylvania) and Taft was left with only eight electoral votes from Utah and Vermont. Chester County went Democratic for the first time since before the Civil War, giving Wilson 6,901 votes. Roosevelt received 6,596 votes and Taft trailed with 5,708. Although his party took a whipping, Butler emerged victorious, polling better than 19,000 votes in the Delchester district to Bonniwell's 12,225 and Howard's 7,647. Over 3,000 of Butler's votes came from supporters of Roosevelt who voted the Bull Moose ticket. Commenting on the returns the *Local* said:

> "About the Court House today there is some little talk of presenting a token in the way of a big apple or a fragrant perfecto to Howard S. Conner, Prothonotary, for his dilligence and skill in leading the Bull Moose Party to a place of recognition in the recent campaign. Apparently the Bull Moose ticket was necessary in order to pull through the (Republican) candidates who had been nominated last Spring."

The counting of the ballots, however, was not the end of the 1912 congressional election story; there was a postscript when Bonniwell filed papers in Washington recommending the unseating of Butler for violation of the election laws. These charges were rejected by a unanimous vote of the House Election Committee.

THE LIQUOR QUESTION

The Eighteenth Amendment to the Constitution prohibiting the manufacture, sale and transportation of intoxicating liquors was not passed by the Congress and referred to the state legislatures for action until late 1917, but the liquor question was always a bothersome one for Congressman Butler. It was a factor in his unsuccessful judgeship campaign in 1889 and became the overriding issue in the 1914 congressional campaign. Prohibitionists had been politically active in the county for years, and many persons shared their views, but their party had never been effective. By 1914, though, under the leadership of Charles L. Huston of Coatesville, a prominent Lukens Steel Company executive and Presbyterian Sunday School teacher, a war against the licensing of drinking establishments was being waged by the militant Chester County No-License Committee. Candidates for public office who were "wets" or held opposing or unsympathetic views were rejected as unfit for office by the No-License Committee in its crusade to consign liquor traffic to "the bottomless pit."

Butler's chief opponent in this campaign was Norris Slack, one of the county's pioneer automobile dealers and chairman of the Democratic Party's county committee. He was also a staunch Methodist and longtime temperance advocate. His position on the liquor question was well known and he had many friends on the No-License Committee. Advertisements placed in the newspapers by the Democrats and Slack's Prohibitionist friends charged that "Thomas S. Butler is endorsed by, and will receive the united support of every liquor dealer in Chester and Delaware Counties." These advertisements also claimed the congressman had done nothing to advance the temperance cause and that if elected he would not be able to "use his influence to bring about Local Option because he will owe his election and allegiance to the liquor interests."

Finally, the No-License Committee was persuaded in late October to send three of its members—the Rev. Washington Laird of West Chester's First Presbyterian Church, the Rev. Robert Green of Phoenixville's First Baptist Church, and Frank L. Campbell of Coatesville—to question Congressman Butler on his views. "My attitude on this issue is so plain that everybody ought to know it," Butler told his visitors.

> "During my life I have been in many a bar room, but no man ever saw me take a drink over the bar. Our family, which has been known in this county for over 200 years, has never been given to liquor. My father, in the days when everybody used liquor in the harvest field, said he would rather burn down the farm buildings than have liquor used about them. I put my name on a petition

> without being solicited—the fourth name on it—asking that the bill for a national expression on this question be brought up in December for consideration. No sir, you need not have any doubt as to where I stand. When the church people line up on one side and the liquor people on the other, depend upon it, I am going to be found with the church people."

Butler's response was apparently convincing. Huston issued a statement advising voters that all the congressional candidates were pledged to "proper anti-liquor legislation" and that they (the voters) could therefore "exercise their personal preferences" at the polls. However, the liquor question remained the paramount and seemingly only issue in the 1914 campaign. To combat statements implying Butler was friendly to the liquor interests, Republican County Chairman Fred T. MacDonald issued a statement pointing out that the congressman had "upon every opportunity voted for and advocated national prohibition." Newspaper advertisements with headings in bold face type saying "Thou Shalt Not Bear False Witness" and "Thou Shalt Not Lie" were also used by the Republicans to strike back at Slack.

There was also a third candidate in the 1914 congressional race. Roosevelt's followers in the Washington Party (known as the Progressive Party in most parts of the country) were still active in Pennsylvania. They had no time for the Republican Party and its state boss, United States Senator Boies Penrose, and had slated Gifford Pinchot, former chief of the United States Forest Service and close friend of Roosevelt, for the Senate and Arthur Tomlinson as their nominee for Butler's congressional seat. The third party effort this time, however, was a feeble one. Butler scored an easy victory, polling 23,239 votes to Slack's 8,340 and Tomlinson's 4,096. As the votes were being tabulated on election night Butler told newsmen "it makes a good birthday gift, for tomorrow I am just sweet sixty years old."

The political war between "wets" and "drys" in this country continued throughout Butler's lifetime. Battle after battle was fought year after year between the two forces. Butler was involved in one of the most dramatic of these battles by being a member of the House on Dec. 18, 1917, when the prohibitionists finally succeeded in persuading the nation's lawmakers to adopt a resolution proposing an amendment to the federal Constitution that would prohibit liquor traffic throughout the country. The *New York Times* announced this historic event with a front page streamer that read "Prohibition Wins In National House By 282 To 128." Butler was among those recorded as favoring the resolution. Neither party could be credited or blamed for the resolution as an equal number of Republicans (137) and Democrats (141) were on the "dry" side and an equal number of Democrats (64) and Republicans (62) were on the "wet" side. Six other lawmakers not affiliated with either major party split four-to-two in favor of the amendment. Thirty-six states subsequently ratified the Eighteenth Amendment and on Jan. 16, 1920, national prohibition went into effect.

THE SUFFRAGE ISSUE

The question of giving women the right to vote was debated many times during Congressman Butler's long career of public service, but for him personally it was not nearly as troublesome an issue as was prohibition. He had been just a boy in 1869 when the National Woman Suffrage Society and the American Woman Suffrage Society were founded. Although never at the head of the parade carrying a banner for the suffragettes, he was sympathetic to their cause. More importantly, he gave them his vote when it was needed.

One of the many dramatic chapters in the long struggle for women's suffrage occurred during the third session of the "lame duck" Sixty-third Congress. Returning to Washington after his 1914 election win Butler found the suffrage question on the front burner. A showdown vote was set for January 12. According to the *Local*, a driving rain storm failed to discourage a record-breaking crowd from flocking to the Capitol for the all-day debate. Women began arriving at eight in the morning and when they " doffed their water-proof coats the purple and yellow banners and sashes of the suffragists filled the galleries with a wave of color."

But it was not a happy day for the suffragettes. The House rejected the amendment resolution by a 204 to 174 vote. Butler voted with the minority. One of the chief reasons for the rejection was that Democrat leaders voiced the attitude of their party that suffrage was a state issue. There were, however, some congressmen who felt politics was a man's game and the "weaker sex" was unequipped to play it. An Ohio legislator caused a storm of hissing in the galleries when he commented "the women of Washington are beautiful, but they have no interest in the affairs of State."

For Pennsylvania suffragettes the months following this setback were very busy ones. In his inaugural address Gov. Martin G. Brumbaugh came out in favor of an amendment to the Pennsylvania Constitution providing for female suffrage. This was followed by a decision to hold a referendum in 1915. A number of Chester County women campaigned throughout the state in an effort to secure support for the amendment, only to be disappointed when the results were announced. Chester County's men favored the suffrage amendment by a 7,429 to 6,035 vote count, but statewide the men of Pennsylvania were not yet ready to trust women with the ballot. The women, of course, were not to be denied. The following year both the Republicans and Democrats had planks in their platforms that gave approval to "state action" in granting suffrage and in eleven states women were able to vote in the 1916 presidential election. Montana's voters went so far as to elect a woman—Jeanette Rankin—to represent them in the Congress.

It was not until after World War I, though, that the Nineteenth Amendment was ratified and not until the Harding-Cox election in 1920 that women were able to vote on a national scale for president and members of Congress. The resolution referring the suffrage amendment to the states for ratification came before the House on May 20, 1919, after President Wilson convened the Sixty-sixth Congress in an extraordinary session. It was the first item of business taken up by the new Republican-controlled House and it had easy sailing. Most of the opponents from the earlier Congress were no longer around or had changed their minds. President Wilson had also buoyed the spirits of the suffragettes by giving his endorsement to the so-called Susan B. Anthony amendment in a message to Congress. After only three hours of debate the resolution was passed by a vote of 304 to 89. Congressman Butler voted with the majority. Two weeks later the measure won approval in the Senate by a 56-to-25 vote, moving the suffrage question from Washington to the state legislatures for ratification.

WORLD WAR I

Prohibition and women's suffrage were topics always good for a lively argument during this period, but for President Wilson, Congress and most Americans the main concern was the war in Europe. It had erupted in August 1914 after Archduke Francis Ferdinand, heir to the Austrian throne, was assassinated. The president shortly thereafter announced the neutrality of the United States, but some leaders in Congress foresaw trouble on the horizon. Butler, the ranking Republican on the House Naval Affairs Committee, was one of these leaders. The first and most persistent "Big Navy" advocate in the House, he played a leading role in preparing the United States for its eventual entrance into the European conflict. His bill for strengthening the Navy received considerable publicity in 1916, but failed by two votes when first introduced. It was eventually adopted, however, and provided for the building of 156 ships.

One of the important claims made by the Democrats in 1916 when Wilson was seeking re-election was "he kept us out of war." The election turned out to be an extremely close one and this claim probably contributed to Wilson's victory. He defeated Charles Evans Hughes, the Republican nominee, by only twenty-three electoral votes. Had the outcome been different in California, that state's thirteen electoral votes would have given the election to Hughes. The Democrats also retained control of Congress in 1916, but they were unable to make any inroad in the Seventh Congressional District where Butler was re-elected with a 12,000-plus vote majority over Edward Buchanan Cassatt of Chesterbrook Farm, Berwyn. A grand-nephew of President Buchanan, the Democratic challenger was a member of one of the Main Line's most prominent families. His father, A. J. Cassatt, had been president of the Pennsylvania Railroad (1899-1906) and his aunt, Mary Cassatt, was one of the country's most talented painters.

Newspaper accounts of his election triumph seem to indicate Butler felt politically secure. He told the *Local* he retired early on election night and didn't join in what proved to be a premature GOP victory celebration in West Chester. "I went to bed and slept well, occupying a room which does not front on the street," he told a reporter. "When the parade came along I was waked by Mrs. Butler, who told me that 2,000 of my friends were outside, but I said I would not go out at that hour unless I could invite them all to supper at my home tomorrow evening." As dean of the Pennsylvania delegation in the House, Butler's seniority began receiving considerable attention about this time both at home and in Washington. On March 3, 1917, a memorandum of respect was read in the House, honoring him for the completion of twenty years of service. It was noted that only nine other lawmakers were still around who had served with him when he entered the Fifty-fifth Congress.

War clouds from Europe continued to gather after the 1916 election. The United States broke off diplomatic relations with Germany in February and finally on April 2, 1917, President Wilson asked Congress to declare war on Germany, saying "the world must be made safe for democracy." Four days later war was declared. It was the second time Chester County's congressman voted for war, the first being against Spain in April of 1898 during the McKinley administration. From the war's outset to the armistice in November 1918, Butler was actively engaged in the military effort. County Republicans commended him at their 1918 spring convention for "the intelligent support and assistance" rendered the administration "in mapping out a Naval and War programme for the successful prosecution of the present conflict with Germany." Several months later Butler traveled with a congressional committee to France and spent time on the front with American troops.

There was little time for politics that year since most everyone in public life was preoccupied with the war effort. Front pages of county newspapers were filled with war stories, and if press coverage is any indication, the campaigns for public office generated little interest. The *Local's* interview with Butler on his trip to France—"You may say that I was six days and six nights on the firing line, and I talked with dozens of our boys"—received more attention than any campaign utterances. Butler had no trouble at the primary defeating Luther Kauffman of Drexel Hill to gain the Republican congressional nomination a twelfth time, nor did James G. Milbourn, the Democratic Party nominee, give him any difficulty at the general election.

In passing, it might be noted that the 1918 campaign for the Pennsylvania governorship involved both an old political foe of Congressman Butler as well as a political ally. The foe was Eugene Bonniwell, whom Butler had defeated in the 1910 and 1912 congressional campaigns. The friend was William Cameron Sproul, a state senator from Delaware County who led the Republican Party to victory. Bonniwell was the second of Butler's vanquished opponents to aspire for the state's highest elected office. William H. Berry, twice beaten by Butler, was the Keystone Party's choice for governor in the memorable three-way gubernatorial race in 1910.

NAVY SPOKESMAN

With the convening of the Sixty-sixth Congress in May 1919, Butler assumed a new leadership role on the national political stage. The Republicans, after being in the minority for eight years, took control of the House. Congressman Frederick H. Gillett of Massachusetts, a longtime friend of Butler's, replaced Missouri Democrat Champ Clark as speaker and Butler became chairman of the House Naval Affairs Committee, a position he held until his death in 1928. During the postwar years this committee frequently was in the limelight and its chairman gained widespread recognition for his expertise on the Navy and its operations. "His knowledge of the Navy and its needs was unsurpassed by any member of Congress," observed Virginia's Rep. Patrick H. Drewry at a 1929 memorial service, "and I doubt if many high-ranking officers of the Navy knew as fully as he did the complex legislative needs of the service."

The story of how Republican leaders in the Senate refused to go along with Wilson's recommendation that the United States enter the League of Nations is a familiar one. Not nearly as well known, though, is the story of the efforts made during the 1920s to place a limit on naval armaments. A congressional resolution calling for a major power conference to consider reducing the size of navies was signed by President Harding in the summer of 1921. Later in the year delegates from nine nations met in Washington and were stunned when Secretary of State Charles Evans Hughes not only called for a ten-year naval holiday with limits on construction, but proposed the scrapping of battleships and cruisers already built in an effort to halt the military preparedness race then underway. His proposition was accepted by England, Japan, France and the other large naval powers.

Congressman Butler went along with the disarmament program, recalling some years later that he "voted with joy in my heart to scrap those ships." With disarmament the United States made a great sacrifice—a sacrifice Butler came to regret. "Do you suppose . . . I could have voted to scrap twenty-nine vessels, to destroy $300,000,000 of the best ships known if I had suspected that within five years we'd have to replace them," he was quoted as saying in a full page story that appeared in *The Philadelphia Ledger* in early 1927. "Do you suppose I could have let that money be thrown away if I had known that probably $400,000,000 more would have to be spent for a virtually new navy?"

Referred to as the "Fighting Quaker" by some reporters, Butler frequently made the front pages of metropolitan newspapers as well as those in his home county as he attempted to correct the scrapping mistake by urging his colleagues in the House to appropriate what he felt was the necessary money to rebuild the fleet. A *Coatesville Record* headline on May 21, 1924, read: "Butler Urges 8 New Cruisers For U.S. Navy." The story beneath it reported how Butler told the House during a debate that Congress must put through a $150-million building program because "this Navy of ours has run down." Another *Record* headline eight days later read: "Butler Directs Passage Of Navy Bill In House." The bill, passed by a 166 to 138 vote, authorized the president to spend $111-million to recondition six battleships and construct eight cruisers. Three years later Butler was involved in another fight for the Navy after the House Appropriations Committee failed to allocate the money he wanted to modernize other battleships. Butler took the matter to the floor of the House, received considerable publicity, and persuaded House members to restore by a 215 to 75 vote the $940,000 appropriation he wanted for his battleships.

The expansion of Great Britain's fleet during the 1920s was disturbing to Butler. Although he maintained that "we must stop the race with other nations and provide just what is needed for national defense," the Chester County congressman grew up and lived in an era of heady nationalism that fostered his desire to see the United States Navy second to none. The United States had loaned its allies more than $10 billion for the prosecution of the war and reconstruction, and it annoyed him to see the British and others building ships while neglecting to pay their war debts. "The most difficult task that has faced the country since the war is the problem of getting our debtors to pay their debts," he complained to the men's Bible class of the First Presbyterian Church of West Chester in early 1927. The *Local* further quoted him as saying, "if France and England were willing to cut down on their armaments fifty percent I would be willing to vote for wiping out their war debts, but I don't propose voting for a cancellation of their debts so that they can use the money to build ships in order to beat us."

THE LAST CAMPAIGNS

Winning elections came easy for Butler during the 1920s. When over 20,000 men went to the polls in the 1916 presidential election it was heralded as the greatest turnout of voters in Chester County's history. Butler polled almost 28,000 votes in Chester and Delaware counties in that election, his largest vote-harvest ever. With women voting in the district (beginning in 1920) his majorities were greater than ever. Against Democrat Freeland S. Brown in 1920 he polled more than 52,000 votes in the Delchester district and won with a 36,000 vote plurality. In his final three runs he also carried the district with handsome majorities over Democrat challengers William T. Ellis, Gordon Cilley and Franklin H. Rhodes.

These campaigns during the 1920s were not especially noteworthy. Ellis branded Butler as an "Eyre-McClure-Sproul Machine Man" in the 1922 battle and tried to engage him in debate, saying a return to the Lincoln-Douglas style would be desirable. He proposed at least one public debate a week, but Butler replied that he could not see where a joint discussion would be of "much assistance to the voters" and went on to win again with a 12,000-vote plurality. With Calvin Coolidge heading the ticket in 1924, Butler scored his greatest triumph. He polled more than 63,000 votes; Democrat Gordon Cilley, a newspaperman from North Carolina who later founded the *Main Line Daily Times*, received fewer than 13,000 votes.

By and large, Butler managed to avoid the petty party squabbles at home during his long tenure in the House. He enjoyed a close rapport with state Senator Eyre, the GOP boss of Chester County, and with the Republican leaders of Delaware County during most of his years in Washington. During the early 1920s, though, an intra-party fight in Delaware County between the McClure and Sproul factions spilled over into Chester County. It resulted in an unsuccessful effort in 1920 on the part of Thierry Van Casteel Phillips, grandson of the Duke of Warsaw, to unseat Butler in the Republican primary. Two years later state Sen. Richard Baldwin of Delaware County, a former speaker of the Pennsylvania House of Representatives, tried to capture the GOP nomination for the Delchester congressional seat. Being a native of Chester County and coming from an old and well established family with numerous political connections (one of his brothers had served as chairman of the Chester County Republican Committee and another brother had served as county commissioner), Baldwin and the McClure forces were expected to give Butler a real battle in the 1922 primary. When the ballots were counted, though, the veteran congressman was a winner with some 20,000 votes to spare.

Just what part the women voters played in these contests is difficult to judge, but it should be noted that Butler's sister-in-law, Isabel Darlington, was very active in politics during this period and undoubtedly worked hard in his behalf. Shortly before the suffrage amendment was ratified Miss Darlington helped organize the first Women's Republican Committee in Pennsylvania and became its chairwoman. She later became the Republican Party's first state committeewoman from Chester County.

With Butler's election to a thirteenth term in 1920 county newspapers proudly noted that the only older member in point of continuous service in the United States House of Representatives was speaker Gillett. A few years later the Massachusetts congressman left the House to join the Senate, causing the *Local* to speculate on May 18, 1927, that "if Congressman Butler's health does not fail him and his political constituents feel that he should be returned to the House for another term, the Eighth Congressional District will come into fame by having a representative who has surpassed all others in the number of consecutive years spent within the halls of the House in Washington."

As already noted, the Chester County legislator's service in the House spanned the tenures of six presidents in the White House, from McKinley to Coolidge. He also served under six speakers of the House, beginning with Thomas B. Reed of Maine, and including David Henderson of Iowa, "Uncle Joe" Cannon of Illinois, Champ Clark of Missouri, Gillett, and Nicholas Longworth of Ohio. At one time there was some talk that Butler himself might be elevated to the coveted post. "Butler Likely Next Speaker" was among the *Coatesville Record* front page headlines on May 20, 1924. The story underneath reported United States Senator Pepper was booming Butler for the job when

Gillett stepped down. Nothing came of this, of course, and one can only speculate as to what motivated those who started the story. Butler certainly didn't need the publicity since he had already earned a reputation as a heavyweight among Washington's lawmakers.

The *Local* recorded his death with a streamer—"Nation Mourns Death of Congressman Thomas S. Butler, Long a Trusted and Faithful Servant"—across the top of its first page on May 28, 1928. Elsewhere throughout the nation newspapers noted the passing of the Navy's greatest champion within the Congress. *The Philadelphia Ledger* said his career was "inextricably bound up with the growth and progress of the American Navy" and that he did more than many world-famous diplomats "to pave the way for an actual naval parity among the leading maritime powers." *The Philadelphia Inquirer* said that Butler, "a Quaker in life and lineage, was nevertheless one of the strongest advocates of military and naval preparedness for the United States during his long lifetime" and that "his career was contemporaneous with and completely bound up in the modern Navy."

CHAPTER 24

KINZER—A NEW DEAL FOE

Chester County was without its "own" congressman for almost nineteen years following the death of Thomas S. Butler in 1928. During this period its interests were looked after briefly by a Delaware Countian and then by a Lancaster Countian whose service in the House of Representatives paralleled Franklin D. Roosevelt's long residency in the White House. Not until Paul B. Dague was sworn in as a member of the Eightieth Congress in January of 1947 did Chester County again have one of its "own" back on Capitol Hill.

Since Congressman Butler had been nominated by the Republicans of Chester and Delaware counties for a seventeenth term shortly before his death, responsibility for finding a replacement nominee fell upon the party organizations of the two counties. Over thirty years had elapsed since a Delaware Countian occupied the Delchester seat so Chester County's Republican Committee headed by state Senator William Clark indicated a willingness to support the choice of the neighboring county's GOP organization. Aside from just being the fair thing to do, Clark and company realized that political clout now rested with Delaware County, the more heavily populated of the district's two counties. At the turn of the century the population of the two counties had been about equal, with Chester County holding a slight edge. Since then Delaware County had experienced phenomenal growth and its population was now twice that of Chester County.

The nominee finally agreed upon by the Republican leadership of Delaware County was James Wolfenden, a prominent manufacturer and banker from Upper Darby Township. Endorsement by the GOP High Command in those days was tantamount to election. Consequently, the Democratic Party did not even bother to run anyone against Wolfenden at a special election held in the fall of 1928 several weeks prior to the regular general election. His only opponent at the special election was Prohibitionist Walter L. Moore whom he clobbered by a vote of 116,504 to 2,579. This victory was followed by another impressive triumph at the regular general election in November over Democrat Henry W. Davis.

Wolfenden was in his late thirties when he presented his election credentials to the Seventieth Congress on Nov. 6, 1928. Although his legislative career in Washington would span the Great Depression and World War II, Wolfenden's association with Chester County was relatively short. He was re-elected in 1930, defeating Democrat Harry D. Wescott by better than 64,000 votes, and continued to represent the Delchester district until reapportionment dissolved the eighty-year marriage of the two counties. Beginning in 1933 and continuing until his retirement from the House in 1947, Wolfenden's constituency was limited to his home county.

The reapportionment following the 1930 census resulted in a major reshuffling of House seats in the Seventy-third Congress. Twenty-one states, including Pennsylvania, saw the size of their congressional delegations reduced. The Keystone State's contingent shrank from thirty-six to thirty-four members, and under the plan finally approved by the state's lawmakers Chester County (population 126,629) was linked with Lancaster County (population 196,882) in Pennsylvania's new Tenth Congressional District. Representing Lancaster County in the Congress at the time of this reshuffling was J. Roland Kinzer, an attorney in his late fifties.

A lifelong resident of the Pennsylvania Dutch county, Kinzer was born and reared on a farm near Terre Hill and educated at Franklin and Marshall College in Lancaster. A conservative Republican, Kinzer was Lancaster County's solicitor for a number of years and had been a delegate to the 1928 national convention that had nominated Herbert Hoover for president. In January 1930, fourteen months after Hoover's election, Kinzer's congressional career was launched at a special election to fill a vacancy caused by the death of veteran Congressman William Walton Griest. Backed by Graybill Diehm's Republican organization in Lancaster County and acceptable to Clark's organization in Chester County, Kinzer had no difficulty securing his party's congressional nomination at the 1932 spring primary. Similarly, he had no trouble getting elected in November even though President Hoover and the Republican Party were losers as the nation turned to FDR and the Democrats for leadership.

Kinzer's opponent that year in both the spring and fall contests was a Princeton-educated farmer from Lampeter Township in Lancaster County named Richard P. McGrann who wanted to ring down the curtain on Prohibition. During the spring primary campaign the Chester County Division of the Women's Organization for National Prohibition Reform carried on an extensive advertising campaign urging people to "Vote for Richard P. McGrann and Help Repeal the 18th Amendment," but the Tenth District was "dry" country and the Lanchester district's Republicans gave Kinzer, a "dry" Lutheran, the nomination. He received 22,000 votes to McGrann's 11,000. During the summer McGrann switched his party allegiance and accepted the Democratic Party's nomination for congressman. In the fall rematch he was again a loser—this time by some 25,000 votes.

GENERAL BUTLER'S CANDIDACY

For the Chester County history buff Kinzer's first vote-getting foray in the Tenth District is of special interest because he was teamed with one of the county's most famous native sons—Smedley Darlington Butler, a candidate for the Republican nomination for United States senator. Never one to leave doubt as to where he stood on an issue, the retired Marine hero told Pennsylvania voters "I am a dry candidate, D-R-Y, and I will run as such." General Butler's opponent was the Republican incumbent James J. Davis whose views on Prohibition angered the Women's Christian Temperance Union and Anti Saloon League. These and other dry organizations endorsed Butler, as did some county Republican organizations such as Clark's in Chester County and Diehm's in Lancaster County, but Senator Davis had the backing of those in control of the Pennsylvania Republican Committee.

Butler made a better showing than his opponent in forty of the state's sixty-seven counties, but Davis won the primary by some 400,000 votes. Big majorities in "wet" Philadelphia and Allegheny counties paved the way for the Davis triumph. Although out of step with a nation tired of the Prohibition laws, Butler's cures for the country's economic ills make interesting reading today. Speaking to several hundred followers at an open-air meeting in Coatesville on a cold and blustery Saturday night in April, Butler sketched economic recovery plans very similar to those employed a year or so later by President Roosevelt.

> "Right now the country is in very serious trouble. I've been in forty-two states and know what I'm talking about. My plan is to build roads, public buildings and veterans' hospitals to make this a better country and furnish employment. We borrow in war times and pay it back later. If an enemy shelled New York we'd go to war at once, depression or no depression. We're in worse trouble today than when in war. But we have resources without limit. Let's have an imaginary war, if necessary, to get things moving."

The old saw that politics makes strange bedfellows was certainly true in the case of Butler and Kinzer. Disappointed and disillusioned with President Hoover and the Republican Party, Butler wired congratulations to Roosevelt after the Democratic Party's national convention and saluted the New York governor's nomination for the presidency as being a "great blessing" for the nation in an hour of desperate need. Kinzer remained loyal to Hoover and spoke on his behalf while politicking about the Tenth District in the summer and fall of 1932.

Congressmen Wolfenden and Kinzer both returned to Washington several weeks after the 1932 election for the second or "lame duck" session of the Seventy-second Congress. Little was accomplished towards relieving the nation's economic ills during this eighty-nine day session that ended on March 3, 1933—the day before Roosevelt's inaugural. It was nevertheless a noteworthy session. As had happened before in other periods of national crisis, there was little those about to assume power could do other than mark time during the long wait between Election Day and Inauguration Day. Fortunately, it was the last time there would be such a lengthy interregnum.

On Feb. 6, 1933, the Twentieth or "Lame Duck" Amendment to the Constitution was ratified. It abolished hold-over short sessions such as the one Wolfenden and Kinzer were attending and called for the convening of newly-elected Congresses on the January 3 following an election, instead of thirteen months later. It also changed the date of presidential inaugurations from March 4 to January 20.

Perhaps realizing the nation's economic problems would demand the full attention of the next Congress, the lawmakers at this "lame duck" session decided to transfer the troublesome question of national prohibition from Washington to the state houses throughout the nation. For decades the liquor question had divided the populace into two classes—wets and drys—and the Eighteenth Amendment, which prohibited the manufacture, sale or transportation of intoxicating liquors, had intensified, rather than mollified, the animosity between the two groups. Almost from the day (Jan. 16, 1920) the Prohibition Amendment went into effect the campaign to have it repealed began, but the wets in Congress always came up short in the votes needed to launch a repeal amendment. But on Feb. 21, 1933, fifteen years and two months after the Sixty-fifth Congress proposed the Prohibition Amendment, the wets finally corralled enough votes to overcome dry resistance, and the House, by a 289 to 121 margin, adopted a Senate resolution proposing repeal of the Eighteenth Amendment. Congressman Wolfenden was among those who supported the resolution that passed on to the states the question of ending national prohibition. Congressman Kinzer was among those who opposed the measure.

Chester County was hard-hit by the Depression, but the front pages of county newspapers did not reflect the hardships experienced by the county's businesses and citizenry during the closing weeks of the Hoover administration. A few articles provided insights into the state of the county's economy on the eve of the New Deal, but as a general rule the newspapers tended to downplay the Depression woes rather than provide their readers with detailed or in-depth coverage of the social-economic problems caused by widespread unemployment. In mid-February when the Chester County Trust Company placed its business in the hands of the Pennsylvania Department of Banking, wiping out the life savings of some of its depositors, the catastrophe was reported in a matter-of-fact way by the *Daily Local News*. There were no boldface headlines or human interest stories describing how the collapse of the local financial institution affected its customers. Nor did the *Local* place a big headline over its March 1 story telling of five truckloads of hunger marchers passing through West Chester enroute to Harrisburg to join in an appeal to the General Assembly for relief. Nor was much coverage given the next day to the decision of the State Emergency Relief Board to allocate $6,203,000 to county boards for relief purposes in March. Chester County's share of this relief handout was a paltry $18,160—but there was no editorial cry of indignation at this pittance.

Almost as if by design, the Depression story seemed to be suppressed. Buried on the inside page of the *Local* on February 17 was an account of the Emergency Relief Council in which it was reported 2,950 county families were being cared for at a cost of approximately $30,500 per month. The account noted "real economy is being practiced." This same story also mentioned "the recent wreck of a coal train at Atglen proved a blessing in disguise" as the coal was "secured for distribution among the needy."

On the eve of Roosevelt's inaugural most everyone hoped the changing of the guard in Washington would result in an upswing in the economy. Politicians of the Democratic faith were especially optimistic, but some were way off the mark in their predictions as to how their new leader would bring about an economic recovery. The *Local's* lead story on February 28 pertained to a speech given by former county party chairman John M. Hemphill to the newly-organized Chester County Democratic Club. Having been his party's gubernatorial nominee in 1930, Hemphill was no run-of-the-mill county politician. He had led the fight in Pennsylvania to repeal the Eighteenth Amendment and knew many of the nation's leading Democrats. But his views on ending the Depression would soon place him at odds with the party's New Dealers. "A return of states rights and a big reduction in the tax load now being born by each taxpayer is necessary before the country can shake off the present depression," Hemphill told his West Chester audience three weeks before FDR took office. The return to the principles of Jeffersonian democracy advocated by Hemphill, however, were not in Roosevelt's game plan.

For the conservative Kinzer most of the solutions to the nation's economic problems offered by the New Dealers were anathema, but with the number of unemployed estimated at about fourteen million the country was ready to try anything. Upon taking office Roosevelt immediately called a special session of Congress and launched an energetic and full-scale frontal attack on the Depression. During his first hundred days, some historians have claimed, more important legislation was produced than during any other time in American history. Congress placed its stamp of approval on a long list of New Deal measures, including the Emergency Banking Act, the National Industrial Recovery Act, the Agricultural Adjustment Act, and the Tennessee Valley Authority Act. Kinzer's opposition to the New Deal was not very loud, but his voting record and performance met with the approval of the Republican leadership back home and he was endorsed for another term.

Kinzer's Democrat opponent in 1934 was Charles T. Carpenter of Glenmoore, who described himself in newspaper advertisements as "A Dairy Farmer Who Knows How Badly The Farmer Is Treated And Has Been Treated By The Republican Organization For Years." A newcomer on the Chester County political scene, Carpenter maintained a winter residence in Philadelphia and had been a Republican until 1928 when he switched his allegiance to the Democrats and campaigned for Al Smith. His effort to unseat Kinzer was for naught. Over 102,000 Tenth District voters went to the polls on

Election Day and Kinzer won by a comfortable 15,500-vote margin. In the governorship race, though, Carpenter's close personal friend George Earle led Pennsylvania's Democrats to their first state house victory since 1890. Commenting on the election, which also saw Democrat Joseph Guffey win a seat in the United States Senate, the *Local* said "Chester County remained loyal to the principles of the Republican Party . . . while other sections of Pennsylvania rolled up majorities for the New Deal." Although a loser in the congressional race, Carpenter soon became one of the county's most influential Democrats. Governor Earle made him a member of the Pennsylvania Milk Control Board and later appointed him to the Pennsylvania Turnpike Commission.

Returning to Washington for the opening session of the Seventy-fourth Congress in January 1935, Kinzer and his Republican colleagues were again greatly outnumbered in the House. They occupied 104 seats; the Democrats 318. The session proved to be a significant and historic one with far-reaching effects. The Works Progress Administration (WPA) was established and both the Wagner Labor Relations and Social Security acts were passed. Although critical of the New Deal and its programs, Kinzer's criticisms received little ink in county newspapers. Never one to seek headlines, his speeches while campaigning were frequently overshadowed by those given by more forceful and dynamic speakers. For example, when the GOP held a big county rally shortly before the 1936 election the *Local* mentioned Kinzer was one of the speakers and succinctly summarized his remarks by reporting that he "emphasized the waste and wantonness of the administration."

Kinzer and the majority of the voters in his Lanchester district did not approve of the New Deal, but most of the nation did. In his second term bid Roosevelt garnered 523 electoral votes from forty-six states while his Republican opponent, Gov. Alfred M. Landon of Kansas, collected only eight from Maine and Vermont. In Chester County the Democratic Party was stronger in 1936 than at any time since the Civil War, but efforts to unseat Kinzer and end Republican dominance once again were for naught. Lancaster County's H. Clay Burkholder made a good showing in the congressional race, but his vote total of 62,768 was 9,413 under Kinzer's.

It was the only time Kinzer's victory margin fell below the 10,000 mark. Still, he fared better than the vast majority of Republicans seeking public office in 1936. Many of his Republican colleagues were Election Day casualties and the following January when the House convened Kinzer could count only eighty-eight other members of his political persuasion on the Republican side of the aisle. As a result of the misfortunes suffered by his former GOP colleagues, Kinzer became the ranking Republican on the Census Committee and his party's second ranking member on the Agricultural Committee.

With such a small group of legislators in the House, and with only seventeen United States senators and a handful of governors, the Republican Party's fortunes hit an abysmal low. Except for the Supreme Court, conservative opposition to the President's programs had been virtually eliminated. Conservatives on the Supreme Court, one of whom was Chester County's Owen J. Roberts, declared one New Deal statute after another unconstitutional during Roosevelt's first term, causing liberals to complain the court was in the grip of hidebound reactionaries who refused to recognize the need for broadening the authority of the federal government. As a consequence when the Seventy-fifth Congress convened the majority leader in the Senate, Joseph Robinson of Arkansas, said he wanted a constitutional amendment giving Congress the power to pass minimum wage, maximum hour, and anti-child labor laws.

President Roosevelt, however, took another approach. In his 1937 state of the union message he said "the vital need is not in alteration to the fundamental law but an increasingly enlightened view with reference to it." He followed this pronouncement with a recommendation that shook Washington and reverberated throughout the land. His proposal for the reorganization of the judicial branch of government became known as Roosevelt's court-packing plan. To change the predominantly conservative structure of the Supreme Court, he sought to appoint one additional judge for each justice over the age of seventy who declined to retire. Six of the nine justices at the time were over seventy and the average age of the court members was seventy-two.

Few proposals (if any) in the 200-year history of Congress have created as much furor as this ill- conceived measure. The judiciary reorganization bill died in committee, but the Supreme Court thinking changed and the argument that nine old men were stifling the nation's economic recovery lost its validity. In five separate cases the Wagner Act was upheld and in another four cases the Social Security Act was upheld. The man responsible for this change was Justice Roberts, who began siding with the more liberal members of the Court to make a majority. In Washington's political folklore he became "the switch in time that saved nine."

By mid-term election time in 1938 the fortunes of the Republican Party were on the upswing. Kinzer was challenged by Democrat Thomas Jefferson McClelland, a retired tax attorney who resided near Unionville. A native of Missouri and onetime federal government employee, McClelland had become a familiar figure in the Chester County political arena during the 1930s, having twice campaigned unsuccessfully for state senator. He was no match for Kinzer. Approximately 123,000 votes were cast for congressman in the Tenth District and Kinzer won with a whopping 35,000 majority. Elsewhere, the returns gave Pennsylvania Republicans reason to celebrate. They recaptured the governorship and returned James J. Davis to the United States Senate.

When Kinzer took his seat in the Seventy-sixth Congress he was pleased to find eighty additional Republicans seated on his side of the House aisle. Unlike previous sessions, though, attention was diverted away from economic problems at home to the troubles in Europe. War broke out in September of 1939 and by campaign time in 1940 the United States was beginning to prepare for its eventual entrance into the conflict. Isolationists, however, were quite vocal at this time and there was a sharp division in public opinion as to what aid should be given to the foes of Nazi Germany. One of the most controversial stands taken by Congressman Kinzer during his long career in Washington occurred several months prior to the 1940 election when he voted against the Selective Training and Service Act.

In Lancaster County strong opposition to the draft was expressed by some religious groups and in mid-August the Pomona Grange of Chester and Delaware counties went on record as being opposed to conscription during peace time. Other groups held another viewpoint and not only Democrats, but some Republicans lambasted Kinzer for his vote against the draft. Speaking to a Chester County audience in mid-September, Gen. Edward C. Shannon, a former lieutenant governor of the Commonwealth and past commander of the Pennsylvania National Guard, called for the Lancaster County congressman's defeat at the polls. "I am a Republican, but I'm telling you to vote against Kinzer," the World War I hero from Phoenixville declared. "I don't have any time for the man who votes against the conscription bill just to win the votes of the plain people." George M. May, the Democratic Party's congressional nominee, also lashed out at Kinzer for his votes on the Selective Service and Neutrality acts, but the majority of voters in the two counties either approved of Kinzer's stance or were willing to overlook his opposition to Roosevelt's military preparedness program. Over 126,000 votes were cast in the district; Kinzer won by almost 20,000.

President Roosevelt won a third term in 1940, bettering Wendell L. Willkie in all but ten of the forty-eight states, but his victory was not of the landslide proportions it had been four years earlier. When the Seventy-seventh Congress convened the Democrats still outnumbered the Republicans by over one hundred, but partisan differences were no longer as pronounced as they had been during the 1930s. The lawmakers were preoccupied with preparations for war. Kinzer joined with the majority of his colleagues in voting for lend-lease in the spring of 1941 and in December, after the Japanese attack on Pearl Harbor, he voted for war.

The wartime elections did not arouse a great amount of interest in Chester and Lancaster counties (now the Ninth Congressional District). Only about 77,000 persons voted in the 1942 election and only about 117,000 participated in the 1944 election. Kinzer won handily both times, defeating Phoenixville's Daniel J. C. O'Donnell in the first of these elections and his old rival from Lancaster County, H. Clay Burkholder, in the second. Kinzer retired as a legislator at the conclusion of the Seventy-ninth Congress and returned to his law practice in Lancaster where he was honored in 1950 on the fiftieth anniversary of his admission to the bar. He died on July 26, 1955, at age eighty-one.

CHAPTER 25

DOWNINGTOWN'S CONGRESSMAN

For the Republican Party 1946 was a vintage year. The midterm congressional elections went against the Democrats and the Republicans scored a victory of landslide proportions, winning control of both the House and Senate for the first time in sixteen years. They also captured a majority of the state governorships. The party's luminaries were many. New York's Gov. Thomas E. Dewey and California's Gov. Earl Warren were re-elected. Irving M. Ives became the first Republican from New York to be elected to the United States Senate in twenty years and in Ohio John W. Bricker, an ex-governor, scored an impressive triumph in his run for Senate. Other Republicans elected to the Senate who would figure prominently in the news in the years to follow were William E. Jenner of Indiana, Henry Cabot Lodge Jr. of Massachusetts, and a thirty-seven-year-old World War II veteran and circuit judge from Appleton, Wisconsin, named Joseph A. McCarthy.

In Pennsylvania the Republican Party also did well in 1946. "Big Jim" Duff moved to the forefront and was elected governor; the state's voters denied Joseph A. Guffey, a New Deal Democrat from Pittsburgh, a third term in the United States Senate, replacing him with Edward Martin, the Commonwealth's outgoing governor; and in the Ninth Congressional District the voters of Chester and Lancaster counties elected Paul Bartram Dague of Downingtown as their representative in the Eightieth Congress.

At the time of his election Dague was Chester County's sheriff. Not since 1808 (when Daniel Hiester was prothonotary and clerk of courts) had a county officeholder jumped directly from the small courthouse political stage in West Chester to the large national political amphitheater in Washington. A lifelong resident of Chester County, Dague was born in the old Thomas farmhouse at Whitford on May 19, 1898. Educated in the Downingtown school system, Dague served with the Marines during World War I and afterwards was employed for a short period by the Pennsylvania Railroad. There was no GI Bill to help veterans obtain an education when Dague was discharged from the Marines. Twice he made an effort to earn a college degree, first at the West Chester Normal School and later at Drexel Institute, but both times he was forced to abandon this pursuit for financial reasons. His political career unknowingly began in 1921 when he went to work for the Pennsylvania Highways Department, one of the Republican Party's main dispensers of patronage jobs. A dedicated and hard-working Republican,

Dague advanced over a period of some twenty-plus years from the bottom to the top of the GOP political ladder in Chester County. During this same time (the 1920s and 1930s) the congenial Dague became one of the county's most popular Legionnaires.

The American Legion, conceived in Paris by a group of military officers in 1919, had a large membership after the war and as an organization wielded great influence in community and national affairs. At the grass roots level Dague was a very active member. A founder of the Charles F. Moran Post in Downingtown, he served as its commander for a time and later was elected to several terms as county commander. Elected vice commander of the Pennsylvania American Legion at its convention in 1934, Dague continued to hold high elected and appointed offices in the American Legion at the state level for many years.

By 1925, the year he married Virginia Williams of Willistown, Dague was an assistant highways superintendent. His American Legion activities along with his work for the Highways Department was rapidly moving the ex-marine to the forefront on the county political stage. His job remained secure during the early days of the Depression, but in 1935 Dague joined the ranks of the unemployed following George Earle's gubernatorial victory and the Democratic Party take-over at Harrisburg. With Republicans in control of the courthouse at West Chester, though, he quickly found new employment. Accepting a deputy sheriff position, Dague continued to work hard for the Republican Party during the lean 1930s. Among his political mentors during this period was Kennett Square's George B. Scarlett, who replaced William Clark as state senator and Republican county chairman in the mid-thirties. Dague was chosen to serve as toastmaster at a testimonial banquet honoring Scarlett in 1936—an early indication of his popularity in the county GOP family. Two years later Scarlett asked deputy sheriff Dague to direct Gifford Pinchot's campaign for the party's gubernatorial nomination in Chester County. It was just one of many chores for the party performed by the future congressman during his long political apprenticeship.

Perhaps due to his long association with the American Legion, Dague was far more vocal in speaking out against Nazi Germany in the late 1930s and early 1940s than was Congressman Kinzer. Addressing a Memorial Day gathering in 1940, when isolationist sentiment was still strong throughout the country, Dague declared "we must give all possible aid to Great Britain if we wish to have the principles of a free people survive." Shortly thereafter when the nation began preparing for war he was called upon to accept a leadership role on the home front. To head up the local civilian defense effort the county commissioners selected Judge W. Butler Windle because of his military background, political connections, and leadership ability. In turn, Judge Windle named Dague as his chief of staff and announced the Chester County Defense Council would be organized along semi-military lines.

Dague's election as sheriff in 1943 was not an exciting event by any stretch of the imagination, coming as it did during the war when most persons regarded courthouse politics as inconsequential. Nevertheless, it was a noteworthy election for several reasons. First, the ticket offered by GOP Chairman Scarlett certainly ranked among the best ever presented by the Republican Party. In addition to Dague the row office nominees included C. Gilbert Hazlett of Kennett Square for register of wills, Miss Marjorie Johnson of Coatesville for prothonotary, J. Martin Kurtz of Honey Brook for recorder of deeds, and Phoenixville's Joseph McKeone for district attorney. Hazlett, who was Scarlett's protege, some years later took over the party helm and served three terms as county commissioner. Miss Johnson's nomination was significant in that it marked the first time the Republican organization endorsed a woman for a major courthouse office. Another unusual feature of this wartime election was the willingness on the part of the Democrats to almost allow it to go by default. They fielded candidates for only three of the five positions, one of whom (West Chester's James McNair) was soundly whipped by Dague. All three incumbent commissioners (Edward Baldwin, Harvey M. Thomas and Herbert E. Crossan) were re-elected, an unusual occurrence. The two Republicans had an easy time of it, but Democrat Crossan had some stiff competition for the minority post from Coatesville's Gladys Fisher, the first woman in either party to run for commissioner.

Dague's career as sheriff was short-lived. When Congressman Kinzer decided to resume the practice of law and escape the political whirlwind of Washington the GOP commanders of Chester and Lancaster Counties—state Senator Scarlett and state Senator Graybill Diehm—agreed Dague should be the Ninth District's next representative. Both senators had a firm grip on the party reins in their respective counties and as a consequence the road from the courthouse in West Chester to the Capitol in Washington was relatively free of obstacles for Dague. He was unopposed at the Republican primary in 1946, which was held just a few days before his forty-eighth birthday. His Democrat opponent in the fall was Edgar Campbell, an insurance man with offices in Philadelphia, and a newcomer to Chester County politics who resided at White Horse Farm, Berwyn. Campbell was not a real challenge in the strongly Republican district, but Dague nevertheless campaigned hard throughout the two counties during the summer and fall months and on election day scored an impressive victory. His two-county vote total was 64,311; Campbell's was 24,175.

It was the first of ten times Dague would be elected to the United States House of Representatives by the voters of the Lanchester district, and always with sizeable majorities in the 30,000 to 64,000 range. Against W. Roger Simpson, a Lancaster County attorney, he polled almost 75,000 votes to win a second term by a two-to-one margin. This was in 1948—the year Harry Truman surprised most everyone by beating Republican Thomas Dewey in the presidential sweepstakes. Next, Dague scored two wins over Philip Ragan, a Willistown Township Democrat, and two wins over Edward G. Wilson, a

Lancaster County Democrat. In his second encounter with Ragan in 1952—the year Dwight D. Eisenhower provided the GOP with its first presidential triumph in twenty-eight years—Dague became the first Chester County congressman to poll more than 100,000 votes. The official vote count gave Dague 100,578 and Ragan 51,268.

Against Wilson in 1954 and James C. N. Paul, a law school professor at the University of Pennsylvania, in 1958—years in which Democrats George Leader and David Lawrence won the Pennsylvania governorship—the vote spread between Dague and his challengers for the Ninth District seat narrowed considerably, but in 1960—the year John F. Kennedy edged out Vice President Richard M. Nixon for the presidency—Dague's vote total hit an all time high of 128,917. His opponent that year was Howard Halsey, an industrial arts teacher at West Chester's Henderson High School. Halsey received 64,659 votes, at that time the most ever recorded by a Democrat congressional candidate.

The last of Dague's Democrat challengers were Richard Keller and John A. O'Brien, both of Lancaster County. With William Scranton heading the GOP ticket for governor, Dague's majority exceeded 58,000 votes in 1962. Two years later this victory margin was cut in half as President Johnson carried both Chester and Lancaster counties enroute to his landslide triumph over the Republican conservative Barry Goldwater. O'Brien polled almost 82,000 votes, establishing a new high for a Democrat in the Lanchester district, but the fact that Dague could win his tenth and final race by almost 30,000 votes in a time of great Republican adversity is testimony to his popularity within the two counties.

In their book, *Congress—The Pennsylvania Dutch Representative,* Edwin D. Eshleman and Robert S. Walker wrote that Dague "became the first man without Lancaster ties to get the endorsement for the Pennsylvania Dutch Seat." Actually, his family roots were in Lancaster County since both his grandfather, William S. Dague, and his father, William J. Dague, were born there. After service with the Union Army, his grandfather returned to Lancaster County and took up farming at Leaman Place. Later, in the early 1880s after he had married and started a family, William S. Dague moved his family to Lionville and then to Whitford. The congressman's father was also a farmer and operated a farm at Whitford for many years. As with nearly all of his predecessors who represented Chester County in the Congress, Dague had a farm background or upbringing.

Dague's move from the relatively quiet and familiar Chester County political environs to Washington's noisy and unfamiliar political whirlpool came during a time of postwar turmoil. Labor unrest and crippling strikes plagued the country during 1946 and most certainly contributed to the voter swing away from the Democrats to the more conservative policies promised by the Republicans. In addition to the many strikes, which made conversion from a wartime to peacetime economy difficult by prolonging the scarcity of consumer goods, some parts of the country experienced food shortages as farmers held back wheat and cattle for higher prices. Price controls, an annoyance since the war's end, became a major issue in 1946, forcing President Truman to reluctantly sign a compromise bill in July reviving limited price controls for another year. Dague and other Republicans running for Congress campaigned on a "Had Enough—Vote Republican" platform, blaming the Truman administration for labor tie-ups, scarcities of consumer goods, and inflation. They also charged Democratic Party officials with graft and corruption as well as being soft on communism. Commenting on his victory on election night, Dague told a reporter the conservative and God-fearing people of the Ninth District were tired of fiscal irresponsibility in Washington and "theories of government which run counter to basic laws of economics and finance."

Dague's arrival in Washington was coincidental with the arrival of two other freshman representatives who thirteen years later would vie for the presidency in one of the nation's closest and most spirited political battles. John F. Kennedy and Richard M. Nixon were the most famous members of Dague's class in the House, but the House membership in January of 1947 also included a number of other lawmakers destined to become world and/or national leaders in the years ahead. On the Democratic side of the aisle were Lyndon B. Johnson and Sam Rayburn of Texas, Montana's Mike Mansfield, Tennessee's Estes Kefauver, and Washington's Henry "Scoop" Jackson. On Dague's side were Philadelphia's Hugh Scott, who shortly would become chairman of the Republican National Committee, New York's Jacob Javitts and Kenneth Keating, Everett M. Dirksen of Illinois, and Charles Halleck of Indiana. Two years later a fourth future president of the United States—Gerald Ford of Michigan—entered the House and became friendly with Chester County's congressman.

The Republicans were in fine shape when Dague entered the Eightieth Congress. With a 245 to 188 majority in the House they elected Joseph Martin of Massachusetts as speaker and were already thinking about next year's election and winning the White House. Dague's picture appeared on the front page of the *Local* on Jan. 3, 1947, under a two-line streamer telling readers "Republicans Take Over Control Of Congress" and "Flood Of Bills To Restrict Labor Unions In The Offing." Four days later the *Local* reported:

> "President Truman and the Republican-controlled Congress headed for a showdown battle over taxes today with other policy conflicts developing rapidly."

The next day the *Local* reported Speaker Martin was predicting the first important measure to be passed by Congress would be a Constitutional amendment limiting presidential tenure to two terms. The battle between Truman and Congress continued throughout 1947 and into the presidential election year, with Truman eventually emerging the winner after taking his case to the people in his memorable "give 'em hell" whistle stop campaign.

One of the most controversial and far-reaching pieces of legislation approved during Dague's early days as a congressman was the Labor Management Relations Act, better known as the Taft Hartley Act. Described by Truman and some Democrats as harshly anti-labor, the bill contained provisions designed to strengthen management's hand in collective bargaining disputes and strikes. Dague voted with the majority (331 to 83) to pass the bill in the House over the president's veto. Another far-reaching decision made during Dague's first term authorized the president to furnish aid to Greece and Turkey to combat communism. Dague voted against the measure, which became known as the Truman Doctrine, explaining later he did so "since the action was taken outside the United Nations and tended to weaken the influence of that body."

Dague, who sometimes described himself as the last of the horse-and-buggy congressmen, served at a time when the nation moved swiftly from one international crisis to another. His vote against the Truman Doctrine and other measures caused some people, particularly his Democrat opponents, to brand him as an isolationist. Philip Ragan, the Malvern documentary film producer who ran against him in the 1950 and 1952 campaigns, was one of the first to tag Dague with an isolationist label. He lashed out at his GOP opponent's voting record, taking him to task for his votes against appropriations for the Voice of America and National Science Foundation, and for being against the Truman Doctrine, the Military Assistance Act, and the Korean Aid Act. He also raked Dague over the coals for suggesting the United States break diplomatic relations with the Soviet Union and for voting against statehood for Alaska and Hawaii.

Responding to the charge that he had an isolationist attitude, Dague said in a letter to the editor of the *Upper Main Line News* that he supported the Marshall Plan, but it was his belief that the United Nations was the only available medium through which "grave international problems can be resolved." He added, however, that in his opinion "the U.N. will never be effective until Russia is expelled from the Community of Nations, thus enabling the peace-loving peoples of the world to unite for the preservation of democracy." This view, it might be noted, was shared by the American Legion's national commander who was advocating a severance of diplomatic relations with Russia.

If Dague's hard line views seem extreme, one must remember the nation had just gotten over one war and had been thrust into another. Among the numerous Cold War crises President Truman and the congressional lawmakers were called upon to deal with during the late 1940s and early 1950s none was of graver concern than the one they faced in June of 1950 when the North Korean communists crossed the 38th Parallel and invaded South Korea. The ensuing war dominated American life during the next two years and led directly to the defeat of the Democrats in 1952. "We support the President wholeheartedly in the war effort," Dague told a *Local* reporter in the early summer of 1950, "but we of the Republican Party reserve the right to point out the cause. The country is in a perilous condition . . . because of the vacillation and uncertainty of the persons in charge of our Government."

The weak foreign policy theme continued in Dague's letters and speeches throughout the Truman years. "Our boys are dying among the rice paddies of Korea," he wrote, "for no other reason than the State Department has been following a program of doing nothing to contain the Communists in the Asiatic area."

Some historians have called the early 1950s the "McCarthy Years." The nation was on the verge of hysteria as the junior senator from Wisconsin made headlines with his charges that government agencies in Washington were riddled with either card-carrying members of the Communist Party or persons sympathetic to the Soviet Union. McCarthy's sensational allegations, the conviction of the State Department's Alger Hiss for perjury, the successful detonation of the atomic bomb by the Soviets, the North Korean invasion, and the triumph of the Chinese communists over the demoralized forces of Chiang Kai-Shek all contributed to the fear and hysteria of the period and re-enforced the "soft-on-communism" shibboleth of right-wing Republicans such as Dague. Although the amiable Ninth District congressman certainly never ranted and raved as McCarthy did during this period of demagoguery and shallow partisanship, Dague's speeches back home in Chester and Lancaster counties did nothing to build up confidence in the State Department or Truman's foreign policy. A partisan from head to foot, Dague followed the party line and was extremely critical of the administration's handling of foreign affairs. Speaking to a local Rotary Club in 1950, he was quoted as saying Washington was "full of security risks" and the country's foreign difficulties started at Yalta where "our delegation included Alger Hiss."

The twenty-fifth national convention of the Republican Party, held at Chicago's International Amphitheatre in early July 1952, featured one of the most spirited contests for the presidential nomination in the party's one hundred year history. Ohio's Sen. Robert A. Taft, longtime leader of the party's conservative wing in Congress and son of the nation's twenty-seventh president, lost out to Gen. Dwight D. Eisenhower, a war hero who had earlier been courted by Democrats in search of a presidential standard-bearer. California's Richard M. Nixon was chosen as Eisenhower's running mate for the vice presidency. Commenting on the GOP ticket shortly after the convention, Dague told the *Local*:

> "General Eisenhower has proven qualifications as an administrator and is basically a conservative, as I am. I know Senator Nixon personally, and can say without equivocation that he is an able young man and will do a good job. The only thing we have to worry about are the party factions, but it was a good omen for unity

> when Eisenhower and Taft got together immediately after the nomination was assured."

The Eisenhower-Nixon ticket was heralded as being a progressive one by Republicans. As always, Dague took a very active part in the 1952 campaign, speaking at numerous meetings and political functions on behalf of not just his own candidacy, but the entire GOP ticket. His Democrat opponent, Philip Ragan, found it hard to believe Dague could run on a "progressive" platform, charging that his opponent's voting record was far from progressive. Ragan branded Dague as "the greatest spendthrift in the history of Chester County." The charges by the Democratic challenger had little effect; Dague was elected to a fourth term, winning in the Ninth District by a two-to-one margin. Eisenhower's triumph was also decisive; he captured the electoral votes of all but nine states in his landslide win over Adlai Stevenson and helped the Republicans win a majority of the races for the House of Representatives.

With their 221 to 213 majority, Dague and his Republican colleagues again took control of the House and again elected Joseph Martin of Massachusetts as speaker of the Eighty-third Congress. It was the second and last time during his twenty years in the Congress that Dague would serve in a Republican-controlled House. Although he continued to be a strong party man and a loyal supporter of the president during the eight-year Eisenhower era, Dague's voting record continued to be a conservative one. He opposed legislation authorizing Canada and the United States to jointly construct the St. Lawrence Seaway—a project endorsed by Eisenhower and a majority of the House's Republican and Democrat lawmakers. Another key vote during the Eighty-third Congress was on the Eisenhower Administration's Housing and Redevelopment Bill—a measure attacked from both the left and right and finally rejected by thirty-five House votes, one of which was Dague's. His conservative viewpoint was also reflected in votes against school construction assistance and a 1954 bill to revise and extend unemployment compensation.

Throughout the Truman and Eisenhower years the question of granting statehood to Alaska and Hawaii was debated by House and Senate legislators on numerous occasions. Here too, Dague maintained a consistent record of opposition to their joining the Union. In 1958, when this writer raised a question in his *Coatesville Record* column as to why Dague opposed Alaska statehood, the Ninth District congressman quickly responded with a letter stating:

> "My opposition is based primarily on the firm conviction that areas remote from the continental limits of the United States should never be admitted to the Federal Union. Aside from that, I do not believe Alaska is ready for statehood since only about one-half of her 200-odd thousand residents are bona fide citizens. The fact that she would be given representation equivalent to that of the 435 thousand people in Pennsylvania's Ninth District in the House, or of the ten million in the Senate is one more objection,

although probably only academic. A personal reason, but one that motivated much of the opposition in the House, stems from the fact that Alaska's lone representative would replace a Congressman representing an established district, since the House membership is fixed by statute at a total not to exceed 435."

Congressman Dague continued to do well at the polls in conservative Chester and Lancaster counties during the late 1950s and early 1960s, but these years were not good ones for the Republican Party's congressional candidates in many parts of the country. After the Soviets launched their Sputnik—the first man-made satellite—there was a weakening in the confidence of the Eisenhower administration's defense and space program. The Democrats were able to capitalize on these issues, miscellaneous Republican shortcomings, and a recession in 1958 to score their most sweeping victory since the New Deal era. When the Eighty-sixth Congress convened they held a 282 to 154 majority.

Some observers regard John F. Kennedy's victory in the 1960 presidential sweepstakes as a turning point in the nation's history. The triumph of the young and charismatic senator from Massachusetts over then Vice President Nixon was certainly one of the most exciting and fascinating chapters in the nation's political history. Although the vote spread, both popular and electoral, between the Democrat winner and Republican loser was extremely thin nationwide, this was not the case in Dague's Ninth Congressional District. Here, Kennedy and his Texan running-mate Lyndon B. Johnson did not fare well. Nixon carried Chester County with a healthy 23,000 vote plurality and did even better in Lancaster County where he won by over 45,000 votes. Dague won in the district by a similar margin over Democrat Howard Halsey and returned to Washington in 1961 to begin the third and final phase of his long legislative career. As had been the case during his first six years as a representative, the executive branch of government was controlled by the Democrats during Dague's final six years. As had been the case during Truman's "Fair Deal" days, Dague's conservative political philosophy made it difficult for him to go along with the "New Frontier" and "Great Society" programs advocated by Kennedy and Johnson. More often than not he was recorded as being against administration bills such as the Housing Act of 1961 and the Economic Opportunities Act of 1964.

Dague was both lauded and lambasted for his voting record during the Kennedy-Johnson years. His critics said he was out of step with the times. His general opposition to expansion of the federal bureaucracy and his conservative approach on fiscal matters, however, won for him praise from the Americans for Constitutional Action. It conferred upon him a distinguished service award in 1961 for his voting record on issues bearing upon the integrity of the Constitution of the United States. It also endorsed him for re-election, stating "an analysis of Dague's voting record reveals that he consistently voted for sound money, private competitive market, local self-government, private ownership, individual liberty, safe-guarding the God-given dignity of the individual, and against appeasement of the Communists and a socialized economy through centralization of power in a mammoth bureaucratic government."

The Supreme Court decisions of the 1950s outlawing various forms of segregation touched off numerous demonstrations throughout the country, and as a consequence Congress was preoccupied with the question of civil rights during much of the time Dague served in Washington. He supported both the Civil Rights Act of 1957, which provided for the creation of an executive commission on civil rights, and the Civil Rights Act of 1960, which made obstruction of court orders for school desegregation a crime. His stance here remained the same during the Johnson administration when he voted for the Civil Rights Act of 1964—one of the most far-reaching pieces of legislation ever approved by Congress. It not only guaranteed blacks voting rights in every state on the same qualifications as whites, but prohibited discrimination in places of public accommodation and established an Equal Employment Opportunity Commission at the national level to see that neither unions nor employers discriminated in jobs because of color. In discussing his vote later, Dague said, "I voted for civil rights on the single premise that no one should be denied the rights to which I am entitled as a white man."

He also voted for the Medicare bill the following year, again placing him in concert with his more liberal colleagues in the House. In explaining his vote, Dague said that to reject it would have penalized people who need help the most.

County newspapers had nothing but good to say about Dague when he announced his decision not to seek re- election in 1966. The *Coatesville Record* wrote:

> "The Chester County political scene won't be the same without Congressman Paul B. Dague in the running. . . . He was a 365-day a year campaigner. He made himself available to the public and eagerly listened to opinions and problems. Rarely did he receive a letter from a constituent that he did not offer an immediate answer—not a week or two, but often the day it was received. . . . Paul Dague did not beat around the bush. He was straight forward. He was and still is a conservative, and a man who displays patriotism no matter where he is. . . . He has few equals as a speaker—one who packs plenty of humor and one who can get across a serious message whether it be at a Memorial Day service, Flag Day program, political rally, firemen's parade, testimonial dinner, school assembly or a post office dedication. . . . He mingles with the people year 'round. . . . He is not like the candidate who makes his appearance when he wants something. This is the difference between the politician with his constituents

> at heart and the man who is campaigning with only himself in mind."

The *Local* described Dague as "an effective and responsible congressman" who listened to his constituents yet "never lost the larger vision where his country was concerned." In a February 16 editorial, it said:

> "Rep. Dague has stood on a platform which is opposed to astronomical spending for programs which he feels are not essential to the nation's best interests; he has opposed piling up of the national debt to a point where even our best economists wonder where we are going to get off, and finally, he has opposed all moves which tend to undermine the soundness of the American dollar."

Over the years many organizations honored Dague with testimonial dinners. His home town Chamber of Commerce named him "Downingtown's Man of the Year" in 1963. His retirement spawned many more testimonial tributes. Among the organizations that honored him were the Fraternal Order of Police, the American Legion, and the Chester and Lancaster County Farmers' Associations. Several years after his retirement—in May of 1971—a county office building at New and Market streets in West Chester was named in his honor. Downingtown's much-respected and well-liked congressman died on Dec. 2, 1974, at age seventy-six.

CHAPTER 26

A NEW CONGRESSIONAL DISTRICT

Had it not been for a 1964 ruling of the United States Supreme Court on an apportionment dispute in Georgia it is unlikely G. Robert Watkins—a Delaware Countian—would have ever represented the citizenry of Chester County in Congress. Chester and Lancaster counties remained glued together in the Ninth Congressional District under the Pennsylvania redistricting plan first approved by the General Assembly following the 1960 census. Population imbalance among congressional districts had been overlooked in years past, but during the early 1960s the Supreme Court rendered new interpretations of the Constitution insofar as the protection of individual rights were concerned. In the area of congressional and state legislature apportionment the justices handed down a series of landmark decisions, and in one of these, Wesberry v. Sanders, it was decreed congressional districts must be as equal as practicable in population. The "one man, one vote" standard set forth in this Georgia case ruling was soon felt in many other states, including Pennsylvania.

In addition to the baby boom that occurred throughout the United States after World War II, there were dramatic shifts in the nation's population from the industrialized North to the Sun Belt states. This growth and movement resulted in significant changes in the distribution of the 435 seats in the federal House of Representatives. California and Florida were the big winners following the 1960 census; together they gained a dozen seats in the House. Pennsylvania was the biggest loser; the size of its House delegation was reduced from thirty to twenty-seven.

Redistricting is always a politically sensitive issue, one that lawmakers handle with kid gloves, and the state's legislators were reluctant in 1962 to make any more changes than were absolutely necessary. Philadelphia lost one of its six congressional seats and there was some shifting of counties from one district to another as new lines were drawn to divide the Commonwealth into twenty-seven districts. Philadelphia's suburban counties continued to be underrepresented. In drawing the new congressional map, the political cartographers in Harrisburg did not violate county lines; no county was broken up and spread over two or more congressional districts. As a result the twenty-seven districts were very unequal in size. At the two extremes were the Seventh District (Delaware County) with a population of 553,000 and the Fifteenth District in the Poconos (Carbon, Monroe, Northhampton and Pike counties) with a population of 303,000.

Congressman Paul B. Dague's Ninth District was the fifth largest of the Pennsylvania districts with a population of almost 489,000. Since its creation in 1932 it had sent just two men—Lancaster County's J. Roland Kinzer and Chester County's Dague—to the House of Representatives. Over the years the Republican leaders of the two counties had developed a close working relationship and even though their citizens were underrepresented they voiced no complaints concerning the apportionment made by the state legislators. As a result of the Wesberry-Sanders decision, though, the Lanchester marriage became unglued. Responding to Supreme Court pressure, some states began to realign district boundaries to implement the "one man, one vote" standard. Pennsylvania was one of these states. Under a new apportionment approved March 8, 1966, Chester County was divorced from Lancaster County and combined with the City of Chester and twenty-one other Delaware County municipalities to form a new Ninth Congressional District.

The reapportionment caught Republican and Democrat politicians in both counties by surprise. Early in the 1966 political season (February 14) Congressman Dague announced his retirement plans. Since no one expected the dissolution of the Lanchester district it was politics as usual during the month of February. The day after Dague's announcement county newspapers carried stories of Louis F. Waldmann's intention to seek the Democratic Party nomination for congressman. A key figure in county politics for a number of years, Waldmann was in his mid-thirties and resided near Glenmoore. A graduate of a high school and college in Lake Forest, Illinois, he had been transferred to Downingtown as district manager of the Pressed Steel Tank Company, a Milwaukee-based firm. In the Republican camp Edwin D. Eshleman, a state representative from Lancaster, quickly gained the inside track for his party's nomination for the seat in Congress being vacated by Dague. Following endorsement by the party organization of Lancaster County, Eshleman was given a similar endorsement on March 3 by the Republican Committee of Chester County at a meeting held at the Covered Wagon Inn in Strafford.

However, when the new redistricting plan was announced several days later Theodore Rubino's Chester County Republican organization was without a candidate and Eshleman found himself residing in a new Sixteenth Congressional District comprised of Lancaster and Lebanon counties, plus several Dauphin County municipalities. Just over the Chester County line in one of the Delaware County municipalities (Birmingham Township) of the new Ninth District the incumbent congressman from the old Seventh District, G. Robert Watkins, made his home.

Watkins wanted to return to Congress. There were those who felt a Chester Countian should occupy the new Ninth District seat in the House of Representatives, but Republican Party leaders felt otherwise and at a meeting of Chester County's GOP executive committee on March 11 an endorsement was given to the Delaware County congressman. Watkins, who two years earlier had been elected to the Eighty-ninth Congress, was a familiar figure on the political stage in Delaware County where he had served as both sheriff and county commissioner before being elected three times to the Pennsylvania Senate. A native of Virginia, he learned the trade of a ship fitter as a young man in Newport News, Virginia, and afterwards organized and headed the Chester Stevedoring Company. In 1932, at the age of thirty, he and a partner organized the Blue Line Transfer Company.

Endorsement of Congressman Watkins by the Republican establishment in Chester and Delaware counties did not frighten off other would-be congressmen. There was considerable interest in the nomination on the GOP side where four hats—two from Chester County and two from Delaware County—were tossed into the ring with Watkin's. They belonged to Dr. Charles H. Butler, a Coatesville physician and a prominent leader in the National Association for the Advancement of Colored People, Elwood Webster of Pocopson Township, and Delaware countians Harold Bram and Edwin E. Colletta.

As might be expected, not everyone was pleased with the turn of events that occurred during early March. Alexander C. Kovach, chairman of the Chester County Democratic Committee, called the new apportionment unfair and inequitable. Newspaper stories indicated he and other Democrats in the suburban counties were considering legal action to set aside the new districts. The redistricting, however, did not alter Waldmann's plans to make a run for Dague's seat in the House.

One of the issues that received some attention during the spring campaign was the war in Vietnam. Congressman Watkins was critical of President Johnson's war policy and was quoted as saying "we ought to get out of this war if we can find a way." Candidate Colletta called for a "more rapid escalation" of the war effort, saying "we must provide military and educational assistance to freedom-loving people of the world who are resisting Communist takeover." Democrat Waldmann said he would not endorse the withdrawal of United States troops under any circumstances and that he supported the administration's efforts to secure a reasonable and honorable peace.

Issues, however, were not the deciding factor when it came to deciding the nominations. The Democrats gave their nomination to Waldmann and the Republican organization in Chester County turned in a big vote for Watkins even though Pocopson Township's Webster felt the Ninth District congressman should be a Chester Countian. "Is our Chester County so poor in 'Timber' that we have to go to Delaware County and endorse a machine-made man to represent us—Chester County?" he asked in his political advertisements.

Overshadowing the congressional nomination contests in the spring of

1966 was the battle for the Democratic Party gubernatorial nomination. Milton Shapp scored a stunning two-to-one victory over state Sen. Robert P. Casey, the organization-backed candidate. Next, he defeated Lt. Gov. Raymond P. Shafer, the Republican nominee, at the general election in November.

Congressman Watkins had no difficulty winning in the new Ninth District. He polled 81,516 votes; Waldmann finished far behind with 48,656. Two years later he was re-elected, defeating Democrat Philip L. Harding of Chester. But in 1970, after having initially said he wasn't interested in another term, Watkins ran into some Republican opposition in Chester County when he changed his mind and said he wanted to return to Washington. County Commissioner J. Carl Empie in announcing his candidacy for Watkin's seat in the Congress told the *Daily Local News* Chester County had been "both patient and courteous in cooperating with Delaware County" to permit the incumbent to accumulate time enough to be eligible for a congressional pension. About the same time Empie tossed his hat in the ring Russell B. Jones, a former county commissioner and onetime president of the county Association of Township Supervisors, announced he was also interested in the GOP congressional nomination. At an area GOP meeting in mid-February thirty-two committee people from West Chester and surrounding townships gave Jones their endorsement.

Shortly thereafter, however, at a Sunday night meeting of Rubino's Republican executive committee held at the 1796 House in Downingtown, Watkins was endorsed for another term. Both Empie and Jones accepted the executive committee's decision and retired to the sidelines. Another candidate, Anthony Z. Giampietro, then made a bid for the Republican nomination, but he was brushed aside at the primary by incumbent Watkins. On the Democratic side there was also a little excitement as Waldmann, now a county commissioner, and Manfred Mueller vied for their party's nomination. Waldmann emerged the winner.

The primary race against Giampietro was the last election race in the long political career of G. Robert Watkins. He died of a heart attack on Aug. 8, 1970.

CHAPTER 27

REPUBLICANS PICK WARE

Republican conferees from Chester and Delaware counties met at the Penn Oaks Country Club in late August of 1970 and chose John H. Ware III of Oxford to replace the late G. Robert Watkins as their nominee for the United States House of Representatives from Pennsylvania's Ninth Congressional District. A state legislator in his early sixties with almost ten years experience on Harrisburg's capitol hill, Ware was subsequently elected to serve the balance of Watkins' unexpired term in the Ninety-first Congress as well as a full two-year term in the Ninety-second Congress.

It was not the first time the Oxford businessman had been picked to fill a ballot slot after the death of a nominee chosen in the Republican primary. Ten years earlier during the summer of 1960 a similar situation had arisen when state Senator Thomas Harney died after being nominated for a third term. Ware was selected as the replacement nominee and elected. His financial contributions and work for the party behind the scenes had long been appreciated by county GOP chieftain C. Gilbert "Jim" Hazlett and other party bigwigs, but at the time of his nomination for state senator the highest public office he had been elected to was that of burgess in his home town of Oxford, a small municipality of some 3,300 persons in the southwestern corner of Chester County. He was widely known then as a civic leader, not as a major domo in the Republican Party.

Forgotten by 1960 voters and most political observers was Ware's entry into the county's political arena in 1936, just six years after his graduation from the Wharton School of the University of Pennsylvania. On that occasion he had sought the Republican nomination for state representative from the First District, an election area comprised of forty-three precincts stretching from Coatesville west to the Lancaster County line and south from the steel city to the Mason-Dixon line. His political debut came at a most inopportune time; the Republican Party was divided. On the one side were party regulars friendly to state Senator William Clark, the party's county chairman who had been convicted of malfeasance and extortion; on the other side were Clark's enemies and independents who called themselves anti-Clark Republicans. Each side entered a slate of candidates at the primary. Ware was the organization's candidate; his opponent was Raymond Webster, a Coatesville school teacher. Overshadowed by other contests, the Ware versus Webster battle nevertheless provided both suspense and excitement at election night headquarters as the returns were tabulated. The young Oxford bachelor did well (620 to 148) in his home town, but Webster scored better (1,775 to 556) in his Coatesville bailiwick. When all the returns were in and counted Webster was the victor by fewer than 200 votes, the final tally being 3,257 to 3,061 in his favor.

In addition to his youth (he was only twenty-eight), Ware had two other things working against him in his first election try. To begin with his opponent, a World War I veteran active in the American Legion, was well-known and well-liked. Additionally, the Republican organization had been besmirched as a result of Clark's trial and Ware's friendship with the GOP chieftain was misunderstood by some voters. After stubbing his toe, Ware put aside thoughts of becoming a legislator and channeled his talents and efforts elsewhere. Twenty-four years later, in a *Daily Local News* account telling how the Oxford burgess was nominated for state senator by garnering 207 of 268 county committee votes, reporter and longtime political observer Hugh V. "Butch" McDevitt succinctly described Ware as a "veteran party worker, an industrialist, utilities company executive, newspaper publisher, and community-spirited county resident."

In the business world, Ware had followed in the footsteps of his father—a self-made man who had become a millionaire at age thirty-six heading the American Water Works Company, the largest waterworks system in the nation. Like his father, Ware was first and foremost a utility executive. He was chairman of the board of American Water Works for twenty-three years and was connected with the natural gas industry for over sixty years. During the administrations of both presidents Truman and Eisenhower he was a member of the Gas Industry Advisory Council. In 1960 when he entered politics on a fulltime basis Ware was president of Penn Fuel Gas, Inc., but when asked about his occupation his modest reply was usually that he was "in the gas and water business." He was also publisher of the *Oxford Press*, to mention just one of his numerous other business involvements, and a trustee on a number of college and university boards.

Born in Vineland, New Jersey, Ware was twelve when his family moved to Oxford. It was here as a youth that he became interested in scouting and attained the coveted Eagle rank. This interest in scouting continued throughout his adult life and in 1947 he received the Silver Antelope Award, one of the highest honors scouting bestows on its leaders. An active Rotarian and lay leader in the Presbyterian Church, he also served as chairman of the Coatesville YMCA and was associated with numerous other civic and charitable organizations. Undoubtedly, these outside activities over many years prepared him well for the political life he was to lead during the 1960s and 1970s as a state senator and congressman.

Married for twenty years, and the father of four children, the personable pipe-smoking Ware received the overwhelming support of the county's committeemen and committeewomen when picked as the party's replacement nominee for state senator in 1960. But the late summer politicking that preceded the Republican gathering at the Elks Club in West Chester is worthy of note since a number of prominent party members actively sought, or were considered for, the nomination. One of these was Monroe Nute, the Kennett Square automobile dealer and past president of Lions International who would later become a county commissioner. Nute at the time was heading the Nixon for President Club of Chester County. Another aspirant for the senatorial post was Whitney R. Kerchner, an executive of the Firestone Tire and Rubber Company in Pottstown. He resided in North Coventry Township and was a member of the party's thirty-seven member executive committee. Some committee people from the Upper Main Line area were backing Robert DiSerafino, a Tredyffrin Township justice of the peace who would later become county controller. Still another hat in the ring belonged to William C. Brown of New London Township. He had served as Secretary of Welfare for the Commonwealth under governors Duff and Fine. Other names mentioned were G. O. Carlson, a prominent steel manufacturer and state committeeman from Caln Township; Benjamin Reynolds, a New Garden Township supervisor who would later become a state representative; William Ashton, a member of the Pennsylvania House of Representatives; and West Chester attorneys Philip Reilly and Morris Moore.

The behind-the-scenes campaigning that culminated in a victory for Ware just days before his fifty-second birthday was beneficial for it brought him in contact with the rank and file of the organization—the workers who would continue to loyally support him throughout his political career. The publicity given to the wild scramble for the nomination was also helpful. Two years earlier Republican Chairman Hazlett had proposed Ware as a "favorite son" candidate for governor at a meeting of GOP leaders held at the Warwick Hotel in Philadelphia. At that time Hazlett told reporters he thought Ware would make an excellent governor, but admitted his Oxford friend could not be considered as a serious candidate because he was not well known throughout the state.

By most accounts Ware's career as a lawmaker was a creditable one at both Harrisburg and Washington even though he is not remembered for introducing or advancing any particular legislation. Winning elections was no problem, thanks to the large Republican registration advantage. But beyond this, Ware's congenial and down-to-earth manner made him a popular personage among Republicans from all walks of life. He won by handsome pluralities all four times he was a candidate for state senator. In his first time out he defeated Democrat Francis Wampler by more than 22,000 votes. Four years later (1964) Ware survived the Democratic landslide (Chester County gave Lyndon Johnson a plurality of 7,000 votes) and turned back a strong effort on the part of West Chester attorney William D. Mitman. Along with other state senators elected that year, he was forced to run again in 1966 after the Pennsylvania Supreme Court invalidated the state's legislative districting and came up with a new apportionment plan. Opposed again by Democrat Mitman, he breezed to victory with a 22,000 vote plurality. Two years later, in his final run for the Senate, he defeated Democrat challenger Fred T. Cadmus III by a comfortable 15,000 vote margin.

Ware earned good grades as a hard working and conscientious senator serving on committees concerned with agriculture, banking, labor, industry, corporations, judiciary, and law and order. He also served with distinction on the Task Force on Modernization of State Government and was chosen by his Senate colleagues as the Republican caucus chairman. His nomination for congressman from the Ninth District by ninety conferees from Chester and Delaware counties took place on Aug. 28, 1970, the day before his sixty-second birthday. It occurred during the early period of Theodore S. A. Rubino's reign as chairman of both the Republican Committee and Board of Commissioners of Chester County and before the start of the long "organization-independent" fight within the GOP ranks. Two by-products of the nomination are noteworthy; John Stauffer of Phoenixville was chosen to succeed Ware as state senator and Richard Schulze of Tredyffrin Township was selected as Stauffer's replacement for state representative from the 157th legislative district.

Ware, Stauffer and Schulze were all elected in 1970 and in ensuing years assumed prominent places on the county political stage, but there was little cause for rejoicing at Republican headquarters in West Chester on election night. Despite the party's tremendous registration advantage (80,235 to 28,746) in the county, Republican gubernatorial nominee Raymond J. Broderick was unable to stretch his plurality to 5,000 votes. His Democrat opponent Milton Shapp polled over 35,000 votes in the GOP citadel of Chester County and won statewide by more than half a million votes. Additionally, the Democrats gained control of the Pennsylvania Senate and retained control of the House, picking up six additional seats—one a Chester County seat captured by Samuel Morris. When he defeated Coatesville's C. Timothy Slack in the 155th district Morris became the first county Democrat elected to the General Assembly in sixty years. Ware himself had no trouble defeating Louis F. Waldmann who at the time was perhaps the most flamboyant and most publicized Democrat in Chester County. Having won election three years earlier as the minority county commissioner, Waldmann made headlines on a regular basis as he debated Commissioner Rubino on a wide range of issues ranging from the environment to assessments. The publicity gained from these commissioner meeting diatribes was not enough, however, to advance Waldmann from the political minor league in West Chester to the big league in Washington. Ware carried the Ninth District with 76,535 votes; Waldmann received 52,852.

Ware arrived on the Washington scene as a freshman congressman at the midpoint of Richard Nixon's first term in the White House. The vacillating and quarrelsome Ninety-first Congress was controlled by the Democrats and there was considerable friction between the legislative and executive branches of government. When the new Congress convened the Democrats continued to be in command, outnumbering Republicans in the House, 254 to 179, and in the Senate, 54 to 44. Carl Albert of Oklahoma was speaker of the House, Gerald Ford of Michigan was the minority floor leader, and Thomas "Tip" O'Neill of Massachusetts was the majority whip.

The involvement of the United States in the Vietnam War was entering its second decade in 1971 as the Ninety-second Congress began its deliberations and the nation was divided over whether its boys should be fighting there. In the spring some 200,000 protesters massed peacefully at the capital and called for a complete withdrawal from Vietnam. More than 540,000 Americans had been stationed in Vietnam when Nixon took office. Since then the number of ground combat forces had been decreasing steadily, but many persons felt the withdrawal was not fast enough. Ware supported the president's withdrawal policy of bringing home American soldiers while at the same time training and equipping the South Vietnamese to do their own fighting. "It's easy to get into a war," Ware told reporters, "but more difficult to get out and still maintain our bargaining power in NATO, the Middle East, and other trouble spots."

Nixon dominated the world news in 1971 and was selected "Man of the Year" by *Time* magazine. In the federal legislature the congressman from Oxford was one of the president's most loyal supporters. *Congressional Quarterly* credited him with supporting administration programs ninety-three percent of the time on eighty-eight key issues. It was the highest rating achieved by any congressman. In appreciation for this support President and Mrs. Nixon invited Ware and his wife to the White House for dinner in the spring of 1972.

During his congressional stay Ware served on the House Administration Committee, which had jurisdiction over the "housekeeping" functions of Congress, and the Committee on Interstate and Foreign Commerce. He also took a keen interest in natural resources and environmental matters. On more than one occasion while speaking before county groups he warned of a potential energy crisis, saying that supplies of oil and natural gas were becoming seriously depleted. His warnings were prophetic; within a few years Americans were experiencing long lines at the gas pumps.

From the outset of Ware's career as a congressman there was concern among Republican politicians as to whether he would be gerrymandered out of his seat at the next election. It was general knowledge the Ninth District (all of Chester County and parts of western Delaware County) would be obliterated by reapportionment, but just how the Harrisburg lawmakers would realign Pennsylvania's congressional districts was a big question mark. Because the state's percentage of the national population had declined during the previous decade the number of seats allotted to Pennsylvania in the federal House had to be cut from 27 to 25. Under the "one-man, one-vote" principle, the optimum population size for a congressional district in the Keystone State was 451,756. Ninth in the county standings, Chester County with a population of 277,746 fell far short of this mark. Consequently, there was a real fear the legislature, dominated by Democrats, might carve the county in such a manner that it would be virtually impossible for a Republican from Chester County to be elected to Congress.

The year 1972 commenced on an uncertain note insofar as the upcoming election was concerned. The deadline for resolving the apportionment problem was January 25, but the lawmakers were still without a solution as the new year began. Rumors were rife as to how Chester County's Ware would be affected by the wheeling and dealing in Harrisburg. The newspapers reported Congressman Ware and his Republican friend from Lancaster County, Congressman Edwin D. Eshleman, were on a collision course and one or the other would lose his seat in the Ninety-third Congress. These reports had it that Chester County was being carved in such a way that it would have municipalities in three different congressional districts, one of which contained the residences of both Ware and Eshleman. Fortunately, this plan was scrapped and the one ultimately adopted assured the county of real representation and erased fears that its townships and boroughs would become just appendages to its larger neighbors—Montgomery, Delaware and Lancaster counties. Forty-five of Chester County's municipalities, including Ware's Oxford hometown, were placed in the new Fifth District; the remaining municipalities were assigned to the new Sixteenth District, which included all of Lancaster County and parts of Lebanon County. Ware's new district stretched into Montgomery County, embracing thirty-two townships and boroughs, and into Delaware County, taking in eleven political subdivisions.

With the redistricting problem out of the way the politicking began in earnest. Incumbents Ware and Eshleman enjoyed party organization support and were heavy favorites in 1972, but both faced opposition at the polls. Challenging Ware for the GOP nomination were Boyd Miller, a thirty-seven-year-old environmental engineer from Birmingham Township, and Charles C. Holt III, a thirty-five-year-old educator turned businessman from Radnor. Although Ware was never in trouble, his opponents kept him busy on the hustings proving his age (sixty-three) was no handicap and that he could speak out on the issues. The so-called independent movement was beginning to crystallize in the county at this time, but Ware was not targeted for removal by the independent leaders interested primarily in ousting Ted Rubino from the party helm and winning control of the courthouse. Consequently, the anti-Rubino approach used by Miller to discredit Ware was ineffectual. Acknowledging the county chairman was his friend and that "the machine" was an issue in the campaign, Ware told a reporter for *Today's Post* he preferred "to work from within, rather than outside." He explained "people are never against their own organization, but the organization in power somehow becomes a machine and then they're against it." Ware's other primary rival, the well-to-do Holt, conducted an advertising blitz that created the illusion the race might be close, but when the returns were in Ware's victory was a decisive one. On the Democrat side there was also a contest for the Fifth District congressional nomination. It was won by Pottstown's Mayor Brower B. Yerger, who turned back a challenge from East Goshen Township's John Franco. In the fall showdown, though, the Pottstown mayor was no match for Congressman Ware. Besides, it was a Republican year; President Nixon won in forty-nine states, burying Democrat George McGovern under an avalanche of votes. Yerger was crushed in this GOP landslide. Ware polled 121,346 votes in the Fifth District to Yerger's 66,329.

On election night Ware told newsmen he was "looking forward to returning to Washington where we still have two-thirds of the Nixon program to get through." As things turned out, though, the Nixon program was put on a sidetrack and Ware experienced firsthand what President Gerald R. Ford later described as "our long national nightmare." Without question, the Oxford congressman's final two years in the House were both eventful and historic, but they were also unpleasant and painful ones. The trial of the seven Watergate defendants began on Jan. 8, 1973, a few days after the convening of the Ninety-third Congress. By March the Watergate incident—which started out as a bumbling burglary at the Democratic Party's national headquarters and ended up as a tragic and unsuccessful attempt to subvert the Constitution—was a major news story. Two of President Nixon's top aides—John Ehrlichman and H. R. Haldeman, resigned on April 30. Then came the Senate hearings on Watergate.

At the same time the inquiry was being made into the White House's involvement in the break-in at the Democratic Party headquarters the vice president of the United States was under investigation for charges of conspiracy, extortion and bribery. It was alleged that Spiro T. Agnew accepted payoffs while serving as Baltimore County's chief executive officer and governor of Maryland. On Oct. 10, 1973, Agnew resigned as vice president. Several weeks later, on December 6, Congressman Ford became vice president. Elected to Congress in 1948—two years after Chester County's Paul Dague became a congressman—Ford had become the House minority leader in 1965 and had served as the permanent chairman at both the 1968 and 1972 Republican Party national conventions.

The Watergate saga stretched into 1974, culminating in August with Nixon's resignation and Ford's becoming the nation's thirty-eighth president. The resignation of Nixon came after the House Judiciary Committee voted to approve Article I of a proposed two-count bill of impeachment—the first offered against any president since Andrew Johnson was brought to trial over a hundred years earlier. As the nation watched the televised proceedings of the committee, Ware made very few public comments other than to say the bulk of the mail pouring into his office from the Fifth District was supportive of the president and against impeachment.

Later, on December 19, just a few days before Ware concluded his congressional career, former New York Governor Nelson Rockefeller took the oath of office as vice president. For the first time in its history the nation had a president and a vice president chosen under the Twenty-fifth Amendment to the Constitution rather than by a national election. Although he had been eyewitness to perhaps the nation's most publicized political drama, the experience during his last term had not been a pleasant one for Ware and he was glad to leave Washington and take up life again as a private citizen in Oxford.

Ware was not actively engaged in electioneering during his final year in office. On Jan. 16, 1974, he issued a statement saying he had decided against seeking another term. This decision, he said, was made because he felt he could better serve society as a private citizen rather than as a public official. He explained:

> "I have found that interest in community, church and social causes is misconstrued by some as an effort to curry favor with the electorate, particularly if they are unaware that I was so engaged long before I held public office."

Throughout the 1970s and much of the 1980s Ware continued to take an active interest in Republican Party affairs and served on a number of campaign committees. The Chester County Historical Society was one of his many outside interests and in 1976 he became president of its board of directors.

CHAPTER 28

SCHULZE BECOMES CONGRESSMAN

With the exception of a few short tranquil interludes the story of the Republican Party in Chester County during the twentieth century has been one of almost constant feuding between party regulars and anti-organization dissidents or independents. More often than not these intraparty fights were over jobs and control of the courthouse rather than important issues. Some were squalls that blew up suddenly a few weeks before the primaries and then subsided quickly afterwards and were forgotten. Others were prolonged struggles that stretched out over years.

Richard T. Schulze's election as register of wills occurred during one of those rare intervals when—on the surface at least—there was peace and unity within the Chester County Republican ranks. His election came during a transition period in county politics when the Hazlett era was ending and the Rubino era was beginning. For a number of years C. Gilbert Hazlett wore two hats—one as chairman of the county commissioners and the other as chairman of the Republican Party. He had already given his party chairmanship hat to Sheriff Theodore S. A. Rubino when Schulze was slated for the register of wills post in the spring of 1967. By the end of the year the transfer of political power had been quietly accomplished. Hazlett finished his third commissioner term and his other hat was donned by Rubino, who succeeded him as chairman of the county governing body.

Election as register of wills was an important milestone on the road that took the thirty-eight-year-old Schulze to Washington and the United States House of Representatives. Winning came easy for the Paoli businessman; unopposed in the spring primary, he scored a better than two-to-one victory over his underdog Democrat challenger Herbert Wiley on Election Day. As with the other row offices, the register of wills position seldom attracts much attention. Consequently, for many politicians elevation to an elected courthouse office is the end of the line. Not so with Schulze. He remained politically active and kept in the public eye. Rubino tapped him for county director of the 1969 and 1970 primary political campaigns—a job he had previously undertaken for the party in 1964 and 1966.

A partner in a retail electric appliance business, Schulze became involved in politics shortly after his discharge from the Army in 1953. He took over leadership of the Upper Main Line Young Republicans and in due course was elected president of the Chester County Federation of Young Republican

Clubs. He also became a committeeman in Tredyffrin Township. His spare time, however, was not exclusively devoted to politics. He was active in the Junior Chamber of Commerce during the 1950s and in recognition for his leadership was awarded the Upper Main Line club's Jaycee of the Year award in 1959.

While register of wills, Schulze served as chairman of the Tredyffrin Township Republican Committee and as a member of the party's county executive committee. He was therefore in a good position to take advantage of any opportunity for political advancement that might present itself. As noted earlier such an opportunity occurred in August of 1970 when the Republican County Committee was forced to change its slate of candidates due to the death of Congressman Watkins. In this ticket reshuffling Schulze became the party's nominee for state representative from Pennsylvania's 157th Legislative District—a district that then embraced Phoenixville borough and the townships of Tredyffrin, Charlestown, East Pikeland, East Whiteland and Schuylkill. It was a strong Republican bastion and Schulze had an easy time turning back his Democrat opponent, Michael F. Beausang Jr. of Strafford.

CHESTERBROOK

During Schulze's first term in the General Assembly a private developer, Greenview Associates headed by Richard J. Fox, kicked up what was to become one of the most controversial zoning and land use disputes in the history of Chester County. The Chesterbrook proposal called for the erection of garden apartments, townhouses and other structures on an 865-acre tract adjoining Valley Forge Park. The "new town" plan for this historic area was about as popular as the tax on tea levied by King George III two centuries earlier. The Paul Reveres of Tredyffrin sounded the alarm, quickly mobilized a volunteer army known as Citizens Organized to Reclaim Chesterbrook (CORC), and began a long but unsuccessful struggle to block the development. Schulze eventually was drawn into the controversy, Chesterbrook being situated in his legislative district, and he joined those calling for the annexation of the property for park purposes. Under a three column headline advising *Suburban Advertiser* readers there was "Lots of Money for Park Available from State," he was quoted in January 1972 as saying the state was going to end up with a substantial fiscal year surplus and that he could "see no better way to use part of that money than to acquire the Chesterbrook land."

In succeeding months the Chesterbrook hassle continued to make headlines. Meanwhile, as the 1972 primary approached, three of the Republican organization's candidates for the General Assembly were challenged by independents. It first appeared as if Schulze would go unopposed, but three weeks before the primary he too faced opposition when Donald C. Smith, vice president of both CORC and the Valley Forge Civic Association, launched a write-in campaign for the 157th Legislative District seat. Smith maintained the Republican-dominated five-man board of supervisors in Tredyffrin Township had ignored the wishes of residents by placing a stamp of approval on the plan for Chesterbrook and that Schulze, despite sympathetic utterances, had failed to sponsor a bill to have the state annex the property for park purposes.

Smith's write-in campaign failed. Schulze captured his party's nomination and later defeated Democrat Annamaria Malloy by almost 6,000 votes in the general election. As had been the case during his first term as a legislator, Schulze continued to be preoccupied with Chesterbrook when he returned to Harrisburg. Scarcely a week went by during 1973 and 1974 when Chesterbrook failed to make at least one splashy headline in county newspapers. One such headline in the *Suburban Advertiser* on Dec. 20, 1973, read: "Schulze Seeks $15 Million to Purchase Chesterbrook." The story beneath it told of legislation he had introduced to enable the Pennsylvania Historic and Museum Commission to purchase the 865-acre property. "I feel the tide is finally turning our way," he was quoted as saying. "I would hope that this historic site will be saved as open space for ourselves and succeeding generations to enjoy." Several months later other newspaper accounts told of his being in Washington attempting to obtain federal funding for park purposes and meeting with James G. Watt, then the Interior Department's bureau of outdoor recreation director, who would later make the cover of *Time* and other magazines when he served as President Reagan's controversial secretary of the interior.

THE 1974 PRIMARY

It was with this background—three years in the courthouse and three years in the state house—that Schulze made his move to go to Washington after John Ware said he would not seek re-election. The scramble for the Republican nomination—the likes of which had not been seen in Chester County for nearly a hundred years—made the 1974 Republican primary a fascinating one. No precise moment marked the beginning of the primary campaign season, but the jockeying for position by would-be congressmen was well underway on January 16 when the *Daily Local News* splashed a tasteless six column streamer across its front page stating "Ware's out; Rubino likes Stauffer." Four months and five days later the season ended with Schulze being designated by the Republican voters as Ware's heir-apparent.

Like a hockey game, the contest for the GOP nomination was divided into three periods. During the first period the congressional aspirants skated onto the ice and presented themselves to the news media and influential party leaders. During the bruising second period the goal of most of the contenders was that of endorsement by the party establishment. With the endorsement of Schulze some of the skaters left the ice; for others the real battle in the third period was just beginning. This battle after the filing of nominating petitions was for the votes of the Fifth District's rank-and-file Republicans.

State Sen. John Stauffer's involvement in this congressman selection saga was a very minor one. Reportedly he was Rubino's "personal choice," but the Phoenixville lawmaker declined to enter the fray, saying he was content to remain in Harrisburg. A story in the January 17 edition of *The Evening Bulletin*, a Philadelphia newspaper, said Schulze was preferred by GOP leaders in Delaware County, but consideration was also being given to two other lawmakers—Edwin G. Holl, a state senator from Lansdale, and Herbert K. Zearfoss, a state representative from St. Davids. This same account included Patricia Crawford, a state representative from Devon, on the list of possible candidates.

The field of entries was not limited to state legislators. James Milne, a West Chester State College professor, and Edward G. Conroy, an attorney who once served as chief counsel of the federal Economic Development Administration, tossed their hats in the ring at an early date. Neither was regarded as an "organization" man. Milne said he favored an open primary and was critical of GOP chieftain Rubino. Conroy, a West Goshen Township resident in his late thirties, initially sought party endorsement, but charted his own course when he was unable to get this backing. A third independent interested in the nomination was John Harding, a young financial analyst from Willistown Township who some years later became one of the party's ruling elders. Another independent aspirant for the congressional post was Rex S. Morgan, a fifty-two-year-old cable television consultant who was well known for having once hosted a children's television show.

The Chester County Government Study Commission, used as a launching pad by several of its members with political ambitions, was making headlines at this time. Serving on this nine-member study group were three more congressional aspirants. Earl Baker, a Temple University political science instructor, was interested in the nomination as was John Robinson (Robin) West, a Unionville lawyer in his late twenties whose credentials included a period of service as a White House aide. Failing to receive support from the party's leaders, Baker removed himself from the race. But West remained and became Schulze's chief rival for the Republican nomination. The third member of the study group desiring to go to Washington was County Commissioner Leo McDermott, a Democrat who would assume a major role in the fall, rather than the spring, political production.

Forty-three of the Fifth District's eighty-eight voting precincts were in Delaware and Montgomery counties, but county newspapers, and some of the would-be congressmen, seemed to either ignore or forget this during the early phases of the campaign. The general impression was created by these newspapers that Rubino and his organization would handpick the nominee and party leaders in the two neighboring counties would dutifully tag along. Dick Schulze knew this was not the case. He clinched support from Harry McNichol's GOP machine in Delaware County and Daniel Beren's organization in Montgomery County while making his bid for support of the executive committee of the Republican Party in Chester County. This politicking was important, but didn't make headlines.

Throughout February the politicking for the nomination received a big play in the newspapers. Several meetings were held by the county's GOP executive committee before an endorsement decision was reached. Ten names reportedly were considered at the final session presided over by attorney John Halsted in the absence of chairman Rubino, who was in the hospital recuperating from a gall bladder operation. Schulze was the overwhelming choice of the committee. The endorsement rated a "County GOP Executive Committee Backs Schulze" streamer on the front page of the *Coatesville Record* and signaled the beginning of an all-out fight for the nomination between the organization-backed Dick Schulze and the rejected Robin West, who would spend many thousands of dollars on a slick media campaign. Downplaying the organization endorsement, one of West's aides told reporters party backing "wasn't worth a hell of a lot" and the contest was "a question of the old politics versus the new politics."

"Old politics versus new politics" was one of many catchy, but vague, phrases bandied about during the spring of 1974. It was the time of Watergate and the general public was fed up with politics. For organization candidates such as Schulze the Watergate issue was a bothersome one. Additionally, the Republican organization in Chester County was under fire and there were some who believed Ted Rubino's machine was falling apart. Anti-Rubino Republicans had elected two of their leaders—Lawrence Wood and Stewart Deery—to courthouse offices the previous year. This victory by the independents came on the heels of setbacks suffered by three organization-backed candidates for the General Assembly in 1972.

Even though West's professionally-run, well-financed campaign earned for the highly visible and attractive young candidate numerous laudatory press stories, including a piece in *Time* magazine, West was soon to learn that party endorsement was still worth something in Chester County. The Wood-Deery independent faction—primarily concerned with courthouse politics—could not or would not unite behind a single candidate, and as a consequence the anti-organization vote was divided amongst West and three other candidates (Milne, Conroy and Morgan) who stayed in the race after Schulze received the blessings of the Republican organizations in the three counties.

Schulze emphasized his legislative experience in campaign talks, stressing that he was "not owned by political bosses." Although he received less than half of the nearly 53,500 votes cast in the Republican primary, Schulze came out on top in the five-man race, polling 24,263 votes. West received 15,666 votes, followed by Morgan (5,713), Conroy (5,445) and Milne (2,405). On the Democratic side nearly 16,700 votes were split between Chester County's minority commissioner Leo McDermott and Jacob M. Scholl, a North Coventry Township builder. McDermott claimed his party's congressional nomination with 9,470 of these votes.

The Schulze-West contest was one of Chester County's more exciting and memorable congressional election battles; the Schulze-McDermott contest that followed in the fall was anticlimactic. The Republican newcomer won easily (83,526 to 56,626) even though in most areas of the country the Democrats capitalized on the Watergate scandal and worrisome economic problems. "Weary of Watergate and worried by inflation," *The Evening Bulletin's* election story reported, "American voters yesterday gave the Democratic Party its greatest number of governors in 38 years and massive majorities in Congress." Among the Democrat winners was Pennsylvania's Gov. Milton Shapp, who won handily over Republican Drew Lewis. The state's voters, however, continued their split-ticket tradition and returned Republican Richard Schweiker to the United States Senate.

THE NINETY-FOURTH CONGRESS

The Ninety-fourth Congress had ninety-two freshmen representatives, more than any Congress since the Eighty-first, which had 118. Schulze gave early indications of being a standout in this freshman class. Chosen president of the freshmen Republicans and appointed to two House committees (Armed Services and Banking, Currency and Housing), he was also named an advisor to the Conference on Disarmament and sent to the ongoing Strategic Arms Limitation Talks (SALT), held in Geneva, Switzerland. His being the only freshman lawmaker in the twelve-member delegation to Geneva gave some observers reason to believe Schulze was on the fast track to a place of prominence in the House.

Among the bills passed by the Ninety-Fourth Congress and signed into law by President Ford was one that created the Valley Forge National Park, which a short time later was one of the chief focal points of the nation's bicentennial Fourth of July celebration. For Chester County and the Fifth Congressional District this bill—for which Schulze took credit as he began his re-election campaign—was a very significant one in that it guaranteed the preservation of one of the nation's most historic landmarks. Campaign literature proclaiming Schulze "a man of action . . . not just words" stated:

> "When Dick Schulze first discussed the possible acquisition of Valley Forge Park by the Federal Government, he was told that with a lot of hard work, it might be accomplished in 3 - 5 years. Dick went to work and less than 18 months later President Ford signed the bill creating Valley Forge National Historical Park. It took action, not just words."

Unlike the spirited 1974 Republican primary that received widespread press attention, the 1976 primary was an uneventful one for Schulze. He went unopposed. Being the nation's bicentennial year as well as a presidential election year, though, there was plenty of excitement on the county, state and national political fronts. In the fall campaign his Democrat rival was Anthony

Campolo Jr., a Baptist minister and former missionary to the Dominican Republic. Chairman of the sociology department at Eastern College in St. Davids, Campolo was described as a liberal activist whose views on most issues were diametrically opposite those of his GOP opponent, who had been rated as one of the House's most conservative members during his first term. On military preparedness, for example, Schulze supported increasing the Pentagon budget; Campolo said he favored selective cuts in defense spending. As with previous political campaigns, though, issues were not a determining factor. With the tremendous Republican registration advantage Campolo posed no serious threat and Schulze won with a 38,000-vote plurality. But for the Republican Party, the election was one of many disappointments, chief of which was President Ford's loss to Jimmy Carter. Chester County, of course, remained in the GOP column, providing the Ford-Dole ticket with a plurality of nearly 25,000 votes.

WINS THIRD TERM

Schulze won re-election to a third term in 1978. In the spring primary he rolled up an impressive 50,000 vote majority over Edmund (Pharaoh) Hairston, a thirty-year-old Vietnam war veteran from Oxford. Later in the year another Democrat scalp was added to Schulze's collection when he trounced Murray P. Zealor by nearly 74,000 votes.

In the eyes of many observers the country was in bad shape as the 1970s ended. The economy showed signs of slipping into recession, inflation was surging at a double-digit pace, and interest rates were at their highest level since the Civil War. One of the last things that Congress did in 1979 was pass the Chrysler Loan Guarantee Bill in an effort to bail out the giant automobile manufacturer and save the jobs of 600,000 workers. But most demoralizing of all was the situation abroad where Iran's Ayatollah Khomeini was threatening to try as spies some fifty American hostages snatched by a mob of students from the United States embassy in Tehran.

When Ronald Reagan said he would seek the presidency in 1980, Schulze and Lancaster County's Bob Walker reportedly were the first Pennsylvania congressmen to endorse his candidacy. In capturing the Republican Party nomination and then scoring a landslide victory in November, the former movie actor and California governor had top billing in the nation's 1980 political extravaganza. For Schulze, there were no big obstacles to winning a fourth term. He had no competition in the Republican primary. His Democrat opponent in the fall was thirty-one-year-old Grady Brickhouse of Spring City, a high school social studies teacher who called for alternate energy sources as he campaigned about the Fifth Congressional District in a horse-drawn wagon. Brickhouse charged that oil companies were "looking out for the dollar interest rather than the country's interest." Most of Schulze's campaign salvos were directed at President Carter and the Democrats in Washington whom he criticized for overindulgence and reckless spending.

The Fifth District ran true to form, returning Schulze to Congress by an overwhelming margin—148,898 to only 47,092 for Brickhouse. For the Republican Party it was one of the happiest election nights in years. In addition to Reagan's landslide win over President Carter, the GOP wrested control of the United States Senate from the Democrats for the first time in twenty-six years. Among the victorious candidates was Arlen Specter, who defeated Democrat Peter Flaherty in the contest for the Pennsylvania senate seat being vacated by Richard S. Schweiker. The Democrats remained in control of the House, but the Republicans registered a net gain of thirty-two seats.

REDISTRICTING

Pennsylvania lost two seats in the House of Representatives as a result of 1980 census findings, but only minimal changes were made in the boundary lines of Schulze's 700 square mile congressional territory. The restructured Fifth District encompassed eighty-five municipalities in central and eastern Chester County, southwestern Delaware County, and northern Montgomery County. Its population was recorded at 515,528.

Social Security and unemployment were two major concerns as the 1982 political campaigns got underway. Newspapers were reporting Social Security was running out of cash and the unemployment lines were growing longer across the country. The nation's farm problem was also in the news. In this connection, the national spotlight focused on Chester County on May 15—three days before the primaries—when President Reagan, accompanied by United States Secretary of Agriculture John Block, paid a visit to Leon Wilkinson's Landenberg farm. It was the president's first farm visit since taking office and proved to be one of the year's major news events for Chester County.

Issues were not really a deciding factor as Schulze made his bid for a fifth term. He again had the backing of the Republican organizations in the suburban counties and neither of his two challengers for the congressional nomination—Paul J. McGarvey, a seventy-year-old real estate company employee from East Norriton, and Robert G. Hill of Limerick—made much of a showing at the primary. Schulze garnered ninety percent of the votes cast. The Democrats did not have a name on their ballot for congressman, but planned to nominate Robert Burger, a Delaware County businessman from Thornbury, through the write-in method. Some of Schulze's friends had another idea, however, and created a bit of a furor when they appeared outside polling places on Election Day wearing "Democrats for Dick" buttons. This last minute effort by the congressman's friends, who were accused of being Republicans by Chester County Democratic Party Chairman Andrew Dinniman, failed and Burger was able to challenge Schulze in the general election. His campaign platform contained a plank calling for an immediate freeze on the proliferation of nuclear arms. Another issue raised, but which had little influence on the outcome, was campaign funding by political action committees.

Newspaper headlines the day after the 1982 election proclaimed Schulze a winner. He polled over 90,000 votes; Burger received less than half this number. Republican Dick Thornburgh was elected governor and Republican John Heinz was returned to the United States Senate, but 1982 was not a banner year for the GOP. Rising unemployment was cited as one of the chief reasons for the Republican ranks in the federal House being thinned by twenty-six members. The reapportionment and election changed a Republican majority (13-12) in the Pennsylvania delegation to a Democrat majority (13-10) in the Ninety-eighth Congress.

THE 1984 ELECTION

Ronald Reagan, one of the most popular presidents in American history, enjoyed a smooth road to renomination at the 1984 Republican National Convention. The country was enjoying economic prosperity; there was low inflation and reduced unemployment. Tax reform and arms control were the big issues in 1984, along with the deficit, an issue Reagan was able to finesse. At the November election Reagan and his running mate George Bush scored a smashing victory over the Mondale-Ferraro ticket, winning every state but Minnesota and capturing 525 of the 538 electoral college votes.

Schulze was also a winner in 1984, brushing aside Priscilla J. (P.J.) Leonard, a Marcus Hook housewife, in the Republican primary and Democrat Louis J. Fanti, a Coatesville attorney, at the general election. Mrs. Leonard faulted Schulze for having voted against an effort to revive the Equal Rights Amendment and for his "unavailability to constituents," but at the time Schulze was still in the good graces of Philadelphia's leading newspaper. An editorial page endorsement in the April 8 edition of *The Inquirer* said: "He has served his constituency in three suburban counties reasonably well, growing in effectiveness as well as seniority." Later, as the general election approached, *The Inquirer* gave Schulze another editorial page boost in its October 21 edition, saying:

> "In his 10 years in Congress, particularly in recent terms, Rep. Schulze, 55, has grown in the job. With a small business background of his own, he has given knowledgeable attention to small-business proprietors and family farmers. He has developed as well an impressive understanding of economic development problems and opportunities across the board. As a member of the House Ways and Means Committee, Mr. Schulze has given thoughtful study to the need for tax reform and should be a positive force in moving Congress toward that goal."

The presidential tide was powerful, but not powerful enough for Republicans to win control of the House. They picked up fourteen of the twenty-six seats they lost in 1982, but the Democrats still outnumbered them

253 to 182. Among the major problems confronting the Ninety-ninth Congress was the federal government's debt. Annual deficits were hovering at the $200 billion level, and in an effort to get a handle on this critical problem the Congress passed, and President Reagan signed into law, the Gramm-Rudman-Hollings Balanced Budget and Emergency Deficit Control Act in December 1985.

THE RINGGOLD CHALLENGE

Unlike his previous Democrat challengers—Leo McDermott, Anthony Campolo, Murray Zealor, Grady Brickhouse, Bob Burger, and Louis Fanti—Schulze's opponent in 1986 was able to capture headlines and stir up a little interest in the Fifth District congressional election. To do battle with Schulze for the $72,000-a-year legislative post the Democrats chose Tim Ringgold, a thirty-three-year-old West Point graduate and former Army officer. Taking time out from his insurance, real estate and financial consulting business in West Chester, Ringgold held weekly press conferences during which he struck out at the Republican incumbent on a variety of issues. He criticized Schulze for having moved his home to Virginia, for being "out of touch" with his constituents, for traveling too much at public expense, and for ignoring local industries such as steel and mushrooms. Late in the campaign the *Local* observed:

> "For a change, U.S. Representative Richard T. Schulze is in an election race. Republican Schulze . . . has what is considered a 'safe' House seat because of the 2-to-1 majority of GOP voters in the district. So Schulze has faced only token challenges from Democrats in past years. But Democrat Timothy Ringgold, 33, of Downingtown, has conducted a full-time campaign which has challenged Schulze's loyalty to his constituents and his Congressional voting record. . . . Each week Ringgold picked a different topic and attacked what he characterized as Schulze's stand on the issues. Schulze and his campaign responded to some of the allegations and ignored others."

Then, as the campaign was drawing to a close, Ringgold got a boost from *The Inquirer*, which in the past had been in Schulze's corner. Under an editorial headlined "It's Ringgold over Schulze," the metropolitan paper said:

> "In a decision not reached easily or lightly, *The Inquirer* endorses Mr. Ringgold. The choice is made in full recognition that Rep. Schulze has acquired valuable seniority during 12 years in the House and has built up a storehouse of knowledge on complex issues such as trade policy, economic development, military procurement and farm problems. He has had an important role in bringing shipbuilding jobs to Chester and has been helpful, but hardly a leader, in regional cooperation. His record, acceptable but undistinguished, does not stack up favorably against the promise of Mr. Ringgold. The Democratic challenger . . . is persuasive on

> a number of counts. . . . As an Army commander, he saw firsthand an enormous amount of waste in the military. . . . He's for a strong defense, as would be expected, but believes it can be achieved more effectively at less cost. He is well versed on other issues, blending fiscal conservatism with a healthy sense of what Congress ought to be doing not only to reduce the deficit but also to deliver social services. . . . He would bring an energetic breath of fresh air to the Fifth District and to the Pennsylvania delegation in the House."

But the favorable newspaper publicity was not enough to put Ringgold over the top. When the returns were all in Schulze had added still another Democrat scalp to his collection. He polled 87,593 votes; Ringgold received 45,648.

The Democrats remained in control of both the Senate and House when Schulze returned for the opening of the 100th Congress. The Iran-contra affair was the big news story out of Washington then and for a time it threatened to hurt the Republicans at the next election. Improved relations with the Soviet Union and a strong economy more than compensated for the arms-for-hostages fiasco, however, when Vice President George Bush and Gov. Michael Dukakis of Massachusetts battled for the presidency in 1988. Bush led the Republican Party to victory, winning in forty states and bettering Dukakis in the electoral college, 426 to 112, and Congressman Schulze was re-elected to an eighth term, defeating Democratic challenger Donald A. Hadley of Drexel Hill, a follower of the jailed political extremist Lyndon H. LaRouche Jr., by some 108,000 votes.

The problems and issues facing Schulze and his House colleagues when the 101st Congress convened in January 1989 were a far cry from those that confronted the county's early members in the national legislature. Not in their wildest dreams could Thomas, Hemphill, Anderson, Davis, the Hiesters or the Darlingtons ever have imagined a Congress debating subjects such as the greenhouse effect, clean air, Medicare and Medicaid, birth control and abortion, star wars and outer space, child care assistance, farm subsidies, gun control, gay rights, Social Security, sexual harassment, capital gains, nuclear disarmament and massive retaliation, *glasnost* and *perestroika*—all topics Schulze was expected to offer opinions on when questioned by reporters. Nor could these early county congressmen, who endured several bumpy days in a carriage or coach traveling to and from Washington, ever have dreamed their 1989 counterpart could vote on House bills at the Capitol, travel home for a political function in his district, and return to Washington all in the same day.

But some things never change. When the Constitution was being drafted there was much debate as to how much congressmen were to be paid. Ben Franklin proposed a modest stipend rather than a liberal one, and James Madison argued legislators should not be allowed to put their hands in the public purse to convey it to their own. Several years later during William

Darlington's time in the House there was a public outcry when the lawmakers increased their wages to ten dollars a day. With the convening of the 101st Congress there was again a public outcry as Congress proposed to give its members a hefty fifty-one percent pay hike. The raise finally settled upon brought the salary of the legislators, exclusive of fringe benefits and perks, to over $120,000.

History continued to move at a headlong pace after the bicentennial inaugural of George Bush as the nation's forty-first president. Under Mikhail Gorbachev the Soviet grip on Eastern Europe was relaxed, the Berlin wall came tumbling down, and the Cold War ended. But happenings throughout the world continued to have an impact on decisions made by the government in Washington. Although not regarded as a high profile congressman, Schulze came to the forefront after one of these happenings—the June 1989 massacre of pro-democracy demonstrators in Beijing's Tiananmen Square—when he urged the Bush administration to take a harder line towards China and waged a losing battle against granting it most favored nation trading status.

As a senior member of the House Ways and Means Committee, Schulze was by this time a leading spokesman for tax relief for middle-income Americans and small business. He was also regarded as a champion of protectionist trade and import legislation. Among the Republican Party's movers and shakers his efforts were appreciated and no roadblock was placed in his way when he announced his candidacy for a ninth term in early 1990.

On the Democratic side, though, there was a bit of excitement when Donald Hadley, the Drexel Hill Democrat who had been an embarrassment to many rank and file Democrats in the previous election, announced he would again seek the party's congressman nomination and run against West Chester attorney Samuel C. Stretton, the choice of the party's regulars.

Schulze, who went unopposed, and Stretton were primary winners, but most of the campaign noise during the summer and fall months was generated by a third candidate—Lewis duPont Smith of Philadelphia, an ardent follower of Lyndon LaRouche. A duPont family heir who had obtained enough signatures to have his name placed on the ballot as an independent candidate, Smith's farfetched charges received a great deal of publicity as did his court battle to reverse Judge Lawrence E. Wood's decision that he was not competent to handle his own financial affairs. Few took Smith's candidacy seriously. As for the forty-two-year-old Stretton, a onetime Republican committeeman who had campaigned for district attorney and judge after switching his party allegiance, even the *Local* was unable to give him its endorsement, saying "he is so liberal his interests are definitely out-of-step with the vast majority of the constituents in this largely Republican district." On Election Day Schulze was again a winner, polling 74,988 votes to Stretton's 50,548 and Smith's 5,789.

CHAPTER 29

THE PENNSYLVANIA DUTCH SEAT

The seat in the United States House of Representatives now occupied by the congressman from Pennsylvania's Sixteenth District has been referred to as the "Pennsylvania Dutch Seat" and is commonly thought of as belonging to Lancaster County, just as the Fifth District seat was thought of as belonging to Chester County. A sizeable piece of real estate in the Sixteenth District, however, lay outside Lancaster County in Chester and Lebanon counties and a substantial number of voters reside in these two counties. But the political realities are such that one must be a Lancaster Countian, and a Republican, to be elected to Congress from the Sixteenth District. This, of course, may change, but since the Supreme Court's "one man one vote" decision the Sixteenth District seat has been occupied by Lancaster County Republicans Edwin D. Eshleman and Robert S. Walker, two conservative lawmakers who several years ago wrote an interesting book entitled *Congress - The Pennsylvania Dutch Representatives*. Because of their large Chester County constituency a few paragraphs about these two legislators and their elections are in order.

As noted in earlier chapters the political ties between Lancaster and Chester Counties have always been close, and at other times prior to the establishment of the Sixteenth District the two counties were linked together when congressional maps were drawn. For thirty years during the first half of the nineteenth century they were part of the same three-member congressional district. Many years later, following the 1930 census, the two counties were combined in a one-member district; and for thirty-four years this Lanchester district was served in Congress first by John Roland Kinzer, a Lancaster Countian, and then by Paul B. Dague, a Chester Countian.

Ed Eshleman, a state assemblyman in his mid-forties, was rounding out his sixth term at Harrisburg when Republican Party chieftains picked him as their choice to succeed Dague after the veteran Downingtown lawmaker announced his retirement plans in early 1966. A World War II veteran and former school teacher, Eshleman was majority leader of the Pennsylvania House of Representatives during the 1963-64 session and later served as minority whip when the Democrats were in control. A recipient of the Junior Chamber of Commerce's distinguished service award and the Pennsylvania Young Republicans Hall of Fame award, he had early been marked as a comer in Lancaster County politics.

Endorsements for Dague's congressional seat had already been given Eshleman by the Republican county committees in Lancaster and Chester counties when the Pennsylvania General Assembly came up with an eleventh hour congressional districting plan in early 1966 that dissolved the Lanchester marriage by placing Lancaster County in a new district with Lebanon County and several Dauphin County municipalities. Eshleman was not hurt by this reshuffling. Nominated by the Republicans of this new district, he was elected to the Ninetieth Congress with a huge 45,000 vote majority. He was subsequently returned to Washington by voters of the new district in 1968 and 1970.

Congressman Eshleman again found himself closely associated with Chester County politics in 1972. Under a new apportionment Pennsylvania lost two congressmen, reducing its membership in the federal House to twenty-five. In drawing a new congressional district map for Pennsylvania the General Assembly's cartographers assigned the City of Coatesville and twenty-seven other Chester County municipalities to the Sixteenth District along with all of Lancaster County's political subdivisions and some of Lebanon County's. Eshleman had easy sailing that year when he sought a fourth term in his revamped Sixteenth District. It was a Republican year; the Nixon-Agnew ticket overwhelmingly defeated the McGovern-Shriver ticket, and in his new district Eshleman rolled up a 71,000-vote majority over Democrat Shirley S. Garrett. Two years later, though, when he made his last run for Congress it was a different story. The impact of Watergate was felt in the Sixteenth District and Eshleman's plurality over Democrat Michael Minney was reduced to less than 33,000.

Eshleman's congressional aide, Robert S. Walker, succeeded him in the Ninety-fifth Congress. A resident of East Petersburg, Walker had just turned thirty-three when he announced his intention to seek his party's nomination for congressman. As with his mentor, Walker was a former school teacher, graduating from Millersville State College in 1964 and later earning a master's degree in political science from the University of Delaware. Although supported by Eshleman and some mainstays of the Republican Party, Walker did not have the nomination handed to him on a silver platter. Other Republicans in the three counties wanted to be congressman, causing a wild scramble at the spring primary. A dozen hats were thrown in the Republican ring, including one belonging to Marvin Miller, a state representative from Lancaster.

Over 60,000 votes were cast by the Republican voters of the Sixteenth District in the 1976 primary election; Walker received only 11,669 votes, but they were enough to carry the day. Miller was runner-up with 9,138 votes, followed by Al Lewis Jr. with 8,894 and Darvin E. Boyd with 8,045. On the Democratic side the congressional nomination went to Michael J. Minney, a young Lancaster attorney making his second try for the "Pennsylvania Dutch" seat in the national legislature. Minney was again unsuccessful in the general election, losing to Walker by almost 40,000 votes. Elsewhere, though, it was a good year for the Democrats. In addition to the presidency, they captured eighteen of Pennsylvania's 25 seats in the federal House.

Walker had no difficulty getting re-elected in 1978. Norman O. Aamodt of East Fallowfield Township, Chester County, one of the unsuccessful contenders in the previous primary, again sought the Republican nomination. He did not pose a serious challenge, however, and Walker was awarded the nomination by a 35,976 to 11,299 count. Next, Walker registered a win over Democrat Charles W. Boohar in November by some 64,000 votes. In 1980, as he went after a third term, Walker had an even easier time; unopposed at the primary, he brushed aside Democrat James A. Woodcock of East Hempfield Township, Lancaster County, at the general election by almost 91,000 votes.

Pennsylvania, a state that once elected thirty-six of the nation's 435 congressmen, was adversely effected for the sixth time in a row when results of the 1980 census were disclosed. With the new apportionment its membership in the House was reduced to twenty-three, but there was only minor shifting of the Sixteenth District's boundary lines when Harrisburg's lawmakers redrew the state map with two fewer congressional districts. Twenty-four Chester County townships and six boroughs—Oxford, Atglen, Honey Brook, Parkesburg, Elverson and Spring City—were assigned to the Sixteenth District along with all the municipalities in Lebanon County and nearly all of those in Lancaster County. The total population of the district was reported at 515,832.

By this time Walker's reputation as an effective and energetic conservative congressman was well established and he had no election worries. But Earl Pfoutz Jr., at age sixty-seven, still had hopes of becoming a congressman and filed a nominating petition at the start of the 1982 election season. A perennial candidate from Millersville, Pfoutz had years earlier campaigned against Paul B. Dague in the Republican primaries. He presented no threat to Walker, who handily won the GOP primary and then was elected to a fourth term in the fall, defeating Lancaster County's minority county commissioner, Jean D. Mowery, by nearly 56,000 votes.

With the televising of House proceedings by the Cable Satellite Public Affairs Network, Walker's evening soliloquies on Democratic misdeeds in an almost deserted House chamber resulted in his receiving national recognition and the wrath of Speaker "Tip" O'Neill, who was infuriated by the attacks being made by Walker and other Republican lawmakers on his Democrat colleagues "in front of an empty hall when there was nobody around to refute what they were saying." The widespread publicity given to O'Neill's tiff with Walker over the use of C-Span in the spring of 1984 didn't hurt the Lancaster County legislator one bit back home. He buried his Democrat opponent, Martin L. Bard, in an avalanche of votes that November, winning a fifth term by nearly 99,000 votes.

The Democratic Party continued to send challengers into the ring against

Congressman Walker, but the results were always the same. James D. Hagelgans lost by some 66,000 votes in 1986 and Ernest Eric Guyll was an Election Day casualty in both 1988 and 1990. As the Republican Party's chief deputy whip in the House, Walker was one of the most vocal supporters of President Bush during the 100th and 101st Congresses. On some issues, such as the controversial tax increase question, though, he took conservative positions that differed from those espoused by the administration.

CHAPTER 30

FIFTH DISTRICT VAPORIZED

Pennsylvania had very little population growth during the 1980s. Elsewhere, especially in the South and the West, it was a different story. In some states growth had been dramatic. As a consequence of this growth and population shifts within the United States the Keystone State once again was adversely affected when the congressional apportionment was made following the 1990 Census. California, Florida and Texas were again the big winners, gaining fourteen seats in the decennial congressional map redrawing, and Pennsylvania was one of thirteen states targeted to lose seats in the House of Representatives when the 103rd Congress convenes in 1993.

Back in the 1920s Pennsylvania's cadre of thirty-six congressmen had been surpassed in size by only New York's delegation. Since then this representation in the national legislature has steadily declined. Under the new apportionment Pennsylvania loses two congressmen and its House delegation is reduced to twenty-one members. Under the "one man, one vote" standard each district is to have a population of nearly 565,800 persons.

Unlike many counties in the state that had a population decline during the '80s, Chester County experienced growth—almost nineteen percent—and with a population of over 376,000 it ranked seventh among the Commonwealth's sixty-seven counties. The 1990 head count and past experience led county Republican leaders to be optimistic when the redistricting process first got underway. In apportionment wheeling and dealing in the past their predecessors had fared well. There was no reason to suspect Chester County would this time be the big loser. In 1972, when it appeared Oxford's John H. Ware was going to lose his congressional seat due to redistricting, an eleventh-hour deal was cut whereby the Republican Party Chairman Theodore Rubino guaranteed the Democrats a Common Pleas Court judgeship in exchange for an acceptable redistricting plan. With the creation of a new Fifth Congressional District that included some forty-five Chester County municipalities, Ware was able to return to the Ninety-third Congress and Chester County was able to have representation in the federal House for the next twenty years.

This time many congressional maps were drawn and some two dozen apportionment plans were considered by the Pennsylvania House and Senate. County GOP leaders hoped to see adopted a plan that contained a "Chester County driven seat"—one that would guarantee the election of (or at least give an advantage to) a county Republican. In a number of the schemes advocated by the county's representatives at Harrisburg a large portion of Chester County would have been linked with municipalities in Berks County. But no deals were made to preserve Chester County's seat in the national legislature. This time when the politicians, legislators, and judges all had their say, and when the dust finally settled shortly before the 1992 primaries, the Fifth Congressional District was vaporized and Dick Schulze, Chester County's nine-term congressman, was on his way toward retirement.

As in the past, Republican and Democrat cartographers in the state legislature were guided by selfish and partisan motives as they attempted to divide the state into twenty-one districts. With Republicans in command of the Senate and Democrats in control of the House, no agreement could be reached in the General Assembly and the matter was turned over to the courts. Serious consideration of the congressional apportionment did not begin until mid-January, and after about four weeks of political conniving, squabbling, and bartering by the legislators, Commonwealth Court President Judge David W. Craig in late February handed down a plan—one that closely mirrored the redistricting scheme of Senate Democrats and one strongly denounced by Chester County GOP leaders as well as some Democrats.

Judge Craig's new congressional district map placed most of Chester County (61 municipalities) in the Lancaster-based Sixteenth District. The dozen remaining municipalities (Phoenixville, Charlestown, Easttown, East and West Pikeland, Schuylkill, Spring City, Malvern, Tredyffrin, West Vincent, East Whiteland, and Willistown) were placed in the Seventh District with municipalities in Delaware and Montgomery counties. For county GOP leaders Craig's plan was a bitter pill to swallow.

Although Schulze had made a decision not to seek re-election months before, it was a very closely kept secret. He had not wanted his decision to adversely influence the apportionment negotiations and purposely held off publicizing it until March 16—three weeks after Judge Craig, a Democrat, split Chester County between the Seventh and Sixteenth districts. In announcing his plans to retire, the veteran lawmaker told reporters he favored limits on congressional terms and that he was especially proud of having sponsored the Taxpayer's Bill of Rights, which he said shifted the burden of proof in tax disputes to the Internal Revenue Service. He also cited the obtaining of federal funds for the Exton Bypass, the much-talked-about and long-sought-after county highway improvement project, as one of his major accomplishments while in Washington.

Barring a dramatic change in voter preferences, both the Seventh and Sixteenth districts in the new plan are expected to remain Republican bastilles, but it is unlikely either congressional seat will be occupied by a Chester Countian any time soon. For Congressman Robert S. Walker, whose constituency has included residents of western Chester County since he began serving in the House in 1977, the new plan removes Spring City and West

Vincent from his present district, but adds thirty-three county municipalities to the thirty he is currently representing. Approximately seventy-eight percent of the county's residents will live in this new Sixteenth District. The Seventh District, to which some 81,000 county residents have been assigned, is currently served by Curt Weldon, a resident of Aston, Delaware County, who was first elected to the House in 1986.

EPILOGUE

"Let men be good, and the government cannot be bad; if it be ill, they will cure it. But if men be bad, let the government be ever so good, and they will endeavor to warp and spoil it to their turn."

When William Penn launched his "Holy Experiment" and spoke these words some three hundred years ago he expressed the belief that government depended upon men, rather than men upon government. Some one hundred years later after his Pennsylvania colony and twelve other colonies had achieved independence, another great experiment in self-government under the United States Constitution was begun. Throughout the preceding chapters the author has endeavored to acquaint his readers with the Chester Countians who have participated in this great experiment by serving in the Congress of the United States.

Publication of this effort comes at an inopportune time when few accolades are given the Congress and those serving in it. As the nation begins its third century of government under the Constitution many of its citizens are disenchanted with their lawmakers. They have lost trust in government, feel the country is in a state of economic decline, and believe the federal bureaucracy is too large and too costly. Congress is being criticized for failing in its most basic responsibility—funding the vast federal government operation. The huge budget deficits and astronomical national debt are of great concern to the citizenry. So are the political action committees that have corrupted the election process by pouring millions and millions of dollars into congressional election campaigns. On top of this the nation's capital continues to experience dreary seasons of scandal involving prominent members of the government. The newspapers and nightly television news programs are filled with accounts of abuse of power and other misconduct. Somewhere and somehow the moral values of those running our government seem to have been misplaced. From the news media accounts one might conclude those in command of the government are endeavoring "to warp and spoil it to their turn."

Like many other citizens far removed from the Washington scene, this writer is concerned and unhappy with many of the things happening in the government today. At the same time, though, he believes many congressmen are dedicated public servants faced with awesome responsibilities as they attempt to steer the nation though difficult and uncertain times. He is also both hopeful and optimistic that there will soon be a turning point and a time when good men will prevail and strive to cure an ill government.

The research journey to learn about the county's representatives in the national legislature went back two hundred years, a long time span, and the old newspaper accounts found in the Chester County Historical Society's files were fascinating reading. No troublesome scandals were uncovered and the chronicler was able to conclude that those who served in the *Chester County*

Line since the days of George Washington were for the most part hard-working, highly committed and highly decent men. As said at the outset, there were no congressional giants in this line, but neither were there any scoundrels who brought shame on Chester County. The American experiment in democracy, with all its faults and shortcomings, has been a great success story, and while often unappreciated by their contemporaries, the county's representatives in the national legislature were able to leave Washington with the satisfaction of knowing they had had a small voice in this success story.

THE CONGRESSIONAL CAST
CHESTER COUNTY CONGRESSMEN

ANDERSON, Isaac (1760-1838) Member of 8th and 9th Congresses. A Jeffersonian Democrat and lifelong resident of Charlestown Township. Presidential elector in 1816. Great-grandfather of Gov. Samuel Pennypacker.

BARNARD, Isaac D. (1791-1834) United States Senator from March 1827 to December 1831. West Chester attorney and Democratic Party leader. Elected to Pennsylvania Senate in 1820 and was later named Secretary of the Commonwealth.

BUTLER, Thomas S. (1855-1928) Member of House of Representatives from March 1897 until his death in May 1928, the longest tenure of any Chester County congressman. Born in Uwchlan Township, the son of onetime state treasurer Samuel Butler. Served briefly as a county judge. Delegate to 1892 Republican National Convention.

DAGUE, Paul B. (1898-1974) Member of House of Representatives from January 1947 to January 1967. Lifelong Chester County resident, longtime Republican Party politician, and sheriff when elected to 80th Congress. World War I veteran. Active in the American Legion.

DARLINGTON, Isaac (1781-1839) Federalist member of 15th Congress. Born in Westtown Township. Admitted to the bar in 1801. President judge of courts of Chester and Delaware Counties from 1821 until 1839.

DARLINGTON, Smedley (1827-1899) Member of 50th and 51st Congresses. Born in Pocopson Township. One of founders of Republican Party in Chester County and a wealthy, powerful and controversial political leader. Second cousin of three other Darlingtons (William, Isaac and Edward) who served in the Congress. Father-in-law of Congressman Thomas S. Butler.

DARLINGTON, William (1782-1863) Member of 14th, 16th, 17th Congresses. A physician, scientist, botanist and president of National Bank of Chester County for 33 years.

DAVIS, Roger (1762-1815) Member of 12th and 13th Congresses. A physician, onetime state legislator, and lifelong Charlestown Township resident. Ardent Democrat and supporter of President Madison during War of 1812.

DICKEY, Jesse C. (1808-1890) Member of 31st Congress. An educator, he operated the Hopewell Academy, near Oxford. Active in Whig Party and later one of the founders of Republican Party in Chester County.

EVANS, Joshua Jr. (1777-1846) Member of 21st and 22nd Congresses. Lifelong resident of Tredyffrin Township and owner-manager of famous hostelry known as "The Paoli." An uncompromising Democrat, he was Paoli's first postmaster, a state legislator, and a brigadier general in the state militia.

EVERHART, James Bowen (1821-1888) Member of 48th and 49th Congresses. Born in West Whiteland Township, the son of Congressman William Everhart, he was admitted to the bar in 1845. Served in Pennsylvania Senate prior to becoming a congressman.

EVERHART, William (1785-1868) Member of 33rd Congress. Born in West Vincent Township, the son of a Revolutionary War soldier. A key figure in development of West Chester, he served the borough as burgess and justice of peace.

HEMPHILL, Joseph (1770-1842) Elected to 7th Congress by Federalists of Chester and Delaware counties and was later returned on five occasions to serve in the House by voters of Philadelphia. Born in Thornbury Township. Admitted to the bar in 1793 and practiced law in the county before moving to Philadelphia where he became the city's first president judge.

HICKMAN, John (1810-1875) Elected to first of four terms in Congress in 1856. Born on a farm in what is now Pocopson Township. One of county's leading attorneys and a staunch Democrat for many years, he was a delegate to his party's 1844 national convention. Earned a national reputation for his stand against extension of slavery. Considered for vice president nomination by Republicans at their 1860 national convention.

HIESTER, Daniel (1774-1834) Member of 11th Congress. A native Chester Countian and son of Congressman John Hiester, he was one of several political personages instrumental in establishing the National Bank of Chester County. Served as clerk of courts, prothonotary, register of wills, and recorder of deeds.

HIESTER, John (1745-1821) Member of 10th Congress. A farmer-soldier-politician from Coventry Township. Fought at the Battle of the Brandywine. Later served in Pennsylvania Senate and as a brigadier general in the militia.

JAMES, Francis (1799-1886) Member of 26th and 27th Congresses. Born in Thornbury Township. Admitted to the bar in 1825. Served as state senator and burgess of West Chester.

McILVAINE, Abraham R. (1804-1863) Member of 28th, 29th and 30th Congresses. Active in Whig Party and a presidential elector for the

Harrison-Tyler ticket in 1840. Later identified with Republican Party. A well-to-do Quaker farmer, he owned the Springton Manor estate now owned by the County of Chester.

MINER, Charles (1780-1865) Member of 19th and 20th Congresses. Editor of the *Chester and Delaware Federalist,* later named *The Village Record.* An ardent Federalist, he was one of Pennsylvania's most influential newspaper editors during the early part of the nineteenth century.

MORRISON, John A. (1814-1904) Member of 32nd Congress. Born in Lancaster County, he established his residence and medical practice at Cochranville following his graduation from Jefferson College. A staunch Democrat, he frequently was a delegate to his party's state and national conventions.

POTTS, David Jr. (1794-1863) Elected to the first of four consecutive terms as a congressman in 1830. Warwick Furnace ironmaster and member of family largely responsible for establishing iron industry in Pennsylvania. Associated with Anti-Masonic and Free-Soil parties.

SCHULZE, Richard T. (1929-) Congressman from 1975 to 1993. Tredyffrin Township Republican leader. Served as register of wills and state legislator before becoming a congressman.

THOMAS, Richard (1744-1832) First Chester Countian elected to Pennsylvania Senate and United States House of Representatives. Member of 4th, 5th, 6th Congresses. Served as colonel of First Regiment of Chester County Volunteers during Revolution.

TOWNSEND, Washington (1813-1894) Elected in 1868 to first of four terms in House of Representatives. Banker, attorney, and lifelong county resident. Delegate to Whig National Convention in 1852 and Republican national convention in 1860. President of Bank of Chester County from 1879 until 1894.

WARE, John H. (1908-) Elected in 1970 to first of two terms in the Congress. Born in Vineland, New Jersey, he grew up in Oxford and later served as the borough's burgess. Elected state senator in 1960. Newspaper publisher and president of several utility companies. For many years active in a wide variety of civic and charitable organizations as well as the Republican Party.

WAYNE, Isaac (1772-1852) Member of 18th Congress. Born in Easttown Township, the only son of Revolutionary War hero Anthony Wayne. A prominent Federalist, he also served in both the Pennsylvania House and Senate.

THE CONGRESSIONAL CAST
NEIGHBORING CONGRESSMEN

During the past two hundred years Chester County has been linked in a variety of ways with Delaware, Lancaster, Montgomery and Berks counties for the purpose of electing members to the United States House of Representatives. The roster of congressmen from these neighboring counties include the following:

ANDERSON, William (1762-1829) A Jeffersonian Democrat from Delaware County. Served in 11th, 12th, and 13th Congresses when Chester County was part of a three-county district.

BOUDE, Thomas (1752-1822) Revolutionary War soldier and wealthy Lancaster County lumber dealer. Served in the 7th Congress when Chester County was linked with Berks and Lancaster Counties.

BROOMALL, John M. (1816-1894) Delaware County attorney. Member of 38th, 39th, 40th Congresses. Delegate to the Republican National Convention and presidential elector in 1860. Numbered among Republican Party radicals during Reconstruction era.

BROWN, Jeremiah (1785-1858) Lancaster County businessman elected on the Whig ticket to the 27th and 28th Congresses.

BUCHANAN, James (1791-1868) Served in the House of Representatives from March 1821 to March 1831 during period when Chester County was combined with Lancaster and Delaware Counties. A United States senator from 1834 to 1845, he later became the nation's fifteenth president.

DARLINGTON, Edward (1795-1884) Delaware County legislator. Served in the Congress from 1833 to 1839 during the period Chester County was combined with Delaware and Lancaster Counties.

DAVIES, Edward (1799-1853) Lancaster Countian elected by Whigs of three county district to 25th and 26th Congresses.

EDWARDS, John (1786-1843) Delaware County lawyer and manufacturer elected to 26th and 27th Congresses on Whig ticket by voters of Chester, Lancaster and Delaware counties.

EDWARDS, Samuel (1785-1850) Delaware County Federalist and member of Congress from March 1819 to March 1827. During his last two terms he was one of three representatives chosen by voters of Chester, Lancaster and Delaware counties.

ESHLEMAN, Edward (1920-1985) A Lancaster Countian elected to Congress in 1966 after serving for twelve years in the Pennsylvania General Assembly. Served as one of Chester County's representatives in 93rd and 94th Congresses following reapportionment of 1972, which placed a goodly portion of western Chester County in revamped Sixteenth District.

GROSS, Samuel (1774- 1884) A Montgomery County farmer- politician elected to 16th and 17th Congresses from Chesmont district.

HAHN, John (1776- 1823) Montgomery County physician and member of 14th Congress.

HIESTER, Joseph (1752-1832) Berks Countian who became governor of Pennsylvania. Elected to 8th Congress when Chester County was part of the three-county district. Also was House member from 1797 to 1805 and from 1815 to 1820.

HIESTER, William (1790-1853) Lancaster County leader of the Anti-Masonic Party elected to 22nd, 23rd and 24th Congresses from three-county district.

HYNEMAN, John M. (1771-1816) Member of the 12th and 13th Congresses from Berks County.

JACOBS, Israel (1726-1796) One of Montgomery County's first colonists to advocate union of colonies. Member of 2nd Congress.

JENKINS, Robert (1769-1848) Lancaster County ironmaster and Jeffersonian Democrat elected to the 10th and 11th Congresses from three-county district.

KINZER, Roland (1874-1955) Represented the Lanchester district in the House of Representatives during the presidency of Franklin D. Roosevelt. A Lancaster County attorney, he served in the House from January 1930 to January 1947.

LEFEVER, Joseph (1760-1826) Lancaster County Democrat elected to the 12th Congress from three-county district.

LEIPER, George (1786-1868) Delaware County Democrat elected to the 21st Congress from three-county district.

LOWER, Christian (1740-1806) A Berks Countian elected to 9th Congress from three-county district.

PAWLING, Levi (1773-1845) Montgomery County lawyer elected to 15th Congress by Federalists of Chester and Montgomery counties.

RICHARDS, Mathias (1758-1830) Berks Countian elected to 10th and 11th Congresses from three-county district.

ROBERTS, Jonathan (1771-1854) A Montgomery Countian elected to 13th Congress from Chesmont district. Later served in the United States Senate from 1814 to 1821.

ROBINSON, John B. (1846-1933) Delaware County lawyer and owner of the *Media Ledger*. Served in Pennsylvania House and Senate prior to representing Delchester District in the Congress from March 1891 to March 1897.

WALKER, Robert (1942-) A Lancaster County school teacher and congressional aide prior to being elected in 1976 to 95th Congress from Sixteenth District, which embraces a goodly portion of western Chester County. Returned to Washington in elections since then and has earned a reputation of being one of the House's most conservative members.

WARD, William (1837-1895) A Chester attorney who represented Delchester district in the 45th, 46th and 47th Congresses.

WATKINS, G. Robert (1902-1970) Delaware County political leader elected to Congress in 1964. Represented Chester County in the 90th and 91st Congresses.

WHITEHILL, John (1729-1815) Lancaster County patriot active in the independence cause. Elected to 8th and 9th Congresses by Jeffersonian Democrats of Chester, Lancaster and Berks counties.

WOLFENDEN, James (1889-1949) A Delaware County manufacturer elected to 70th Congress by Delchester district Republicans to fill a vacancy caused by the death of Congressman Thomas S. Butler. After Delaware County became a separate district he continued to serve in the House until 1947.

THE CONGRESSIONAL CAST
CHALLENGERS

The list of persons wishing to represent Chester County in the national legislature is a long one. Among these would-be lawmakers involved in convention struggles or election campaigns were the following:

AAMODT, Norman O.—Candidate for 16th District nomination in 1976 and 1978 Republican primaries.

ALISON, Oliver—Chester County sheriff and state legislator from London Grove. Democratic Party leader and presidential elector in 1832 and 1836. Loser by 285 votes to Abraham McIlvaine in 1843 congressional race.

ASKINS, John Henry—Democrat loser in 1870 congressional race.

BALDWIN, Richard—Native of Chester County elected to Pennsylvania House and Senate by Delaware County voters. A 1922 Republican primary loser in bid to unseat Congressman Thomas Butler.

BARD, Martin L.—Democrat nominee for 16th District congressional seat in 1984.

BEATTY, William—Democrat loser to Congressman John Broomall in 1864.

BERRY, William H.—Prominent Pennsylvania politician. Elected state treasurer in 1905. Keystone Party gubernatorial nominee in 1910. Defeated in 1894, 1896 and 1898 Delchester congressional contests.

BONNIWELL, Eugene—A resident of Wayne, Delaware County, and prominent Democrat twice nominated for governor. Defeated in 1910 and 1912 Delchester congressional contests.

BOOHAR, Charles W.—Democrat aspirant for 16th District congressional seat in 1978.

BOWEN, John S.—West Chester attorney nominated for Congress by Chester County Republicans at 1856 convention.

BRAM, Harold—Candidate for Congress in 1966 GOP primary.

BRICKHOUSE, Grady G.—Democrat nominee for Congress in 1980.

BRINTON, John H.—West Chester attorney and Jeffersonian Democrat defeated by Congressman John Hickman in 1860. Presidential elector in 1856 and a delegate to his party's national convention in 1872.

BROWN, Freeland S.—Democratic Party's nominee for Congress in 1920. General store operator and postmaster at Cochranville for many years.

BUCKLEY, John J.—Lifelong Phoenixville resident and justice of the peace. Democrat loser in 1906 congressional race.

BURGER, Robert—Democrat nominee for Congress in 1982.

BURKHOLDER, H. Clay—Lancaster County Democrat defeated in 1936 and 1944 Lanchester congressional contests.

BUTLER, Charles—Physician and NAACP leader from Coatesville defeated in bid for Congress nomination in 1966 GOP primary.

BUTLER, Smedley Darlington—Marine hero and son of Congressman Thomas S. Butler. Loser in 1932 primary race for U.S. Senator nomination.

CAMPBELL, Edgar—Democrat opponent of Paul B. Dague in 1946 congressional race.

CAMPOLO, Anthony Jr.—Democrat nominee for congressman in 1976.

CARPENTER, Charles T.—Glenmoore Democrat defeated by Congressman Roland Kinzer in 1934. Later a member of Pennsylvania Milk Control Board and Pennsylvania Turnpike Commission.

CASSATT, Edward B.—Son of A. J. Cassatt, president of the Pennsylvania Railroad, and nephew of artist Mary Cassatt. Resided at Chesterbrook Farm, Berwyn, when nominated for Congress by Democrats in 1916.

CILLEY, Gordon—Founder of *Main Line Daily Times*, onetime chairman of Democratic County Committee, and 1924 candidate for Congress.

COLLETTI, Edwin—Candidate for Congress in 1966 GOP primary.

CONROY, Edward G.—Candidate for Congress in 1974 GOP primary.

CORNWELL, Robert T.—Civil War hero and foe of Congressman Smedley Darlington at 1888 GOP convention.

CUNNINGHAM, John W.—Democrat nominee for Congress in 1836. Onetime state legislator and presidential elector for Andrew Jackson in 1828.

CUSTER, Bethel M.—Democrat aspirant for Congress in 1878.

DAVIS, Henry W.—Democrat nominee for Congress in 1930.

DICKINSON, O.B.—Democrat loser in 1886 congressional race.

ELLIS, Nathaniel—Democrat nominee for Congress in 1900.

ELLIS, William T.—Swarthmore Democrat defeated by Congressman Thomas Butler in 1922.

EVANS, Henry—West Chester newspaperman and Whig politician. Served in

Pennsylvania House and Senate. Candidate for GOP congressional nomination in 1868.

FANTI, Louis J.—Democrat nominee for Congress in 1984.

FARRELL, John—Prominent West Chester Democrat nominated for the United States Senate in 1920. Defeated by Boies Penrose, the Republican incumbent. Onetime president of Chester County Medical Society and member of board of trustees of West Chester State Teachers College at the time of his death in 1938.

FORWOOD, J. Larkin—Civil War veteran and four times mayor of Chester. Democrat loser in 1874 Delchester congressional race.

GARDNER, Francis—Federalist loser in 1812 congressional race.

GARRETT, Shirley S.—Democrat nominee for 16th District congressional seat in 1972.

GIAMPIETRO, Anthony—Loser in bid for Congress nomination in 1970 GOP primary.

GREENWOOD, Samuel—Valley Township Democrat defeated by Smedley Darlington in 1888 congressional race.

GUYLL, Ernest Eric—Democratic Party's candidate for Congress in 16th District in 1988 and 1990.

HADLEY, Donald A.—Democratic Party's nominee for Congress in 1988.

HAGELGANS, James D.—Democrat aspirant for 16th District congressional seat in 1986.

HAINES, Townsend—One of Chester County's most prominent political figures for three decades prior to the Civil War. An unsuccessful candidate for Congress in 1828 on the Adams or Administration ticket, he became the county's first elected president judge in 1851.

HAIRSTON, Edmund—Republican primary loser to Congressman Richard Schulze in 1978.

HALSEY, Howard—Democrat nominee for Congress in 1960.

HARDING, Philip L.—Democrat loser to Congressman G. Robert Watkins in 1968.

HARTMAN, William D.—West Chester physician nominated for Congress by Democrats in 1876.

HECKEL, Frederick W. Jr.—Democrat nominee for congressman in 1884.

HEMPHILL, Joseph—Prominent West Chester attorney and Democratic Party leader. Nephew of Congressman Joseph Hemphill. Defeated by Whig Party's Jesse Dickey in 1848 congressional race.

HIBBERD, Dilworth P.—Philadelphia attorney defeated by Congressman Thomas Butler in 1908.

HOLDING, Archibald M.—Longtime Democratic Party leader and president of Pennsylvania and Chester County bar associations. Loser in 1904 Delchester congressional contest.

HOLT, Charles C.—Loser to Congressman Ware in 1972 GOP primary.

HOWARD, Frederick—Loser in 1912 Delchester congressional race.

HUTCHISON, David W.—Candidate for GOP congressional nomination in 1868.

KELLER, Richard—Democrat loser in 1962 congressional race.

KELTON, James—Federalist candidate for Congress in 1818. Served in Pennsylvania House and Senate.

LEONARD, Priscilla—A Marcus Hook housewife defeated by Congressman Schulze in 1984 GOP primary.

MacVEAGH, Wayne—Prominent Chester County attorney and member of President Garfield's cabinet. Unsuccessful candidate for GOP congressional nomination in 1868.

MANLEY, Charles—Delaware County state legislator and Democratic Party nominee for Congress in 1858.

MAY, George—Democrat nominee for Congress in 1940.

McCALL, George A.—West Point graduate and military officer defeated by Republican Party's John Broomall in 1862 congressional contest.

McCLELLAN, Robert—Cochranville dentist and state legislator. Candidate for GOP congressional nomination in 1882.

McCLELLAND, Thomas Jefferson—Unionville Democrat nominated for Lanchester congressional seat in 1938.

McDERMOTT, Leo—Chester County minority commissioner for three terms, onetime chairman of Democratic County Committee, and party's nominee for Congress in 1974.

McGRANN, Richard P.—Loser to Congressman Roland Kinzer at both spring and fall elections in 1932.

MILBOURN, James—Democrat nominee aspirant for Congress in 1918.

MILLER, Boyd—Aspirant for GOP congressional nomination in 1972.

MILNE, James—Loser in 1974 Republican scramble for 5th District nomination.

MINNEY, Michael J.—Lancaster Democrat beaten in 1974 and 1976 races for 16th District seat.

MONAGHAN, Robert Emmett—State legislator and burgess of West Chester. Delegate to Democratic Party's 1876 and 1880 national conventions. Loser in 1868 congressional race.

MONAGHAN, R. Jones—Democrat nominee for Congress in 1880.

MORGAN, John—Phoenixville businessman, carpenter and politician. Served as postmaster, state legislator and justice of the peace. Democrat nominee in 1832 and 1834 congressional races.

MORGAN, Rex S.—Candidate for GOP congressional nomination in 1974 primary.

MOWERY, Jean—Lancaster County commissioner and Democratic Party nominee for Congress in 1982.

MURPHY, Andrew—Sadsbury Township physician and Democrat nominee for Congress in 1852.

O'BRIEN, John A.—Lancaster County attorney defeated by Congressman Paul Dague in 1964.

O'DONNELL, Daniel J.C.—Phoenixville attorney and Democratic Party leader nominated for Congress in 1942.

PARKE, Robert—State legislator from Sadsbury Township defeated in bid for Whig congressional nomination at 1848 and 1850 conventions.

PARKE, Thomas Edge—Chief burgess of Downingtown. Democrat candidate for Congress in 1894.

PAUL, James C.N.—University of Pennsylvania law school professor nominated by Democrats for congressman in 1958.

PENNYPACKER, Nathan—Physician and state lawmaker. Candidate for GOP congressional nomination in 1882.

PFOUTZ, Earl—Lancaster County opponent of congressmen Dague and Walker in several GOP primaries.

PHILLIPS, Thierry Van Casteel—Grandson of the Duke of Warsaw and loser to Congressman Thomas Butler in 1920 GOP primary.

PIERCE, Thomas—Onetime district attorney and chairman of Republican County Committee. Nominated by Democrats for Congress in 1890.

PRATT, Nathaniel—Congressional nominee of Democrats in 1866.

RAGAN, Philip—Democrat candidate for Congress from Lanchester district in 1950 and 1952.

RHODES, Franklin H.—Democratic Party nominee for Congress in 1902.

RHODES, Frank B.—President of Media Title & Trust Company. Democrat opponent of Congressman Thomas Butler in 1926.

RINGGOLD, Timothy—Democrat nominee for Congress in 1986.

RUTTER, John—West Chester attorney nominated by Democrats for Congress in 1846.

SIMPSON, W. Roger—Lancaster County attorney nominated by Democrats to opposed Congressman Paul Dague in 1948.

SLACK, Norris—Pioneer Chester County automobile dealer and longtime temperance advocate who headed Democratic Party for a number of years. Defeated in 1914 congressional race.

SMEDLEY, Garrett E.—Delaware County attorney and Democrat loser in 1892 Delchester congressional race.

SMITH, Lewis duPont—Lyndon LaRouche follower and 1990 independent candidate for Congress.

SMITH, P. Frazer—West Chester attorney and onetime state legislator defeated in 1860 congressional race.

STRETTON, Samuel C.—West Chester attorney and Democrat nominee for Congress in 1990.

TAYLOR, Franklin—Editor of *Kennett Square Free Press* and Liberal Republican Party's candidate for Congress in 1872.

TOMLINSON, Arthur—Washington Party's candidate for Congress in 1914.

WADDELL, William Bell—State senator and later president judge of Chester County Courts. One of the principal contenders for the congressional nomination at marathon GOP conventions in 1882 and 1884.

WALDMAN, Louis F.—County Commissioner and Democratic Party nominee for Congress in 1966 and 1970.

WEBSTER, Elwood—Candidate for Congress in 1966 GOP primary.

WESCOTT, Harry D.—Democrat loser in 1932 congressional race.

WEST, John Robinson—Candidate for GOP congressional nomination in 1974.

WILSON, Edward G.—Lancaster County Democrat defeated by Congressman Dague in 1954 and 1956.

WOODCOCK, James A.—Democrat nominee for Congress from 16th District in 1980.

YERGER, Brower B.—Mayor of Pottstown and Democratic Party nominee for Congress in 1972.

ZEALOR, Murray P.—Democrat loser in 1978 congressional contest.

CONGRESS AND CHESTER COUNTY TIMELINE

1787 United States Constitution drawn up in Philadelphia.

1789 First Congress assembles in New York City.

1790 National government moves to Philadelphia.

1791 Pennsylvania divided into eight congressional districts with Chester and Montgomery counties combined to form Third District.

1793 Cornerstone laid for Capitol in Washington.

1794 Richard Thomas becomes first Chester Countian elected to Congress from new Chester-Delaware County district.

1800 National capital moved from Philadelphia to Washington.

1802 House of Representatives increased to 141 members. . . . Isaac Anderson and two others elected to Congress from new district comprised of Chester, Lancaster and Berks Counties.

1803 Louisiana Territory purchased from France.

1812 Congress declares war against England. . . . Chester and Montgomery Counties combined to form new congressional district.

1814 British burn Capitol and White House.

1816 Public debt of United States exceeds one million dollars for first time. . . . Isaac Darlington, a Federalist, unseats his cousin, Dr. William Darlington, in congressional race by seven votes.

1820 Congress passes Henry Clay's Missouri Compromise bill.

1822 New apportionment entitles Pennsylvania to 26 of 213 House seats. . . . Isaac Wayne elected congressman from new district comprised of Chester, Lancaster and Delaware Counties.

1824 Chester Countians show preference for Andrew Jackson in controversial presidential election and help elect James Buchanan, Charles Miner, and Samuel Edwards as their congressmen.

1827 Pennsylvania's state legislators elect Isaac Barnard, prominent Chester County Democrat, to United States Senate.

1830 Two Chester Countians—David Potts Jr. and Joshua Evans Jr.—elected to 22nd Congress.

1843 New apportionment reduces Pennsylvania's membership in House to 24 members and Chester County is made separate congressional district.

1845 Florida and Texas admitted as states.

1846 War is declared against Mexico.

1848 Cornerstone for Washington Monument laid.

1850 California admitted as the 31st state. . . . Fugitive slave law enacted. . . . District of Columbia's population recorded at 51,687; Chester County's at 66,438.

1851 Thomas U. Walter, architect for recently built Chester County Courthouse, named architect for U.S. Capitol project.

1852 Chester and Delaware counties joined in congressional district marriage that will last for eighty years.

1854 John Hickman elected to first of four terms as Delchester congressman.

1856 N.P. Banks, a Free-Soiler from Massachusetts, elected Speaker of the House on 133rd ballot.

1857 James Buchanan becomes nation's fifteenth president. . . . Salaries of congressmen raised to $3,000 per year.

1861 Civil War begins after establishment of Confederate States of America and attack on Fort Sumter, S.C.

1865 Slavery abolished by adoption of 13th amendment to the Constitution. . . . Civil War ends. . . . President Lincoln assassinated.

1867 Alaska purchased from Russia.

1868 Impeachment proceedings instituted against President Andrew Johnson. . . . Washington Townsend elected to first of four terms in Congress.

1869 National Woman Suffrage Association submits resolution to Congress calling for suffrage amendment to the Constitution.

1870 Blacks permitted to vote for first time, causing county congressional election campaign to be marred by racial bigotry.

1872 President Ulysses S. Grant re-elected.

1874 Scandals and depression, along with Liberal Republican defections, give Democratic Party victory in nation's congressional elections for first time since Civil War.

1881 President James A. Garfield assassinated.

1882 James Bowen Everhart elected to 48th Congress after fierce struggle for Republican Party nomination.

1888 Washington Monument opened to public.

1897 Thomas S. Butler begins 31-year career as member of House from Delchester district.

1898 Congress declares war against Spain. . . . Hawaii annexed to United States by act of Congress.

1900 District of Columbia's population recorded at 278,718; Chester County's at 95,695.

1908 Cannon office building for House members completed.

1911 Apportionment approved by Congress entitles Pennsylvania to 36 representatives in federal House.

1913 17th Amendment to Constitution providing for direct election of United States senators is ratified.

1916 Jeanette Rankin of Montana become first woman elected to House.

1917 United States declares war against Germany.

1919 Prohibition Amendment ratified.

1920 Women participate in election of president for first time following 19th Amendment ratification.

1922 Lincoln Memorial dedicated.

1932 Pennsylvania's congressional delegation reduced from 36 to 34 members. . . . New Tenth District comprised of Chester and Lancaster counties elects J. Roland Kinzer as its congressman.

1933 Prohibition ends and New Deal era begins with inauguration of Franklin D. Roosevelt as president.

1935 Congress passes Social Security Act and Wagner Labor Relations Act.

1941 Congress declares war on Japan after Pearl Harbor attack.

1945 President Roosevelt dies. . . . World War II ends with surrender of Germany and Japan.

1946 Paul B. Dague elected to first of ten terms in Congress by voters of Lanchester district.

1947 Eightieth Congress convenes with Republicans in control of House for first time since 1931.

1948 Harry S. Truman defeats Thomas E. Dewey in presidential election upset.

1949 Congress passes minimum wage bill raising wages to 75 cents per hour.

1950 Korean War begins. . . . District of Columbia's population recorded at over 802,000; Chester County's at 159,141.

1951 22nd Amendment to Constitution limiting presidents to two terms is ratified.

1953 Dwight D. Eisenhower begins presidency. . . . Truce signed ending Korean War.

1957 Congress establishes Civil Rights Commission.

1959 Alaska and Hawaii become states.

1960 John F. Kennedy elected president.

1962 Pennsylvania's congressional delegation reduced to 27.

1964 Supreme Court mandates congressional districts must be as equal in population as practicable.

1965 U.S. 7th Cavalry fights first major battle of Vietnam War.

1966 Pennsylvania's 27 congressional districts realigned with Chester County and sections of Delaware County in new Ninth District.

1970 Eighteen-year-olds allowed to register under new federal voting registration law. . . . John H. Ware III, of Oxford, elected to Congress.

1972 Voters elect representatives to U.S. House of Representatives from districts of nearly equal size for first time in nation's history. . . . New apportionment reduces Pennsylvania's seats in House to 25 and places some Chester County municipalities in Fifth District and others in Sixteenth District.

1974 President Nixon resigns and Gerald Ford becomes nation's 38th president. . . . Richard Schulze elected congressman from Fifth District.

1976 Edwin Eshleman steps down as congressman from 16th District and Robert Walker is picked as his replacement.

1980 Ronald Reagan elected president. . . . Republicans win control of Senate for first time in 26 years.

1989 Congress increases salaries of its members from $89,500 to $125,000.

1991 United Nation forces defeat Saddam Hussein's Iraqi invaders in Gulf war.

1992 Pennsylvania loses two more seats in U.S. House of Representatives. . . . Congressman Schulze announces retirement after Fifth District is eliminated in realignment.